VOICE, TRUST, AND MEMORY

VOICE, TRUST, AND MEMORY

MARGINALIZED GROUPS AND
THE FAILINGS OF
LIBERAL REPRESENTATION

Melissa S. Williams

PRINCETON UNIVERSITY PRESS   PRINCETON, NEW JERSEY

Library of Congress Cataloging-in-Publication Data

Williams, Melissa S., 1960–
Voice, trust, and memory : marginalized groups and the
  failings of liberal representation / Melissa S. Williams.
      p.   cm.
Includes bibliographical references and index.
ISBN 0-691-03714-0 (cloth : alk. paper)
  1. Minorities—Political activity. 2. Ethnic groups—
Political activity. 3. Women in politics. 4. Representative
government and representation. 5. Equality.
6. Fairness. I. Title.
JF1061.W55 1998
328.73′07347—dc21   98-9642

To David

Contents

Acknowledgments ─────────────────────────

WRITING THIS BOOK has taken a long time, and in that time I have been the beneficiary of many generous people. I am humbled to reflect on the bountiful gifts of time, careful thought, and friendship I have received from these talented people, and on the inadequacy of my words to express my gratitude to them.

It is a particular sorrow that I am unable to thank Judith Shklar, who advised the doctoral dissertation out of which this book grew. Like so many others who learned from her, I miss the sparkle of her intellect and the integrity of her example. But her voice, always challenging, always calling on me to reach for a higher standard, is a still audible presence projecting over my shoulder, a sometimes irksome but always salutary companion.

Dennis Thompson also advised my dissertation and has continued to be an important source of insight and criticism for this and other work. One of his gifts to me was to perceive clearly what I was up to at a time when others did not. My own commitment to bridging the distance between the normative concerns of democratic theory and the structure of political institutions has received important sustenance from Dennis and his work.

The relationship between democratic theory and institutional design is mediated by myriad empirical questions. It was for this reason that I asked Sidney Verba, who so elegantly combines empirical inquiry with democratic theory, to serve as an additional adviser to my dissertation. It is a pleasure to thank him publicly for his many helpful comments on my work.

My good fortune in teachers has a history. I would especially like to thank Stephen Salkever, whose exemplary teaching first kindled my love for political theory, and who also took the time to read the entire manuscript and to offer instructive and insightful suggestions.

Two people deserve special thanks for their extraordinary friendship. Annabelle Lever has read this manuscript many times, and each time has given her distinctive and perceptive comments. Our conversations about matters both personal and political sustain me on many levels. Joseph Carens read various parts of the manuscript at various times, and again read the whole thing through at a critical juncture. His guidance on both substance and procedure has been golden, and his generosity as a friend and as a colleague is immeasurable.

I am especially grateful to Will Kymlicka and Iris Young for their thoughtful readings and constructive criticisms of the manuscript, from which it benefited considerably. I would also like to thank Judith Baker, Rainer Bauböck, Keith Bybee, Joshua Cohen, Jenny Mansbridge, Steve Wasby, and three anonymous reviewers for reading the entire manuscript and offering helpful comments and challenges.

Many others have helped along the way with thought-provoking comments, suggestions, criticisms, and support, including Chloë Atkins, Sylvia Bashevkin, Nancy Burns, Betty Ann Donnelly, Marion Dove, Karen Feaver, Peter Feaver, David Fott, Jeanne Heifetz, Bonnie Honig, Veronica Jarek-Prinz, Evert Lindquist, Victoria Kamsler, Laurence McFalls, Daniel Markovitz, Tim Prinz, Arti Rai, Michael Sandel, Debora Spar, Allison Stanger, Shannon Stimson, Rob Vipond, Alec Walen, and Carolyn Warner. Many thanks also to Ann Wald at Princeton University Press for her patient and knowing performance of the role of editor.

I would also like to express my gratitude for the support I have received from all my family, especially to my parents for educating me. My siblings Diane Paul, Shelley Cummins, and Michael Williams have bolstered me throughout the process of writing this book. Thanks also to Katharin Welch for her considerable support.

Several people provided me with superb assistance in researching and preparing the manuscript. Sharon Krause did a tremendous job in editing the manuscript. Julie Bernier, Pak-cheong Choo, Troy Goodfellow, and Tom Jones acted as research assistants. Sandra Clancy, Catherine Frost, and Benjamin Moerman did painstaking work in finalizing the manuscript, and Rita Bernhard copyedited it with thoughtful care. I very much appreciate all their hard work. The reference staff at the Schlesinger Library, Radcliffe College, and at the Robarts Library of the University of Toronto provided essential research support for chapters 4 and 5, respectively.

I presented portions of the book or summaries of its argument in several academic forums and would like to thank the organizers of and participants in those forums for the opportunity to share my work and for their comments. They include the Department of Government of the University of Virginia, the Department of Political Science of St. Thomas University, the Department of Political Science at Rochester University, the Duke University Law School, the Law and Philosophy Reading Group at the University of Toronto, and the Canadian Centre for Philosophy and Public Policy.

I gratefully acknowledge permission to reprint material that has been published elsewhere. An earlier version of chapter 5 was published as "Memory, History, and Membership: The Moral Claims of Marginalized Groups in Political Representation," in *Do We Need Minority Rights? Conceptual Issues*, ed. Juha Räikkä (The Hague: Martinus Nijhoff, 1996), pp. 85–119, © Kluwer Law International. Brief sections of chapter 1's discussion of Edmund Burke were originally published in my article, "Burkean 'Descriptions' and Political Representation: A Reappraisal," *Canadian Journal of Political Science* 29 (1) (1996): 23–45.

I would also like to acknowledge with gratitude the financial and institutional support of the Social Sciences and Humanities Research Council of Canada, the Connaught Fund of the University of Toronto, the Department of Political Science at the University of Toronto, and the Program in Ethics and the Professions of Harvard University.

Words are least adequate to express my gratitude to David Welch. I can only hope that words are also least necessary in this case. David is not my harshest critic, as he claims that I am his; but he is my staunchest friend, and he has read every word of this book many times. He is also very good with a word processor. Lastly, I thank my son Nathaniel for knowing how to put even very big books in their proper place.

VOICE, TRUST, AND MEMORY

Introduction

Voice, Trust, and Memory

THE RIGHT TO fair legislative representation is a centerpiece of modern representative democracy. But what does fair representation entail with respect to the identity of the people who sit in legislatures? This book takes as its starting point the fundamental intuition that *when historically marginalized groups are chronically underrepresented in legislative bodies, citizens who are members of those groups are not fairly represented.* The American electoral system reliably produces legislatures in which marginalized groups hold a disproportionately small share of the seats, a system that hardly seems fair to the distinctive political interests of these groups. In particular, it is difficult to ignore the suspicion that the "underrepresentation" of historically marginalized groups is related to the history of discrimination against them. Certainly, members of those groups have been vocal in their criticism of governments from which people like themselves are chronically absent. But claims for representation, like other claims for political recognition, are not self-validating. In what ways, and to what extent, does the fair representation of marginalized groups depend on their presence within legislative bodies?

Recent political events have brought greater attention to the idea that the legislative presence of marginalized groups is an important part of group members' equality as citizens. Consider two groups that have been the focus of heated debates over the relationship between citizens' political equality and group members' electoral success: African Americans and women. For African American citizens, the Voting Rights Act of 1965, together with its 1982 amendments, ushered in a "Second Reconstruction." Like the first Reconstruction, voting rights reform began by vastly extending the free exercise of the vote to incorporate citizens who had been forcibly excluded from full citizenship. Again, like the first Reconstruction, the first wave of democratic change in the form of an expanded franchise was followed by a second wave: a massive increase in the legislative representation of African Americans by African Americans. Yet in June 1993, only six months after legislative reform yielded a momentous increase in the number of African American members of Congress, the Supreme Court began dismantling the legal structure supporting race-conscious districting that had made these gains possible.[1] The Court's decision in *Shaw v. Reno* began a reversal of the understanding of fair representation that had developed during the preceding twenty years of judicial decisions and congressional legislation on minority voting rights.[2] Just as the first Reconstruction had its reactionary movement in the "Redemption" of the

South, we are now witnessing a second "Redemption" in the *Shaw* decision and its growing progeny.

For women, anger over the all-male Senate Judiciary Committee's treatment of Anita Hill during Supreme Court Justice Clarence Thomas's confirmation hearings helped to spur a record number of women's candidacies in the 1992 elections, and many female candidates were successful.[3] The mobilization of women's political organizations such as Emily's List and the Fund for the Feminist Majority supported these campaigns, and these organizations continue to be active. Yet the prospects for further increases in women's representation are by no means certain. In the 1994 elections a disproportionate number of the new female representatives lost their seats.[4] Moreover, studies of electoral systems show quite clearly that single-member district systems are inherently less likely than other electoral systems to result in the election of large numbers of women.[5] Without electoral change, women's recent gains in representation may be quite insecure.

There is good reason, then, to be concerned about the ongoing underrepresentation of historically marginalized groups. If we turn to existing theories of representational fairness, however, we discover that the intuition with which I began my own inquiry—that fair representation for historically marginalized groups requires their presence in legislatures—is exceedingly difficult to sustain on theoretical grounds. Within the American legal and political tradition, "fair representation" has been defined largely in terms of a highly individualistic understanding of procedural fairness. Its epitome is the slogan, "one person, one vote," and it holds that as long as all citizens have an equal opportunity to influence the electoral process, the outcome of that process is fair, whatever it happens to be. The Voting Rights Act, and especially its 1982 amendments, attempted to give an expansive meaning to procedural fairness so as to prevent electoral structures from "diluting" minority voting strength (and so effectively giving minorities' votes less weight than those of White citizens). But as I show in chapter 3, even an expansive reading of procedural fairness fails to justify measures that aim specifically at increasing the legislative presence of African Americans or Latinos. There is nothing in the procedural account of fairness with which one can rationally defend the claim that the fair representation of historically disadvantaged groups depends on the presence in legislative bodies of their own members.

Debates over the increased legislative presence of marginalized groups reflect a broader tension in American politics, law, and culture between color- and gender-blind procedural conceptions of fairness, on the one hand, and, on the other, the view that the deep structure of contemporary inequalities along the lines of race and gender can be transformed only if we take social difference into account. As a political matter, this debate is now being won by the difference-blind proceduralist view. If advocates of enhanced representation for marginalized groups are to have any hope of resisting the current tide of difference-blind conservatism, they must develop theoretical arguments that can justify group representation. Despite the persistence of intuitions about the unfairness of the chronic underrepresentation of women and minorities, we have yet to articulate a complete and coherent theory of fair representation for marginalized groups that can justify those intuitions. My aim in this book is to offer such a theory.

I. Problems with Group-Based Views of Fair Representation

When I first began thinking about representation, scholars were just beginning to address the relationship between political equality and social difference. No one had yet written extensively about the ways in which this relationship might play out in the sphere of political representation. As so often happens in political theory, however, others were turning their attention to the topic at the same time as I. There is an emerging zeitgeist concerning the place of social difference in schemes of political representation of which this book is a part. In particular, political theorists Iris Young and Anne Phillips, and legal scholar and practitioner Lani Guinier, have made critically important contributions to our understanding of the fair representation of disadvantaged groups.[6]

In one way or another, all the recent work on representation grapples with the theoretical underpinnings of the intuition with which I began this study: that the chronic legislative underrepresentation of historically marginalized groups is unfair. There is a considerable amount to grapple with, since the task of defining fair representation for marginalized groups is fraught with difficulty. Four problems stand out as particularly nettlesome and important.

The Problem of Group Essentialism

The claim that fair representation for women and minorities depends on their presence in legislative bodies seems at first glance to imply that members of such groups somehow share an identity of interests or concerns for which their representatives can advocate. Yet there is clearly a wide diversity of both opinion and interest within any social grouping, and women and minorities are no exception. Women may be pro-choice or antiabortion; African Americans may be middle class or poor; Latinos may be Mexican American or Cuban American, Democrats or Republicans. In order to defend a conception of representational fairness that focuses on marginalized groups, and to sustain the intuition that the fair representation of such groups requires their legislative presence, one must adduce something that members of these groups share without falling into the trap of essentialism. Further, one must justify the claim that whatever they share both warrants and requires the presence of group members in legislative bodies in a proportion roughly comparable to their proportion of the population as a whole.

No defensible claim for group representation can rest on assertions of the essential identity of women or minorities; such assertions do violence to the empirical facts of diversity as well as to the agency of individuals to define the meaning of their social and biological traits. Yet these groupings do have a social significance which stands independently of the meanings their members voluntarily attach to them. In particular, they define the contours of important patterns of social, political, and economic inequality, and thus help to determine the life prospects and to constrain the life choices of most of their members. Like some other defenders of enhanced representation for marginalized groups, I conclude that what members of such groups share is the *experience* of marginalization and the distinctive *perspective* on matters of public policy that comes of that experience.[7] The claim I defend in chapters 4 and 6 is that even though the experiences and perspectives of marginalized group members are themselves diverse, the social positions of group members are sufficiently similar that there are good reasons to believe that members of marginalized groups, *on average*, are more likely to represent the concerns and interests of citizens from those groups than are nonmembers.

The Problem of Accountability

A corollary of the problem of group essentialism is the problem of accountability. While fair representation for marginalized groups may depend in some ways on their legislative presence, it would be absurd to claim that a representative, simply because she is a woman, therefore represents the interests or perspectives of women generally, or that an African American representative is automatically representative of all African Americans. The mere presence of members of marginalized groups in legislatures is not *sufficient* for the fair representation of citizens from those groups, even though it is often *necessary*. We can all think of examples of female or minority political figures who represent the antithesis of what many regard as women's or minorities' interests (Phyllis Schlafly and Clarence Thomas are frequently invoked for this purpose). But the task for a defender of a group-based conception of fair representation is not to specify, a priori, who can serve as the "authentic" representative of a marginalized group, a project that inexorably falls back into the problem of essentialism. Rather, as Anne Phillips and Lani Guinier argue cogently, a group-based account of fair representation must identify the mechanisms of accountability that ensure the fidelity of marginalized group representatives to their constituencies.[8] As I discuss in chapters 5 and 7, elections are among the most important mechanisms of accountability for marginalized group representatives as for other representatives. The key is to create electoral connections between representatives and constituencies defined around group identity. In addition, numerous political and technological innovations promise to provide ways of strengthening legislator-constituent communication that would further strengthen accountability.

The Problem of Legislative Marginalization

Even where it is possible to overcome the challenge of electing "authentic" representatives for marginalized groups, a group's marginalization may simply be reproduced at the level of the legislature. In legislative bodies with simple majoritarian decision rules, representatives of ethnic and racial minorities may be unable to influence policy decisions if they are consistently outvoted. Moreover, the internal diversity of marginalized groups may hinder the legislative solidarity that would secure their representatives greater influence over policy. Arguments that increased legislative presence will enhance the fairness of political representation for marginalized groups must confront the institutional dynamics and mechanisms that translate presence into policy influence.[9] For legislative minorities, the capacity of legislative presence to yield policy influence depends critically on whether the legislative process encourages a *deliberative* exchange among representatives rather than a *competitive* or *bargaining* mode of decision making. Although legislative presence can contribute to marginalized groups' influence even in the absence of deliberative dynamics by giving group representatives more clout in forming coalitions, increasing the deliberativeness of legislative decision making is the most promising avenue of change for these groups. I develop these arguments in chapters 4 and 7.

The Problem of Group Proliferation and "Balkanization"

The claim that marginalization supports the specific representation of identifiable groups runs certain risks, including the risk that all social groups will have an incentive to identify themselves as "marginalized." Critics of difference-conscious policies often focus on the possibility that special forms of group recognition will generate an unworkable proliferation of demands on the state. They also argue that recognizing group differences perpetuates social conflict and that we should instead aim to eradicate conflict by pursuing an ideal of equality that treats all citizens alike. Any defense of a group-based conception of fair representation, then, must be able to specify *which* groups have a claim to special solicitude in the field of political representation and to offer criteria by which to distinguish stronger from weaker claims for representation. Moreover, it must offer reasons why the risks of group recognition are worth the price. All the defenses of enhanced representation for marginalized groups regard the deep history of inequality along group lines as a compelling reason for giving special priority to these groups in the quest for political equality, even if the price for such attention is an increase in conflict. Without denying that some sociopolitical conditions may generate a tension between the claims of equality and the claims of stability, between justice and peace, defenders of marginalized group representation do not agree with its critics that stability should always take priority over equality. My analysis in this book focuses on African Americans and women as important examples of historically marginalized groups whose claims to representation are especially strong, but does not mean to suggest that these are the only groups with strong claims. In chapter 6, I offer criteria aimed at assisting us in reaching judgments about which groups have strong claims to self-representation in legislative bodies, and I defend the inclusion of a history of marginalization among those criteria.

This book addresses each of these problems within the framework of a comprehensive theoretical defense of the intuition that fair representation for marginalized groups requires their legislative presence.

II. The Structure of the Argument

Each of the following chapters constitutes a distinct part of the central argument of the book as a whole, which defends a group-based theory of fair representation as an alternative to the theory I call "liberal representation." The first chapter serves as the foundation of the argument, for it raises the general question of how we are to evaluate competing conceptions of representational fairness: *What constitutes a coherent theoretical account of fair legislative representation?* The chapter lays out certain requirements that any complete and coherent theory of fair representation must meet. Because the processes that constitute political representation are complex, any theory of fair representation must be similarly complex. The complexity of representation arises from the fact that its institutions and processes mediate between citizens' concerns and governmental decisions in several ways, each of which has a profound impact on the expression public policy gives to citizens' political aims. In the view I call "representation as mediation," I discuss three forms such mediation takes: the dynamics of legislative decision making, the nature of legislator-constituent relations, and the basis for aggregating citizens into representable constituencies. With respect to the first dimension of representation as mediation, I will argue that a concern for marginalized group representation should yield efforts to encourage the deliberative rather than competitive dynamics of legislative decision making. Second, I argue that the capacity of citizens from marginalized groups to trust their representatives is greater when those representatives are also group members. Third, I claim that marginalized group identity should play an important role in defining legislative constituencies; relying on single-member geographic districts as the principal mode of constituency definition will not provide fair representation for historically marginalized groups. As in any theory of representation, a group-based conception of representational fairness offers both a political sociology and a normative understanding of the place of social groups in the constitution of the common good.

The latter part of the chapter explores the interaction of the three aspects of representation as mediation in the thought of four prominent and insightful theorists of representation: Edmund Burke, James Madison, John C. Calhoun, and John Stuart Mill. These studies reveal an important contrast between theories of representation that seek to *express* intergroup differences in the political process and those that regard intergroup differences as dangerous and destabilizing and therefore something that well-designed political institutions will *suppress*. The distinction between *expressive* and *suppressive* approaches to group conflict runs throughout the book as a whole, and is particularly relevant to contemporary debates over the dangers of "balkanization." My argument throughout the book is that for societies committed to the principle of democratic equality, expressive strategies of political representation are far superior to suppressive views. Yet the predominant American understanding of fair representation—particularly in the form it takes in recent critiques of race-conscious districting—is undoubtedly a suppressive view.

While chapter 1 answers the question of what, in general, constitutes a coherent theoretical account of fair representation, chapter 2 offers an interpretation of the dominant theory of fair representation in the United States and explains why that theory stands in deep tension with the fundamental intuition underlying this book's project. Chapter 2 answers affirmatively to the question, *Is it possible to identify a coherent theoretical account of fair representation that informs American political culture, political science, and jurisprudence?* Because the dominant American understanding of fair representation rests firmly on the liberal principles of individual equality and individual autonomy, I give it the name "liberal representation." Like other liberal doctrines of equality (particularly the doctrine of equal opportunity), liberal representation's conception of fairness is deeply individualist and proceduralist. It consists of two strands, both of which embody the ideal of what John Rawls describes as "pure procedural justice," i.e., procedures we can count on to produce fair outcomes because they begin with conditions of individual equality and treat individuals impartially at every stage. Where this is the case, the theory holds, the outcome is fair, "whatever it happens to be"; we neither possess nor need an independent standard of justice against which to measure a fair procedure's results.[10]

The first strand of liberal representation is the principle of "one person, one vote." This principle holds that electoral outcomes are fair, whatever they happen to be, so long as every individual has an equally weighted vote in the electoral process. The second strand of liberal representation is the normative theory of interest-group pluralism, which applies at both the electoral and the legislative stages of representation. At the electoral stage, interest-group pluralism holds that electoral outcomes are fair as long as every citizen had an equal opportunity to organize with other citizens—whether in parties or in interest groups—to support candidates' campaigns. At the legislative stage, interest-group pluralism holds that the interests which receive substantive recognition and protection in legislative policies are and should be those around which individuals have formed large or energetic interest groups. Thus legislative decisions are fair, whatever they happen to be, so long as every citizen has an equal opportunity to mobilize politically around the interests that are important to her.

Although both strands of liberal representation define standards of fairness that are proceduralist and individualist, they articulate slightly different standards of fairness in political representation. The standard of "one person, one vote" expresses a simple, formal principle of democratic equality and yields a standard of *equal* representation. The pluralist strand of liberal representation, in contrast, does not predict the equal satisfaction of every citizen's interests. Rather, it specifies a social decision function that will translate the number and intensity of individual policy preferences into legislative policies. It thus yields a standard of *equitable* representation. Throughout the book I use the term *equal representation* to refer to the formal equality of individual citizens as expressed in an equally weighted vote, and I use *equitable representation* to refer to a fair method of aggregating citizens' interests.[11] Together the two strands constitute a perfectly coherent and defensible theory. While the fact of geographic districting adds a challenge to liberal representation's pluralist conception of fair methods for aggregating citizens' interests, and so complicates liberal representation's account of equitable representation, it is nonetheless possible to approximate liberal representation's standards of fair representation within a system of district-based elections.

Within the theory of liberal representation, the social identity of elected legislators is entirely irrelevant to the question of whether representation is fair. In this theory, fair representation for marginalized groups does not depend on their members' legislative presence; it is guaranteed by the principle of "one person, one vote," in open and free elections. If women or minorities fail to organize around their identities in the electoral process and fail to elect candidates who share their identities, this reflects either their lack of a sense of the political salience of those identities or the fact that they are minorities. In the latter case there is still no cause for complaint, for in our electoral system majorities win and minorities lose. Moreover, if African Americans and women do not or cannot influence elections, they may still influence legislative policy through the interest-group process. On this view, fair representation does not require attention to the identity of those who sit in the legislature—indeed, it precludes it. In sum, then, chapter 2 does not present a general view of liberalism and of its implications for representation. Rather, it offers an account of the reasons why, within the liberal view of fair representation that dominates American discourse, the chronic underrepresentation of historically marginalized groups is not problematic.

Liberal representation is not only theoretically coherent; it also contains important elements of justice that must be preserved in any adequate account of fair representation. Yet because it does not do justice to the claims of marginalized groups for self-representation in legislative bodies, it requires supplementation. Chapter 3 explores one strategy for supplementing liberal representation's proceduralist view with a more substantive standard of fairness and shows how this strategy has failed both politically and theoretically. More specifically, the chapter traces the course of liberal representation through judicial and legislative treatments of minority voting rights and shows how the legacy of racial discrimination in voting led both Congress and the Supreme Court to modify the pure proceduralism of liberal representation.

The doctrine of minority vote dilution that emerged from these efforts aimed at protecting racial and ethnic minorities from the invidious consequences of past and present discrimination in the sphere of electoral politics. The process of devising this remedy for an evident wrong led both Congress and the Court to substantive standards of representational fairness. Their goals were the electoral success of minority candidates and effectual guarantees that geographically concentrated minority communities would be able to elect the candidates of their choice. Yet these goals, it soon appeared, clashed with even the most expansive reading of liberal representation. Without a theoretical alternative to liberal representation's procedural conception of fairness, such substantive standards could only appear as "excesses." The Supreme Court, accordingly, has recently done its utmost to reverse them. The consequence is a confused jurisprudence that not only threatens recent gains in minority representation but also clothes profound racial biases in the guise of a "color-blind electoral process," biases I discuss separately in the appendix to chapter 3. In short, chapter 3 raises the question, *Can liberal representation be modified to acknowledge the claims of historically marginalized groups to representation by their own members?* The answer is that while liberal representation can go some distance toward justifying measures such as race-conscious districting, it cannot justify deeper claims to the legislative presence of marginalized groups. The remainder of the book turns to the task of justifying those claims.

Chapters 4 through 6 constitute the heart of the book's argument. It is here that I develop the themes of "voice," "trust," and "memory" through which each of the three dimensions of representation as mediation is given a content that supports the claims of historically marginalized groups to legislative self-representation. These chapters begin with the question, *How should we move beyond liberal representation in order to understand the requirements of fair representation for marginalized groups?* My assumption in addressing this question is that we increase our understanding of the meaning of fair representation for marginalized groups if we turn to group members' own views about political equality and political representation. In exploring the normative foundations of group claims to representation, I thus move back and forth between marginalized groups' own understanding of their need for self-representation and the three dimensions of representation as mediation, puzzling out the implications of the former for the latter. This dynamic constitutes the method of the book as a whole, a method that shares what Iris Young describes as the strategy of "listening": "While everyday discourse about justice certainly makes claims, these are not theorems to be demonstrated in a self-enclosed system. They are instead calls, pleas, claims *upon* some people by others. Rational reflection on justice begins in . . . hearing, in heeding a call, rather than in . . . mastering a state of affairs, however ideal."[12]

A commitment to democratic equality, I am convinced, carries with it a commitment to take seriously citizens' persistent sense of injustice, to attempt to understand the nature of the equality to which they lay claim. As Judith Shklar wrote, we can be sure that our judgments will be unjust "unless we take the victim's view into full account and give her voice its full weight."[13] I have tried to follow through on that commitment by examining the claims to political representation made by and on behalf of members of marginalized groups at times when their status and rights as equal citizens were at stake. Two historical cases of the political arguments of marginalized groups claiming political recognition constitute most of the "listening" undertaken in this project: the claims for political rights of the woman suffrage movement and Black political arguments during Reconstruction after the Civil War. My strategy here is to develop a theory of group representation by examining the historical experience of women and African Americans in their movements for political equality. Chapters 4 and 5 trace the shift within each of these movements from a stress on individual natural rights to a greater stress on group-oriented self-representation.

The use of historical case studies runs the risk that issues of political equality relevant in other times and places are less relevant today. But this approach also has advantages. By looking at arguments from different eras, we gain some distance from the models of politics that dominate current understandings. If specific demands for group-conscious political equality cut across different groups and different historical periods, they cry out even more for a system of representation that is responsive to them. In addition, political action produces creative political thinking. These historical moments offer great insight into the different meanings of political equality for members of marginalized groups. Thus my method reinforces Jane Mansbridge's insight that political theorists can learn by looking at what ordinary people think about the meaning of our ideals, particularly when those ideals are "under stress."[14]

Although some of the conclusions I reach through an exploration of the themes of "voice" and "trust" correspond quite closely to the insights of other theorists of group representation, my path to these conclusions relies on sources indigenous to American political culture. These conclusions gain support both from principled argumentation and the lessons of our history. Both their longevity and their location *within* the American democratic tradition sustain confidence that arguments for the self-representation of marginalized groups are here to stay. They are no passing intellectual fancy.

Although several themes of political equality emerge in both case studies, each study emphasizes a different aspect of group-conscious equality and a different implication for a group-based theory of fair representation. Chapter 4 examines the arguments of the woman suffrage movement in which arguments for political equality and political representation emphasize women's distinctive "point of view" or "voice." The suffragists argued that because of their history of subordination, women's experiences of the world are substantively different from those of men. Further, this difference of perspective is relevant to politics in general and to the equal representation of women in particular. It means that women are often best represented by other women, as they have an understanding of what equality means for them that is not readily available to men.

Fulfilling the need for women's self-representation depends on a mode of legislative decision making that is fundamentally different from the mode presumed by liberal representation: the capacity of the distinctive voices of marginalized groups to inform policy decisions depends heavily on the *deliberative* qualities of legislative decision making. Because it is their distinctive experience of policies and practices that sets marginalized groups apart from relatively privileged groups, legislative responsiveness to marginalized group concerns is most likely when that experience can be fully expressed and thoughtfully considered. While a log-rolling approach to legislative decision making may sometimes enable marginalized group representatives to pressure others to change their votes, it is not designed to change their minds. Yet in the long run, changing the structural inequalities that marginalize these groups requires changing minds. In this way the "voice" argument for the self-representation of marginalized groups also offers an image of the first aspect of representation as mediation within a group-based theory of fair representation.

The fifth chapter addresses African American claims to full political equality during Reconstruction. This history raises the question of *trust*—in particular, whether Black citizens could trust White representatives to protect their political interests. The experience of newly enfranchised Black citizens shows that in a deeply divided society the relationship of trust between legislator and constituent, and between citizen and government, is imperfectly fulfilled for those on the less privileged side of the divide. Black leaders' arguments also show how those relationships of trust can be at least partially mended if the disadvantaged group is represented by its own members. A shared similarity in descriptive traits between legislator and constituent is not, of course, sufficient to secure a constituent's rational trust. Representatives of marginalized groups are not immune to the temptations that produce a betrayal of their constituents' trust. A fuller relationship of trust rests on the *accountability* of representatives to constituents, an issue I discuss in both chapter 5 and chapter 7. Accountability secures trust for historically marginalized groups by allowing those groups to define the constituencies from which representatives are elected. Together, reflections on the themes of trust and accountability generate a solution to the second aspect of representation as mediation within a group-based theory, the relationship between legislator and constituent.

In chapter 6, I employ the theme of "memory" to develop an answer to the question, *How are we to distinguish groups with strong moral claims to enhanced representation from groups whose claims are relatively weak?* My answer to this question consists in a political sociology that provides content for the third aspect of representation as mediation, the problem of constituency definition. The premise of my argument throughout the book is that contemporary American society (like many other democratic societies) is characterized by patterns of *structural* or *systemic inequality* that are presumptively unjust.[15] The groups with the strongest claims for enhanced representation, I argue, are those whose members are subject to long-standing patterns of structural inequality and who share a sense of political identity with other group members.

I distinguish between "objective" and "subjective" forms of group identity and argue that both must be present to sustain the strongest moral claims to political recognition through representation. "Objective" sources of group identity include a history of state-supported discrimination against the group and the continuance of contemporary patterns of social, economic, and political inequality along group lines. "Subjective" sources of group identity include a shared memory of that discrimination and a conviction of shared political interests in the present. Objective group identity distinguishes those groups toward which other members of the political community have strong justice-based obligations. Subjective group identity creates an identifiable group interest which group members can claim to represent more effectively than nonmembers. Together, objective and subjective sources of identity provide a standard for distinguishing stronger from weaker group claims, and so for overcoming the critiques of group representation grounded in concerns over balkanization and ungovernability.

No theory of representation is complete without an account of the institutions which it entails. Indeed, the moral defensibility of any conception of fair representation may turn on its institutional arrangements. Throughout the book I argue that although the group-based theory of fair representation reaches beyond liberal representation, the theory itself is not only compatible with but indeed is required by liberalism's core commitments to individual equality and individual autonomy. But we cannot be sure of that consistency without examining the institutional requirements of the theory I defend. Chapter 7 thus raises the question, *Is it possible to design institutions of fair representation for historically marginalized groups without compromising democratic commitments to individual equality and individual autonomy?* The chapter explores the institutional desiderata of the group-based theory of fair representation and begins by exploring alternative institutional devices for ensuring that marginalized group membership defines at least some of the constituencies that receive political representation.

Here I argue that within a single-member district system of elections race-conscious districting is a morally defensible means of enhancing the legislative presence of marginalized groups. But this method has defects. Various forms of proportional representation are more desirable institutional tools for achieving fair representation. In the legislature itself, various institutional innovations would encourage the deliberative exchanges necessary for making marginalized groups' voices effective within legislatures. The chapter next considers the mechanisms of accountability that can secure a relationship of trust between legislators and constituents. It concludes with an overview of a scheme of electoral institutions that would enhance marginalized group representation with no greater compromise of the principles of individual equality and autonomy than exists in the current American system.

The remainder of this introduction further clarifies some of the book's key concepts in order to avoid possible misunderstandings and to provide a further conceptual framework for the reader. In particular, it addresses the nature of the groups that are my main concern in this book, the relationship between substantive and procedural conceptions of fairness in the theory of representation I offer, and the domain of the argument for group representation.

III. What Is a Marginalized Group?

Throughout the book I use the terms *marginalized group* and *marginalized ascriptive group* interchangeably. Although I do not claim to offer here an exhaustive theory of social groups, I distinguish marginalized groups from other kinds of groups in arguing for their specific representation in political bodies. As I use the term, *marginalized ascriptive groups* have four characteristic features: (1) patterns of social and political inequality are structured along the lines of group membership; (2) membership in these groups is not usually experienced as voluntary; (3) membership in these groups is not usually experienced as mutable; and (4) generally, negative meanings are assigned to group identity by the broader society or the dominant culture. Historically marginalized ascriptive groups, then, are groups that have possessed these features for multiple generations. Each of the characteristics distinguishes marginalized groups from the voluntary associations that populate the theory and practice of interest-group pluralism.

The first feature of marginalized groups points to the fact of structural (or systemic) inequality, i.e., the fact that the dynamics of social, economic, and political processes reliably reproduce patterns of inequality in which members of these groups lie well below the median of the distribution of resources. Although conscious acts of discrimination may contribute to the reproduction of group-structured inequality, the concept of structural inequality refers to the fact that patterns of inequality may be reproduced by social practices even without intentional discrimination. Some of the sources of structural inequality are discussed at greater length in chapter 6.

The last three features of marginalized groups warrant my use of the term *ascriptive* to characterize these groups. In the sociological literature the term *ascriptive* signifies that a person's role or status in society is a product of unchosen characteristics such as sex, race, or age rather than a result of his or her actions. It thus stands in contrast with "achievement" roles and statuses, which are based on what an individual has actually done. In individual interactions, a member of an ascriptive group will often be treated by others on the basis of attributes they *ascribe* because of race or gender or kinship ties, rather than attributes actually displayed.[16]

It is important to note that while the identities ascribed to individuals may include allegedly natural behaviors, nothing in the concept of ascriptive groups as such supports the claim that any essential identity attaches to individuals because of their possession of ascriptive traits. Cultures assign social meaning to certain traits, and members of those cultures treat individuals who have those traits differently from individuals who do not. The traits that carry ascriptive meanings often vary from one culture to another. Class might be an ascriptive trait in some societies but not in others, or in some social contexts but not in others. Ascriptive traits—and the meanings they carry—are neither chosen voluntarily by the individuals who bear them nor can they be (readily) changed by them. For marginalized groups, some of the social meanings attached to the traits they possess are negative, helping to reinforce (and provide a rationalization for) structural patterns of material inequality.

The marginality of the groups that concern me here, then, is doubly constituted by their disadvantaged position in the distribution of social, economic, and political resources and by the fact that their ascriptive traits carry stigmas or other social meanings that limit individuals' agency. To borrow Nancy

Fraser's helpful conceptual framework, members of these groups are burdened simultaneously by *cultural injustices* and *economic injustices*, by injustices of recognition and injustices of distribution.[17] Indeed, patterns of structural inequality frequently result from the interaction of these two forms of injustice. As Fraser puts it, "[c]ultural norms that are unfairly biased against some are institutionalized in the state and the economy; meanwhile, economic disadvantage impedes equal participation in the making of culture, in public spheres and in everyday life. The result is often a vicious circle of cultural and economic subordination."[18] One of the principal claims underlying the "voice" argument for enhanced representation is that the relationship between cultural and economic inequality is more likely to be apparent to those who suffer its consequences than to those who do not.

In the United States African Americans and women offer paradigmatic examples of historically marginalized ascriptive groups. By focusing on women and African Americans, however, I do not want to suggest that these are the *only* marginalized ascriptive groups or that the argument for group representation should apply only to them. Rather, I presume that if *any* marginalized groups have strong moral claims for recognition, these two groups must be among them, and that if arguments for enhanced representation are persuasive for any group, they should be persuasive *at least* for these two groups.

History plays an important role in defining the groups whose moral claims are strongest. The groups most profoundly disadvantaged in contemporary society have also been the subjects of legal exclusions from citizenship and of state-sponsored discrimination. The causal connection between marginalized group identity and state-supported discrimination runs in both directions: the cultural stigmas that dominant groups have historically attached to marginalized group identity have helped sustain discriminatory practices; and discriminatory practices have themselves been causally connected to the ongoing group-structured patterns of distributive inequality. The more egregious the historical forms of domination and the deeper the history of inequality, the more firmly entrenched we would expect to find the patterns of both distributive and cultural inequality likely to be. Contemporary cultural injustice toward members of a marginalized group can even take the form of a public failure or refusal to acknowledge the injustice of a group's historical experience (as when, for example, White Southerners advocate flying the Confederate flag from their state assemblies). Finally, the concept of structural inequality, which constitutes a part of my definition of marginalized groups, itself contains a temporal dimension, for it is difficult to determine whether patterns of group-structured inequality are both *systemic* and *unjust* unless they are reproduced over time.

I intend my definitions of the features of marginalized groups and of subjective and objective dimensions of group identity to be open-textured enough to allow debate over which social groups are marginalized and which have the strongest claims to enhanced representation. The content of the category "marginalized group" or "disadvantaged group" should be a subject of political disagreement. My purpose is not to offer a final catalog of marginalized groups but to provide a critical conceptual framework through which we can arrive at reflective judgments about group claims. This framework leaves open the possibility that changing social circumstances and new understandings of intergroup relations will yield revised judgments about the content of the category "marginalized group."

What, then, do members of marginalized groups share? Most important, they share the experience of cultural and structural obstacles that nonmembers do not face, including the experience of group-based stereotypes. Not all group members experience the marginalization of their group in the same way or to the same degree. Not all members attach the same significance to group identity. But at the most general level the objective fact of marginalization gives group members a shared interest in overcoming that marginalization, even though they may interpret this interest very differently.[19] Group members also have divergent interests, since membership in a group is not the whole—or even, for some, the most salient element—of individual identity. In short the existence of structural inequality does not mean that the marginalized groups it creates will automatically share a unitary social or political purpose. Like other social groups, marginalized groups are internally diverse, and the formation of a shared political purpose can only be the product of political *action* among group members. Successful political mobilization around a group identity depends on the creation of a shared subjective sense of the political importance of that identity. The objective factors of structural inequality and a history of marginalization provide both the material preconditions for such a mobilization and the reasons why a group should receive moral recognition from others.

The internal diversity of groups poses interesting and difficult challenges to theorists of social difference. My focus on the distinguishing features of marginalized ascriptive groups is not meant to be an exhaustive theory of social groups. If that were its aim, it would undoubtedly fall short. Rather, my characterization of marginalized groups has a *practical political* purpose, namely, to provide a rationally and morally defensible way of coping with the fact of group-structured inequality within a scheme of political representation and to provide a means of distinguishing stronger from weaker claims to legislative self-representation. Max Black's reflections on the difficulty of defining the concept of a mathematical set has relevance to the challenges of defining marginalized groups: "Perhaps 'set' cannot be defined, upon some restrictive interpretation of definition; but its employment can surely be elucidated. The point is not to 'define' the word, but to delineate its functions—and that, too, deserves to be called definition."[20] Whatever the limitations of my account of marginalized groups, I am hopeful that it can at least perform the pragmatic functions I have set out for it.

IV. Substantive Justice, Procedural Fairness, and Group Representation

The definition of marginalized groups, and the concern to develop a theory of fair representation of those groups, turns on the critique of the injustice of patterns of structural inequality. But one might fairly ask why, if my ultimate concern is about social injustice, I have chosen to focus on legislative representation. My answer to this question is that, notwithstanding the size of this project, its aims are relatively modest: it claims that the legislative presence of historically marginalized groups will help significantly in ameliorating structural injustice, not that it will complete the job. The sources of marginalization are manifold, and dynamics of intergroup relations in civil society are undoubtedly more important in determining the shape of social hierarchy than anything government can do. If a substantial proportion of organizations in civil society incorporated principles of marginalized group representation into their decision-making processes, this might do far more to ameliorate structural injustice than changes in the system of political representation. But legislative institutions are, and for the foreseeable future will remain, immensely important in shaping our individual and collective lives. So long as they remain so, the legislative presence of marginalized groups promises to be an important source of social change and of increased political legitimacy.

But the question about the relationship between systemic injustice and group representation also raises a deeper theoretical question: given that my critique of liberal representation claims that we must look beyond proceduralism to substantive standards of justice, what, precisely, is the relationship between substantive conceptions of justice and procedural conceptions of fairness in my defense of group representation? The general answer is that both procedural and substantive conceptions of justice play essential roles in the group-based view of fair representation that I defend in this book.

Two intuitions about substantive justice inform my project as a whole. One is a standard for judging electoral outcomes; the other is a standard for judging other social and political processes. The first intuition is the one that launches the whole inquiry: that the chronic underrepresentation of historically marginalized groups is intrinsically unfair. The second, already noted above, underlies the definition of marginalized groups in terms of structural inequality: that the reproduction of patterns of inequality along the lines of ascriptive group identity is presumptively unjust. This understanding of social justice is a close relative of the liberal intuition that one's life chances—one's prospects of attaining one's life goals—ought not to be determined by one's social position at birth. For members of marginalized groups, life chances *are* limited by the fact of their membership in the group. Thus, although I am critical of some liberal understandings of procedural fairness, there is a close affinity between the intuitions with which my inquiry begins and those that liberals would affirm.

As I have already stated, my main purpose is to give a reasoned, theoretically coherent defense of the first substantive intuition about fair representation. But that defense turns on the argument that the two substantive (or results-oriented) standards of fairness are closely related. It is because the experience of marginalization is relevant to the representative agency of the legislator that fair representation often requires the *self*-representation of marginalized groups. At the same time, one of the core interests of marginalized groups that is served by self-representation is the amelioration of the patterns of structural inequality that constitute them as marginalized.

I demonstrate in chapter 3 that both intuitions about substantive fairness are deeply embedded in American political culture and jurisprudence. At the same time, ideals of procedural fairness are also deeply embedded in the American political and legal tradition. Now, pure procedural justice defines an allocative or decision-making procedure whose outcome is "correct or fair, whatever it is, provided that the procedure has been properly followed,"[21] under circumstances where there is no independent standard of the justice of the outcome. Principles of procedural fairness have three great advantages for dynamic, modern democratic societies in which individuals are regarded as free and equal and which are characterized by a plurality of moral commitments. First, procedural approaches allow people to agree on the *fairness* of an outcome or decision, even when they disagree substantively about what the outcome should be.[22]

Second, fair procedures provide a means for managing complex and iterative social interactions without the need for constant interventions. If one has successfully identified the elements of a fair procedure, "it is no longer necessary in meeting the demands of justice to keep track of the endless variety of circumstances and the changing relative positions of particular persons."[23] Third, procedural approaches in which all individuals are formally equal perform the expressive function of reaffirming the idea of equal respect for persons whenever they are employed.[24] It is, arguably, important to have such symbolic representations of equality in democratic institutions.

As discussed above, liberal representation contains two forms of procedural fairness: "one person, one vote" and interest-group pluralism. But despite the fact that liberal representation is open to a range of interpretations, it cannot, by itself, yield results that square with the substantive intuitions about fair outcomes. Adhering to principles of pure procedural fairness will neither erase structural inequality nor yield substantial increases in the legislative presence of marginalized groups. While some conclude that we should therefore abandon the substantive intuitions, I conclude that, once we have developed a moral defense of those intuitions, we should relax our embrace of pure procedural fairness and focus our energies on redressing our neglect of the substantive principles.

However, acknowledging the limitations of proceduralism does not mean we must reject the idea of procedural fairness altogether. The three advantages of proceduralism are genuine, and we should strive to secure them wherever possible. Instead, the failings of pure proceduralism should lead us to the conclusion that it is not a sufficient account of justice and that we should recur to outcome-oriented standards of fairness to judge our procedures and, if necessary, revise them. In this sense, my argument is a species of what Charles Beitz calls "complex proceduralism," i.e., a commitment to hold institutions simultaneously to substantive and procedural conceptions of fairness.[25] Beitz's view, and my interpretation of it, bear important similarities to what Rawls calls "imperfect procedural justice." Imperfect procedural justice stands as a contrast to pure procedural justice because it *does* articulate an independent substantive standard of justice, as well as a set of procedures which will generally (though imperfectly) realize that standard.[26] Rawls and others offer criminal justice as the paradigmatic example of imperfect procedural fairness.

The difference between imperfect procedural fairness as Rawls describes it and complex proceduralism is twofold.[27] First, complex proceduralism's substantive standards of fairness may be multiple, and they may also designate a *range* of substantively fair outcomes rather than a single outcome. Thus, in contrast to criminal justice in which the fair outcome is that guilty defendants should be convicted and innocent ones acquitted, complex proceduralism's account of fairness may simply rule some substantive outcomes out of bounds and regard as legitimate any outcome that falls within the acceptable range. Thus complex proceduralism might modify pure proceduralism's motto by defining outcomes as fair, "whatever they happen to be, *so long as they lie within this range.*" Second, whereas the formal statement of imperfect procedural justice appears indifferent to the qualities of the procedures themselves and are interested only in their efficacy at yielding the right outcomes, complex proceduralism applies standards of fairness directly to the procedures. Most important, it favors those procedures that embody the principles of equal respect for persons and of individual autonomy over those that do not.[28] In short, complex proceduralism defines the ideal of fair representation in terms that are "more than process, less than substance" and so occupies a middle ground between procedural and substantive fairness.[29]

It is important to note, however, that acknowledging the moral requirement of attention to substantive as well as procedural standards of fairness does not, in itself, justify any *particular* substantive standard; nor does it indicate whether or to what degree procedural fairness should give way to it. These issues require independent justification, which is why so much of my argument is focused on defending a standard of legislative presence for members of marginalized groups. This standard defines a range of morally permissible outcomes from legislative procedures; it aims at the roughly proportional presence of marginalized group members in legislatures. Yet I argue in chapter 7 that in fact we can go a long way toward realizing this standard through procedures that do respect individual equality and autonomy, but that finding the right procedural solution to the problem of fair representation may, in some social circumstances, require a recursive revision of electoral procedures in light of the electoral outcomes they produce; that is, electoral institutions which produce the continued systematic underrepresentation of historically marginalized groups should be subject to review aimed at discovering the reasons for those outcomes. To the extent that unequal outcomes reflect unjustifiable biases in electoral procedures, there is good reason to experiment with alternative electoral systems that will be less likely to produce the bias.

V. The Domain of the Argument

My defense of enhanced representation for marginalized groups is squarely situated within the American political tradition. Although I draw extensively on comparative research and on other countries' experimentation with diverse electoral systems in chapter 7's discussion of institutions. I do not mean to claim that my argument is valid for, or applicable to, all democratic societies. In particular, judgments about which groups merit special forms of recognition in politics are necessarily context-specific, contingent on the history and social dynamics of particular societies. For these reasons, the domain of my argument is limited to the case of American constitutional democracy. I nonetheless explore other countries' systems of representation because I believe there to be heuristic advantages in reflecting on our own practices in light of other countries' experiences, and because we may find there some concrete institutional alternatives that will be useful to us.

At the same time, I am hopeful that my discussion of the themes of "voice," "trust," and "memory" will contribute to broader debates about marginalized group claims for special recognition.[30] The central claims of this book are that a group's distinctive experience gives its members a perspective on social and political life that is relevant for collective decisions; that citizens' capacity to trust in institutions is a component of democratic legitimacy and that such trust may be compromised by a historical pattern of betrayal and domination; and that the history of a group's social and political experience is relevant to our moral judgments about its claims against the rest of society. In their most general form these arguments may illuminate discussions of group-based justice claims beyond the borders of the United States and beyond the sphere of political representation; but whether they indeed have such potential is a question I do not attempt to resolve here.

1

Representation as Mediation

I. The Problem of Fairness and the Complexity of Representation

What constitutes fair political representation? To begin with, a system of fair political representation would have to meet the broader standards of fairness that apply to a political order more generally. Most fundamentally, fair political institutions must treat citizens as equals, that is, they must not systematically sacrifice some citizens' interests to those of other citizens. Yet the question of which institutions of political representation can meet democratic standards of fairness is extremely difficult to answer, for institutions of representation mediate between individual citizens and governmental actions in multiple and complex ways. Consequently, deciding what constitutes "fairness" or "treating citizens as equals" in a system of political representation is itself a complex task.

In a representative government, the citizen's relation to the state is mediated in a number of ways, and any coherent theory of representation must give an account of the nature of these mediations. Moreover, and especially important for our purposes, a coherent theory of representation in a regime with democratic aspirations must make sense of the idea of political equality as it relates to these different ways in which political representation mediates between state and individual. Because representation is so complex, any conception of fair representation must be similarly complex. In other words, *a coherent theory of fair representation must give an account of the way in which political equality is served by each of the aspects of representation as mediation.*

When I use the term *representation as mediation* I mean that the different institutions and practices of any scheme of representation operate to shape and transform individual citizens' political concerns and interests into governmental decisions and policies. In stating it this way, however, I should make clear that I am not proposing a functionalist view of representation, in which a "system" of government transforms the "inputs" of individual preferences into the "outputs" of policy. One of the important differences between this view and functionalist ones is that I do not assume that citizen preferences are "given" in advance of politics. Nor do I wish to argue that there are fixed processes of representative government, which, given the same preferences, will always operate to produce the same policy outcomes. Rather, the idea of representation as mediation is that representative government per se inserts at least three distinct institutions or processes between individuals and policy outcomes. These three aspects of the mediative dynamics of representative government are (1) the nature of legislator-constituency relations; (2) the process of legislative decision making; and (3) the criteria for defining constituencies, that is, for identifying politically relevant groups.

First, the relationship of the individual to the state is mediated by the more direct relationship between representative and constituent, a relationship whose own complexity is illuminated by Hanna Pitkin's definition of political representation in her masterful work on the concept of representation:

> [R]epresenting here means acting in the interest of the represented, in a manner responsive to them. The representative must act independently; his action must involve discretion and judgment; he must be the one who acts. The represented must also be (conceived as) capable of independent action and judgment, not merely being taken care of. And, despite the resulting potential for conflict between representative and represented about what is to be done, that conflict must not normally take place.[1]

Thus representation requires that we recognize the agency of the represented; the agency of the representative; and the fact that the represented have real, discernible interests of which both they and their representative can be aware.

By focusing on the agency of the represented, we can see that the relationship between representative and constituent is partially constituted by the mechanisms of accountability by which constituents can hold their representatives responsible for looking after their interests. In a society committed to democratic equality, such mechanisms should embody a recognition of the equal agency of each citizen, her capacity for "independent action and judgment" in matters concerning her essential interests in politics. Whatever institutional form it takes, the principle of accountability would seem to require that representatives are equitably responsive to citizens' interests.

Before government can act in a manner that is responsive to the interests of individual citizens, those interests must be articulated by a representative in a decision-making body such as a legislature.[2] This draws our attention to the role of the representative's agency. But the expression a representative gives to constituent interests will be markedly different depending on the operative conception of the proper relationship between legislator and constituent. What are the obligations of the representative to the constituents? This is the aspect of political representation that is at stake in the many debates over the "delegate" and "trustee" models of representation. These debates concern the question of whether representatives ought to act strictly according to constituents' views of their own interests or whether the representative has a duty to act on his or her independent judgment, either of constituents' interests or the public interest.[3] But there are additional aspects of the relationship between legislator and constituent that are relevant: How does the representative become aware of constituent interests? Does the burden lie with the representative to discover those interests? Is he or she presumed to be familiar with constituency views by virtue of familiarity with their circumstances? What obligations do representatives have toward those who did not elect them? If constituencies are defined by territorial districts, for example, do representatives have obligations toward electoral minorities in their districts? Any coherent theory of political representation will offer some account of the relationship between the agency of both representatives and constituents, and the contribution of each to the government's capacity to act in a manner responsive to citizens' interests.

Second, a scheme of political representation mediates between individual and state through the dynamics of legislative decision making; that is, the ways in which final policies respond to and reflect citizens' political interests and preferences will be shaped not only by the attitude the representative takes toward them but also by the dynamics of the interactions between legislators. Are representatives expected to make strong claims only about issues that directly affect their constituents, or is it acceptable for them to take stances on issues about which their constituents may have no distinct views? Given that conflicting interests or preferences must somehow be reconciled if needed policies are to emerge from legislatures, what is the accepted method of reconciliation? The clearest contrast here would be between a deliberative model of decision making and a compromise or bargaining model.[4]

Finally, representation mediates between individual and state by the way in which it aggregates citizen preferences for the purposes of responsiveness. No matter how individualistic the premises of a political system, all political representation is group representation insofar as legislators represent constituencies and constituencies are defined by some shared characteristic, that is, as a group.[5] As Justice Powell put it in his opinion in *Davis v. Bandemer*, "The concept of 'representation' necessarily applies to groups: groups of voters elect representatives, individual voters do not."[6] Individual citizens can only be represented insofar as they have identifiable interests, and the act of identifying the interests that ought to be reflected in public policy is necessarily an act of defining a group of citizens who share those representable interests. In other words, no system of representation can escape the need to aggregate citizens for the purpose of assigning a representative to them. By identifying a basis for aggregating citizens, however, a system of representation identifies, at least implicitly, *communities of interest* whose recognition is relevant within the political arena.

However, to say that interests must somehow be aggregated or grouped together in order to be represented is not to specify the basis for aggregation. As I discuss in chapter 2, the predominant theory of representation in American political culture acknowledges two methods of interest aggregation: the voluntary organization of shared interests into pressure groups and the definition of territorial constituencies. There are other options, however. Consociational democracy, for example, defines the relevant interests according to subnational groups, usually defined along lines of language or religion. In neocorporatist systems, structural interests (labor, capital, and sometimes agriculture) are what receive representation. Party list systems of proportional representation aggregate citizens on the basis of party allegiance or ideology.

A system of representation's mechanism of aggregation carries normative weight because, implicitly or explicitly, it must distinguish the communities of interest that merit recognition in the political arena from those that do not. Clearly the decision to define constituencies along one line rather than another will have significant consequences for the political agenda, and consequently for different citizens' prospects for having their interests represented. A consociational democracy is much more likely to lead to the embodiment of ethnic minorities' interests in public policies than is a scheme of representation based solely on single-member territorial districts, for example. Choosing the former over the latter implies that there are good reasons to promote the representation of ethnic minorities.

But even modes of aggregation that do not explicitly affirm the political merit of particular substantive group interests will have the *effect* of favoring some interests over others. It is a well-established principle, for example, that schemes of representation that use single-member territorial districts tend to produce two-party systems in which the majority is overrepresented, whereas proportional representation schemes produce multiparty systems.[7] The political agenda in a two-party system will be narrower than that of a multiparty system,[8] and thus will generally be more likely to exclude political minorities' interests. Theories of fair representation that attempt to defend one electoral system over another do so precisely in terms of which groups' interests will receive expression in the political agenda. For example, some believe that a two-party system's amplification of majority preferences is desirable insofar as it prevents the agendas of radical or fringe political groups from appearing in the political arena.[9] In short, since every scheme of representation will lead to the greater representation of some kinds of interests than others, *every coherent theory of fair representation must have a correlative theory of groups.* The defense of a scheme of representation must rest, at least in part, on the claim that it aggregates citizens' interests in a manner that is salutary for politics. The latter part of this chapter examines this point in greater detail by exploring the place of groups in a number of historically prominent views of representation.

There is a fourth aspect to representation as mediation, namely, the nature and origin of the citizen preferences that are filtered through the processes of representation on the way to becoming policies. A common criticism of the dominant view of representation is that it assumes preferences are given prior to politics, and so does not recognize the formative influence of political insti tutions on the preferences themselves.[10] I think this criticism is correct: notwithstanding the assumptions of liberal theory, *any* institutions of representation (and probably political institutions in general) create circumstances favorable to the formation and expression of some kinds of preferences and unfavorable to the emergence of others. But it seems likely that the institutions that flow out of different theories of representation will influence the shape of citizen preferences in different ways, sometimes consciously and sometimes unintentionally. The influence of representative institutions on citizens' preference formation is crucially important to democratic theory and enters into my analysis at several points. Tracing the intricacies of this relationship is beyond the scope of my project here; I leave that work to others.[11] However, particularly in light of the importance of the moral psychology of group-based claims to fair representation, it is worthwhile to keep this more subtle dimension of representation in mind.

II. Groups and Representation:
The Need for a Political Sociology of Groups and the Flaws of Descriptive Representation

At first glance the statement that every theory of representation has a correlative theory of groups appears to run counter to individualistic views of representation. In particular, a claim that groups lie at the foundation of any theory of representation would seem to be undermined by a strong commitment to individual equality as against the political representation of collective entities such as territorial districts, economic sectors, or classes. As Chief Justice Warren put it in *Reynolds v. Sims*, "Legislators represent people, not trees or acres. Legislators are elected by voters, not farms or cities or economic interests."[12] Against John Adams's characterization of American society as comprised of the classical orders of "the one, the few, and the many," which he argued were represented by the president, the Senate, and the House, respectively, John Taylor of Caroline insisted that society was "made of individuals" who distributed their power "into a multitude of hands."[13] John Stuart Mill, criticizing those who opposed proportional representation for fear it would undermine the local character of representation, argued that it made no sense to speak of the representation of such collective entities as towns or counties apart from the representation of their individual inhabitants.[14]

It is true that some activities of elected representatives may reasonably be identified as cases of the representation of individuals. It makes sense, for example, to view constituency service as one such sort of personal representation.[15] But as I have suggested above, in most senses in which we use the term, *political representation* means the representation of a constituency, an aggregation or collection of citizens. Ultimately, the conduct of elected representa-

tives is judged according to the extent to which they have fulfilled their obligations to their constituencies taken as wholes, and not on the performance of
particular acts of service for particular citizens.

The need to articulate a principle for constituency definition has not been
reliably met by all theorists of representation. Indeed, some views of representation seem studiously to avoid articulating a theory of groups that could
support such a principle. For example, a group theory would certainly seem
to be absent from views of "descriptive" or "microcosmic" representation.[16] In
these views, what makes an assembly "representative" is its similarity to the
people themselves, its accuracy in reflecting or mirroring their characteristics.
As Melancton Smith expressed the idea during the New York debates over the
ratification of the Constitution, Congress "should be a true picture of the people."[17] John Adams similarly declared that a legislature ought to be "an exact
portrait, in miniature, of the people at large, as it should think, feel, reason
and act like them."[18] Indeed, the claim that more women and minorities
should hold government office often echoes these earlier statements of mirror
representation.

Left at this, theories of descriptive representation are rightly ridiculed.
Clearly, there is more to political representation than mere similarity to one's
constituents. First, in most views of representation the activities of the representative flow out of a broader view of the ends of government, which requires
the exercise of sound judgment or at least political astuteness, and an ability
to comprehend the complexities of public policies. In this light, descriptive
representation would seem to be a distinctly ill-suited device for securing
good political representation, as most of the theorists who regard the capacity
for judgment and comprehension as important attributes in politics do not
believe them to be evenly distributed across the population.

More to the point, descriptive representation appears absurd without some
specification of *which* attributes of the citizenry are relevant for the purposes
of political decision making.[19] Chancellor Livingston answered Melancton
Smith's demand for the representation of classes other than the "natural aristocracy" of wealth, education, and talent with a reductio ad absurdum that is
frequently invoked for this purpose. Smith, he said, "would have his government composed of other classes of men: where will we find them? Why, he
must go out into the highways, and pick up the rogue and the robber; he must
go to the hedges and ditches, and bring in the poor, the blind, and the lame."[20]
Lord Boothby expressed a similar idea even less diplomatically in a 1960 English radio program: "Ideally, the House of Commons should be a social mi-
crocosm of the nation. The nation includes a great many people who are
rather stupid, and so should the House."[21]

These mocking critiques are not altogether fair to advocates of descriptive
representation, who generally do not propose the equal representation of the
idiotic. But the critics do point up a gap in descriptive theorists' views: with-

out specifying *which* attributes of citizens especially deserve to be represented in an assembly, the idea of descriptive representation does not present a very compelling view of political representation at all.[22] It leads either to the kind of absurdity that critics relish, as noted above, or it articulates a view of representation that is likely to be unworkable because it would require too large a number of representatives. More important, as Pitkin points out, descriptive representation, if taken literally, destroys the mediative distance between representative and elector and renders meaningless the distinction between these two roles; it fails to specify what activities the representative performs on the elector's behalf that merit the name "representation."[23] On its face, descriptive representation does not present a compelling understanding of political representation because it is neither possible nor desirable to represent all aspects of citizens. Something more is needed, namely, a set of defensible standards by which to distinguish those attributes of citizens that deserve representation from those that do not.

The latter part of this chapter examines the ideas of four prominent theorists of representation in Anglo-American political thought—Edmund Burke, James Madison, John C. Calhoun, and John Stuart Mill—and focuses especially on the place of groups within their theories. Each of these theorists offers a scheme of political representation which he regards as serving "the interest of the represented, in a manner responsive to them," yet each scheme differs importantly from the next. It is instructive to examine these prominent theories of representation in some detail, as such an examination reveals some of the relationships between the different aspects of representation as mediation. In particular, they reveal that stating a principle for constituency definition is a more profound step than it might initially appear. Ultimately it rests on both an *empirical hypothesis* about the group structure of society and a *normative vision* of the manner in which a nation's common good is constituted through the activities and institutions of political representation. The relation between a theorist's empirical analysis of the social "matter" and of his or her normative vision of the common good, it turns out, dictates a great deal of the structure of representative institutions. If we alter our characterization of the social groups that are most relevant for purposes of political representation, we are very likely to have to alter our conception of the most desirable processes of political decision making and of the ideal relationship between the representative and the represented.

The examination of the theories of Burke, Madison, Calhoun, and Mill serves three functions in the project as a whole. First, it reminds us that there are alternatives to our contemporary habits of mind concerning the representation of social groups. Consequently it provides us with conceptual resources for examining contemporary issues of political representation that we might otherwise tend to overlook and that can fruitfully inform our current thinking about political representation. I draw instruction from the insights (and errors) of these thinkers throughout the remainder of the book. Second, by drawing attention to the relationship between constituency definition and other aspects of representation as mediation, I hope to show what other treatments of political representation have tended to overlook: that how we conceive of the social groups that are relevant for politics radically affects our conclusions about what constitutes fair representation. Given that the project of the work as a whole is to evaluate the claims of marginalized groups to political representation *as* groups, it is useful to see how, in general, a different understanding of politically relevant groups might unsettle assumptions about fair representation as well. As we shall see in the following chapters, the challenge that marginalized groups present to the prevailing conception of fair representation consists largely in a challenge to the appropriateness of that conception's definition of politically relevant groups. Finally, a comparison among these theories reveals a disagreement not only over the *identity* of politically relevant groups but also over how best to manage conflict among groups. Some theorists of representation regard intergroup conflict as salutary for the discovery of a common good; others regard it as destructive of the common good; still others regard some group differences in a positive light and some in a negative light. Thus one of my purposes in this chapter is to elucidate the distinction between what I call *expressive, suppressive,* and *mixed* theories of representation.

The relationship between a theory's political sociology and its view of the nature of the common good is, fundamentally, a partial account of what constitutes political legitimacy, and therefore of what the theorist believes justifies rational trust in government. Before turning to examine the theories of Burke, Madison, Calhoun, and Mill, therefore, it is fruitful to attend more closely to the question of the contribution of political representation to political trust.

III. Trust and Political Representation

In constitutions based on institutions of representation, it is not practical for governments to have constant recourse to citizens' active consent or approval of every state action. Consequently a politics of representation must draw on a fund of popular *trust* in the government's fairness in protecting and advancing citizens' interests. The concept of fairness, whether in institutions of political representation or in other political institutions, provides the standard for evaluating whether popular trust is justified in any particular instance. The conformity of political institutions to principles of fairness is what makes government worthy of popular trust. Indeed, this interdependence between the concept of fairness and citizens' ability to trust their government to protect their essential interests is commonly expressed by political theorists' characterization of political office as a "trust," and of officeholders as "trustees" for the public welfare.[24] Clearly citizens' ability to trust in government is an integral element of political legitimacy. What elements of a system of representation inspire the trust necessary to sustain government legitimacy?

An inquiry into political trust benefits from Hobbes, who tells us that

> Trust is a Passion proceeding from the *Belief of him* from whom we *expect* or *hope* for Good, so *free* from *Doubt* that upon the same we pursue no other Way to attain the same Good: as *Distrust* or Diffidence is *Doubt* that maketh him endeavour to provide himself by other means.[25]

Hobbes's definition of trust tells us something of its complexity. It is a passion, an affective state, which we know by the fact that we cannot will ourselves to trust another any more than we can will ourselves to love another. But, at the same time, trust is a cognitive state, a belief regarding the likely actions of another. This cognitive aspect is revealed by our capacity to judge whether trust is well- or ill-placed; when we trust someone, we should have *reason* to believe that he or she will act for our good. Moreover, trust involves a transference of *agency*, a relinquishment of the prerogative to act on our own behalf, to rely exclusively on our own capacities. It is more than a *hope* that the person we trust will act in a way that delivers some "Good" to us, for hope does not imply that we will not take other measures to secure the end in question. When we entrust our interest to another's care, as when we allow others to look after our children, we simultaneously surrender the option of looking after the interest ourselves. In the absence of trust, or in the face of a failed trust, a betrayal, reason dictates that we must act on our own behalf. It would clearly be foolish to give over our welfare to the care of one who was demonstrably unwilling or unable to look after our interests. Relations of trust are epitomized by the making and keeping of promises, which always involve an initial expression of faith despite uncertainty that, when promises are observed, becomes transformed into a belief justified by reason. As John Dunn puts it, trust is both a "modality of action" and a state of mind, but it is possible that by acting on trust under conditions of uncertainty we may "convert a *policy* of trust into a condition of confidence."[26]

The idea that trust lies at the heart of representative government is a longstanding and familiar one. Most important, conceiving of representative government as a relationship of trust means recognizing that the power governors exercise is not for their own benefit but for the benefit of the governed, "the people," however they may be defined. Moreover, representation as a fiduciary relationship is a two-sided affair, creating "trust and obligation" for both the representative and the represented.[27] On the side of the representative, it incurs the obligation to advocate policies that will serve constituent interests. On the side of the represented, representation creates an obligation to obey the laws so long as government has acted in good faith. Others use the legal concept of the trust to describe both the responsibilities of government in general and the role of the representative in particular. As Hanna Pitkin explains, a legal trust involves the transference of a property title from a principal to a trustee with the restriction that it must be administered in the principal's interest. However, she is careful to note, the idea that the representative should act as trustee for the represented entails no necessary obligation to *consult* constituents regarding their preferred course of action. As we shall see, this point is abundantly clear in Burke's conception of the representative as trustee.[28] John Stuart Mill even characterizes the franchise itself as a trust, not to be exercised in the interest of selfish desires but as an expression of individual judgment regarding the public interest.[29]

John Locke is the theorist of trust par excellence, and his conception of limited government as a trust most powerfully informs all the rest. In the *Second Treatise*, Locke states that

> the Legislative being only a Fiduciary Power to act for certain ends, there remains still in *the People a Supreme Power* to remove or *alter the Legislative*, when they find the *Legislative* act contrary to the trust reposed in them. For all *Power given with trust* for the attaining an *end*, being limited by that end, whenever that *end* is manifestly neglected, or opposed, the *trust* must necessarily be *forfeited*, and the Power devolve into the hands of those that gave it, who may place it anywhere they shall think best for their safety and security.[30]

As in Hobbes's definition, Locke's view makes clear that a betrayal of the people's trust in government leaves only one option, that of reclaiming the agency, the "*Power*," they delegated and exercising it again on their own behalf. Moreover, in representative democracies Locke's logic operates at two levels. Not only do the people retain the right of resistance against a government that has fundamentally betrayed their trust, but periodic elections return constituencies' political power to them, enabling them to reject an individual representative who has failed to protect their essential interests. Indeed, it seems fair to say that the relationship of trust that exists between the people and the government as a whole is reproduced in miniature in the relationship between a representative and his or her constituents: constituents' power to hold their political agents accountable is a critical foundation of their capacity for political trust. Further, representative democracy assumes that the more effective an electoral system at securing a relation of well-founded trust between representative and constituents, the less likely that government as a whole will betray its trust.

Locke's view of limited government as a trust contains an important element, however, that tends to get obscured in contemporary discussions of representative democracy: that a moral relationship of trust between people and government must be undergirded by a trust among the people themselves. In Locke's view, these two different stages of trust are contained in the contract that creates political society and in the delegation of the collective power of the body politic to a government created by majority decision.[31] In modern representative democracy, given the fact of social diversity, it is more difficult to assume the possibility of a body politic unified by trust. Yet some degree of trust among citizens would appear essential to a society's capacity for legitimate government, government that can be trusted with the tremendous powers that governments now possess. At a minimum, "citizens must trust one another to constitute parties, electoral constituencies, and majorities. . . . Finally, when those in office betray their trust, citizens must trust one another enough to organize resistance to unlawful rule."[32]

Just as every theory of representation contains a theory of groups, no theory of representation that claims to articulate a vision of *legitimate* government is complete without an account of trust. Every scheme of representation must offer citizens a *rational basis of trust* in government, a set of reasons why institutions of representation will function to make government responsive to their essential interests. Moreover, because, as Locke shows us, some degree of trust *among* citizens is a precondition of trust in government, there is an important relationship between the characterization of the group structure of society and the capacity of a system of representation to sustain popular trust. Since the definition of politically relevant groups depends on the contours of social and political conflict, it seems clear that a system of representation can uphold citizens' trust in government only to the extent that it is able to mediate that conflict. As we shall see in the following overview of prominent theories of representation, this last aspect of representation as mediation may take a number of different forms. In short, different systems of representation offer different reasons for citizens to trust in government.

IV. Burke

Edmund Burke's views on political representation are well known for their elitism, particularly for the idea that Parliament should be composed of a "natural aristocracy" of merit and judgment. Burke was a self-declared Whig and thought it important that members of the House of Commons be elected—not primarily because it would make them more responsive to the people, but because it was only by owing their seats to a power independent of the crown that they could be trusted to remain morally independent of the crown. The purpose of government was to protect and preserve the interests of the people, and the House of Commons would be kept to that purpose only by its accountability to electors who would turn members out of office if they were seen abusing the public trust. "The House of Commons," he wrote, "can never be a control on other parts of government unless they are controlled themselves by their constituents; and unless those constituents possess some right in the choice of that House which it is not in the power of that House to take away."[33] But it was not by enacting the will of the people that their protection was best secured. Rather, representatives fulfilled their functions through the exercise of their superior judgment in deliberations with other members of Parliament about the content of the common interest in particular cases. The role of the representative, therefore, was not to follow the wishes of his or her constituents, which would tend to be short-sightedly self-interested, but to act as the people's trustee, taking on the responsibility for acting in the best long-term interests of the nation as a whole. If this were done, Burke was confident, the interests of each part of the nation would be abundantly fulfilled: the wise know that the interests of the whole nation, despite surface appearances, do not conflict with the interests of the parts. In his famous speech to the electors of Bristol, his constituents, Burke summed up these ideas in a single, grandiloquent statement:

> Parliament is not a *congress* of ambassadors from different and hostile interests, which interests each must maintain, as an agent and advocate, against other agents and advocates; but Parliament is a *deliberative* assembly of *one* nation, with *one* interest, that of the whole—where not local purposes, not local prejudices, ought to guide, but the general good, resulting from the general reason of the whole.[34]

Defining the common interest means moving among the apparently conflicting interests of the several parts in order to locate the solution that harmonizes them all and, in so doing, preserves the whole.

Burke's view of the corporate structure of society was based on a certain sociology, that is, on empirically grounded judgments about what the relevant elements in society were rather than on a theory of a natural order. Burke partly carries over the functional-corporatism of the medieval view of society. But whereas the functional groupings in the medieval view were regarded as divinely ordained, Burke's functionalism is based on a vision of Britain as a commercial nation and empire, a vision that defines the relevant "interests" in society in terms of broad economic sectors. Thus there is "a mercantile interest, an agricultural interest, a professional interest,"[35] each of which plays an integral part in the economic flourishing of Britain as a whole. In addition to such functionally defined groups, however, Burke also defends "descriptions" of people whose claims for political representation are at least as strongly grounded in equity and justice as in economic and political prudence.[36] His discussions of "virtual representation," particularly as they relate to Irish Catholics and American colonists, display an alternative, contractualist Burke whose insights into the relationship between fair or just representation and the correct identification of politically relevant groups are particularly significant for contemporary efforts to define fair representation for historically disadvantaged groups.

Virtual representation, in Burkean theory as in the general views of his age, stands in contrast with the "actual" representation of constituencies that send

representatives to Parliament. Citizens are virtually represented when, despite
the fact that they lack the opportunity to elect a representative, their concerns
are expressed by representatives whose own electors share similar concerns.
Burke defines virtual representation in this way: "Virtual representation is that
in which there is a communion of interests and a sympathy in feelings and
desires between those who act in the name of any description of people and
the people in whose name they act, though the trustees are not actually chosen
by them."[37] Here Burke speaks of the virtual representation of "descriptions"
of people and not of interests, groups, classes, territories, or sectors. The term
description arises repeatedly in Burke's discussion of the representation of col-
lections of citizens. In a discussion of constitutional reform, for example, he
argues that if constitutional changes were to be made (a prospect he viewed
dimly), they must be made in accordance with the sense of the people, and
that this would require "that the matter should be prepared in open committees, from a choice into which no *class or description* of men is to be excluded."[38] In his scathing critique of the exclusion of Irish Catholics from
representation, Burke states that "the Catholic, as a Catholic, *and belonging to
a description*, has no *virtual* relation to the representative—but the *contrary*."[39]
On the same topic Burke rejects the idea that Irish Catholics were virtually
represented by the candidates chosen by Protestant electors, who had the
exclusive right to vote. For the Catholics, he said, "it is not an *actual*, and, if
possible, still less a *virtual* representation. It is, indeed, the direct contrary. It
is power unlimited placed in the hands of *an adverse* description *because it is
an adverse description*."[40]

It would seem that if the virtual representation of a "description" consists in
a "communion of interests" and "sympathy of feelings," then an "adverse description" would have to refer to a class of citizens whose interests were opposed to the interests of the "description" in question, and who felt antipathy
toward them. Clearly this was the case with the exclusion of the Irish Catholics, who were denied political rights for reasons of sheer bigotry; that is, it was
precisely because of Protestant feelings of animosity toward Catholics that the
latter were denied the franchise, and surely there could be no greater contrast
with the "sympathy of feelings" that defines virtual representation.

The "compact" which constitutes the corporate entity of the nation is a
constantly (if slowly) changing one, whose strength derives precisely from its
gradual adaptation to the changing demands placed on it. The parties to it
have, over time, presented challenges to it that it has answered and, in answering them, it has become a much more creative and resilient compact than any
particular group of individuals could possibly define:

> [A] nation is not an idea only of local extent and individual momentary aggregation,
> but it is an idea of continuity which extends in time as well as in numbers and in
> space. And this is a choice not of one day or one set of people, not a tumultuary and

giddy choice; it is a deliberate election of ages and of generations; it is a constitution made by what is ten thousand times better than choice: it is made by the peculiar circumstances, occasions, tempers, dispositions, and moral, civil, and social habitudes of the people, which disclose themselves only in a long space of time. It is a vestment which accommodates itself to the body.[41]

This is the source of Burke's conservatism: Because the practical adaptations to constitutional arrangements that were wrought by history are superior to the judgments of individual men, Burke was reluctant to make changes to the Constitution. More important for our purposes, he was ever conscious that sustaining the "compact" among the diverse elements of the British nation and empire required a conscientious attention to the interests of each part. Virtual representation plays an important role in his theory because it ensures that any sense among a "description" of citizens that their interests are being violated will be aired, and so can be attended to by Parliament. No element of the nation or empire, he argued, can be kept in it by force without destroying those things which make union valuable: economic prosperity and the liberty of the people.[42] The attachment of the different parts to the nation must be maintained, therefore, by ensuring that each has a tangible motive to remain a party to the compact. As he said in relation to the issue of taxation in the American colonies, "The question . . . is, not whether you have a right to render your people miserable, but whether it is not your interest to make them happy."[43]

It is now easier to see the ways in which Burke's corporate view of the nation includes an understanding of the corporate character of the different parts of the nation. Virtual representation and the concept of "descriptions" of citizens suggest that the groups that are relevant for political representation are those that have both shared interests and a "sympathy of feelings," the combination of which create the capacity to act as a body. The "sympathy of feelings," it appears, might originate in functionally defined powerful interests themselves, or they might be created by a sense of shared history, culture, and values. This characterization would apply equally to territorial units or localities, to major economic sectors, and to religious or cultural groupings; it would describe Bristol as a "commercial city," the American colonists as joined both by a spirit of liberty and economic interests that were being violated by British taxation, and the Irish Catholics as joined by religious belief and an interest in not being economically and politically oppressed. Depending on the nature of the "description" of citizens or subjects, it is perfectly plausible that it could remove itself from the nation simply by refusing its cooperation, the consequences of which are, Burke believed, almost always undesirable for all concerned.

As this makes clear, the task of representation was to ensure that no "description" was pushed to the point of refusal to cooperate. Its performance depended on the House of Commons "being the express image of the feelings of the nation,"[44] well-attuned to the presence of grievances in the nation. The representatives, as trustees of the national interest and reporters of discontent, had the challenging but (Burke seemed optimistically to believe) usually manageable job of harmonizing the various interests within the nation in a manner that would keep everyone sufficiently contented that they would have no cause to rebel. Thus Burke's account of virtual representation yields an *expressive* view of representation, at least with regard to the various "descriptions" discussed here (though not with regard to the lower classes).

The House of Commons, on this view, ought to include the best men from the various "descriptions" of citizens[45]—though it was not necessary that the descriptions receive representation in proportion to population. All that was required for effective deliberation was the *presence* of the different concerns. Moreover, the test of good government, of effective representation, is not whether it is responsive to the various concerns or interests expressed by the various elements in society (not all of which, it should be noted, are necessarily attached to the "descriptions" he has in mind, as would certainly be the case with populist rumblings), but whether it succeeds in keeping the whole together, securing liberty, and promoting prosperity. "In all moral machinery," Burke wrote, "the moral results are its test."[46]

For Burke, the practices that secure trust in government are thus relatively blunt instruments. Popular trust cannot be secured by any particular act of responsiveness or "responsibility"; rather, it is the product of a pattern of governmental actions that demonstrate a recognition of the place that each social description holds in the life of the nation or empire as a whole. Just as it must be created over time, such trust cannot be destroyed in a single moment but will be withdrawn gradually during the course of a Lockean "long train of Abuses"[47] that demonstrates the willful disregard of a particular "description's" interests.

Burke's theory of representation provides a particularly clear demonstration of the important relationship between the definition of the groups that are politically relevant and the other aspects of representation as mediation. As we have seen, Burke identifies as relevant those groups or "descriptions" of citizens that are joined by a "sympathy of feeling" or commonality of interest that has become apparent over time. Such groups are distinct from other elements of society and are substantial enough that their willing cooperation is a necessary component of the prosperity and well-being of the nation or empire as a whole. Given such a view of politically relevant groups, it seems clear that the relationship between representative and constituents cannot be one in which the representative is the delegate of the constituents, allowing their instructions to determine his parliamentary votes. To the contrary, although the representative has a special obligation to ensure that his constituency's principal interests receive expression in Parliament, ultimately his role is to balance their interests against, and integrate them with, other important social interests. Neither the group's existence nor the political relevance of its concerns is a product of constituents' will, and the prudent representative will recognize this. He must have a sense of what historical forces have shaped the constituents' particular interests in order to judge what present political and economic dynamics bode for them.

Further, if this is the individual representative's role, it is clear that the dynamics of parliamentary decision making follow directly: the decision-making process must be a deliberative one in which various social interests are balanced against one another. Since the nation or empire is conceived as a corporate whole whose well-being is constituted by the appropriate relation of its parts, the task of defining the common good can only be that of discerning what that relation is, a task best met through the exchange of rational arguments aimed at mutual persuasion. A national interest so conceived could not be served through mere bargaining or defined by simple majority vote. Burke offers a view of the common good whose identification depends on the quality of representatives' individual and collective judgment.

V. Madison

James Madison's view of the group structure of society differed radically from Burke's in a number of important respects. Most important, Madison saw groups as defined less by what joined them in a "communion of interest" or "sympathy of feeling" than by the opposition of their interests to the interests of others. Interests as such are always particular interests, or "factions," defined in opposition to the common good, and so they can never play a salutary role in the construction of that common good. Whereas a conflict of interests is, in Burke's view, generally only apparent and in most events resolvable, Madison sees conflict as an inevitable and defining feature of political life in a free society. "The latent causes of faction," he wrote in *Federalist* 10, are "sown in the nature of man."[48]

These causes are various in nature and are characterized in part by the inevitable differences of opinion over every conceivable matter that will emerge in a free society. But in another important contrast with Burke, Madison regards the principal and most enduring cause of faction to be class, "an unequal distribution of property." Certainly Madison also emphasizes the sectoral groupings that figure in economic-functionalist readings of Burke; they include "a landed interest, a manufacturing interest, a mercantile interest, a moneyed interest." But unlike Burke, Madison does not believe that any internal harmony of these interests can be worked through a hierarchical ordering of classes.[49] "Those who hold and those who are without property have ever formed distinct interests in society."[50] Moreover, the different interests created by class, opinion, religion, and sectoral concerns all cut across one another, coalescing sometimes along one line, sometimes along another. Madison rejects the idea that "enlightened statesmen" can harmonize these conflicting interests, as Burke believes is possible, on the ground that "[e]nlightened statesmen will not always be at the helm" (p. 80). But this supposes that enlightened men would be capable of harmonizing the interests if they *were* at the helm, a supposition that is contradicted by Madison's general characterization of the clash of factions. Rather, different degrees of property, and of the faculties that produce property, form "insuperable obstacle[s] to a uniformity of interests" in society (p. 78).

Apart from Madison's definition of factions as "adverse to the rights of other citizens, or to the permanent and aggregate interests of the community" (p. 78), it is not yet clear why the free development of factions is undesirable. The reason, Madison argues, is that conflicting interests will elect legislators who will attempt to advance these particular interests against those of other groups and of the whole. Questions of economic regulation and taxation would yield different answers depending on which interests were predominant, and none of the answers would likely be formulated "with a sole regard to justice and the public good" (p. 80). In particular, as Jennifer Nedelsky argues convincingly, the danger in a popular government is that a "majority faction" of the propertyless would form and would enact policies violating the rights and interests of property; they would hasten to act on "[a] rage for paper money, for an abolition of debts, for an equal division of property" (p. 84). These problems were precisely the ones that had created an increasing degree of social and political instability under the Articles of Confederation, and they, above all, had to be remedied if the new nation would endure.[51]

Madison's celebrated solution was "a republican remedy for the diseases most incident to republican government."[52] That remedy was representative government: in contrast to direct democracy, representative government was possible over a broad territory. This "extended sphere" of government meant that a greater variety of interests would be brought into play, which would cause territorial, sectoral, religious, class, and other interests to cut across one another in myriad ways, making it virtually impossible for any one category of interest to dominate. His oft-quoted plan bears repeating: "Extend the sphere and you take in a greater variety of parties and interests; you make it less probable that a majority of the whole will have a common motive to invade the rights of other citizens; or *if such a common motive exists, it will be more difficult for all who feel it to discover their own strength and to act in unison with each other.*"[53] Although elected representatives would still promote the particular interests of their constituents, the competing interests in Congress would cancel one another out. We can therefore be confident, Madison argued, that only those programs that are in the common interest of the whole will command a majority of the representatives, and in this way the public good will be preserved.

I have rehearsed Madison's familiar argument in order to point out those features that distinguish his view of group representation from the view embedded in other prominent theories of representation. The contrast with Burke's view is of special interest, particularly in light of the many similarities between Burke and Madison. Both believed that institutions should be structured so as to encourage the election of a talented elite inclined toward the public interest. The flip side of this similarity was that both distrusted the people's judgment regarding their genuine, long-term interests, and both believed that good government was more likely to be secured through a responsibility to the broad ends of government than through an easy responsiveness to the shifting popular will. Finally, Burke and Madison shared the belief that a national interest distinct from narrow social interests not only exists but can and should provide the aim of legislative activity.

In contrast to Burke, Madison was not confident that elections would always place the most talented men in office or that those who were elected would prefer the common interest to factional interests or to personal aggrandizement. Whereas Burke relied on the character of the people to put good men in office (and to remove those who proved unworthy of the trust) and on the virtue of those men to promote the common good, Madison was not willing to leave the fate of the nation to anything as unreliable as virtue. Instead, he put his faith in the ingenuity of the constitutional convention to create institutions that would substitute interest for virtue, channeling the forces of interest to produce the common good.

This approach produced the contrast between Madison's and Burke's theories of representation that is of the greatest relevance here, namely, the contrast between Burke's belief that the various interests of the nation could be harmonized and Madison's belief that conflict was an ever-present fact of politics. It is true that in Burke's view the concerns and feelings of the different "descriptions of citizens" were not useful guides to policy; while the people were the best judges of their own suffering, they lacked the powers of diagnosis and prescription necessary to make any worthwhile contribution to public affairs. However, it was essential to the vitality of the nation as a whole that their feelings be expressed, for only through an awareness of such feelings—and especially feelings of aggrievement—was Parliament alerted to the potential "schisms" in the nation that "wanted healing." The idea of virtual representation was, in this limited sense, a statement that the various "descriptions" of people within the nation should receive representation as such.

For Madison, the goal of the system of representation in the "extended republic" was to prevent such schisms from emerging in the first place. The only "descriptions" of citizens that had any permanence were those defined by class. But the oppression of one class by the other could be averted by preventing either from organizing along class lines. This goal might appear to be contradicted by his hope and expectation that a "natural aristocracy" would fill governmental offices: although being a member of this group was not solely a function of wealth, it clearly did not include the propertyless. Yet the wealthier classes did not pose a threat to the common interest of society in the same way as the propertyless did. Not only were they naturally inclined to take a longer view of things, but the cross-cutting interests of the well-off would themselves prevent any thorough-going exploitation of office for sectional gain. Moreover, to the extent that the shared interests of property did shape policy, they would do so only in the general direction of stability and prosperity. Despite the beliefs of the propertyless classes, these could only work to their long-term advantage as well. If only the lower classes could be prevented from forming an effective organization of their interests, the benefits of protections for property as a condition of economic development and social stability would soon be apparent to all. Property was both a right and an institution necessary for the general prosperity, yet only the few "can be interested in preserving the rights of property."[54]

Madison certainly was committed to the idea of government by the consent of the people. Yet it is a distinct irony in his theory of representation that the aspect of the scheme that will likely *motivate* popular consent and trust in government (the freedom to elect representatives who will pursue their interests in Congress) is almost contrary to the aspect that *justifies* consent (the inability of partial interests to become policy when they do not accord with the general interest). While this move is Machiavellian in its brilliance, we might well question whether it can satisfy democratic norms of publicity as a ground of legitimacy. What is not clear in Madison's theory, however, is what determines the content of the general interest that *ought* to be realized through representative government. If it is not a product of the various interests in society, then how are we to understand it, and how is a deliberative body of representatives to locate it? At times Madison seems to agree with Hamilton's conception of the common good in terms of "public goods" such as national defense and public peace. Yet these do not seem to offer a sufficient sense of common purpose to sustain the unity of the nation as a whole. As Nedelsky expresses this problem in Madison's theory,

> [F]or all Madison's sophistication about the sources of conflict, he had little more to offer as a solution than the neutralization of that conflict. . . . [H]e offered little about what the public good actually consisted of and how his system would ensure that it was "discerned" and pursued. And he had little to say about what would promote sufficient harmony among the conflicting groups to develop some sense of common purpose.[55]

For Madison, social groups' political relevance is not that they constitute the interests that must be recognized if the common good is to be achieved but, to the contrary, that *the common good depends on their suppression*. This is particularly true for class interests, but it holds for other types of faction as well. How does this reading of the relevance of social groups inform the other aspects of representation as mediation in Madison's theory? In general, it would seem, the most desirable relationship between representative and constituent is one in which the representative acts directly to advance the constituency's interests. Since the mutual cancellation of conflicting social interests is a function of their multiplicity, Madison's scheme would seem to be more effective the greater the number of interests advanced by legislative officials. Moreover, as noted above, such advocacy will inspire constituents' trust and confidence in government, despite the fact that it is the frustration of particular interests that actually warrants their trust. In order to produce this reciprocal canceling out of factional interests, the dynamics of legislative decision making would seem to have to be defined by a bargaining process in which the multiplicity of deals neutralized policy outcomes taken as a whole. As noted above, however, the principal flaw in Madison's theory is that in order for any substantive common good to be achieved the politics of factional competition would have to be supplemented by a politics of deliberation over the common good, something for which he makes no provision.

VI. Calhoun

Government, John C. Calhoun argued, has two sources in human nature: that individuals prefer their own happiness to that of others, producing conflict, and that human beings naturally desire the society of others.[56] The former attribute makes government necessary, and the latter makes it possible. The principal task of constitutional design is to structure institutions so as to encourage and develop citizens' social impulses and render harmless individuals' tendency to put their own interests first.

The need to protect against the abuse of one element of society by another exists in all constitutional governments, Calhoun argued, but it is particularly difficult to resolve in popular regimes. The emphasis on equality in democratic societies encourages a tendency toward majoritarianism or, as Calhoun calls it, government by "numerical majority." In a society governed according to the majority principle, Calhoun argues, the dynamics of politics inevitably divide society into two great parties, which are coalitions of the various interests in society. The majority party then uses its position of power to accomplish its aims, against the interests of the minority, and the minority party struggles to turn the electoral tables, so that it might then do the same. This endless competition between the two parties is destructive of the ends of government for a number of reasons. First, and most obvious, it fails to protect the interests of members of the minority party, who are, after all, part of the nation and equally entitled to the benefits of government. Second, because the parties are constantly vying for the political power necessary to advance their particular aims, no effort is invested in locating a common interest.

The multiple dangers threatening popular government can be avoided, Calhoun argues, by replacing rule by the numerical majority with that of the "concurrent majority." Instead of allowing the majority to decide public policy, this constitutional device (or *organism*, in Calhoun's terminology) would require the assent of "each interest or portion of the community" separately; only when all agree can a policy take effect. It thus would "require the consent of each interest either to put or to keep the government in action," and so would give each a "concurrent voice in making and exercising the laws or a veto on their execution."[57] The sense of each interest must be taken by "the appropriate organ"; in a popular government, this means by its majority.

By giving each social interest or section a veto over governmental action, government by concurrent majority removes all opportunity for groups to violate one another's interests. In the process, it also removes the temptation to narrow self-aggrandizement and encourages groups to find ways of harmonizing their interests with those of their historic competitors. In this way, "individual feelings are . . . necessarily enlisted on the side of the social, and made to unite with them in promoting the separate interests of each, while in those of the numerical majority the social are necessarily enlisted on the side of the individual and made to contribute to the interest of parties regardless of that of the whole."[58] In contrast to the ceaseless competition and maneuvering that characterizes a government by numerical majority, Calhoun argued that government by concurrent majority would force political leaders to deliberate about the common good. Just as the rule of unanimity produces agreement among jury members even where they begin with starkly different positions, the veto power of each social interest would force a consensus on legislation. Calhoun dismissed the likelihood of government paralysis under such a scheme on the ground that the costs of inaction would, in all the important cases, be greater than those of compromise.[59]

Thus, like Madison, Calhoun envisioned his scheme of the representation of diverse and conflicting interests as resulting in the suppression of class-based representation and hence the stabilization of politics. The constitutional protection of certain portions of society through the device of the concurrent majority is likely to deflect attention away from other social cleavages. This would not present a problem for Calhoun's theory if he supposed the social cleavages that warranted expression through concurrent majorities to be permanent features of the society. To the contrary, however, Calhoun emphasized the evolving nature of society and politics. In particular, he argued that changing economic circumstances, driven by technological innovations, would restructure social relations and give rise to new social interests. Yet the institutions of concurrent majorities that Calhoun discusses—and particularly the idea of two presidents elected separately by North and South—crystallize the cleavages of the day by giving them constitutional status. Once a particular definition of the relevant "portions" of the community has been embedded in the Constitution, it is likely to be very difficult to change them in response to changing circumstances. As Richard Hofstadter argues, "[t]he essence of Calhoun's mistake as a statesman was that he tried to achieve a static solution for a dynamic situation,"[60] and this mistake was all the more serious because of Calhoun's own theoretical emphasis on historical change. Ultimately the weaknesses of his view arose from the fact that he was not interested in protecting the rights of minorities *in general*, but only in protecting the interests of Southern planters against the North. By attempting to justify this aim through a general theory of concurrent majorities, Calhoun became entangled in inescapable inconsistencies.

Despite these difficulties, Calhoun's argument provides an insight into the problems of minority representation that eluded both Burke and Madison. Calhoun's central insight was that where a deep and lasting conflict exists, the minority interest will be dominated unless the majority is given no choice but to take minority interests into account. It is ironic that despite his defense of slavery as a "positive good"[61] Calhoun's insight into the failure of rational trust endemic to a deeply divided society has particular contemporary relevance in American society, divided as it is by race.[62] Calhoun saw that when a society has become separated into a majority and a minority that share little commonality of interest or experience, and when the majority "section" controls the government, the minority has little cause for trust in that government's propensity to protect its essential interests. Under such circumstances, the constitutional devices that normally protect against majority tyranny are ineffectual; they have already failed to prevent the emergence of a political majority capable of controlling the various branches of the federal government. These circumstances call for measures that acknowledge the failure of political trust and attempt to repair it. Because the circumstances are so grave, the measures must be radical. Whereas under other circumstances trust might be warranted by a system of checks and balances that keeps political officials attentive to the public interest, under conditions of deep sectional division such as prevailed when Calhoun was writing, nothing less than a minority veto power will suffice to make the minority's continued cooperation rational:

> The nature of the disease is such, that nothing can reach it, short of some organic change—a change which shall so modify the constitution, as to give to the weaker section, in some form or another, a negative on the action of the government. Nothing short of this can protect the weaker, and restore harmony and tranquillity to the Union, by arresting, effectually, the tendency of the dominant and stronger section to oppress the weaker.[63]

It may be the case that more modest measures than a veto are capable of providing a substitute for the failed trust of an oppressed minority. But Calhoun's argument draws our attention to the fact that the popular legitimacy of a representative democracy depends on the belief that society's principal groups receive meaningful representation. In the absence of such representation, a minority group has little ground for believing that government is conducted in its interest, and consequently little reason to offer its willing cooperation in upholding a public order of law. In the wake of such a failure of trust, the only remedy that can mend the social and political fabric is one in which the minority can exercise a substantive political *power* according to its own evaluation of its well-being. Whereas under other circumstances minorities may be willing to entrust their interests to a government in which their power is indirect and the content of their welfare is defined by others on their behalf, a failure of political trust can only be remedied by their own direct exercise of that power. Calhoun's scheme reveals his understanding of the remedy for distrust as Hobbes articulates it: that where trust in another appears unwarranted, one should "provide himself by other means." It was precisely for these reasons that Calhoun advocated concurrent majorities and "negatives" for minorities.

The principal problem with Calhoun's theory is that providing a minority veto involves granting new powers to a *particular* social group or section and entrenching those powers in the constitution. As soon as this is done, however, it grants constitutional status to the cleavage itself, and so rigidly defines the parameters of political conflict.[64] Minority protection is purchased at the price of adaptability to changing political circumstances. The rationale for protecting minority interests is that political power should reflect social interests—yet the institutions that reflect today's conflict will prevent tomorrow's cleavage from being recognized. Institutions of minority representation, Calhoun's argument suggests, must inevitably become obsolete. Yet in Calhoun's view, the common good of the nation as a whole will not be recognized, let alone pursued, if the current minority's role in defining it is left unprotected. In the absence of minority power in governmental decision making, the ends pursued will reflect only the partial good of the majority. Although Calhoun agrees with Burke (and perhaps Madison) that the common good can emerge only out of deliberation among the representatives of the nation's different sections, he has no confidence that such deliberation will emerge voluntarily. The device of concurrent majorities provides a strong inducement to cooperative deliberation, and so supplies the defect of the different sections' will.

VII. J. S. Mill

Representative government, according to John Stuart Mill, is vulnerable to two dangers. First, representative government will fail if the general level of intellectual and moral development in society is low. Second, it is threatened by the influence of interests that are at odds with the general welfare of the community as a whole.[65] Like Madison and Calhoun, Mill was particularly concerned about the form this second danger is likely to take in popular governments: majority tyranny. Rule of the numerical majority, Mill argues, is no protection against the domination of society by "sectional or class interests" inimical to the common good. Indeed, where society is clearly divided between two groups, Mill seems skeptical that the domination of the minority by the majority group can be avoided without some corrective to simple majoritarianism. "Suppose the majority to be whites, the minority Negroes, or *vice versa*: is it likely that the majority would allow equal justice to the minority?"[66] Further, where the social division is not based on racial, religious, linguistic, or cultural differences, Mill—like Madison and Calhoun—thinks it inevitable that a central cleavage will emerge along class lines, that is, between the poor and the relatively rich, or between unskilled and skilled workers.[67] Consequently, in a popular government the natural danger is that the majority working class will legislate in their own interests and against the long-term interests of the whole.[68] Historically, this reasoning has been used to justify the exclusion of the working class from the franchise, a practice Mill rejected both because he thought the systematic exclusion of any interest group contrary to the principle of social utility[69] and because he thought that political participation was important to cultivating good character in the citizenry.[70] To exclude some persons from the processes of representation would be to make bad citizens.[71] This leaves those committed to good government in a quandary, at least in an electoral system based on winner-take-all territorial districts: "There is great difficulty, under the present machinery, in measuring out influence to the working classes, so as to be just to them without being unjust to every one else. They are not represented even as a class, unless they are the majority of the constituency, and if they are, nobody else is represented."[72]

As this passage suggests, the solution as Mill sees it is to change the "machinery" of representative government. The "virtual blotting-out of the minority" is no necessary consequence of popular government; to the contrary, majority domination is antithetical to the "first principle of democracy—representation in proportion to numbers."[73] Instead of single-member territorial districts, Mill advocates the system of proportional representation formulated by Thomas Hare, in which a citizen's ballot is a rank ordering of his or her preferred candidates.[74] The result is that "all interests or classes of any importance" have a voice in the representative assembly.[75] Although it is true that the ultimate decisions about legislation are made by a majority of the representatives, no substantial group or interest in society goes without the opportunity to express its interest, and the likelihood that a majority can violate the interests of a minority or legislate against the common good is radically reduced.

In addition to protecting minorities, proportional representation enhances the effectiveness and scope of citizen participation. Every citizen will feel an attachment to government under such a system, Mill argues, because virtually everyone will have played a role in electing a representative. In a single-member plurality districting system, those who voted for losing candidates have no spokesperson in Parliament, and those whose candidate did win may nonetheless feel that they had to vote for their party's candidate despite the fact that they had little respect for his merits. Moreover, in a system of proportional representation, citizens exercise their political agency not only by participating in elections and making judgments about candidates but also by defining for themselves the lines along which their votes shall be counted. This aspect of proportional representation sets it in sharp contrast to territorial representation, in which constituencies are defined by convention, and to corporate or sectional representation as in Burke or Calhoun, in which the relevant constituencies are defined by historical, social, cultural, and economic forces. Mill emphasizes this aspect of proportional representation as a point strongly in its favor: "I cannot see why the feelings and interests which arrange mankind according to localities should be the only ones thought worthy of being represented, or why people who have other feelings and interests, which they value more . . ., should be restricted to these as the sole principle of political classification."[76]

The voluntary formation of constituencies, Mill acknowledges, may lead to the representation of some marginal groups whose aims are opposed to the general interest. He acknowledges, for example, that there may be a "Temperance ticket[]," which, given his views on the subject of temperance laws in *On Liberty*, he would not be likely to favor. But the multiplication of diverse views in Parliament through proportional representation is desirable for the same reasons that broad social tolerance and the universal franchise are desirable: the clash of conflicting opinions in a public space is the greatest guarantee of social progress, particularly when the views being challenged are those of the dominant power in society, the majority.[77] Parliament will thus become "[a] place where every interest and shade of opinion can have its cause even passionately pleaded, in the face of the government and of all other interests and opinions [and will be able to] compel them to listen and either comply or state clearly why they do not."[78]

This makes clear that Mill adapts an *expressive* approach to political representation. What is not immediately clear in Mill's view, however, is how this diversity of interests and opinions in Parliament gives rise to policies that are in the general interest. Conflict produces nothing of itself, and so Mill's view requires some further account of how conflicting views are translated into or overridden by a view of the common good. Moreover, as Dennis Thompson argues, "[t]he well-being of all members of society . . . cannot be achieved by merely adding up the particular interests of all citizens."[79] Even if it could be so achieved, the addition would have to be performed as an activity separate from the expression of those interests.[80] At some points Mill seems to believe that a deliberative role will be played by the representatives of all the various groups, each of whom will exercise his or her powers of persuasion on the other members. For example, he suggests that if representative members of the working class were to present their views in Parliament on the question of strikes, they would persuade anyone who listened that "the reason of the matter is [not] unqualifiedly on the side of the masters."[81] On the whole, however, Mill does not seem to have faith in the capacity of representatives of the majority of society to be effective participants in the sort of deliberation that produces the public good. Indeed, not only will the representative assembly reflect the broad range of opinion present in society, it will also be "a fair sample of every grade of intellect among the people which is at all entitled to a voice in public affairs."[82] Given Mill's conception of society as containing only a small minority of intellectually talented individuals, the equal representation of all grades of intelligence would not seem to bode well for a general ability among members of Parliament to reach reasoned judgments about the common good as a product of deliberation. At some points Mill seems to abandon all hope that intelligence will play much of a role in the representative assembly itself, and he draws the conclusion that the assembly is an organ for expressing the popular will and for voicing the wants in society but is not well suited to making judgments about what is necessary to harmonize these wants in pursuit of the common good. Consequently, he argues, the intellectually demanding function of fashioning legislation should be given to a special commission of technical experts, and Parliament's function would simply be to approve or disapprove the result. "[T]he Commission would only embody the element of intelligence in construction; Parliament would represent that of will."[83]

At other points in his argument, however, Mill suggests that the common good depends on the presence of some element of intelligence in the representative assembly itself. In fact, Mill's principal concern in advocating a scheme of proportional representation often appears to be that one minority in particular receive representation: the "instructed minority," the intellectual elite of the nation. This class of talented individuals is the only group in society characterized by an inclination toward the public good and an ability to rise above the particular, conflicting interests in society.[84] Mill even projects that the instructed few will form their own political organization, creating a "personal merit" ticket alongside the "Temperance ticket" mentioned above.[85] This elite will, he hopes, even gain seats beyond their proportion in the population as members of the majority recognize their worth.[86]

Because of the general moral or intellectual incapacity of citizens to rise above their narrow interests, the presence of the instructed minority in Parliament is indispensable if parliamentary deliberations are to identify the common good—particularly in the early stages of political development, before the educative effects of participation have taken full effect. In part, this is because they fulfill an important educational role, teaching by the moral example of preferring the general interest to any private interest, and by the intellectual example of using the information provided by particular interests in locating the common good.[87] But even more important is the role the intellectual minority plays by virtue of its independence from partial or sectional interests. In this part of his argument, Mill's reasoning strongly resembles that of Madison, for he conceives of the common good as dependent on a balancing out of the partial, narrow interests in society: "The reason why, in any tolerably constituted society, justice and the general interest mostly in the end carry their point is that *separate and selfish interests of mankind are almost always divided.*"[88] But in contrast to Madison, Mill makes it explicit that in order for this balancing of interests to result in the common good, it is necessary that some other force be present to represent it. This force is the talented minority: because no particular interest is able to enact its aims without the support of some other group, the talented minority can put its vote behind those whose partial interests coincide with the general interest. Not only is the intellectuals' power in the assembly enhanced beyond their numbers by this coalitional function they play, but their presence also heightens the general level of discussion, as sectional interests must address their arguments to the instructed few if they are to achieve their legislative goals.

On the one hand, then, Mill's conception of the role of the representative assembly in achieving the common good turns on the fact that constituencies are self-defining. By sustaining a fluidity of group formation, voluntary constituencies ensure that all the relevant interests in society will be represented in Parliament, and thus that the protective function of the assembly is being fulfilled. By allowing individuals to decide for themselves which of their interests matter most for political purposes, the Hare system develops citizens' sense of public agency and contributes to the educative function of political participation.[89] On the other hand, particularly before the political judgment of a people has developed to a relatively high level, the interests around which citizens are likely to organize and vote are very likely to be narrow and perhaps selfish, and certainly are not guaranteed to be any part of a common good. It is essential that these interests are expressed but equally important that they not be allowed to control decisions on legislation. As we have seen, it is not necessarily the case that the common good is created through harmonizing or aggregating all the particular goods in society: more likely, some of those partial interests will turn out to be on the side of the general interest, and others will not. What is needed to ensure that the common good is realized, therefore, is the presence of the independent class, the competent minority, who have the capability to identify the relationship between the common good and the particular interests. Moreover, it is not enough for their judgment to have a role in the deliberative process; like Calhoun, Mill thought that achieving the general interest also depended on ensuring a share of political *power* to this important minority. Mill did not adopt Calhoun's solution of granting the minority a power equal to that of the majority, but he did favor institutions that gave them at least proportional, and preferably larger than proportional, representation, whether through the a scheme of proportional representation or through the device of plural voting.

Mill's theory of representation follows from his characterization of the genesis and character of the social groups that ought to be represented in politics; it is not hard to see the relationship between the different aspects of representation as mediation. The multiplicity and ever changing nature of groups, combined with Mill's view that individuals must ultimately be the judges of their own interest, means that constituencies should be self-defining. But unlike Madison, Mill does not hope that the manifold interests of social groups will cancel one another out in the process of legislative decision making. To the contrary, he favors a *deliberative* process in which conflicting interests will be weighed against one another to produce the greatest common good possible. In order for such deliberation to occur, it is important that representatives be familiar with the interests of their constituents and act in part as mouthpieces for those interests. Nonetheless, the legislative process must have sufficient distance from groups' various interests to enable those with prudent political judgment to evaluate the relationship between particular social interests and the common good. Thus Mill quite pointedly rejects a choice between the idea of the representative as a delegate of his constituents, acting on their instructions, and that of the trustee whose judgment of constituents' true interests may be better informed than their own.[90] By separating the work of designing legislation from that of deliberation, Mill makes it possible for representatives to move between the two roles with relative ease. In so doing, he creates a role for the representative which, more clearly than the other theorists here considered, simultaneously respects the agency of both the representative and the represented.

VIII. Conclusion

The review of these contrasting theories of representation, and of the views of social groups embedded in each, allows us to draw a few general conclusions about the role of group theories within theories of representation, the place of groups in a theorist's conception of the common good, and the processes of representation that produce that common good.

First, in the theories of representation examined here, the theory of social groups defines those interests in society among which there is conflict or potential conflict. Groups whose interests never conflict, or never even appear to conflict, with the interests of other groups are of no concern in politics. Thus the identification of politically relevant groups is a *political sociology*, an account of the sources of group identity and group interests and of the nature of the conflicts that are likely to arise between groups. To this extent, every theory of representation is grounded in a statement of the empirical reality of social groups and their constitutive interests.

The function of the theory of representation, in each of these cases, is to mediate conflicts or potential conflicts so they are not destructive of society as a whole. But the fact that institutions of representation are designed to mediate group conflict does not dictate the manner in which the mediation is achieved. In some views, such as Madison's, group interests are always opposed to the general interest, so that the only way of preventing the conflict between groups from being destructive is to prevent them from being expressed in a way that makes any difference to political outcomes. In these *suppressive* views of representation, the role of political representation is to minimize the effect of conflicting group interests.

In other theories, however, group conflict is potentially valuable, as the common good is comprised at least in part of the well-being of the different groups in society. It may be the case, as in Burke's and Calhoun's theories, that the common good is a product of the good of discrete and identifiable groups. Alternatively, as in Mill, the general interest is not always defined as a harmony or product of all the interests in society but rather coincides sometimes with certain interests, sometimes with others. All three of these views regard the expression of group interests as a valuable and indispensable part of the process of good government; at least with respect to some groups, they are *expressive* views of representation. The key difference between them is that whereas for Burke and Calhoun an intelligent observer can identify the groups that constitute the community and hence whose interests are relevant in locating the common good, Mill regards the long-term interests in society as sufficiently open-ended that it is not possible to know in advance of deliberation which particular interests will be relevant to the general interest. In part for this reason, Mill's embrace of the expressive approach to representation is unqualified, whereas Burke and Calhoun adopt a *mixed* strategy: expressive with respect to some groups, suppressive with regard to the lower classes.

In short, the theory of representative institutions can be seen as standing between a particular political sociology and a particular view of the common good. A coherent theory of representation will give an account of the connection between the empirical understanding of the nature of groups, the normative theory of the general interest, and the processes by which representative institutions produce the latter from the former. In metaphorical terms, we may think of the difference between suppressive and expressive views of group representation by likening conflict to a river and representative institutions to dams: some dams are designed to prevent flooding, whereas others also generate electricity.[91]

It might be helpful for illustrative purposes to foreshadow the place of these points in my own argument. The group-based theory of fair representation that I defend in this book is an expressive view. Its political sociology rests on the empirical claim that structural inequality creates a social divide between marginalized groups and privileged groups, and on the normative claim that such inequality is unjust and against our shared interests in democratic equality. The political representation of marginalized groups can serve our interest in ameliorating structural inequality by creating legislatures more capable of generating policies that do not reproduce systematic bias against marginalized groups.

For those who hold an expressive view of group representation, the general aims of representative government can only be achieved given a background commitment of politically relevant groups to share each others' fate, to continue in a cooperative project with one another. In other words, there must be some underlying agreement that binds competing groups to one another even in the face of conflict and enables them to sustain their cooperation long enough for the conflict to be translated into a general good. For Burke, this commitment is renewed through reflection on the place of a "description" of citizens in the character and welfare of the British nation or empire: by invoking the benefits that accrue to Britain as a whole from the participation of one of its parts, he hopes to encourage others to guard the welfare of those who are not protected by virtual representation in Parliament. In part, then, the political will to cooperate is a product of a visionary leadership that reaches out to such excluded "descriptions." Calhoun, in contrast, believes that the two great sections of North and South would only acknowledge the interdependence of their long-term interests if they are bound to each other with a very strong institutional rope. The conflict between them did not obviate the actuality of their interest in cooperation, but it has progressed to the point where nothing but the force of institutional necessity will move them to cooperate with each other. For Mill, the bonds between members of society have sufficient natural strength that no extraordinary energies must be exerted to sustain them—so long as they are not too different from one another to begin with. However, it does seem likely that Mill's view of political education would bring with it a strengthening of those bonds, as an increase in moral virtue would increase citizens' inclination to define their own good in terms of the good of others, and their intellectual development would lead them to perceive the interconnectedness of their interests with the welfare of other groups.

All these theories of representation were developed during historical periods radically different from our own. All preceded the extension of the franchise to all competent adults and the full political mobilization of the working class, as well as the growth of a modern state that regulates a much wider sphere of social activity than any (except perhaps Mill) would have supported or anticipated. Nonetheless, the foregoing exploration of their views of representation discloses a number of questions and concerns that are highly relevant to contemporary considerations of representation. Some of these concerns follow directly from the theories themselves. Burke offers us a way of conceiving of society as a scheme of cooperation that depends vitally on protecting the interests of any group whose noncooperation will hamper collective aims. Calhoun develops this point a step further by showing that once a substantial group's interests have been repeatedly thwarted, its trust, or willingness to cooperate, will not likely be restored without an increased measure of political power to enable it to protect itself. Madison offers us the insight that the mere existence of certain social groups need not translate directly into a legitimate claim for their political recognition; there are some groups whose recognition may be damaging to the general welfare. Mill shows us that any scheme of representation that defines constituencies independently of citizens' expressed will fails to respect their agency to know and communicate their most essential interests.

As we shall see in the coming chapters, my own view draws on each of these insights. In a society dedicated to the ideal of democratic equality, sharing one another's fate requires a commitment to combat structural inequality. From Burke I take the suggestion that the failure to take up that commitment eventually produces a refusal to cooperate from those who are most injured by it, and the view that a willingness to combat unjust inequality requires strong political leadership.[92] From Calhoun I conclude that fair representation for marginalized groups requires institutional innovations aimed at pressing representatives of groups with conflicting interests toward legislative deliberation.[93] Madison's insight about potentially dangerous groups leads me to qualify my preference for expressive approaches to representation in societies where they would threaten stability, and to take the challenge of balkanization more seriously than I might otherwise.[94] And Mill's insights contribute to my preference for institutional devices that increase the legislative presence of marginalized groups by allowing for the voluntary formation of constituencies rather than by constitutionalizing group identity.[95]

In addition to revealing the enduring insights of profound theorists of representation, a comparison of these theories confronts us with a choice between different ways of conceiving social conflict and its relation to representation. On the most general level we must choose between expressive and suppressive theories of representation. In making these choices, we must recognize that they are always relative to the specific groups that figure in our political sociology. Two sorts of considerations might lead us to choose suppressive institutions of representation over expressive institutions, with their obvious advantages in terms of political fairness and openness. First, we might choose to suppress intergroup conflict in the name of stability in circumstances where intergroup conflicts are so potentially destabilizing that they threaten the very survival of the public order that is capable of delivering the public good of justice or equity. Although American neoconservative critics of policies of group recognition freely invoke the dangers of balkanization, it is difficult to believe that such policies would ever yield dangerous political instability.[96] In the real Balkans, however, political hindsight might well recommend replacing the power of the Yugoslavian central state to suppress ethnic conflict with representative institutions that had a comparable capacity.

Second, we might wish to create suppressive institutions of political representation with respect to groups whose interests are inimical to the common good as we understand it. Calhoun and Burke (and, to a slightly lesser degree, Madison) did not resist the representation of the lower classes not only because they believed class conflict was dangerously destabilizing (as they believed it was), but also because they believed that the common interest of society lay in the preservation of property, and that yielding too much power to the lower classes would produce a substantive threat to that interest in the form of redistributive legislation. Even if one prefers expressive over suppressive theories of representation on grounds of political fairness and inclusiveness, as I do, one cannot avoid confronting the question of suppression altogether, since *there is no such thing as a "neutral" system of representation*. In practice, all institutions of representation will have the effect of favoring some groups over others or of disadvantaging some groups more than others. Thus a coherent and defensible theory of representation will have to make choices about which sorts of group difference should receive expression within a system of representation.[97]

The comparison of the theories also illustrates that despite the complexity of group identity and group formation, especially under contemporary circumstances of social fluidity, no one who is interested in fair representation can rightly ignore the problem of how to characterize the group structure of society. In particular, a theory of representation's characterization of social groups must address *the nature of individual membership in social groups* and *the place of the group within society*, especially the relationship between group interests and the interests shared by all members of society as such. It is useful to articulate the considerations that arise under each of these headings:

a. *The nature of individual membership within social groups.* First, membership in social groups may be a *dichotomous* or a *continuous* characteristic; that is, membership may be an all-or-nothing affair so that it is clear who is a member and who is not, as in a geographic district in which one must be a legal resident in order to vote. Another example might be the landed aristocracy whose representation Burke so fondly favored. Or membership might be a matter of degree, as in a Millian social group such as the temperance movement, in which one might be a stronger or a weaker advocate of prohibition or regulation of alcohol. Second, membership in a politically relevant group might be *voluntary* or *involuntary*. An example of the former would clearly be Mill's self-defined constituencies; an example of the latter would be social class or perhaps place of residence. Third, membership might be *shifting* or *immutable*. Although one might live in the geographic district in which one was born, so that one cannot rightly be characterized as having *chosen* membership in that collectivity, such membership is not an immutable characteristic: one can shift from district to district. In contrast, Calhoun might argue that although you can take the Southerner out of the South, you can't take the South out of the Southerner. Once acquired, the identity and outlook that comes from having been raised in Southern culture is something *immutable*, irrevocable.[98]

   b. *The place of the group within society.* First, a group might have a *permanent* place in the social structure or it might have a *changing and shifting* role, advancing and receding in political relevance. An example of the former would be Burke's "natural landed interest," which he argued should have a permanent (and exaggerated) representation in Parliament.[99] An example of a social group whose political relevance was shifting rather than permanent might be, again in Burke's view, the financial class, whose importance emerged only with capitalism and might decline once governments ceased relying too heavily on public debt to finance their operations.[100] Second, the recognition of a particular group's interest may be either *necessary* or *antithetical to the common good.* As noted above, the implications of this distinction for a theory of representation is clear: a group interest that is integral to the collective interest should be expressed and recognized in the political process, whereas, at least for some theorists, a system of representation should have means of suppressing those groups (or "factions") whose interest conflicts with the common good. Finally, theories of representation should generally attend to the *systemic effects of the relations between groups.* Since the distinction between politically relevant groups always defines boundaries of political conflict, the question arises whether patterns of conflict between social groups are salutary or harmful to the society as a whole. For Madison and Mill, intergroup competition clearly has beneficial systemic consequences, albeit for different reasons. (For Madison, the benefit is that the factional interests that are antithetical to the common good tend to neutralize one another in the course of competitive politics; for Mill, the benefit of competition is that it ensures that all relevant social interests are expressed, so that the selection of policy options is based on the fullest information possible.) In contrast, both Burke and Calhoun see untrammeled intergroup competition as damaging to the common interest, as it reinforces social division and discourages cooperation.

As the remaining chapters will show, these different ways of conceiving of social groups continue to carry tremendous consequences for our definition of fair and effective political representation. In particular, the challenge of marginalized ascriptive groups to the prevailing conception of fair representation consists precisely in a challenge to its characterization of the nature of the social groups that matter for contemporary politics, of individual membership in those groups, and in the relationship between social groups in contemporary American society. Whereas membership in the interest groups that are so central to liberal representation tends to be continuous, voluntary, and shifting, membership in marginalized ascriptive groups tends to be dichotomous, involuntary, and immutable. And whereas liberal representation generally conceives of intergroup competition as salutary, members of marginalized groups tend to regard competition as inimical to their most fundamental political interests. Before we examine the substance of marginalized groups' challenge to liberal representation, however, it is necessary to articulate more precisely what the prevailing conception of fair representation is. Such is the purpose of the next two chapters.

2

Liberal Equality and Liberal Representation

INTUITIONS about the injustice of marginalized groups' chronic underrepresentation are not universally shared. Some regard the group identity of those who sit in legislatures as entirely irrelevant to their capacity to represent their constituents well. For them, even the utter absence of African Americans or women or any other marginalized group members from legislative bodies would not, in itself, warrant a sense of injustice. The purpose of this chapter is to show that the view of fair representation that runs through American political culture and American jurisprudence supports those who regard group identity as irrelevant to fair representation. Here I articulate the content of that view and show the reasons why its advocates are not troubled by the legislative underrepresentation of marginalized groups.

Although the dominant American conception of fair representation owes a great deal to the Madisonian theory reviewed in the preceding chapter, it has developed features in this century that make it a distinctive theory of its own. The first section of this chapter offers an overview of the ideal of equality that informs most American thought on representation. The second part articulates the predominant American theory of representation, a view I call "liberal representation." I give it this name because it communicates the centrality of the principles of liberty and equality in mainstream American understandings of fair representation and suggests the consonance of those understandings with other liberal doctrines such as equal opportunity. This is not to say that what I am calling "liberal representation" is the only theory of fair representation that is consonant with liberalism. For example, both Madison's and Mill's views, outlined in chapter 1, are also broadly consistent with liberal principles.

Liberal representation consists of two strands. The first is the judicial doctrine of "one person, one vote," which expresses the ideal of fair representation as an outcome of free and open elections in which every citizen has an equally weighted vote. I refer to the normative principle expressed by "one person, one vote" as "equal representation," since it gives each individual equal weight in the electoral process. The second strand of liberal representation, interest-group pluralism, provides the political sociology which defines the groups that should be recognized in the political process. Interest-group pluralism expresses a social decision function in which the preferences of different interest groups are weighted according to the amount of organizational effort they expend. In its normative guise, interest-group pluralism provides a standard of "equitable representation" against which to judge electoral and representative processes. By combining the doctrine of "one person, one vote" with interest-group pluralism, the theory of liberal representation aims to serve both equality and equity. Despite the differences between them, both strands articulate procedural understandings of representational fairness.

The coherence of liberal representation on the theoretical plane becomes compromised in American political practice for a number of different reasons. In particular, while liberal representation presents its own normative and sociological account of constituency definition, the practices of political representation in the United States are based on traditions of geographic representation whose normative justification is often at odds with the principles of liberal representation. The third section of the chapter explores the extent to which liberal representation may be reconciled with the constraints of geographic districting.

Liberal proceduralism has come under serious criticism in recent years for its tendency to obscure the ways in which facially neutral procedures actually function to reproduce the oppression of certain groups, particularly historically marginalized ascriptive groups. These critiques have been focused with particular force on liberal theories of distributive justice and on the doctrine of equal opportunity that so powerfully informs liberal conceptions of fairness. In the final section of this chapter I draw attention to some parallel critiques of the pluralist strand of liberal representation and discuss the response offered by defenders of that doctrine. In the end, I argue, the conservative defense of liberal representation fails to do justice either to the critiques themselves or to the considerable efforts, evident in the history of voting rights legislation and jurisprudence, to recognize the distinctive claims of marginalized groups within the liberal conception of fair representation. Those efforts provide the focus of chapter 3.

I. Liberal Equality

Equality, as J. R. Pole has noted, is an idea whose survival through the ages can be credited to its evolutionary adaptability to changing social circumstances, its remarkable capacity for "meaning different things to different minds."[1] Biological metaphors often generate more confusion than clarity, but this one is particularly well-suited to the contemporary question of how to reconcile pluralism and equality. Until recently it seemed clear that liberal conceptions of equality had mastered the challenge that social difference posed to its coherence, principally through the doctrine of equality as difference-blindness. But recent feminist and other group-based critiques of equal opportunity have unsettled that solution, creating a need for another transformation (or mutation) of democratic equality, one whose precise contours are not yet clear.

Before proceeding to address issues of representation, it is worth reviewing liberal views of equality and the reasons why equality must mean something different to the "different minds" currently challenging them. Not only are debates over equality central to any conception of fair representation, but (not coincidentally) there are also important parallels between the group-based critiques of equal opportunity and group-based claims to representation.

Whatever liberal equality may be—its precise character is subject to manifold interpretations—there seems to be general agreement on where it begins. First and foremost, liberalism insists on the essential moral equality of all persons as such. The foundation of democratic equality commands us to regard all individuals with an equality of respect "which is owed to persons irrespective of their social positions," as John Rawls has put it.[2] In moments of uncertainty about what equality requires of a liberal democratic polity, this is the principle of last resort: the respect owed to all persons by virtue of their status as thinking and feeling beings.[3]

In the public sphere, equality is operationalized as equality before the law. Equality demands that citizens are treated impartially by the state, that they are neither favored nor disadvantaged because of personal attributes which are "arbitrary from a moral perspective."[4] In particular, the liberal view of legal equality rules out distinctions among citizens on the basis of attributes given by birth, such as race and sex. Justice Harlan, in his famous dissent in *Plessy v. Ferguson*, gave the classic statement of this view of equality: "Our Constitution is color-blind, and neither knows nor tolerates classes among citizens."[5] Although legislation invariably creates classes insofar as, for example, regulations apply to some groups or sectors and not to others, the classes they create must not be based on morally arbitrary distinctions.[6]

The notion that citizens ought to be treated equally without regard to birth-given characteristics leads naturally to a debate over what attributes *should* be considered in the distribution of social goods, especially scarce goods such as quality education, jobs, income, and political power.[7] It is these scarcer goods that create the problem: since the demand for them exceeds supply, the final distribution is unavoidably unequal. What ought to be the criterion by which such goods are distributed? The answer given by liberal theory is based on the idea of individuals' moral autonomy. Social goods should be distributed on the basis of attributes over which individuals have a measure of choice or control, so that their "fate is determined by their choices, rather than their circumstances."[8] At the same time, some benefits, such as jobs or educational opportunities, can neither benefit individual recipients nor fulfill their social purpose unless some standard of merit is used in distributing them. Together, these two ideas give rise to the doctrine of equal opportunity, which dictates that "those who are at the same level of talent and ability, and have the same willingness to use them, should have the same prospects of success regardless of their initial place in the system."[9] The methods that equal opportunity doctrine prescribes for making distributive decisions regarding social goods thus include (a) eliminating from consideration all "morally arbitrary" attributes over which individuals have no choice or control; and (b) counting traits that have a specific relation to the good at stake (such as grades or test scores for admission to universities, or creativity and productivity for high-paying jobs).

Advocates of equal opportunity present it as a case of what Rawls calls pure procedural justice, "whose outcome is . . . correct or fair, whatever it is, provided that the procedure has been properly followed."[10] If equal opportunity did define such a procedure, Rawls suggests, "*distributive justice could . . . be left to take care of itself.*"[11] In other words, a great advantage of equal opportunity is that once the machinery of pure procedural justice has been put in place, it will produce fair outcomes automatically, without need of further supervision or adjustment.[12]

The central flaw of equal opportunity doctrine might best be called "history": individuals do not, in fact, arrive at life's many starting lines with the equal resources that equal opportunity assumes. Their prospects for success at any given stage are far from equal, even given the same level of talent and motivation, because they have received different amounts of the resources necessary to cultivate their talents and to reinforce their motivation. This is true no matter what the stage at which we decide thoroughly to equalize resources, because inequalities will always have existed in an earlier phase of the individuals' histories. We may guarantee an elementary and secondary education to all children, and yet by the time they enter kindergarten familial influences have already shaped the self-perceptions and attitudes toward learning that, to a large extent, determine whether they will succeed in school. Precisely those factors that were supposed to be "morally arbitrary"—race, class, sex, and so on—are the ones that correlate most highly with relative advantage and disadvantage at earlier stages of an individual's life. Consequently a procedure that purports to treat all individuals alike will likely result in the success of the advantaged and the failure of the disadvantaged given equal levels of talent and ambition. To take the case of women, "[a]t least in the present social context, sexual equality in procedure often may ensure rather than obliterate sexual *inequality* in outcome."[13] The flaw of equal opportunity is infinite regress; we cannot draw the line even at birth, since malnutrition and other poverty-related factors can retard fetal development, permanently limiting the opportunities a child can expect during his or her lifetime.[14] Thus "equal opportunity," in Brian Barry's words, "is a Holy Grail: It disappears as one approaches it."[15] Moreover, critics argue, the inequalities hidden by equal opportunity doctrine undercut one of the procedural advantages of equal opportunity: the automatic legitimacy of its outcomes. Even if it is procedurally fair, that is, attends only to morally relevant criteria in reaching a decision, the background conditions of an equal opportunity process are not likely to be fair (because some start out with disadvantages rooted in their social origins). Both standards of fairness must be met in order for a procedure's outcome to be fair, "whatever it happens to be."[16] Instead, critics argue, equal opportunity's legitimacy is based on the false claim that it is a case of pure procedural justice.

In addition, some critics charge that the "impartial" criteria that are used to decide how scarce social goods are allocated are in fact biased in favor of those who are already in advantaged social positions. Equal opportunity's claim to impartiality is a sham because impartiality itself is impossible: any selection of criteria will be influenced by conscious or unconscious social values.[17] Since criteria tend to be defined by people who are in positions of power, what *appears* to them to be an impartial standard actually affirms the traits they have. As Iris Young expresses this idea:

> Where social group differences exist, and some groups are privileged while others are oppressed, this propensity to universalize the particular reinforces that oppression. The standpoint of the privileged, their particular experience and standards, is constructed as normal and neutral. If some groups' experience differs from this neutral experience, . . . their difference is constructed as deviance and inferiority.[18]

In an example that would be humorous were it not so damaging, the Supreme Court has upheld a health insurance scheme that covered such peculiarly male medical needs as prostate surgery but did not cover pregnancy on the ground that it was a "unique" and "additional" disability. No sex discrimination was involved, the Court held, since the policy made no gender distinctions. Rather, "[e]mployers were simply drawing a distinction between . . . 'pregnant women' and 'non-pregnant persons.'"[19]

Most difference-based critiques of equal opportunity assert, in sum, that equality means *both* regarding individuals as fundamentally equal moral beings *and* recognizing that social difference will affect the ways in which equality becomes translated into the distribution of social goods. Catharine MacKinnon captures both the puzzlement and insistence with which these seemingly incompatible claims are expressed:

> To treat issues of sex equality as issues of sameness and difference is to take a particular approach, here termed the differences approach because it is obsessed with sex difference. The main theme of its fugue is, "we're the same, we're the same, we're the same." The contrapuntal theme (in a higher register) is "but we're different, but we're different, but we're different."[20]

What would a defensible approach to difference-conscious equality require? At a minimum, it would seem to require both acknowledging and attempting to address the background inequalities that are structured around social difference, for example, through affirmative action programs. In addition, a difference-conscious equality would seem to require that these groups have greater power in defining the terms by which social goods are identified and allocated. In other words, social groups would have to have a greater role in setting the social, economic, and political agenda. As we shall see, both these difference-based responses to equal opportunity—eradicating structural inequality and creating a political space in which the voices of marginalized groups can be heard—are integral parts of group-based critiques of the existing system of representation as well.

II. Liberal Representation

Complex though the problem of equal or fair representation is, the theory and practice of liberal democracy in America have, over the course of the twentieth century, worked together to produce a generally coherent view of political representation that preserves the fundamental liberal commitment to individual equality and autonomy. As noted above, liberal representation comprises two distinct strands. The first strand of liberal representation is the principle of "one person, one vote," the standard of equal representation that regulates elections in single-member legislative districts. The second strand is interest-group pluralism, the theory of the organization of shared social interests with the purpose of securing the equitable representation or reflection of those interests in public policies. "One person, one vote" compensates for the inequalities permitted within interest-group pluralism by requiring that each citizen has an equally weighted say in determining electoral outcomes. Both strands of liberal representation bear a number of similarities to equal opportunity doctrine, the import of which is that the theory legitimizes inequalities in political influence. Together they articulate a coherent theory of fair representation, one that gives content to each of the aspects of representation as mediation while remaining consistent with an underlying commitment to political equality.

"One Person, One Vote"

The fair representation of citizens in a liberal democracy depends critically on their ability to exercise the sanction of the vote and to do so in a manner that reflects their essential equality as citizens. How does liberal representation affirm and secure the principle of equality within free and open elections?

The Supreme Court began addressing the question of fair representation in the early 1960s. The early reapportionment cases were occasioned by the fact that many states had not reapportioned their legislative districts in decades. Because of population movements, and particularly the shift of population from rural to urban areas, many states' districting plans were severely malapportioned, that is, there was a wide discrepancy between the largest and smallest legislative districts.[21] Consequently, plaintiffs argued, voters in small rural districts were overrepresented in the legislatures, and those in the large urban districts were underrepresented. In effect, they argued, the votes of citizens in large districts were worth only a fraction of those in the smaller districts, and this violated the principle of equality enshrined (among other places) in the Equal Protection Clause of the Fourteenth Amendment.

After deciding in *Baker v. Carr* in 1962 that apportionment was a justiciable question, the Warren Court developed the notion that fair representation requires the equal weight of citizens' votes into the doctrine of "one person, one vote."[22] As the Court made clear in *Wesberry v. Sanders*[23] and *Reynolds v. Sims*,[24] the principle of electoral equality was not satisfied by the mere fact that citizens had an equal right to cast a vote and have it counted. Beyond that, the Court held, "as nearly as is practicable, one man's vote . . . is to be *worth as much as another's*."[25] At a minimum, the equal "worth" of citizens' votes has been taken to require that districts must be drawn to contain roughly equal numbers of inhabitants. Again, as with equal opportunity, fairness rests on a rejection of "morally arbitrary" criteria of distribution: the weight of a citizen's vote must not vary according to any such arbitrary factor as place of residence.[26] To permit any alternative, Chief Justice Warren argued for the *Reynolds* Court, is to deny citizens a fundamental right of democratic government: "The right to vote freely for the candidate of one's choice is of the essence of a democratic society, and any restrictions on that right strike at the heart of representative government. And the right of suffrage can be denied by a debasement or dilution of the weight of a citizen's vote just as effectively as by wholly prohibiting the free exercise of the franchise."[27]

The Court did concede in *Reynolds* and other cases that there were other representational values that might sometimes justify a slight divergence from strict numerical equality in the drawing of legislative districts. In particular, the Court acknowledged that the boundaries of traditional political subdivisions ought to be preserved as much as possible. Still, Warren was adamant that the political equality of *individual* citizens be regarded as the paramount value in political representation. Drawing district lines with regard for existing communities was a good idea,[28] but it could not be used to justify great disparities in district size. Although the standard of "precise mathematical equality"[29] is stricter for federal congressional districts than for state legislative districts, any divergence from equality must be justified by a "rational state policy."

The Supreme Court's doctrine of "one person, one vote" has come under attack because of its emphasis on the purely formal aspect of equally weighted votes. As a doctrine of fair representation, critics argue, numerical equality is pathetically thin, ignoring as it does the fact that legislators cannot represent individuals as such. Rather, as I argued in chapter 1's discussion of representation as mediation, the activity of representation requires grouping individual citizens together according to some understanding of their interests, and then speaking on behalf of those interests in the course of the legislative process. The relevant criterion for aggregation may be the specific geographic community defined by the district, or it may be some other kind of "community of interest." As Justice Harlan put it in his dissent in *Reynolds*, "people are not ciphers and . . . legislators can represent their electors only by speaking for their interests—economic, social, political—many of which do reflect the place where the electors live."[30]

Interest-conscious critics of "one person, one vote" are correct to point out its limitations. Although the principle that citizens should have an equal vote in elections is a crucial element of the democratic accountability of representatives, and so an important part of a coherent theory of liberal representation, the doctrine of voter equality cannot suffice as an account of fair representation. Most important, "one person, one vote," taken alone, fails to give an account of the third aspect of representation as mediation, the principle of constituency definition: it tells us nothing of how citizens' interests should be aggregated for purposes of political representation. To see how liberal representation resolves this problem, we must turn to its second strand, the theory of interest-group pluralism.

Interest-Group Pluralism

The central idea of interest-group pluralism, first systematized by Arthur F. Bentley in 1908, is that political processes in general, and public policy in particular, are best explained and most clearly understood as the product (or, as early pluralist thinkers were wont to say, the "resultant") of the dynamic interactions of social groups. Bentley's view challenged formal institutionalism, the then prevailing framework that explained political processes in terms of the legal and constitutional roles of governmental institutions. Instead, Bentley argued,

> All phenomena of government are phenomena of groups pressing one another, forming one another, and pushing out new groups and group representatives . . . to mediate the adjustments. It is only as we isolate these group activities, determine their representative values, and get the whole process stated in terms of them, that we approach to a satisfactory knowledge of government.[31]

Bentley's new view of politics lay dormant for several decades. In the 1950s, however, it was taken up and developed by political scientists such as David Truman, whose *The Governmental Process* is the classic statement of interest-group pluralism, and Robert Dahl, whose work on "polyarchy" developed the normative aspects of the theory.[32] Despite recent theoretical revisions to pluralist models of politics, its basic understanding of the nature of political groups, and of the processes by which group interests attain representation, remains intact.[33]

In the world according to pluralist theory, interest groups are the actors occupying center stage. But what exactly is an interest group, and what distinguishes it from other social groupings? First, it is clear that an interest group is more than a category of individuals, an aggregation of those who share some particular characteristic that in itself has no social or political significance. For example, until they join together to protest against society's unfair characterization of them as unintelligent, blonds do not constitute an interest group.[34] Rather, an interest group is a collection of individuals who share a common interest, broadly defined, and have formed an organization whose purpose is to advance that interest. David Truman's seminal work in pluralist theory defines an interest group in terms of this activity of interest advancement: "As used here 'interest group' refers to any group that, on the basis of one or more shared attitudes, makes certain claims upon other groups in the society for the establishment, maintenance, or enhancement of forms of behavior that are implied by the shared attitudes."[35]

A great many different interest groups exist in society, organized around a seemingly endless variety of economic, political, and social issues. Although the prototypical political interest groups are those organized around economic issues (the National Association of Manufacturers, the AFL-CIO and other labor unions, chambers of commerce, sectoral interests such as agriculture, etc.) the concept includes any group whose activities include attempts to shape governmental policies. Thus, in addition to the dominant interests of capital and organized labor, some interest groups are organized around particular policy issues (ranging from the abortion issue to the environment to the advocacy of prayer in public schools) as well as broader concerns (e.g., Common Cause or the National Organization for Women). The term *pluralism* is apt not only because of the number and variety of interest groups, but also because, in the United States at least, government offers many different points of access, including contacts with legislators and bureaucrats, financial contributions to electoral campaigns, testifying at congressional committee and administrative agency hearings, launching grass-roots letter-writing campaigns, and so on. This multiplicity is compounded even further by the fact that individuals may belong to a number of different interest groups.

With a logic similar to that of the market-clearing processes guided by a Smithian hidden hand, all this seemingly chaotic activity is said to result in legislative and other policies that effectively represent the significant interests in society. The pressures exerted on individual legislators in the form of lobbying and other activities leads representatives to act as advocates for those interests in framing legislative policies. But because many conflicting claims are being made on all the legislators, stable legislative policies are always the product of a great deal of bargaining, adjustment, compromise, and accommodation.[36] In its simplified form, interest-group pluralism views the legislative process as a calculus of physical pressures, and the legislative outcome a vector sum of all the different groups' claims.

Pluralist theorists sometimes argue that the representation of social interests achieved through the give-and-take of interest group conflict is superior to the more formal processes of representation, particularly representation through elections in territorial districts.[37] This is not to say, however, that they overlook or deny the place of other institutional and social influences in the policy-making process.[38] The system of district-based elections is perhaps the most significant of these influences, essentially operating as an additional and particularly compelling set of interests to which the legislator must attend. Dahl argues, for example, that it is the juxtaposition of the two systems of representation that best guarantees the responsiveness of representatives to the people.[39]

At the same time, although the classical sources of pluralist theory tend to focus on the role of interest groups as *pressure* groups, i.e., as exerting pressures on legislators during the formation of legislative policies, the theory of interest-group pluralism does operate at the electoral as well as the legislative stage of political representation. Interest groups organize during the electoral process to support candidates and to claim attention from parties and candidates alike. Indeed, parties themselves are often characterized as umbrella organizations for or coalitions among a variety of narrower, issue-focused interest groups. Clearly the activity of groups during elections influences both who gets elected and what platforms candidates and parties endorse, both of which have important consequences for legislative outcomes.

Another crucial constraint on legislative decisions is what Bentley and Truman call the "rules of the game." By this they mean the fundamental moral, constitutional, and institutional principles that define the outer boundaries of acceptable government behavior. They include, for example, essential individual rights and freedoms and a basic commitment to democratic equality, as well as institutional standards of legislative behavior to which representatives conform. Although what is included among the "rules of the game" is always somewhat ambiguous, the rules' power to limit policy outcomes is great because they constitute the underlying social consensus that is essential to the stability of any democratic regime.[40] Finally, especially as Truman articulates it, pluralist theory acknowledges the influence on policy of "potential interests," that is, groups of individuals who have interests in common but have not had occasion to form pressure groups. "Any mutual interest," he argues, "is a potential group. A disturbance in established relationships and expectations anywhere in society may produce new patterns of interaction aimed at restricting or eliminating the disturbance. Sometimes it may be this possibility of organization that alone gives the potential group . . . influence in the political process."[41] As we shall see, this possibility that unorganized interests will form pressure groups if their well-being is threatened is at once the source of pluralist theory's moral appeal and its greatest weakness.[42]

The normative power of interest-group pluralism is very similar to that of equal opportunity. Essentially, the idea is that *as long as individuals possess the opportunities (particularly the rights and freedoms) necessary to form interest groups, they will do so as their needs or interests dictate.*[43] When the freedom to organize exists throughout the political system, and a broad range of interest groups is active in politics, we can be confident that the most significant interests in society are being expressed. Since the expression of interests by pressure groups has an impact on policy formation, this means that citizens are receiving representation (understood as policy responsiveness) with regard to their primary concerns. Through protecting individual freedoms of speech, press, and assembly, a polity characterized by interest-group pluralism will secure multiple benefits. First, it benefits individual citizens by responding to their most important needs *as they define them*: like Mill's system of proportional representation, it allows for the voluntary formation of constituencies. Second, it provides the benefit of stability: since citizen demands are vented through the pressure-group system, no urgent or deep-seated claims go unexpressed or unaddressed. This gives the political outcomes considerable legitimacy and minimizes the likelihood that citizens will challenge political authority. Moreover, because policy outcomes are a product of the conflicting pressures exerted on government, it is a self-correcting system. Politics becomes "a business in which you do something, then wait to see who hollers, then relieve the hollering as best you can to see who else hollers."[44]

Further, pluralists argue, this process of response to interest-group pressures responds to the *intensity* of political preferences. This advantage is of particular concern for minorities who value certain political goods very highly but, under a strict majoritarian system, would be outvoted by a majority that nonetheless felt only mild opposition to their aims. Intuitively, majoritarianism seems unfair in such cases, particularly where minorities' urgent needs are at stake.[45] Interest-group pluralism resolves this problem in a manner that is counterintuitive because it initially appears anti-democratic. In other words, the policies it produces are not equally responsive to citizens' preferences; they often favor minority interests over those of the majority, and a cross-section of policies is not likely to reflect the distribution of unweighted political preferences across the population. But, as Dahl argues, most people, most of the time, have no policy preferences one way or the other. Ultimately very few issues arouse strong political feelings in the average citizen. A strict majoritarianism consequently delivers benefits that few people especially want. Instead, says Dahl, we ought to allow the intensity of individuals' political preferences to weigh in along with the content of the preferences themselves. Interest-group pluralism provides the ideal means of accomplishing this end, for the reason that organizing and being a member of an interest group exacts some costs from citizens, whether in the form of time, energy, or money.[46] Individuals' willingness to overcome these barriers to the expression of their interests is an excellent indication of the intensity with which they hold a particular preference. Further, the pitch of interest-group activity, and consequently its impact on policy decisions, will also be a function of the intensity with which its members hold their preferences. "All other things being equal," Dahl argues, "the outcome of a policy decision will be determined by the relative intensity of preference among the members of a group."[47]

Like equal opportunity doctrine, interest-group pluralism so conceived is a self-legitimating process. To recall Rawls's characterization of pure procedural justice, interest-group pluralism is regarded by its proponents as a process whose outcome is fair, "whatever it happens to be."[48] Groups whose interests are not currently represented in the policy-making process have no grounds for complaint; like the intelligent individual who seeks admission to a good university, they have only to assert themselves to achieve their goals. Looking at the system as a whole, the pluralist can be confident of its broad legitimacy. Indeed, legitimacy is not something with which political officials generally need to concern themselves. If ever a group (whatever its size or concern) is alienated, the politicians will be the first to know.

I mentioned above that in addition to the legitimacy that comes from the self-correcting processes of interest-group pluralism, the theory also claims the advantages of political stability. In this respect pluralism shares a great deal with James Madison's argument, in *Federalist* 10, regarding the advantages of representative government in an "extended republic" over pure democracies. Similarly, interest-group pluralism (at least in theory) avoids the instabilities produced by deep and permanent divisions of interest among citizens for two reasons. First, as with the Madisonian republic, a pluralist system contains a seemingly endless number of interest groups, which are constantly coming into being and passing away. Second, not only do individual citizens tend to be members of more than one group, but the membership of particular groups may be in flux. Individuals join and leave interest groups for different reasons, and the social circumstances that impel individuals to join an interest group are constantly changing. Consequently interest groups have overlapping memberships (that is, membership in one group does not necessarily correlate with membership in another), and individuals have shifting attachments to the groups of which they are members (they will not remain as members in a group unless their circumstances continue to dictate that membership is in their interest). The fact of overlapping and shifting memberships not only prevents any particular interest from dominating the political stage, but it also acts as a brake on the activities of group leaders: they are likely to avoid radical proposals in order not to alienate their more moderate members.[49] The fluidity of shifting and multiple memberships combines with the

geographic distance and diversity Madison relied on to produce a political
system that is extremely stable, that is, in which conflict is diffused over a
broad diversity of issues.[50]

As I have suggested above, neither the doctrine of "one person, one vote"
nor the theory of interest-group pluralism is sufficient, by itself, to constitute
a complete and coherent account of fair representation. Views of community-
based or interest-based representation confront the complexity of the processes by which groups of citizens get their representatives to act in their
interests. In so doing, they also express the notion that representational fairness has to do with the capacity of citizens to affect legislators' decisions by
acting in concert (e.g., by lobbying or by persuading voters to support or reject
a candidate). However, as we saw above, the pluralist strand of liberal representation does not, by itself, contain any mechanism for affirming the essential
political equality of individual citizens; it leads to the *unequal* representation
of interests as a function of the different political investments made by different interest groups. The principle of "one person, one vote" provides this
mechanism and works together with interest-group representation to render
the liberal theory more complete.

Another way of viewing the relationship between the two strands of liberal
representation is suggested by Ronald Rogowski. Any theory of fair representation, Rogowski argues, will specify a "social decision function" that determines the relative weights given to the ideal preferences of each subgroup or
member in the process of aggregating those preferences and producing a political policy or outcome.[51] Fair representation is accomplished, Rogowski argues, whenever the representation process performs in accordance with this
social decision function, allocating weights to different preferences as it specifies. This helps to clarify that equitable representation is not the same as
equal representation, since the social decision function may not allocate an
equal weight to the ideal preferences of all members or subgroups.[52] As in the
example Rogowski offers, "equitable representation" may entail weighting
only the ideal preferences of the community elders and ignoring the interests
of other members of the community.

Although he does not use his distinction to characterize the strands of liberal representation I present here, Rogowski's framework is a useful one for
understanding the different role each strand plays. The theory of interest-
group pluralism can be seen to express a doctrine of equitable representation,
defining a "social decision function" in which the preferences of different interest groups are weighted according to the amount of organizational effort
they expend. The greater their investments of time, money, and energy, the
greater the pressure they exert on legislators and the more the final policies
reflect their preferences. So long as the system of representation translates
these "inputs" into policy responsiveness, it is functioning fairly. As Dahl
argues, however, this is not to say that interest-group pluralism provides equal

representation—in fact, it clearly does not. However, the democratic demand for equal representation is met by the principle of "one person, one vote," the principle Rogowski defines as "equally weighted" (as opposed to "equally powerful") representation.

To say that liberal representation has two different strands—one promoting "equitable representation," the other promoting "equal representation"—is not to say it is an incoherent theory of representation. To the contrary, it is remarkably coherent, a theory that ties together all the complexities of democratic representation from the starting point of individual equality and autonomy, through the process of interest aggregation, to the dynamics of legislative decision making and the substance of legislative outcomes. To put it in terms of the aspects of representation as mediation, the liberal theory of representation addresses all three: legislator-constituency relations (constituents place pressures on legislators, who balance out different interests and advocate them on the basis of numbers and intensity); the dynamics of legislative decision making (bargaining and compromise); and the method of aggregation of individuals for representation (spontaneous interest-group formation). Moreover, liberal representation accomplishes all this while remaining consistent with the idea of the individual as morally autonomous. It is true that one strand alone cannot accomplish all these tasks, tasks that are essential to any comprehensive theory of representation. But that is a virtue rather than a failing, as it reflects the fact that political representation *is* complex, and that realizing the ideal of democratic equality in the sphere of representation demands that we recognize and reproduce that complexity. Like the plies of a cabled rope, the two strands of liberal representation are distinct and, in remaining so, add to the strength and integrity of the whole.

III. Liberal Representation, Geographic Districts, and Gerrymandering

The ingenuity of liberal representation consists in the fact that it simultaneously meets two requirements that any democratic theory of fair representation must satisfy: it gives institutional expression to the principle of individual equality, and it fulfills the need for a social decision function that can fairly aggregate individuals into representable constituencies. But despite these strengths, liberal representation does contain one theoretically troubling feature: the principle of "one person, one vote" does not acknowledge that voting is itself a moment of aggregation, with consequences for which interests receive representation. Because the design of geographic districts is the principal determinant of the manner in which interests are aggregated in the electoral process, districting itself performs a "social decision function." To be consistent, defenders of liberal representation in the American context must acknowledge that because of this aggregative dimension of districts, the design of the electoral system should itself be subject to a standard of *equity* as well as a standard of *equality*.

How does the standard of equity translate from the sphere of interest-group mobilization to the sphere of the aggregation of voters in the electoral process itself? First, equity in the electoral process would require that no individuals are systematically disadvantaged in their ability to form a constituency with others who share their interests. Recall that interest-group pluralism's normative theory asserts that fairness requires political responsiveness to both the *number* of citizens who share a given interest and the *intensity* with which they hold that interest. Thus minorities whose interest in an issue is very strong may outweigh the preferences of a majority when those preferences are relatively weak. At a minimum, then, equity in the electoral sphere would seem to require some degree of proportionality, i.e., responsiveness to numbers, so that a significant minority of voters—whatever the nature of its interests— could elect a number of candidates more or less in proportion to its share of the voting population. As I discuss in chapter 7, some versions of proportional representation also attempt to allow room for the expression of the intensity of preferences at the stage of elections. While defining an electoral process that can meet the standard of equity is quite feasible within systems of proportional representation, it is difficult to meet that standard within a geographic system of electoral districts. The remainder of this section explores the troubled relationship between liberal representation and geographic districting.

Territorial representation has its origins in feudal parliaments, which originally comprised lords of feudal estates convened at the order of the crown to consult on matters of state. In the hierarchical vision of feudal society, heads of estates were morally responsible for the welfare of all within their domain; hence their role in parliament was, in theory, neither to advance their personal interests nor the interests of individuals within their communities, but to represent the interests of their community taken as an organic whole. The British parliamentary system grew directly out of this tradition, and the American system, in which towns sent delegates to colonial assemblies, was imported from Britain.[53]

As a quasi-corporatist understanding of the body politic, the normative view underlying geographic representation assumes that local communities coincide with the important socioeconomic interests which need to be balanced against one another in the formulation of public policy that serves a common good—thus providing both the empirical hypothesis and the normative vision that undergird the third aspect of representation as mediation, constituency definition.[54] As Gordon Baker expressed it in the context of the early reapportionment cases, which pitted "rural interests" against "urban interests," "[t]he argument in favor of giving special recognition to various regions of a state through area representation often rests on the assumption that political boundaries conform to social or community boundaries."[55]

Thus the historical origins of systems of geographic representation are quite distinct from those of the normative theory of liberal representation. To the contrary, the principle of individual equality within liberal representation emerged directly out of the *critique* of "rotten boroughs" in Britain and out of population inequalities between towns and counties with equal numbers of delegates in colonial America.[56] Nonetheless, elements of geographic representation persist in American culture and law, not only in the form of geographic districting as the dominant mode of defining constituencies for electoral purposes but also as a normative theory that exists alongside that of liberal representation. As I have noted already, Justice Harlan expressed this normative view in his dissent in *Reynolds* that legislators represent their constituents only by advocating for their interests and that those interests may correspond closely to a geographically defined area.[57] The persistence of the normative side of geographic representation is perhaps most evident in some of the "traditional districting criteria" which many states observe in their districting processes and to which the courts have given substantial deference in their reapportionment and redistricting decisions. In particular, courts have regarded respect for traditional subdivision (county, town, etc.) boundaries and attempts to protect "communities of interest" as justifications for small deviations from strict district equality.[58] Such exceptions to the "one person, one vote" standard, however minor, are nonsensical without some supposition that legislative districts should yield the political representation of geographically defined or geographically bounded communities of interest.

Even if geographic districting were constrained by the strictest requirements of equal district size, however, important tensions with the liberal theory of representation would remain. As Lani Guinier emphasizes, territorial districts form "compulsory constituencies" in which membership is determined not by individual choice and voluntary mobilization but by the more-or-less unpredictable decisions of districting bodies. Citizens are not likely to change their residence in order to be able to vote in a different district. Even were they to do so, they could not rely on remaining in their district of choice because of the continual redistricting mandated by the rule of "one person, one vote."[59] Thus geographic districting stands in tension with the voluntarist understanding of constituency formation that lies at the heart of liberal representation's pluralist strand.[60]

Second, the standard of procedural fairness that is central to the pluralist strand of liberal representation eschews any procedural or systemic bias that advantages some interest groups over others in the political process. In a geographic districting system, the electoral chances of a candidate will be determined by the choices of the majority of voters within a given district. Legislators therefore have an electoral incentive to be responsive to the interests held by a majority of voters in their districts. When a district is drawn in such a way that an identifiable interest group constitutes a majority within it, that group will enjoy a competitive advantage in the political process: they are more likely to have their political preferences looked after by elected representatives than groups that do not constitute majorities within electoral districts. This creates a structural advantage for geographically concentrated interests (such as some economic interests) relative to those that are geographically dispersed (such as women). In fact, in a complex industrial society with its social fluidity and shifting patterns of residence, an eighteenth-century conception of town- or county-based representation seems anachronistic; it is far more likely that communities of interest will be defined along economic, racial, ethnic, or religious lines.[61]

Finally, winner-take-all territorial districts almost inevitably overrepresent the political majority, that is, yield a higher proportion of legislative seats to the majority party than their proportion of the popular vote.[62] A corollary of this tendency is "Duverger's Law," which states that single-member district elections have a propensity to produce stable two-party political systems and to discourage the emergence of third parties.[63] As with the bias in favor of geographically concentrated interests, the exaggeration of legislative majorities arguably stands in tension with liberal representation's standard of equity, as it systematically denies minorities legislative representation in proportion to their share of votes. Advocates of proportional representation, who themselves tend to affirm the principles of individual equality and voluntary constituency formation which I have argued lie at the heart of liberal representation, routinely charge that the systematic overrepresentation of majorities is inconsistent with principles of democratic equality.[64]

This final critique of geographic districting, however, does not follow as a matter of course from an embrace of liberal representation. From the broader standpoint of liberal constitutionalism, the exaggeration of legislative majorities is often regarded as a point in its favor relative to systems of proportional representation—not because it promotes equality, but because it promotes the different but critically important value of political stability.[65] Thus, although geographic districting does not have its historical origins in liberal constitutionalism's concern with stability, it does find its strongest twentieth-century justification there. Pointing to the Weimar experience with proportional representation, in particular, defenders of first-past-the-post electoral districts argue that a constitutional regime must balance different governmental values against one another in the design of political institutions, and that there is ample room for the principle of equality to be affirmed within the framework of territorial districts. Even if single-member territorial districts do not support many representational values,[66] they may support other values of governance. There is no need, therefore, to risk political instability in the name of equity by encouraging the emergence of fringe parties and frustrating the emergence of strong majority governments.[67]

Empirical research shows that the claims on behalf of the relative stability of district systems as compared to proportional representation systems are overdrawn.[68] Nonetheless, it might be possible to approximate the principle of equity within a system of territorial districts. First, the overrepresentation of political majorities may not substantially deprive minorities of representational opportunity except where there are strong overlapping cleavages between majority and minority groups. Where cleavages are cross-cutting, the logic of interest-group pluralism may well overwhelm the fact of majority legislative dominance. District majorities may have only weak preferences on the issues on which minorities have strong preferences, enabling the latter to mobilize effectively to influence even legislators from opposing parties.[69] Second, as Charles Beitz argues convincingly, while proportional representation may give minority voters nearly equal prospects of *electoral* success, it does not solve the problem that their representatives will still constitute a *legislative* minority, "unable except through compromise to effect their constituents' will."[70] This problem has led some defenders of minority representation, notably Pamela Karlan and Lani Guinier, to take the further step of proposing changes to legislative decision rules in order to secure minority influence over legislation. But it is hard to argue that such proposals follow necessarily from the liberal theory of representation, and some may not be consistent with it at all.[71]

Yet if geographic districting is fundamentally incompatible with some principles of liberal representation, it is possible, within the limits defined by geographic districts, to fulfill the principle of individual equality and thus render districting at least partially compatible with liberal representation. The question remains, however, whether it is similarly possible to approximate the principle of equity that forms the core of pluralist theory within a district system. Liberal representation does not presuppose geographic districts, but can it make its peace with them?

The concept of gerrymandering as an unfair political practice stands at the intersection of geographic districting and liberal representation's principle of equity. The critique of gerrymandering claims that the holders of districting power should not exercise that power so as to bias the electoral or legislative process in their own favor. Despite the inherent tensions between districting and equity, liberal representation need not have a serious quarrel with territorial districts so long as they are not drawn so as to produce a *systematic* disadvantage for identifiable interests. As Robert Dixon famously noted, "all districting is 'gerrymandering,'" since regardless of the intent of its authors any districting scheme will have the effect of giving some groups a disproportionate influence in the electoral process.[72] However, as long as there is no long-term pattern of influence that permanently disadvantages some identifiable group, the logic of pluralism prevails: today's winners may be tomorrow's losers, and vice versa. Perfect equality of political opportunity may not be achievable for any single election, but over time different interest groups' influence balances out. Although political minorities may never, in a single-member districting system, have a proportionate share of legislative seats or policy outcomes, neither will they be shut out altogether. And as I have noted above, they always have the opportunity to mobilize independently in order to exert pressure on any and all elected representatives to advance their political agendas.

The best model for such a neutral districting process is probably random districting performed at frequent intervals to prevent the temporarily advantaged legislative majority from becoming too deeply entrenched. It is important to note, however, that the problem of permanent minorities that afflicts pluralist theory in general is all the more salient in the area of districting. Even if such minorities are geographically concentrated and so have the potential to constitute a constituency within a district system, random districting is statistically unlikely to draw districts that would enable them to elect representatives. On rare occasions such a district might happen to be drawn, but they could not rely on it.

Even apart from permanent minorities, there are important limits to the extent to which pluralism's standard of equity can be reconciled with districting. While the two do intersect in theory in moral objections to intentional gerrymandering, the difficulty lies in applying the standard of procedural fairness to particular districting schemes. As Charles Beitz argues, for a principle of districting fairness to have any practical force, "it must specify the kinds of outcomes that fairness forbids."[73] As we shall see in the next chapter's discussion of voting rights jurisprudence, the pluralist conception of procedural fairness is incapable of distinguishing an unfair distortion of the electoral process from a legitimate balancing of the variety of governmental values that (at least in theory) can be served through districting. More specifically, since districting's natural tendency is to overrepresent majorities, it is very difficult to define the threshold at which a minority interest has been unfairly disadvantaged in the electoral process.

IV. The Limits of Liberal Representation

There are many detours on the road between a coherent and comprehensive theory and the realization of fair representation in practice. Thus even advocates of liberal representation frequently acknowledge that it is naive to believe that fair representation will automatically emerge so long as we protect voting rights (even if defined as "one person, one vote") and the other fundamental political rights of free speech and assembly.

Some of the challenges to liberal representation focus on the core of pluralist theory's normative claims. Recall that interest-group pluralism's claim to fairness was that "unorganized interests" are free to become organized if social and political circumstances so dictate, and that the openness of the system of representation made outcomes responsive to the differential efforts of various interest groups. The weakness in this argument again brings out the parallels between interest-group pluralism and equal opportunity doctrine. The critique is raised by questioning the assumption that individuals have roughly equal access to the means or resources necessary to organize and mobilize an interest group. Just as real-world circumstances make it clear that individuals of equal talent do not, in fact, have equal prospects of winning scarce social goods, actual social conditions also give the lie to the notion that interest groups arise spontaneously whenever the need occurs. The principal obstacle is money: among the barriers that "unorganized interests" face in becoming active interest groups, the financial demands are the most obvious. This means that social interests backed by wealth are much more likely to become organized as interest groups than are economically disadvantaged groups. As E. E. Schattschneider said in his classic critique of pluralism, "The flaw in the pluralist heaven is that the heavenly chorus sings with a strong upper-class accent."[74]

Pluralists themselves have not overlooked this problem, but neither do they have an answer to it that is consistent with a purely pluralist politics. Since writing *A Preface to Democratic Theory*, Dahl, for example, has given increasing recognition to the fact that the principles of democratic equality remain unfulfilled so long as radical economic inequality persists. As a result, he concludes, pluralism sometimes fails to produce fair outcomes. Those with fewer economic resources have less initial opportunity to influence the political process, given the extent to which economic resources translate into political resources. In addition, this dynamic of inequality is an iterative process: if those who have greater economic resources are better able to mobilize, policy outcomes will reinforce and reproduce existing patterns of inequality. "If some interests have ready access to organizations and their resources, and others do not, then such a pattern may help to maintain inequalities among citizens, and some of these inequalities may be unjust."[75] Although Dahl's concerns about the political consequences of economic inequality have steadily increased over the years, he has not articulated a strategy for correcting this fault of pluralism that is consistent with pluralist premises. Rather, he suggests that the only remedy for the dynamic of inequality may be to move away from free-market economics toward a more centralized, integrative political economy that aims explicitly at reducing inequality.[76] However, for government to intervene in the economic and political market in this way would involve using an independent standard of equality that is inconsistent with pluralism's reliance on proceduralism to produce fairness. Until such intervention can be defined in a manner consistent with individual autonomy, Dahl suggests, "polyarchy's" resolution of the tensions between pluralism and democracy may be preferable to "any alternative that appears to be available."[77]

A second condition of the fairness of liberal representation is the fluidity of the process of interest-group formation: the overlapping membership of different groups and individuals' shifting membership in groups. As Dahl's analysis demonstrates, however, this fluidity is possible only in a society in which the fundamental social and political cleavages are cross-cutting.[78] But such is not the case for historically marginalized ascriptive groups, and particularly racial minorities: patterns of racial bloc voting make it clear that they regard their interests on a broad range of issues as consistently opposed to the felt interests of dominant or majority groups.[79] In a system of majority or plurality single-member districts, and one in which legislative majorities rule, critics argue, this means that the interests of historically marginalized ascriptive groups often go unrepresented; they are not reflected in policy outcomes. As noted above, meeting liberal representation's standard of equity in the electoral process is especially difficult with regard to permanent minorities.

Dahl briefly acknowledged the problem of permanent minorities in his *Preface to Democratic Theory* and has confronted it more explicitly in recent works.[80] In particular, he examines the various institutional innovations such as consociational democracy that have emerged to cope with the problems of permanent subcultural minorities. But the difficult question—which Dahl tends to skirt—is whether interest-group pluralism can support a right of collective entities to political recognition or whether such rights can only belong to individuals. Although the representation of collectivities such as states and provinces (in federal systems), economic structural groups (such as labor, business, and agriculture, as in neocorporatist arrangements), or cultural groups (in consociational democracy) may have many practical advantages, it is impossible to defend such institutions consistent with the individualistic assumptions of liberal representation. Dahl's own discussion acknowledges as much in his concern over the possibility that granting political status to groups always runs the risk that they might fail to respect the rights of their *internal* minorities.[81] So despite his admiration for the practical efficacy of institutions of consociational democracy, Dahl at least implicitly acknowledges that beginning from the premises of pluralist theory, it is not possible to offer a principled defense of collectivist solutions to the problem of permanent minorities. Although I share Dahl's concerns on all these points, I do not give up on the project of discovering institutions that secure representation for permanent minorities without violating the principles of individual autonomy and individual equality.[82]

Finally, some critics argue that whatever the theoretical fairness of the *processes* that produced them, electoral *outcomes* are not fair when they mean that historically marginalized ascriptive groups are consistently underrepresented in legislative bodies. Similarly, some argue that legislative decisions are unfair when the interests of marginalized groups are consistently subordinated to those of privileged groups. Genuine political equality requires that "representatives of minority, ethnic, or other groups . . . must at least be able to carry the day when significant interests of members of their own group are at issue and they are opposed by groups who have only a marginal interest in the matter."[83] Indeed, this standard of fairness is implied by Dahl's concern with intensity, and it suggests that pluralist theory fails to meet its own principle of equity when it comes to disadvantaged minority groups.

Like the difference-based critiques of equal opportunity doctrine, arguments for the legislative presence of historically marginalized groups focus on the ways in which existing political processes, while facially neutral, function to reproduce existing patterns of social inequality along group lines. Just as genuine equal opportunity can be realized only when the biases of existing standards of evaluation are revealed and overcome, fairness in representation can be realized for disadvantaged groups only when the themes of social difference are interwoven with the concrete practices and institutions of political representation. According to these critics, fairness requires the representation of disadvantaged social groups in decision-making bodies because without their presence it is extremely likely that their interests will be overlooked and that policies will be biased against them. As Iris Young puts it:

> [B]ecause it assures a voice for the oppressed as well as the privileged, group representation better assures that all needs and interests in the public will be recognized in democratic deliberations. Social and economic privilege means, among other things, that the groups which have it behave as though they have a right to speak and be heard, that others treat them as if they have that right, and that they have the material, personal, and organizational resources that enable them to speak and be heard. As a result, policy issues are often defined by the assumptions and priorities of the privileged. Specific representation for oppressed groups interrupts this process, because it gives voice to the assumptions and priorities of other groups.[84]

Defenders of liberal representation stand ready with responses to almost all these criticisms, although not all their responses are equally powerful. The charge—that the ethical justification of interest-group pluralism is based on the faulty premise that interests have an equal opportunity to organize—is the one that defenders of liberal representation have the most difficulty in addressing. The available defenses are akin to the standard response to similar critiques of equal opportunity doctrine itself: that while they must acknowledge that organizational resources do vary according to "morally arbitrary" characteristics such as race and gender, this does not present an insurmountable obstacle to group organization and influence even for those groups. Like the opponent of affirmative action who points to the successful Black businesswoman as evidence that equal opportunity works, defenders of liberal representation are likely to guide attention away from statistical patterns of success and failure across groups and focus instead on individual success stories. Thus critics of race-conscious districting such as Abigail Thernstrom and Carol Swain point to examples of Black representatives elected from majority-White districts, such as Representative Gary Franks, a Republican from Connecticut, and Ron Dellums, a Democratic Representative from California, as evidence that regular electoral processes contain no insuperable barriers to minority representation.[85] As Swain argues, "The fact of black representatives from majority-white districts flies in the face of the conventional wisdom that majority-black political units . . . are needed to elect black politicians."[86] Yet such anecdotal evidence of Black electoral success is not an adequate response to the overwhelming empirical evidence of continuing patterns of racial bloc voting in the United States, particularly in the South, nor of the fact that the vast majority of Black elected officials have been elected from majority-Black districts.[87] Indeed, the evidence is clear that minority gains in representation in the 1990s are almost entirely a consequence of the creation of majority-minority districts.[88]

Defenders of liberal representation are not daunted by the evidence against them. Rather, they turn to arguments that the effective representation of minorities does not depend on the election of large numbers of minority legislators to office. Those who are elected, they argue, enjoy an amplified voice in legislatures because the civil rights environment since the 1960s makes it costly for nonminority legislators to appear to oppose minority rights. Abigail Thernstrom expressed a similar point: "A tarnished image on civil rights jeopardizes the support of not only minority voters but also whites who see themselves as sympathetic to minority concerns and equate such sympathy with uncritical support for policies advocated by civil rights groups."[89]

As for marginalized group concerns that their members are underrepresented among elected representatives, the answer provided by the liberal theory of representation is clear. As a case of pure procedural fairness, liberal representation creates no entitlements to any particular outcome, and certainly not to a threshold level of group presence in legislative bodies. By all means, electoral channels should be cleared of any obstacles to minority group representation that arise out of racial discrimination—but the existing system of voting rights accomplishes this. If marginalized groups claim more, and especially if they seek anything like the proportional presence of their members in legislative bodies, they are demanding more than a fair system of representation entitles them to. In essence, they are asking that they themselves be recognized as a special class of citizens deserving of recognition not granted to others, and claims such as this have been regarded as anathema to American democratic principles since before the Founding. The existing system not only protects all citizens' rights to vote on an equal basis, but it also provides ample opportunities for groups to organize in order to accomplish their political aims. They may organize efforts to influence policy decisions, they may organize to put forward minority candidates, and they may organize to mobilize voters to put those candidates into office on election day. But neither the Constitution nor the Voting Rights Act entitles minority groups to the legislative seats that would make all these organizational efforts unnecessary. Suggesting that the quest for interventions which enhance minority representation is a way of avoiding the hard work of political mobilization, Thernstrom queries, "how much special protection from white competition are black candidates entitled to?"[90] Again, liberal representation maintains that the fairness of representation depends on the *voluntary* formation of constituencies.[91] If a fair system of elections, cleansed of racially discriminatory schemes, nonetheless fails to result in the election of minority candidates, the remedy is not to seek federal action but to step up political organization.[92]

Most important, liberal representation's advocates assert that to the extent marginalized groups claim a threshold number of legislative seats for group members, their arguments contain the disturbing and erroneous premise that Whites are incapable of representing Blacks or other minorities[93] or that men are incapable of representing women. According to liberal representation, such an assumption has a number of serious flaws. First, it utterly misunderstands the nature of the process of representation. Representatives do not serve their constituents by being *like* them, but by acting in their interests. What causes representatives to respond to their constituents' interests is the extent to which they are electorally dependent on a particular group of citizens, combined with more specific pressures exerted by the group. This process of responsiveness has nothing at all to do with race or gender or ethnicity. Thernstrom quotes an aide to a southern senator who supported the Voting Rights Act as an example of this elemental principle of liberal representation. Referring to Blacks, the aide explained, "You have to cater to those interests like you cater to other interests."[94] This argument refers to the aspect of representation as mediation that concerns legislator-constituency relations. The representative fulfills his or her obligation to act in the interests of the represented by *bargaining for* those interests, not by *sharing* them. Minorities who lay claim to representation by members of their own group not only demonstrate a shallow understanding of the process of representation, Thernstrom suggests, but also an unreasonable distrust of Whites. Vernon Jordan remarked during House debates on the Voting Rights Act that "'I don't trust white people in the South with my rights. . . . I didn't before the act; I don't 17 years later.'" Thernstrom responds, "[I]t is hard to imagine what sort of evidence could have overcome such *inbred distrust*."[95]

From the standpoint of the liberal theory of representation, another deep flaw in group-based claims to representation is that they ossify distinctions among classes of citizens rather than reinforce the liberal ideal of difference-blind equality. Chief Justice Burger expressed this idea eloquently in his dissent in *United Jewish Organizations of Williamsburgh v. Carey*, a case in which a Hasidic community challenged a state districting plan that maximized safe Black districts at their expense: "Manipulating the racial composition of electoral districts to assure one minority or another its 'deserved' representation will not promote the goal of a racially neutral legislature. On the contrary, such racial gerrymandering *puts the imprimatur of the State on the concept that race is a proper consideration in the electoral process.*"[96] This argument goes beyond the one frequently presented by opponents of affirmative action, that to favor individuals on grounds of their race, sex, or ethnicity is "reverse discrimination." For whereas affirmative action involves decisions that take individual differences into account, and in any event confers benefits on individuals, the practice of giving state recognition to group claims for separate representation re-creates discrete classes of citizens. Because of the centrality of the institutions and processes of representation in our constitutional system, therefore, accepting racial criteria for districting practices comes very close to the reconstitutionalization of race. To allow such a move is to undercut the central liberal commitment to the freedom and autonomy of individual citizens, for it allows the state to ascribe political beliefs and preferences to individuals on the grounds of their group membership rather than preserving a system that gives them the freedom to express their views on an individual basis. As Thernstrom sums it up, "democratic choice and democratic institutions require a fluidity and freedom that are at odds with the concept of labeling citizens for political purposes on the basis of race or ethnicity."[97]

This argument, however, fails to confront the reality of racial divisions in the United States, of which there is ample empirical evidence.[98] Measures to protect minorities from racial hostility do not create that hostility but attempt to reduce its effects. To suggest that remedies for racial hostilities are the cause of racial divisions is, as the Senate Report of the Voting Rights Act Amendments of 1982 put it so effectively, "like saying that it is the doctor's thermometer which causes high fever."[99]

This concern over balkanization brings out another important similarity between the Madisonian theory of representation and liberal representation: for both, one of the most important benefits of the play of factions or interest groups is that it prevents dangerously divisive conflicts from paralyzing democratic politics. In this sense, both views of representation take what I referred to in the preceding chapter as a *suppressive* rather than an *expressive* stance toward certain kinds of social groups.[100] Defenders of liberal representation turn the vice of the underrepresentation of permanent minorities into a virtue by claiming that the interests that divide the majority from minority groups are damaging to the public good. For them, as for Madison, a pluralistic politics functions to suppress those political conflicts that most deeply afflict American society, and this is something to celebrate rather than challenge. Resolving these conflicts in a manner most conducive to public harmony and the general interest depends precisely on preventing them from dominating political discussion, which will polarize both the legislature and the populace. By resisting the inclination to confer political recognition on class or race, both views of representation create an image of state neutrality toward these social differences and so of a public policy that treats citizens equally without regard to their class status or racial identity.

Liberal representation has strong defenders in scholars such as Thernstrom and Swain. Their defense, however, fails to address several central points in the general critiques of liberal representation that I have summarized here. For starters, their response fails to acknowledge the internal critique of liberal representation, that is, the problem of permanent minorities. It tends to skirt this issue by offering anecdotal evidence for the erosion of racial cleavages without addressing the available statistical evidence concerning the persistence of those cleavages. Equally important, it fails to recognize the possibility that historically marginalized groups as such might have a distinctive claim, grounded in the principle of political equality, to specific representation in legislative bodies. The next chapter shows that while liberal representation is unquestionably the dominant strand in American jurisprudence on voting rights, Supreme Court decisions and congressional legislation have not always embraced the restrictive, pure proceduralist reading of liberal representation advanced by Thernstrom and Swain. Instead, much of the voting rights jurisprudence and the legislation that grows out of it can only be understood as an attempt to acknowledge the distinctive claims to equality of historically marginalized groups and to reconcile those claims with the central commitments of liberal representation, including liberal conceptions of individual equality. These efforts to recognize the contemporary relevance of past discrimination have led Congress and the Court to moderate liberal representation's pure proceduralism with a measure of attention to results. Ultimately, however, this attempt fails both politically and, in several key respects, theoretically as well. Its failure brings to light the need for an independent substantive defense of marginalized group representation, one that is not immediately derived from the principles of liberal representation.

3

The Supreme Court, Voting Rights, and Representation

IT IS NOW a commonplace in legal scholarship that there is no coherent theory of representation underlying the Supreme Court's voting rights jurisprudence.[1] Yet in this chapter I will argue that liberal representation's conception of procedural fairness lies at the heart of all the voting rights jurisprudence from the early 1960s to the present. A great deal of the confusion in these cases arises out of the tension between liberal representation's understanding of procedural fairness, on the one hand, and the persistence of institutions (and consequently of the normative justifications) of geographic representation, on the other. In attempting to understand the place of historically marginalized groups in voting rights doctrine, we come to see that liberal representation itself contains a range of possible interpretations of procedural fairness. In the more *restrictive* readings, the claims of marginalized groups to protection from process distortions are not qualitatively different from the claims of any other kind of political group. In the more *expansive* readings, marginalized groups receive special solicitude because of the ways in which the history of discrimination has systematically distorted the political process to their disadvantage. The more expansive the reading of liberal representation, the greater the modification of its pure proceduralism in light of a standard of fair outcomes.

As we shall see, however, even the expansive interpretation of liberal representation fails to account fully for some of the core intuitions that repeatedly appear in the voting rights jurisprudence and legislation. Most important, it fails to account for the common view that the fair representation of historically marginalized groups requires some threshold presence of group members in legislative bodies. This persistent intuition regarding substantive fairness toward marginalized groups goes beyond what can be justified within even an expansive reading of liberal representation. Thus advocates of the expansive view have tended to support the idea that fair representation for minorities requires their legislative presence, but they have not been able to articulate sound theoretical justifications for measures to enhance that legislative presence.

In its recent redistricting decisions, the Supreme Court has come to embrace a very narrow and restrictive conception of representational fairness at the expense of the expansive conception that had been developed over the preceding twenty years.[2] These decisions are riddled with logical inconsistencies and transparent racial biases, which I demonstrate in an appendix to this chapter. Nonetheless, there is a deeper harmony between liberal representation and the recent decisions that gives them considerable popular legitimacy.[3] In part, the recent reversal of the Court's support for race-conscious districting may be a product of a more general conservative shift in American politics and in the Court's majority. I believe, however, that the recent success of the restrictive interpretation of representational fairness arises, in part, out of the greater robustness of the liberal theory of fair representation as compared to the group-conscious alternative that remains incipient in the legislative and jurisprudential treatments of voting rights. In this context, advocates of minority representation face an urgent need to develop a theoretical account of fair representation that is sufficiently robust to constitute a persuasive alternative to liberal representation.

The purpose of this chapter, then, is to trace the movement of minority voting rights doctrine from the restrictive to the expansive reading of liberal representation and back again, and to explain why the strategy of reading liberal representation expansively has failed to secure legislative representation for disadvantaged minorities. I argue that the theoretical failings of the expansive view of liberal representation are partially responsible for its *political* failure on the Supreme Court and elsewhere. I demonstrate that a theoretical defense of the legislative presence of marginalized groups is unavailable from within liberal representation's procedural conceptions of fairness, even when pure proceduralism is supplemented with attention to outcomes. Instead, the defense of marginalized group representation must rest on an independent substantive justification of the legislative presence of members of such groups. The project I undertake in the remainder of the book is to develop such a justification.

While I do not wish to add to the list of finely detailed accounts of the Court's jumbled history on issues of political representation,[4] I do find it necessary to review some of that history in order to illuminate the theoretical strands within the Court's reasoning. In what follows, then, I begin with a brief sketch of the evolution of voting rights law from the reapportionment decisions to *Shaw v. Reno*, focusing especially on the emergence of the concept and doctrine of minority vote dilution. Next, I trace the development of the restrictive, difference-blind interpretation of liberal representation through these cases, followed by an account of the more expansive reading that emerges in cases concerning the voting strength of historically disadvantaged racial and ethnic minorities. I then turn to the shift in voting rights jurisprudence since *Shaw v. Reno*, which constitutes a victory of the restrictive over the expansive reading of liberal representation. Finally, I address the reasons why advocates of political equality for historically marginalized groups need to move beyond liberal representation to develop an independent substantive defense of representation for marginalized groups. While I believe it is possible to reconcile a concern for marginalized group representation with the fundamental commitments of liberal democracy, to do so requires a more focused inquiry into the relationship between historical marginalization and representational fairness than has been undertaken until now.

I. Voting Rights from *Reynolds* to *Shaw v. Reno*: The Concept of Minority Vote Dilution

The reapportionment decisions' new emphasis on the right to "fair and effective representation" for all citizens intersected in the 1960s and 1970s with legislative and doctrinal changes arising out of the civil rights movement and aimed at enfranchising African American citizens and protecting their right to participate as equal citizens in the political process. Following the Civil Rights Act of 1964 and the Voting Rights Act of 1965,[5] southern White officials followed the example of their nineteenth-century forebears and demonstrated considerable ingenuity in devising alternative methods for minimizing minorities' effective participation in politics.[6] Such practices have been brought together under the heading of minority vote dilution, defined as "a process whereby election laws or practices, either singly or in concert, combine with systematic bloc voting among an identifiable majority group to diminish or cancel the voting strength of at least one minority group."[7]

Judicial and legislative recognition of the phenomenon of minority vote dilution yielded the "second generation" of voting rights law,[8] in which the focus is not simply on whether minorities are able to vote but whether they have the capacity to make their votes *effective* in electing the candidates of their choice.[9] The emergence of a doctrine of minority vote dilution was greatly facilitated by the Court's decision in *Allen v. State Board of Elections* in 1969 that the federal pre-clearance requirements of Section 5 of the Voting Rights Act should extend not only to issues of voting and registration but to all election laws, including electoral systems and districting.[10] *Allen* yielded a massive increase in the number of Section 5 challenges to state election procedures, and most of the new challenges were grounded in vote dilution claims.[11]

It took several years, however, for the Court to reach its own finding of impermissible vote dilution. In 1971, in *Whitcomb v. Chavis*, the Court heard a claim by Black residents of Indianapolis that the use of multimember districts in county elections denied them effective representation by submerging their votes within majority-White constituencies. Rejecting the plaintiffs' claim that the lack of proportional Black representation was evidence of vote dilution, the Court held that they would have had to demonstrate that Black voters "had less opportunity than did other . . . residents to participate in the political process and to elect legislators of their choice."[12] It was not until *White v. Regester*, decided in 1973, that the Court actually disallowed a multimember district system on grounds that it unconstitutionally diluted the votes of African Americans and Mexican Americans in two Texas counties and produced elections in which minorities "had less opportunity than did other residents in the district to participate in the political processes and to elect legislators of their choice."[13] The Court's holding was based on the district court's "intensely local appraisal" of the "totality of the circumstances," which included both a history of discrimination against these groups and evidence of government officials' unresponsiveness to their interests.

Zimmer v. McKeithen, a federal Court of Appeals decision applying the new White standards for minority vote dilution, systematized those standards by specifying eight criteria for evaluating vote dilution claims. Although the Zimmer court did include a history of discrimination among the criteria, requirements for evidence of intentional discrimination were notably absent from its list. The Zimmer criteria included four "primary" factors ("a lack of access to the process of slating candidates, the unresponsiveness of legislators to their particularized interests, a tenuous state policy underlying the preference for multimember or at-large districting, or . . . the existence of past discrimination") and four "enhanc[ing]" ones ("the existence of large districts, majority vote requirements, anti-single shot voting provisions and the lack of provision for at-large candidates running from particular geographical subdistricts").[14]

Nonetheless the White decision was somewhat unclear as to whether the force of minority plaintiffs' claims lay in the discriminatory *effects* they suffered or in the fact that they were the victims of *intentional* distortions of the political process, for which the Zimmer criteria provided circumstantial but not direct evidence. In 1980 a plurality of the Court attempted to resolve this uncertainty in City of Mobile v. Bolden by requiring a direct showing of racially discriminatory intent to sustain a claim of minority vote dilution.[15] Although there was no majority to support this requirement, neither was there a majority opposing it, and so it provided the new standard for lower courts. Not surprisingly, the Court's new "smoking gun" standard of intentional discrimination made it very difficult for minority plaintiffs to mount sustainable vote dilution claims.[16]

Temporary provisions of the Voting Rights Act were due to expire in 1982, which meant that Congress had to consider whether to renew them.[17] In direct response to the Mobile decision, civil rights activists used this opportunity to mobilize congressional support for amending the Act to entrench a set of results-oriented standards of fair representation.[18] After heavy debate, Section 2 was amended to impose a nationwide prohibition on minority vote dilution. In the amended language of the Act, a Section 2 violation exists

> if, based on the totality of circumstances, it is shown that the political processes leading to nomination or election in the State or political subdivision are not equally open to participation by members of a [protected] class of citizens . . . in that its

members have less opportunity than other members of the electorate to participate in the political process and to elect representatives of their choice. The extent to which members of a protected class have been elected to office . . . is one circumstance which may be considered: *Provided*, That nothing in this section establishes a right to have members of a protected class elected in numbers equal to their proportion in the population.[19]

It was not until 1986 that the Court first interpreted amended Section 2 in *Thornburg v. Gingles*,[20] in which minority voters challenged the use of multimember districts for state legislative elections. The district court upheld the challenge after reviewing the "totality of circumstances," including evidence of past discrimination affecting Black registration and voting, the disadvantaged socioeconomic position of Blacks in the affected areas, the presence of racial appeals in recent state elections, and severe racially polarized voting.[21] Affirming the lower court decision with respect to four of the five contested districts, a narrow majority of the Supreme Court defined a three-pronged test for the existence of impermissible minority vote dilution: First, the minority group must be "sufficiently large and geographically compact to constitute a majority in a single-member district"; second, it must be "politically cohesive"; and, finally, the White majority must also vote "sufficiently as a bloc to enable it . . . usually to defeat the minority's preferred candidate."[22] The first prong of the test, the Court argued, is necessary to demonstrate that the minority group has been injured; without the theoretical potential to constitute an effective electoral majority, the minority group has no claim that it has been disadvantaged by the existing scheme of districts. The second prong complements the first, for even a geographically compact minority cannot claim to have been disadvantaged in the electoral process unless it votes sufficiently cohesively to elect the community's preferred candidate. The third prong, voting cohesion among Whites such that they are usually able to defeat the candidates preferred by Black voters, is necessary to "distinguish[] structural dilution from the mere loss of an occasional election."[23] The virtue of the *Gingles* test is that it provides a judicially manageable standard for evaluating vote dilution claims. Notwithstanding some ambiguities in its application,[24] it seems clear that the general purpose of the *Gingles* test has been to "minimize[] unnecessary investigation into historical, social and economic dynamics and intent, and . . . to measure dilution in the same objective way as does the 'one person, one vote' rule."[25]

Before *Shaw v. Reno*, both supporters and detractors of the *Gingles* test tended to agree that because racially polarized voting is the rule rather than the exception in the United States,[26] Section 2 effectively required states to draw as many majority-minority districts as the geographic distribution of minority voters would allow, at least to the point of proportionality.[27] To that extent, Justice O'Connor was justified in her expectation, expressed in her separate concurrence in *Gingles*, that the decision would make *"usual, roughly proportional* success the sole focus of its vote dilution analysis," despite the explicit renunciation of proportionality in the amended statute itself.[28] Clearly a geographic system of electoral districts imposes powerful constraints on the likelihood of actual proportional representation for minority communities. This is true not only because minorities are sometimes geographically dispersed, but also because even where they are concentrated they may overlap with other protected minorities in ways that make it difficult or impossible to draw districts in which each has electoral control.[29]

Further, there is nothing in the *Gingles* test to suggest that an electoral plan's failure to yield minority *representatives* in proportion to the minority's population constitutes a violation of Section 2 (even though the failure to elect minority representatives at all is a factor in "totality of circumstances" analysis). The question, rather, is whether minority communities are able to elect the "candidates of their choice," whether or not those candidates are themselves members of the minority community. *Shaw v. Reno* and its progeny impose at least one additional constraint, that majority-minority districts must meet not only the *Gingles* test but also a test of geographic compactness.[30] Nonetheless, within these constraints, *Gingles* did appear to require states to draw majority-minority districts wherever its test could be met. It was to comply with that perceived requirement (sometimes under pressure from the Department of Justice, as in *Shaw*) that states drew a record number of majority-minority districts following the 1990 census.

On the same day that it handed down its decision in *Gingles*, the Court also decided *Davis v. Bandemer*, which held for the first time that *partisan* as well as racial gerrymanders were justiciable under the Fourteenth Amendment.[31] The Court's reasoning in *Bandemer* turns on the judgment that "each political group in a State should have the same chance to elect representatives of its choice as any other political group,"[32] and that the justiciability of a group's claim to fair representation is independent of the fact that it is "submitted by a political group, rather than a racial group."[33] What matters, Justice White argued for the Court, is that the group alleging discriminatory districting is sufficiently cohesive to constitute a genuine community of interest. Establishing a cohesive group interest capable of representation, however, does not make it easy to receive constitutional protection from vote-dilution schemes.[34] The group must demonstrate not only that a districting plan was drawn with the *intent* of diminishing its electoral power but also that it had that *effect*. Moreover, a simple showing that elections did not result in a return of the group's candidates roughly in proportion to its share of the popular vote was not sufficient.[35] In addition, successful plaintiffs would have to demonstrate that a plan would "consistently degrade a voter's or a group of voters' influence on the political process as a whole."[36] Despite these criteria, for reasons

I explain below, *Bandemer* fails to articulate a manageable judicial standard of unconstitutional partisan gerrymandering. Since *Bandemer* was decided, no districting scheme has been overturned as an unconstitutional partisan gerrymander.

In the next two sections I argue that *Bandemer* and *Gingles* constitute the end points of two distinct logics of representational fairness that are intermingled in the Court's voting rights jurisprudence before *Shaw v. Reno*. While *Bandemer* follows logically from a difference-blind interpretation of liberal representation's pluralist strand, *Gingles*—at least as it was applied before *Shaw*—requires a sensitivity to the historical and sociological distinctiveness of disadvantaged racial and ethnic minorities. Although *Gingles* is still consonant with a procedural conception of fairness, it requires a much deeper and more expansive understanding of the political process than do the arguments supporting *Bandemer*, and also allows greater attention to electoral outcomes. In both, geographic representation functions as a limit on the extent to which procedural fairness can be realized within the American system of political representation.

II. Difference-Blind Proceduralism and Voting Rights Doctrine

As I argued in the above discussion of the relationship between geographic representation and liberal representation, the liberal conception of representational fairness *can* be satisfied, albeit imperfectly, within geographic districting systems. The Court's history of intervention into electoral processes can be read, first and foremost, as an attempt to protect the principles of individual equality and procedural fairness that inform liberal representation. John Hart Ely, in his book *Democracy and Distrust*, eloquently articulates the proceduralist understanding of political fairness:

> Malfunction occurs when the *process* is undeserving of trust, when (1) the ins are choking off the channels of political change to ensure that they will stay in and the outs will stay out; or (2) though no one is actually denied a voice or a vote, representatives beholden to an effective majority are systematically disadvantaging some minority out of simple hostility or a prejudiced refusal to recognize commonalities of interest, and thereby denying that minority the protection afforded other groups by a representative system.[37]

The second distortion of the representation process occasions the need for judicial review to overturn legislation that discriminates against minorities. The first is what occasions the need for judicial review of electoral processes. This "market-corrective" understanding of the role of the courts in overseeing electoral processes and legislative outcomes, Ely argues, constitutes the most defensible justification of the Court's decisions in the areas of reapportionment and voting rights. Certainly it seems to underlie much of the Court's understanding of its role in securing "fair and effective representation."

We have seen already that liberal representation's concern for individual equality receives doctrinal expression in the principle of "one person, one vote" and is embodied institutionally in the requirement of equally populous legislative districts following the reapportionment decisions. Although not as readily apparent, the principle of equity—the normative standard of the pluralist strand of liberal representation—is also present from the Court's first consideration of reapportionment.[38] The main force of the moral objections to extreme malapportionment was not only that it denied individual voters an equal influence over the electoral process, but that it yielded—and preserved—a system in which a minority of voters elected a majority of legislators.[39] Although the Court did not go beyond majoritarianism explicitly to assert a pluralist argument, it came close when it stated that "the fundamental principle of representative government in this country is one of equal representation for equal numbers of people, without regard to race, sex, economic status, or place of residence within a State."[40] As Pamela Karlan notes, "[d]espite the Court's individualist rhetoric, the system it overturned was one that systematically biased the overall legislative complexion in favor of identifiable groups—white rural voters."[41] Malapportionment clearly violated the principle of equity, as Gordon Baker recognized when he wrote (following a discussion of Dahl's *Preface to Democratic Theory*), "[a]n imbalance of representative strength . . . means that accessibility to the decision-making process is rendered difficult or impossible for some groups and easier for others."[42]

The pluralist strand of liberal representation is more explicitly affirmed in the Court's minority vote dilution cases. The guiding principle of those cases, indeed, is that the political process should be equally open to the representation of all cohesive communities of interest, whatever the nature of the interest they share.[43] To the extent that electoral institutions are structured so as to diminish systematically the capacity of an identifiable interest to secure political representation, and so to bias the political process arbitrarily in favor of some interests and against others, those institutions are unfair. The propensity of districting schemes to produce such a bias was first recognized by Justice Brennan in a side remark in his opinion for the Court in *Fortson v. Dorsey*, where he suggested that multimember apportionment schemes might unjustifiably "operate to minimize or cancel out the voting strength of racial or political elements of the voting population."[44]

This insight informed the development of a doctrine of minority vote dilution in the cases I have summarized above. Taken as a whole, those cases support the difference-blind proceduralist claim that the deliberate manipulation of the electoral process to prevent identifiable groups from securing legislative representation is inconsistent with the principle of equality. It is particularly important to note here, however, that within the difference-blind proceduralist framework the defining characteristic of the group targeted for discriminatory treatment is irrelevant to the impermissibility of the discrimination. As Ely states, "[t]here is nothing in the reasoning that establishes the relevance of unconstitutional motivation that limits it to cases involving racial discrimination."[45] What makes discrimination objectionable, rather, is that it creates inequalities on the basis of morally arbitrary distinctions. From this standpoint, racial distinctions are especially suspect not because they are more morally objectionable than other arbitrary distinctions, but because they are more frequently the occasion of unjust inequality. Within the pluralist understanding of procedural fairness, it is important to highlight that when Justice Brennan raised the issue of minority vote dilution in *Fortson v. Dorsey*, his concern applied to "racial *or political* elements of the voting population," and did not single out racial minorities for special protection from dilution. Similarly, in his dissent in *Mobile*, Justice Marshall drew a distinction (which the *Bandemer* Court seems implicitly to have relied on) between the "fundamental rights" branch and the "suspect classifications" branch of Equal Protection doctrine, and regarded minority vote dilution as part of the former rather than the latter. This means, he argued, that there is "a substantive constitutional right to participate on an equal basis in the electoral process that cannot be denied or diminished for any reason, *racial or otherwise*, lacking quite substantial justification."[46] And in his concurrence in *Karcher v. Daggett*, Justice Stevens urged that the Court should be concerned with legislative actions that "serve no purpose other than to favor one segment—*whether racial, ethnic, religious, economic, or political*—that may occupy a position of strength at a particular point in time, or to disadvantage a politically weak segment of the community."[47]

This difference-blind understanding of procedural fairness leads naturally to the Court's conclusion in *Bandemer* that deliberate partisan gerrymandering is justiciable and that a group's claim to relief from a biased political process should not hinge on whether it is organized around a racial rather than a partisan identity. The *Bandemer* decision thus follows the difference-blind procedural logic almost perfectly: As institutions whose purpose is to maintain the fairness of the system of political competition, courts should make no substantive judgments on the relative merits of different groups' claims to representation. Rather, groups merit political representation to the extent that they express a unitary and cohesive set of interests that attach to a discrete segment of the population. In other words, groups deserve representation insofar as they are internally cohesive and act as a unit, as demonstrated, for example, by bloc voting. A system of representation is fair if it does not systematically bias the electoral process against such a cohesive group. Within this understanding of fairness, eliminating gerrymandering would appear to be as strong a moral imperative as overturning laws that exclude racial minorities from full political participation. As is clear from the parallel logic of free market liberalism, then, some intervention in the political process is necessary to keep the channels clear for free competition.[48]

In practice, however, the difference-blind pluralist conception of procedural fairness justifies intervention to protect minorities only under quite narrowly defined circumstances. First, as the holding in *Bandemer* makes clear, minorities wishing to establish that there has been an unfair distortion of the political process would have to show that there has been *intentional* discrimination against them. A group's electoral failure does not mean that the electoral process has been *arbitrarily* biased against them. Thus, in *Whitcomb v. Chavis*, in which Black voters challenged multimember districts in Marion County, Indiana, the Court concluded that "[t]he mere fact that one interest group or another concerned with the outcome of Marion County elections has found itself outvoted and without legislative seats of its own provides no basis for invoking constitutional remedies where, as here, there is no indication that this segment of the population is being denied access to the political system."[49] More recently, Justice Thomas pronounced that "[i]f a minority group is unable to control seats, that result may plausibly be attributed to the inescapable fact that, in a majoritarian system, numerical minorities lose elections."[50] To demonstrate the unfairness of unequal or disproportionate electoral outcomes, groups would need to show that they were specifically and systematically disadvantaged, and it seems unlikely that they would be able to do so without evidence of intentional discrimination on the part of those who control the districting process.

Second, groups could not make a justifiable claim for intervention on their behalf without some evidence that electoral institutions have produced a discriminatory effect, that is, that they have suffered an electoral injury. But it is extremely difficult, if not impossible, to define a standard of fairness by which to judge whether a group's influence in the political process has been unfairly diluted. Articulating such a standard necessarily refers to the *outcomes* of the electoral process, as the claim of minority vote dilution turns on the assertion that a group has not enjoyed the degree of electoral success it would have enjoyed in an undistorted electoral process. Specifying that fair "degree of electoral success" in quantitative terms turns out to be a ticklish challenge. If we were to rely exclusively on liberal representation's view of procedural fairness, then the natural impulse to compare actual outcomes against a standard of proportionality might be warranted. As Samuel Issacharoff has noted, "[t]he minority voting rights cases ultimately rested on an *almost intuitive sense that if a minority population is voting cohesively, it should have a more-or-less proportionate share of representation*."[51] But we have seen already that a winner-take-all geographic system of representation makes it very unlikely that parties or other groups will receive legislative representation in proportion to their share of the vote. Thus Justice White's opinion in *Bandemer* explicitly eschewed the standard of proportionality, arguing that "a group's electoral power is not unconstitutionally diminished by the simple fact of an apportionment scheme that makes winning elections more difficult, and a failure of proportional representation alone does not constitute impermissible discrimination under the Equal Protection Clause."[52]

If proportionality cannot provide a workable standard for judging whether electoral systems are unfairly biased against an identifiable group, then what *would* such a standard look like? When *is* the Court justified in intervening to correct intentional distortions of the political market, and what remedies should it impose? The difficulty in answering these questions arises from the pluralist assumption that the play of political interests is multivariate, and the set of procedurally fair outcomes it can yield may well be quite large. On a theoretical level, it is easy to say that unfair outcomes are those that lie clearly and consistently outside the set of outcomes that an undistorted process could produce. On a practical level, however, we must assume that a wide range of outcomes is consistent with a fair process, and that only very extreme cases of marginalization or exclusion constitute evidence of discriminatory effect.[53] Given these restrictive implications of difference-blind proceduralism, it is perhaps not surprising that the *Bandemer* Court did not overturn an obvious case of partisan gerrymandering that resulted in a legislative majority for a party that had won a minority of the popular vote. Rather, the decision required that a successful challenge would have to show that the group had "essentially been shut out of the political process."[54]

Third, even if a minority group can satisfy this narrow standard of procedural unfairness, critics of *Bandemer* have argued convincingly that few groups will be able to make a strong normative case for intervention. Even if it were possible to determine a group's reasonable (or probabilistic) expectation regarding electoral outcomes, there is no normative reason for regarding this expectation as the standard for fair or "nondiscriminatory" electoral results. The principal reason for this flows from liberal representation's assumptions about the nature of political groups, i.e., that their membership is fluid and overlapping. It may be true that an identifiable group—for example, the Republican Party—consistently wins fewer seats than one would predict given their share of the popular vote and the hypothetical results from an iterated series of random districting schemes. Nonetheless, pluralist theory presupposes that membership in political groups changes according to shifting political circumstances. Thus the fact that the Republican Party consistently wins 45 percent of the popular vote but only 20 percent of the legislative seats, even if it does reflect a systematic distortion of the political process by Democratic incumbents, does not necessarily mean that any *individual's* vote has been diluted or that any *individual* has been denied a fair opportunity to participate in the electoral process. This election's Republican voters might include a large number of individuals who voted Democratic in the last election, and vice versa. In pluralist theory, only if individual voters consistently voted as a cohesive bloc with other voters, election after election, would judicial intervention in gerrymandering be defensible. This point has been the centerpiece of Mark Rush's extensive critiques of the Supreme Court's decision in *Bandemer*:

> The concept of . . . the denial of fair representational opportunity make[s] sense . . . only when certain unrealistic assumptions are made about voting behavior and the nature of political groups: first, that the group in question meets some criteria of cohesion and durability from election to election, that is, the group is identifiable; second, that the group in question is durable and cohesive and the group's size and representational entitlement are measurable; and third, that voters are *party* voters. That is, a Democratic vote in one district will be a Democratic vote in another, regardless of the candidates, and party votes in one part of a state are equatable with party votes in other parts.[55]

Finally, the case for intervention to protect minority groups is limited by liberal representation's assumption that politics as a competitive process is a zero-sum game. In some cases, even where it is possible to show that a group's voting strength has been "consistently degraded," it will not be possible to order remedies to protect that group without impinging on another group's prospects for electoral influence. Without a substantive standard for distinguishing stronger from weaker group claims for electoral power through districting, it is simply impossible to adjudicate among competing group claims for recognition. Where the populations of two distinct ethnic minorities overlap geographically, and where drawing a district to protect one makes it impossible to protect the other, what standard should the courts apply in choosing between them? This was the issue in *United Jewish Organizations of Williamsburgh v. Carey*, in which a Hasidic community challenged a districting plan that divided its members between two districts in order to create a majority-Black district.[56] Although a deeply divided Court upheld the plan, several justices objected that it created an arbitrary bias in favor of African American voters—a bias that cannot be justified consistent with the terms of difference-blind proceduralism.[57]

Taken together, these considerations make for a very restrictive reading of procedural fairness. They justify intervention only when these four concerns are met, that is, when (a) there is evidence of intentional discrimination; (b) there is evidence of discriminatory effect that goes considerably beyond nonproportionality; (c) the minority in question is cohesive over time; and (d) intervening to protect one cohesive minority will not injure the political prospects of a different, similarly cohesive minority. If stringently observed, these requirements would place a substantial barrier in the way of minorities seeking relief from vote dilution.

III. From Restrictive to Expansive Readings of Liberal Representation

Even if Rush is right that partisan minorities cannot establish a strong claim for protection against gerrymandering, it is not the case that *no* group can launch such a claim.[58] The history of voting rights jurisprudence reveals that there have been cases of racial gerrymandering so egregious that they violate even this restrictive reading of liberal representation's conception of procedural fairness. There is little difficulty, for example, in justifying the Court's intervention in *Gomillion* on narrow pluralist grounds. In this section I will argue that there is a continuum of circumstances that supports the protection of minority groups from vote dilution, and I will trace the logic of the Court's decisions from the "easy" cases such as *Gomillion*, which violate even the most restrictive reading of difference-blind procedural fairness, to the principles of minority vote dilution doctrine that have informed courts and the Department of Justice from *Gingles* to *Shaw v. Reno*. In accordance with the more expansive view of procedural fairness expressed by those principles, measures have been taken to enhance minority representation without a direct demonstration of discriminatory intent or minority cohesiveness.

The emergence of the "second generation" of voting rights legislation and jurisprudence clearly begins with the logic of such "easy cases" for intervention as *Gomillion*: deliberate discrimination against a discrete and cohesive minority is clearly impermissible and should be overturned. The clarity of such cases became somewhat muddied when states moved from practices that were overtly discriminatory in intent toward practices that were facially neutral but had discriminatory effects, as was characteristic of many of the electoral changes at issue in "second generation" cases. In such cases, the Court[59] and Congress[60] recognized that those in power may create distortions in the political process to disadvantage minorities without allowing their discriminatory purpose to show on the surface of their legislation. The application of the preclearance provisions of the Voting Rights Act to jurisdictions with a history of discrimination, like the "totality of circumstances" analysis prescribed by *White v. Regester*, implicitly recognizes that to root out intentional but covert discrimination one needs to scrutinize closely those actions that have discriminatory effects when they occur against a background history of intentional discrimination. The "totality of circumstances" analysis suggests that where state actors have shown a propensity to discriminate on racial grounds, where White majorities continue to vote against minority-favored candidates (polarized voting), where minorities see their interests as bound together (political cohesiveness), and where there are ongoing patterns of socioeconomic inequality structured around the lines of race, there is strong circumstantial evidence of discriminatory intent even if such intent is not present on the surface of the state's action.

From this conclusion, however, it is not difficult to move one step further down the continuum toward a results-oriented standard of minority representation to recognize that even in the absence of discriminatory intent, electoral processes may embody patterns of systemic or structural discrimination that follow directly from the history of state-sponsored direct discrimination. It might be, for example, that a state's new districting plan was put in place in order to comply with the rule of one person, one vote, but that patterns of past housing discrimination have created large concentrations of minority voters whose voting strength has been diminished by the current districting scheme.[61]

As Samuel Issacharoff has argued, such circumstances are particularly objectionable when they interact with patterns of what the Court has labeled "societal discrimination," that is, patterns of voting in which Whites consistently vote against minority candidates:

> The creation of stable patterns of political exclusion through the combination of racial voting practices and institutional devices . . . has a specific connotation for groups that emerged from formal and complete exclusion from the political process only a generation ago. These electoral process distortions work a kind a de facto disenfranchisement, the results of which bear an unfortunate and uncanny resemblance to the older regime of formal exclusion of historically disadvantaged groups from the political process.[62]

When patterns of systemic discrimination traceable to a history of state-sponsored discrimination combine with patterns of societal discrimination among majority voters to dilute minority voting strength, there is a strong suggestion that the social attitudes which underlay past state-sponsored discrimination continue to interact with state-mandated procedures to reproduce electoral inequalities. Thus even where there is no evidence that state officials have intentionally discriminated against minorities in these circumstances, there are still strong grounds, fully consistent with the proceduralism of liberal representation, to hold the state morally responsible for the discriminatory effects of its electoral system.

On an expansive reading of liberal representation, any systematic bias against a cohesive, historically marginalized group is good reason for political "market correction" in its favor. The group's history of exclusion or marginalization is relevant in such an analysis for two reasons: First, a historical inquiry might provide circumstantial evidence of discriminatory intent, as the reasoning in *Regester* suggested. Second, even in the total absence of discriminatory intent, a history of racial hostility and state-supported discrimination may produce patterns of systemic discrimination that deny minorities genuine equality of opportunity in the political process. These arguments are never explicitly laid out in the legislative history of the Voting Rights Act or its amendments, nor in the Court's reasoning in *Regester*, but they are implicit in a "totality of circumstances" approach which examines a combination of history, contemporary socioeconomic inequality, and contemporary practices that have discriminatory effects.

The difference between the restrictive and expansive interpretations of liberal representation hinges on whether decision makers are willing to recognize the existence of systemic and societal discrimination. The more restrictive readings of liberal representation—in a manner exactly parallel to restrictive readings of affirmative action, and derivative from them—refuse to recognize patterns of systemic or societal discrimination as occasions for intervention in the political process.[63] In the restrictive reading of procedural fairness, the moral responsibility of the state to remedy inequality is limited to cases where inequality is the immediate consequence of intentional discrimination. To go beyond this, conservatives argue, to protect a specific minority's interest in representation (through, for example, the creation of majority-minority districts) is to give it an unjustified advantage in the political process. Because pluralist politics is a zero-sum game, any preference for a specific minority gives it more than its fair share of electoral influence (even though it is not possible to specify exactly what that "fair share" might be) and gives government actions the appearance of arbitrariness. Whereas the expansive reading of procedural fairness delves deeply into the history of discrimination to identify process distortions, the restrictive view has an obdurately short memory.[64]

IV. *Shaw v. Reno* and Its Progeny: Back to Difference-Blind Proceduralism

Beginning with its 1993 decision in *Shaw v. Reno*, the Supreme Court has almost entirely repudiated the expansive understanding of minority voting rights that had developed in the twenty years since *White v. Regester*. As we have seen, the development of that doctrine had gradually come to support enhanced minority representation through the creation of majority-minority districts. The implications of the Voting Rights Act amendments of 1982 for minority representation were only realized in the redistricting following the 1990 census, and it was in the 1992 elections that minorities enjoyed their first substantial increase in legislative representation. In several southern states, race-conscious districting led to the election of the first African American members of Congress since Reconstruction. They had occupied their seats for only a few months, however, before the Court began to reverse the trend of voting rights jurisprudence that made their elections possible.

Shaw v. Reno, decided in 1993, involved Congressional District 12 of North Carolina, now infamous for its unusual, elongated shape. The district had its origins in the 1990 census, which resulted in the apportionment of a twelfth congressional seat to North Carolina. The state redistricted and, since several of its counties are covered jurisdictions, submitted its districting plan to the Department of Justice for preclearance under Section 5 of the Voting Rights Act. North Carolina's population is 78 percent White, 20 percent African American, and 1 percent Native American. The plan it originally submitted for preclearance contained one majority-Black district. The Justice Department refused preclearance, arguing that North Carolina could have created a second majority-Black district in the southeastern part of the state. Instead, the state created a majority-Black district in the north-central region, stretching 160 miles along Interstate 85 and in places no wider than the highway's corridor. Five White voters challenged the district under the Equal Protection Clause of the Fourteenth Amendment, claiming that the district "is so extremely irregular on its face that it rationally can be viewed only as an effort to segregate the races for purposes of voting, without regard for traditional districting principles and without sufficiently compelling justification."[65] They did not challenge the district on grounds that their own votes were diluted, and they could not have done so because even under the challenged plan, the proportion of seats controlled by White voters was still larger than their proportion of the population.

A divided Court held that the plaintiffs did have constitutional grounds, "analytically distinct" from vote dilution, for challenging the district.[66] While acknowledging that race-conscious districting is not unconstitutional per se, the Court decided that districts whose bizarre shape creates the impression that race predominated over all other considerations in the districting process should be subject to the same strict scrutiny that the courts apply to other invidious racial distinctions in law. As Justice O'Connor expressed it in her opinion for the Court,

> we believe that reapportionment is one area in which appearances do matter. A reapportionment plan that includes in one district individuals who belong to the same race, but who are otherwise widely separated by geographical and political boundaries, and who may have little in common with one another but the color of their skin, bears an uncomfortable resemblance to political apartheid. It reinforces the perception that members of the same racial group—regardless of their age, education, economic status, or the community in which they live—think alike, share the same political interests, and will prefer the same candidates at the polls.[67]

Further, the decision argued, blatantly race-conscious districting sends the "pernicious" message to representatives that "their primary obligation is to represent only the members of that group" which was deliberately concentrated in their districts.[68] The Court remanded the case to the district court to determine whether the plan could survive strict scrutiny, that is, whether it was "narrowly tailored" to serve any "compelling governmental interest."[69]

Two years later, in *Miller v. Johnson*, the Court undertook its first review of the lower courts' application of *Shaw v. Reno*.[70] The *Miller* decision went a step beyond *Shaw* in setting up obstacles to race-conscious districting when it held that, even without a showing of noncompactness, any plan in which race was the "predominant factor" was subject to strict scrutiny: "Shape is relevant not because bizarreness is a necessary element of the constitutional wrong or a threshold requirement of proof, but because it may be persuasive circumstantial evidence that race for its own sake, and not other districting principles, was the legislature's dominant and controlling rationale in drawing its district lines."[71] The decision (written by Justice Kennedy) further held that to show the "predominance" of race, plaintiffs must establish that the districting body subordinated "traditional race-neutral districting principles"—including the geographic criteria of compactness and contiguity, as well as the preservation of "communities defined by actual shared interests"—to race (p. 2488). As in *Shaw*, the Court held that states have a compelling interest in eradicating the effects of past discrimination, but "insist[ed] on a strong basis in evidence of the harm being remedied" (p. 2491).

Again, the *Miller* decision leaves room for doubt whether states have a "compelling interest" in compliance with the Voting Rights Act (pp. 2490–91). But the decision makes clear the majority's view that the creation of the third majority-minority district was driven by a Department of Justice policy requiring covered states to "maximize" the number of minority districts in their plans and that such a policy was not warranted by a correct reading of the Act (pp. 2492–93). Rather, the Court held, Section 5 authorizes the Department of Justice only to ensure that no new districting plan would lead to a retrogression of minority voting strength.[72] Although the Court stopped short of holding that the minority vote dilution provisions of Section 2 of the Voting Rights Act violated the Equal Protection Clause of the Fourteenth Amendment, it hinted at such a possibility.

The right claimed by the plaintiffs in *Shaw* was to "a color-blind electoral process," and the Court seems to acknowledge a constitutional right at least to the *appearance* of color blindness.[73] The Court's reassertion of a color-blind standard of procedural fairness pushes to the limit liberal representation's refusal to recognize "morally arbitrary characteristics" as a relevant basis for identifying the groups that should receive recognition in the political process.[74] Just as the Madisonian view recognizes the existence of class conflict but regards its overt recognition as damaging to political stability and the common good, the Court's doctrine of color blindness does not go so far as to deny the empirical reality of racial conflict but does deny that racial differences should receive any official recognition. As with all suppressive conceptions of representation, the restrictive reading of liberal representation contains a split between its political sociology (in which racial group differences are an acknowledged empirical reality) and its normative account of the groups that should be represented.[75]

To legitimate its refusal to recognize differences of political interest that follow the lines of race, the Court has repeatedly employed the stark language of racial separatism to describe race-conscious policies aimed at enhancing minority representation.[76] Thus, in *Shaw*, Justice O'Connor likened race-conscious districting to "apartheid."[77] Justice Thomas adopted the same rhetoric in his separate opinion in *Holder v. Hall*, where he characterized majority-minority districts as "political homelands" that create "nothing short of a system of 'political apartheid.'"[78] Similarly the Court's opponents of race-conscious districting have invoked images of civil strife in the former Yugoslavia by suggesting that race-conscious districting will "balkanize us into competing racial factions."[79] It is self-evident that such language is inappropriate to the circumstances, since the challenged districts were themselves racially *integrated* and were drawn to integrate the races within legislative bodies. But their clear purpose is to support a conception of fair representation in which institutions are blind to racial difference.

The notion that representational fairness consists in the fair competition of *all* political interests, without any special solicitude for the political opportunities of racial minorities, lies on the surface of some of the majority's statements in these decisions. In *Miller*, for example, Justice Kennedy seemed to characterize the districting process itself as a competition among interest groups to secure representation: "It is true that redistricting in most cases will implicate a political calculus in which various interests compete for recognition, but it does not follow from this that individuals of the same race share a single political interest."[80] Similarly, O'Connor's worry in her concurrence in that case—that the decision should not be read as treating "efforts to create majority-minority districts *less* favorably than similar efforts on behalf of other groups"—suggests that the creation of districts around communities of interest should be the outcome of competition among interests, constrained by neutral procedures in which no group was burdened or advantaged relative to other groups. Given that districting plans are almost universally drawn by state legislatures, whose members clearly have an interest in districting outcomes, it is completely unrealistic to regard districting as a neutral procedure in which all groups have an equal opportunity to succeed.[81] But statements such as these help to reveal that the Court's majority is relying on a difference-blind conception of procedural fairness in these decisions.

The restrictiveness of these decisions' difference-blind proceduralism is also readily apparent. In the spirit of *Mobile*,[82] the majority has explicitly stated that in order to justify a "compelling state interest" in remedying the effects of past discrimination, remedial state action must be directed to "specific, 'identified discrimination'" and the state must have a "strong basis in evidence" that remediation is necessary. Following its decisions overturning affirmative action, the Court holds in these cases that a generalized history of discrimination is not sufficient to justify remedial action on behalf of minority voters. In other words, bizarre district lines might be permissible as a remedy for a "smoking gun" of localized discrimination—though the Court has been very unclear as to what could possibly constitute evidence of "identified discrimination"—but not otherwise.[83] In the same spirit, the Court explicitly disavows any state interest in remedying "societal discrimination."[84]

Although the Court has generally (if grudgingly) acknowledged states' legitimate interest in complying with the Voting Rights Act, the majority in these cases has been very careful not to assert that the law itself is justified. To the contrary, by repeatedly flagging the fact that it "assumes without deciding" that Section 2 is constitutional, the Court has bracketed this question (and seems to invite a constitutional challenge to Section 2). Justices Thomas and Scalia explicitly state their view that race-conscious districting as such is presumptively unconstitutional,[85] and Justice Kennedy's opinion in *Miller* suggests that he agrees.[86] In these decisions, then, the Court acknowledges that states have a very narrow interest in complying with a still valid law but no general or positive interest in avoiding minority vote dilution through the creation of majority-minority districts. Moreover, by rejecting the Department of Justice's expansive reading of its Section 5 preclearance authority, and asserting that its authority extends only to ensuring "nonretrogression" in minority voting strength, as it does in *Miller*, the Court closes off one avenue to the prevention of minority vote dilution. By doing so it effectively requires minorities to launch Section 2 lawsuits if they have suffered vote dilution but not an absolute decline in representation, even in states with a recognized history of discrimination against them.

The restrictiveness of these decisions is also evident in the Court's requirement that states "narrowly tailor" their actions to serve their compelling interests in Section 2 compliance. It has offered slim guidance as to what a successful, "narrowly tailored" majority-minority district might look like. However, the clear implication of the decisions is that "the majority's narrow tailoring requirement . . . forc[es] States to remedy perceived § 2 violations only by drawing the district around the area in which the *Gingles* preconditions have been satisfied."[87]

As a final note, it is worth returning to the question of the role of geographic representation in the Court's voting rights arguments. As we saw in the earlier discussion of the difference-blind reading of liberal representation, the persistence of a geographic system of representation functions as a limit on the capacity of American electoral systems to yield proportional outcomes. Consequently it adds to pluralist theory's general difficulty of articulating substantive standards of fairness against which to evaluate claims of process distortion. In the expansive reading of liberal representation, it similarly functions to proscribe proportionality as the substantive standard of fairness in assessing minority vote dilution claims. But there it also functions as a tool for enhancing minority representation where evidence of procedural bias exists and where minority populations are sufficiently concentrated to draw majority-minority districts.[88] In the *Shaw* decisions, however, it functions quite differently: geography comes in only where invoking it can defeat the expansive account of liberal representation. Thus "bizarreness" or noncompactness is invoked against majority-minority districts but not against majority-White districts. Geographic representation appears in its normative guise when the Court affirms the legitimacy of drawing districts to ensure the representation of communities of interest, yet the Court repeatedly claims that racial identity does not define a genuine community of interest. Although the interaction of geographic representation with competing theoretical accounts of fair representation is a tricky matter in all the Court's voting rights jurisprudence, it is only in the recent decisions that the role of geography in the Court's arguments defies principled justification altogether.

V. Summary and Conclusion: Beyond Liberal Representation to Group Representation

Both the restrictive and expansive jurisprudential readings of liberal representation acknowledge that procedural fairness cannot be achieved without some consideration of results, since facially neutral procedures may yield a systematic bias against some groups. In that sense, both modify, to varying degrees, the pure proceduralism of liberal representation in the direction of complex proceduralism, which allows some attention to outcomes.[89] In the face of systematic bias, no matter how energetic a disadvantaged group's political mobilization, it is prevented by the process itself from yielding an equitable return in the form of political representation. Where results are chronically unequal, therefore, there is some reason to suppose that the process itself treats groups unequally. The amended Voting Rights Act recognizes explicitly that the chronic frustration of the electoral goals of minority communities is a likely sign of an unwarranted bias in the process, a part of the "totality of circumstances" that provides a basis for judgments of unfair procedural inequality.

Nonetheless, giving positive definition to the results standard turns out to be a tricky matter. The statute itself makes clear only that the standard is not the proportional presence of minority group members in the legislature. This caveat makes sense within a system that attempts to balance practices of geographic representation against liberal notions of procedural fairness since, as we have seen, such a system is intrinsically unlikely to yield proportional representation for minorities, however large they may be. The restrictive reading of liberal representation begins with this observation and concludes that only more-or-less permanent exclusion constitutes an unfair result. The expansive reading works harder at defining a results standard which, while falling short of a guarantee of proportionality, recognizes that the mere avoidance of total exclusion is no assurance of fairness.

The standard defined in *Gingles* is an admirable effort to articulate an interpretation of procedural fairness that acknowledges the importance of outcomes. As articulated in that case, it does not (as critics charge) simply substitute a substantive conception of equality for a procedural one. Rather, it searches for the specific distortions of the political process that are wrought by the combination of systemic discrimination (revealed in the broader "totality of circumstances" inquiry) and societal discrimination (revealed in patterns of racially polarized voting). It further acknowledges the need to reconcile the requirements of procedural fairness with the reality of geographic districting by prescribing a remedy only in those cases where doing so is consistent with geographic districting. This it does without affirming or denying the *normative* claims of geographic districting; it rather treats it as a legal fact with which states must cope whether or not it is warranted by moral considerations.

Moreover, given the reality of racially polarized voting and the constraints imposed by geographic districting, the creation of majority-minority districts is a perfectly appropriate remedy. Indeed, no other remedy for minority vote dilution is available within a system of single-member geographic districts, a fact that has led many critics to propose the abandonment of that system in favor of alternative electoral systems. Yet the practice of race-conscious districting *appears* morally suspect in a political culture that extols proceduralism, for two reasons. First, it means that states cannot avoid relying on "morally arbitrary characteristics" in crafting their districting plans. Justified though this may be, it creates an appearance of illegitimacy. Second, because of the electoral solidarity of minority voters, creating majority-minority districts virtually guarantees them legislative representation. Indeed, that is its point. But this creates the appearance of procedural unfairness because it consciously distributes benefits to a group defined by "morally arbitrary characteristics" which it does not distribute to other groups. This appears to much of the White public in the same way affirmative action does, as an attempt to remedy past unfairness toward minorities with a present unfairness toward Whites. An inquiry into the facts would reveal that no unfair bias is involved, but it is difficult to undertake that inquiry in a way that is readily accessible to the general public.

This, however, does not describe fully the reasons why the expansive reading of liberal representation has foundered. While one can understand the resistance of the general public to race-conscious districting, elite decision makers such as members of the Supreme Court cannot be so easily excused. Their resistance to the practice is explicable, first and foremost, as a product of their ideological preference for the restrictive reading of liberal representation. This preference is grounded not in racism but in a belief that the overinvolvement of the state in questions of social equality necessarily expands the state and leads it to contract the sphere of individual liberty. In pursuit of their ideal of civil freedom, conservatives take a near-sighted view of inequality. Regarding general patterns of social inequality as inevitable, they treat as remediable only those sources of inequality that are immediately traceable to deliberate discrimination, that is, the intentional and differential treatment of individuals on the basis of "morally arbitrary characteristics."

Recently, a stable majority of Supreme Court justices has been very effective at establishing the restrictive view of procedural fairness in the field of affirmative action.[90] In the sphere of voting rights, however, the Court's efforts have faced more considerable obstacles. Most important is that Congress, in the Voting Rights Act amendments of 1982, consciously and explicitly chose the expansive understanding of procedural fairness over the restrictive view, in direct reaction against the Court's attempt to impose the restrictive reading in *Mobile*. This means that one of the arguments the Court has frequently invoked for refusing to recognize systemic or societal discrimination—limited judicial competence to review the contextual details that support claims of systemic and societal discrimination—is not easily available in the field of voting rights. Section 2 effectively requires an inquiry into these contextual details by invoking the "totality of circumstances" language, but it imposes the requirement on the states, not on the courts. In order for the restrictive view of liberal representation to prevail entirely, therefore, the Court would have to find grounds for declaring Section 2 itself unconstitutional. This it could do only by denying altogether the reasonableness of the concepts of systemic and societal discrimination and the relevance of racially polarized voting to the political equality of minorities. While clearly some of the Justices (notably Scalia and Thomas) do not lack the will to pursue such a course, others (including Justice O'Connor, who has held the swing vote on these questions) continue to be swayed by the history of voting rights abuses to recognize Congress's reasons for wishing to remedy minority vote dilution.

Despite these constraints on the capacity of the Court's conservatives to overturn the expansive reading of liberal representation, they have succeeded in eroding it substantially. Their success not only derives from their having forged a majority on the Court in the area of voting rights. It also arises out of the fact that the *application* of the *Gingles* test has at least appeared to require a results standard without any accompanying respect for the procedural conception of fairness. This appearance emerges from the suggestion that the Department of Justice, in exercising its preclearance authority under Section 5, has required covered jurisdictions to *maximize* the number of majority-minority districts in their districting plans, and it has done so without any accompanying evidence of racially polarized voting, any requirement of geographic compactness, or any "totality of circumstances" inquiry. Further, to the extent it did pursue this policy (or was perceived by states to do so), the

Department created an incentive for covered states to avoid preclearance denials and Section 2 lawsuits by "playing it safe," that is, by creating majority-minority districts wherever they could, at least to the point of proportionality. In fact, all these claims are subject to disagreement.[91] But whatever the truth of the matter, these charges lend force to the popular perception that race-conscious districting violates norms of procedural fairness. If legislative bodies did pursue a policy of drawing majority-minority districts wherever they could, without any inquiry into polarized voting, a history of discrimination against the minority in question, or patterns of systemic bias, that *would* violate even the expansive view of liberal representation.[92] This apparent disregard for procedural fairness in districting practices thus created an opportunity for a legal challenge to race-conscious districting that might not have been available if the Department of Justice and state legislatures had visibly and conscientiously undertaken polarized voting and "totality of circumstances" analyses.

The foregoing helps to explain the *political* failure of an expansive reading of liberal representation. But liberal representation suffers from important *theoretical* failings as well. The theory of liberal representation as a whole simply does not contain the theoretical resources for a complete or fully coherent account of the fair representation of historically marginalized groups. In particular, there are two powerful and persistent intuitions about fair representation for such groups that liberal representation cannot explain or defend. The first is the notion that fair representation for marginalized groups depends on their legislative presence. The second is the sense that liberal representation's model of interest-group pluralism is inappropriate for marginalized groups because they are different in key respects from voluntary associations.

The intuition that historically marginalized groups are not fairly represented if their members are chronically excluded from legislative bodies is present throughout the legislative and judicial treatments of minority voting rights. Indeed, it is expressed even in the text of the Voting Rights Act amendments of 1982, which states, "The extent to which members of a protected class have been elected to office in the State or political subdivision is one circumstance which may be considered" in evaluating whether a group lacks equal political opportunity. This focus on legislative presence comes directly out of the "totality of circumstances" analysis prescribed in *White v. Regester.* On one level, a concern about the chronic absence or underrepresentation of minorities within legislative bodies is consonant with the expansive view of liberal representation, as it is one of the indications of racial bloc voting and societal discrimination of White voters against minority candidates. In the total absence of discriminatory attitudes, one would predict that a roughly proportionate number of candidates would be elected from all demographic groupings.[93] But the concern about representational fairness would not simply disappear if electoral processes were completely rid of all discernible biases and historically marginalized groups continued to be chronically underrepresented in legislative bodies.[94] If such groups fail to receive some measure of legislative presence, advocates of political equality for the historically marginalized are not likely to be satisfied even if there is no clearly identifiable distortion of the political process.

Justice Souter lucidly expresses these concerns in his dissent in *Bush v. Vera*. The post-*Shaw* doctrine of voting rights, he argues, leaves open two alternative futures. The first would preserve a narrow space for majority-minority districting for geographically compact minorities. The second would banish all considerations of race from the districting process, "either by eliminating the practice of districting entirely, or by replacing it with districting on some principle of randomness that would not account for race in any way." If the latter route were chosen, Souter objects, a policy of color blindness would inevitably submerge minority voters. "While dilution as an intentional constitutional violation would be eliminated by a randomly districted system, this theoretical nicety would be overshadowed by the concrete reality that the result of such a decision would almost inevitably be a so-called 'representative' Congress with something like 17 black members."[95]

Justice Souter's objection to reduced legislative presence for African Americans, however, remains on the level of intuition. He offers no substantive account for believing that the aim of political equality for all citizens is frustrated by the chronic underrepresentation of historically marginalized groups in legislatures. Nor, as I discussed in chapter 2, is such an account available within the boundaries of liberal representation, which regards effective representation as a product of a legislator's responsiveness to and advocacy for constituents' interests and is in no way dependent on a representative's *similarity to* constituents.[96] This leaves us with two alternatives as we reflect on persistent intuitions concerning the legislative presence of marginalized groups. The first is to regard them as comparable to intuitions concerning, for example, district shape, and to conclude that despite their persistence they have no rationally defensible foundation. Not all intuitions are reasonable; not all survive critical reflection. The second alternative is to take their persistence as a datum indicating the possibility that they have underlying reasons that have yet to be excavated and to take up the theoretical challenge of giving them rational expression and coherence. Some efforts in this direction have already been made by theorists such as Iris Young and Anne Phillips; my project in the remainder of this book is to take them further and integrate them into a comprehensive theory of fair representation for historically marginalized groups.

A second prevalent intuition about the fair representation of historically marginalized groups is that the standards of procedural fairness that apply to them are different from those that apply to other groups. This intuition receives partial recognition and explanation in the place of societal and systemic discrimination within the expansive view of liberal representation. But the theory of liberal representation remains incomplete insofar as it fails to give a full account of the distinctiveness of historically marginalized groups and also fails to show why that distinctiveness sustains the sense that their fair representation requires *self*-representation. Rather than spelling out the ways in which such groups differ from the voluntary associations that populate pluralist theory, many claims for special solicitude toward them remain on the level of intuition. Even Samuel Issacharoff, one of the most sensitive and perceptive voting rights analysts who has addressed issues of minority representation, writes only that the de facto underrepresentation of minorities bears "an unfortunate and uncanny resemblance to the older regime of formal exclusion of historically disadvantaged groups from the political process."[97] What is the difference between interest groups and marginalized ascriptive groups, and how does it explain liberal representation's incapacity to make moral sense of marginalized group claims to political representation?

A sharp distinction can be drawn between interest-group pluralism's views of membership in *social* groups and membership in *interest* groups. Recall the pluralist notion that while a great diversity of interests exists throughout society, many of these interests, perhaps even most, are not organized as interest groups. Rather, new interest groups form only under circumstances of social or economic change, when a "disturbance in established relationships and expectations . . . produces new patterns of interaction aimed at restricting or eliminating the disturbance."[98] Whether or not individuals are able consciously to generate their own "wants and preferences," the nature of interest-group formation shows that when they join interest groups they are conscious of those preferences and voluntarily choose to act on them. Moreover, membership in any particular interest group is temporary: not only do the activities and structures of groups change over time, but so do the interests and concerns of individuals.[99] Finally, in a pluralist society individuals belong to a large number of different social groups, and each group has a different set of members.

Justice O'Connor suggests the key difference between membership in a historically marginalized group and membership in a political interest group in her separate opinion in *Bandemer*. There she remarks that racial minorities' constitutional claim to judicial protection related not only to the history of discrimination against them but also to the *immutability* of race.[100] The notion of *immutable* characteristics returns us to the observation that the groups for which legislative presence is most often claimed are *ascriptive* groups, i.e., groups in which membership is given by birth, not by choice. As Iris Young expresses this idea, "one *finds oneself* as a member of a group, which one experiences as always already having been."[101] To say that membership in historically marginalized groups is ascriptive does not deny that the meaning of group membership is socially defined. It is not an argument that marginalized ascriptive groups are "natural" and interest groups are "artificial." Further, it does not mean that members of such groups are not able to form associations and define their own identities; to the contrary, members of such groups are constantly redefining the social meaning of their group identities. What it does mean, however, is that belonging to a historically marginalized ascriptive group will carry a social meaning whether or not the individual member so desires. In a racist society, being Black may be something an individual takes pride in or else regards as irrelevant to his or her sense of self; in either case it will guarantee that the individual is treated by Whites as "other."

Thus membership in a marginalized ascriptive group has two aspects. The first is the meaning the individual group member gives to membership, the way in which she views membership as shaping her outlooks and concerns. This aspect of membership may be similar to some forms of voluntary association. The second aspect, however, is the identity that the dominant elements in society impose on group members. The inescapability of the group differences regarded as meaningful by the dominant society makes membership in ascriptive groups profoundly different from membership in interest groups.[102] This difference is all the more profound to the extent that membership in an ascriptive group coincides with restrictions in one's options as a consequence of structural inequality. Because of these differences between interest groups and historically marginalized ascriptive groups, being a member of a marginalized group carries with it distinctive experiences and interests.

In what ways does the difference between interest groups and marginalized groups render the liberal theory of representation incapable of comprehending the normative force of group-based claims to representation? The answer to this is as complex as the idea of representation as mediation. As we saw, the nature of relevant political groupings was a central feature of the complexity of representation. Consequently the differences between the liberal view of groups and the nature of marginalized ascriptive groups is likely to play out into other differences, including differences in the conception of legislator-constituency relations and the dynamics of legislative decision making. In order to articulate a theory of representation that *can* make sense of the normative claims to group representation, it is necessary to explore the ways in which the character of membership in a marginalized group shapes the different aspects of claims to political representation and, at the same time, understandings of political equality.

Another way of understanding the threatened demise of minority representation, then, is that the procedural approach to understanding fair representation has limited resources for defending the claims of historically marginalized groups. Liberal proceduralism, as a moral theory and a legal ideology, is extremely robust—and so is the theory of representation that flows from it. Any attempt to defend a substantive standard of political equality—such as a threshold of legislative representation for marginalized groups—must respect the moral claims of proceduralism. A procedural conception of fairness can take us a considerable distance toward a persuasive defense of minority representation, but it falls short of a complete and reasoned account of our common intuitions about fair representation for these groups. The alternative, which I pursue in the remainder of this work, is to develop an independent, substantive account of the fair representation of historically marginalized groups, one that attempts to make theoretical sense of our intuitions and complements the procedural account. The result will be compatible with a procedural conception of fairness but will also provide a more robust defense of marginalized group representation than any defense derived directly out of liberal proceduralism can provide. If a widespread moral commitment to the fair representation of marginalized groups is to survive the current challenge, it will require a more solid theoretical foundation than the one that arises out of liberal representation alone.

Appendix: The Racial Bias of Recent Supreme Court Decisions on Minority Vote Dilution

Following the 1993 decision in *Shaw v. Reno*[103] the Supreme Court has handed down a series of decisions that continue to erode the practice of race-conscious districting. In chapter 3, I demonstrate that, to the extent there is any coherent doctrine underlying these decisions, it is a restrictive reading of liberal representation's standards of difference-blind proceduralism. But as I discuss in that chapter, the post-*Shaw* decisions are riddled with inconsistencies. For an institution entrusted with the constitutional "voice of public reason,"[104] these inconsistencies are troubling enough. They are even more troubling, however, once one recognizes the extent to which the decisions' inconsistencies produce standards of legislative districting that must function to disadvantage systematically communities of minority voters relative to White voters. The purpose of this appendix is to demonstrate the racial bias of the post-*Shaw* decisions.

On remand, the District Court in *Shaw* had held that North Carolina's twelfth congressional district survived strict scrutiny because it was "narrowly tailored" to meet the state's "compelling interests" in complying with Sections 2 and 5 of the Voting Rights Act. In *Shaw v. Hunt (Shaw II)*[105] the Court overturned this decision, maintaining that (a) following *Miller v. Johnson*,[106] the district was not necessary to meet Section 5's nonretrogression requirement, and the Justice Department had no authority to require more; (b) although some members of the legislature invoked evidence of past discrimination, it could not have supplied the motivation for the districting plan because "these members did not have enough voting power to have caused the creation of the second district on that basis alone";[107] and (c) the strange shape of the district shows that it could not have been "narrowly tailored" to meet Section 2, which (under the *Gingles*[108] test) requires the existence of a geographically compact minority to sustain a claim of minority vote dilution.

The second case was *Bush v. Vera*,[109] involving three majority-minority districts in Texas. The 1990 census entitled Texas to three additional congressional seats. To comply with the Voting Rights Act, the legislature created a districting plan including a new majority-Black district and a new majority-Hispanic district, and transforming a third district from a minority-influence to a majority-Black district. Six voters challenged the plan as an unconstitutional racial gerrymander, and the district court ruled these three districts unconstitutional.

Despite strong evidence that considerations of incumbent protection were the driving force behind the many twists and turns of the challenged districts' boundaries, and despite the fact that several majority-White districts were at least as noncompact as the ones overturned, the Court concluded that race was the "predominant factor" in the districting decisions and that the districts were subject to strict scrutiny. The Court also ignored evidence that ties of community bound the residents of some of the challenged districts to one another, and so justified the district on racially neutral "community of interest" grounds. Turning to the question of whether the districts were "narrowly tailored" to further a "compelling governmental purpose," the *Bush* Court once again "assumed without deciding" that compliance with Section 2 constitutes such an interest. However, it held, the noncompactness of the districts demonstrates that they subordinated "traditional districting principles" to race and so failed the test of *Shaw I*. This holding is of particular interest because the Court acknowledged that the facts met the first prong of the *Gingles* test, that is, the geographic compactness of the minority populations. The particular districts were not sustainable because they were not themselves compact. Justice O'Connor wrote for the plurality, "If, because of the dispersion of the minority population, a reasonably compact majority-minority district cannot be created, § 2 does not require a majority-minority district; if a reasonably compact district can be created, nothing in § 2 requires the race-based creation of a district that is far from compact."[110] Further, the Court held that the districts do not serve the purpose of ameliorating the effects of past discrimination because there was no demonstration of specific and "identified" discrimination that these particular districts could have remedied. Finally, the Court decided that the one district that included a "covered" jurisdiction was not required to meet Section 5's nonretrogression requirement.

As noted above, these cases weave a tangled web of unprincipled and incoherent arguments whose ultimate consequence is substantial racial bias in the adjudication of voting rights controversies. Their starting point—the bizarre shape of District 12, at issue in *Shaw*—is a popular intuition about the desirable aesthetic of an electoral district. As I discussed in chapter 2's account of geographic representation, however, the normative assumptions underlying this intuition are of limited validity in contemporary, mobile societies, in which the most politically relevant communities of interest may not be those that are geographically compact. Thus, as Lani Guinier has stated concisely, "within a geography-is-a-proxy-for-interest paradigm, the relevant inquiry is not the district's shape but its feel: does it reflect an effort to connect voters who have a relevant community of interest?"[111] Yet in these decisions the Court has consistently refused to recognize evidence of ties of community among the minority voters brought together in the challenged districts, whether in the form of racially polarized voting analysis, which was available in *Shaw*, or in the form of common local newspapers or organizational ties, evidence of which was presented in *Bush*. The principal representational value of compactness (the ease of the representative's communication with constituents) was never invoked by the Court in *Shaw I*. Nor could that value be persuasively invoked in that case, since the very complaint that critics raised against North Carolina's twelfth district—that it followed and often was no wider than Interstate 85—presumably would make travel throughout the district that much easier.

Incumbent protection is also among the "race-neutral" districting criteria that the Court now believes should not be outweighed by considerations of race. This holding is particularly puzzling in a political climate in which term limits are increasingly popular. The Court offers no substantive justification of the representational values served by incumbent protection, nor any argument as to why states should subordinate the goal of recognizing minority constituencies to the goal of incumbent protection.[112] Rather than affirming the legitimacy of incumbent protection as an overriding consideration in districting, one might expect the Court to conclude that the principles of neutrality and political fairness are not met "when legislatures permit and even encourage incumbents to use their positions as public servants to protect themselves and their parties rather than the interests of their constituents."[113]

Shaw I's notion of representational harm—that race-conscious districting encourages representatives to ignore the concerns of the racial minority in their districts—is similarly illogical. The Court here appears to be claiming that representatives normally are expected to represent equally the interests of all their constituents. As a working assumption about the American system of representation, this is clearly absurd. To believe it to be true, one would have to assume that the process of competitive elections does not involve a clash of interests, or at least that there are no conflicts of interest within particular districts. Yet the Court has repeatedly acknowledged the adversarial character of electoral competitions when it asserts that the American system of elections does not guarantee electoral success. Moreover, if it were true that representatives are equally responsive to all their constituents, the question of minority vote dilution as a remediable harm could never arise in the first place, since electoral minorities would be equally well represented whether or not the successful candidate was the one for whom they voted. Instead, the idea of an adversarial political process rests on the supposition that people vote for the candidates who will advocate for their interests or views and that voters whose candidates lose have less of such advocacy than those who win. Thus the creation of majority-minority districts in such a system does not increase the likelihood that White representatives will ignore the interests of minority voters. Rather, it increases the likelihood that minority voters will elect candidates who will not ignore their interests.

The argument that race-conscious districting is somehow "stigmatizing" similarly lacks a foundation in rationality wherever there is evidence of racially polarized voting, as there was in all these cases.[114] Indeed, it was precisely the patterns of racially polarized voting in North Carolina that yielded the three-prong test of *Gingles*. Where racial bloc voting exists, the assignment of voters to districts according to race is simply an acknowledgment of the shared political identity that citizens have already expressed in their voting behavior. Recognizing that members of a racial group have interests in common does not, in itself, stigmatize them. As Justice Ginsburg noted in her dissent in *Miller v. Johnson*, "ethnicity itself can tie people together, as volumes of social science literature have documented—even people with divergent economic interests. For this reason, ethnicity is a significant force in political life."[115]

By far the most troubling flaw of these decisions, however, is that they produce a clear and unmistakable racial bias in the adjudication of districting disputes. In her concurrence in *Miller*, Justice O'Connor stated, with apparent concern that her conclusion might not be clear to others, that "[t]he standard would be no different if a legislature had drawn the boundaries to favor some other ethnic group; certainly the standard does not treat efforts to create majority-minority districts *less* favorably than similar efforts on behalf of other groups."[116] Yet O'Connor was perfectly right to worry. Because the post-*Shaw* analysis considers race "predominant" whenever any other districting consideration is overridden by the goal of creating a majority-minority district, such districts are distinctly vulnerable to legal challenge. In the wake of these decisions, districts drawn to protect communities of interest whose members are White are perfectly legitimate, no matter how irregular or elongated they may be; yet those drawn to protect communities of interest whose members are African American or Hispanic are subject to strict scrutiny.[117]

In *Bush*, for example, the Court noted Pildes and Niemi's important study showing that the three challenged districts were among the least regular and compact in the nation.[118] What the Court failed to acknowledge, however, was that Texas also contains three majority-White districts that were on the same list of least-compact districts. Moreover, since these districts did not border on the challenged ones, their noncompactness is in no way a consequence of the legislature's decision to create the majority-minority districts.[119] Whatever the purpose of these noncompact majority-White districts, the racial bias is clear: a noncompact majority-minority district now automatically raises the prospect that it will be subject to strict scrutiny, whereas a noncompact majority-White district is automatically assumed to have been drawn for valid reasons. Rather than acknowledging the evidence presented that the *Bush* districts did in fact recognize actual communities of interest, and rather than articulating the signs by which such communities may be recognized, the Court now simply assumes that it is an insult to racial minorities to assert that they have any interests in common which warrant recognition in the political process. Yet it is not an insult, in the Court's eyes, to recognize the common interests of White suburbanites (as in the early reapportionment cases) or of predominantly White Florida coast dwellers (as in one of the most noncompact districts in the country).[120]

Even if the Court were right that political institutions should not recognize race, by itself, as a type of shared political interest (a highly contentious claim), the fact remains that other communities of interest that happen to overlap with minority racial identity are also inequitably burdened by these decisions. As Pildes and Niemi state in their influential article,

> [R]ace frequently correlates with other socioeconomic factors. In evaluating oddly shaped districts, this correlation will require courts to attempt to untangle legitimate communities of interest from the now-illegitimate one of race. If blacks as blacks cannot be grouped into a "highly irregular" district, but urban residents or the poor can, how will courts distinguish these contexts, and under what mixed-motive standard?[121]

The racial asymmetry of these decisions is also apparent in the Court's treatment of incumbency protection. Because race correlates highly with partisan identity,[122] there may be cases where it is simply impossible to separate partisan considerations from racial ones in the districting process. If a legislature wished to create a district in order to protect a Democratic incumbent in areas where there is a concentrated African American population, its purpose might well be defeated if it had to ignore racial data in defining the district's boundaries. The racial bias of the Court's treatment of incumbency protection, raised by Justice Souter in his dissent in *Bush*, becomes clear as soon as one acknowledges that where there is racial bloc voting a candidate may well have been chosen precisely for racial reasons. The consequence of *Shaw* and *Bush* is that legislatures may rely on any sort of demographic data to draw districts as irregular and noncompact as they wish if the purpose is to protect White incumbents; but if they draw districts with the aid of racial data, or whose boundaries are irregular, in order to protect minority incumbents who need Black votes to win, they trigger strict scrutiny.

The bias becomes clearer if we examine a hypothetical case whose logic follows from the decision in *Bush*: Assume a primary race between two candidates for a seat in which there is no incumbent. One candidate is White, the other is Black. The district is characterized by racially polarized voting and contains a White majority. The White candidate therefore wins for reasons having to do with race (the majority of White voters will not vote for a Black candidate). In the next round of redistricting, protecting that incumbent by drawing a noncompact district is perfectly permissible. It is not subject to strict scrutiny and is perfectly constitutional. Yet if one reverses the race of the voters and candidates, but otherwise maintains all the facts as they are, the district is both subject to strict scrutiny and constitutionally impermissible. Thus the same set of facts will now be regarded by the Court as impermissible racial gerrymandering if the district's majority is Black, but as permissible partisan gerrymandering (or incumbent protection) if the district's majority is White. As Justice Souter notes, the *Bush* decision yields an "exceedingly odd result, when the whole point of creating yesterday's majority-minority district was to remedy prior dilution, thus permitting the election of the minority incumbent who (the Court now seems to declare) cannot be protected as any other incumbent could be."[123]

The correlation of partisan and racial identity has enabled the Court to treat the same districting practices as partisan in some circumstances and racial in others, depending on which is more conducive to overturning majority-minority districts. Thus in *Shaw* the Court ignored the fact that the legislature did not draw a third, compact majority-minority district in the southeastern part of the state, as the Department of Justice had recommended, because doing so would have threatened the seat of an incumbent.[124] The twelfth district would not have its final shape or location were it not for these partisan considerations, but the Court chose to consider only the fact of its racial composition as relevant. Similarly in *Bush*, although the Court recognized that incumbency protection was a factor contributing to the shape of the challenged district, it concluded that the use of detailed racial data in determining the twists and turns of the districts' boundaries was evidence of the "predominance" of race. While it was true that the legislature employed racial data to draw these districts, however, many of the twists and turns of the boundaries are explicable only in partisan terms, since they incorporated *White* neighborhoods that tend to vote Democratic. As Justice Stevens notes in his dissent, some of the districts' departures from the smooth and compact boundaries preferred by the Court functioned to *diminish* the size of the minority group's majority in the district.[125] This selective definition of "partisan factors" and "racial factors" has led to a "shell game of race or politics,"[126] a game of shifting categories that minority voters seem inevitably to lose.[127]

4

Voice: Woman Suffrage and the Representation of "Woman's Point of View"

IN THE FIRST three chapters we have seen that representation comprehends a complex set of relationships and processes, which may be differently conceived. Further, we have seen that when we articulate a scheme of representation, a great deal follows from the way we characterize the constituencies or groups that ought to receive representation. The prevailing understanding of fair representation in American political culture identifies groups that are relevant for representation in a manner which excludes the possibility that marginalized ascriptive groups can be regarded as having a legitimate claim to political recognition. But chapter 1's exploration of different theories of representation makes clear that there are alternatives to liberal representation's characterization of politically relevant groups as voluntary constituencies. Given the persistence of marginalized groups' claims to political recognition, and of the impulse to recognize those claims through practices such as race-conscious districting, it seems clear that we have more to learn about fair representation than the prevailing view can teach us.

But all this does not explain what difference it makes if we define politically relevant social groups differently. What happens if we take as our starting point the notion that marginalized groups' persistent dissatisfaction with the prevailing scheme of representation *does* indicate their political relevance? How would fair representation look different if we began with the fact that these groups constitute an undeniable component of the American political scene?

Membership in a marginalized ascriptive group is clearly different from membership in an interest group: it is involuntary, immutable, and dichotomous, whereas membership in an interest group is voluntary, shifting, and a matter of degree. Given the extent to which the moral defense of liberal representation rests on its characterization of voluntary associations as the only politically relevant groups, this stark contrast strongly suggests that fair representation would look different if viewed from the perspective of members of marginalized ascriptive groups. But an alternative conception of fair representation does not follow directly from the different characterization of groups; it needs exploring. In particular, if we wish to make sense of group-based claims to fair representation, we must explore the implications of this different characterization of group membership for the various aspects of representation as mediation. How might the demands of political equality play out differently in the complex relationships and processes of representation if we begin with a different political sociology, a different characterization of politically relevant groups?

The answer to this question is not self-evident; to find it, we must employ some method of inquiry. From the outset it seems clear that the inquiry must be empirical and interpretive rather than merely analytic. As we saw in chapter 2, it was precisely the formalism of equal opportunity doctrine which obscured that doctrine's capacity to justify inequalities between socially privileged and marginalized groups. We saw that only by attending directly to the experience of marginalized groups can we perceive how practices that are "fair" under prevailing definitions of fairness nonetheless function to reproduce the marginalization of certain groups. My method in this chapter and the next builds on this insight by looking to marginalized groups' own expressions of their aspirations for political equality in order to understand how their understandings of equality (and so of political fairness) might differ from the understandings that permeate liberal representation. In other words, I have looked to marginalized groups' own arguments for political equality as a source of insight into the ways in which prevailing understandings of equality might function to disadvantage them in politics.

In this chapter I turn to American arguments for woman suffrage in the late nineteenth and early twentieth centuries in the hope that the meaning of political equality to those who were denied it so completely might shed light on the meaning of political equality today, when its existence or nonexistence is more contestable and ambiguous. The different claims for political inclusion are brought into sharper relief by the stark exclusion of women from politics— and, as I examine in the next chapter, of Blacks' marginalization even after they won the franchise. Certainly elements of these arguments differ from those of contemporary debates over political equality because of the radically different times we live in. Yet, as it happens, the contours of suffragist understandings of political equality have shifted very little. In contemporary arguments for women's equality in particular and for the recognition of historically oppressed groups in general, the predominant themes are strikingly similar to the ones sounded a century ago. This is particularly true for suffragists' diverse understandings of women's identity as a political group and, consequently, for the relationship between group identity, political equality, and fair representation. As the discussion in the latter part of the chapter makes clear, contemporary claims to the self-representation of women rest on the same normative foundations as those of suffragists. These continuities show that arguments for women's legislative presence are not a fleeting phenomenon of our age but have long been present in American political culture and are not likely to disappear.

I should point out that my project here is to explore the understandings of political equality implicit in arguments for woman suffrage; I do not claim to survey suffragists' understandings of fair representation per se, mainly because the various arguments for the vote were not always developed into clear conceptions of what women's equal representation would require. Indeed, some suffragists (but certainly not all) simply did not look beyond the vote. For them, the franchise was a *symbolic* affirmation of their equal standing as members of the political community, and that was all they required.[1] As we shall see, however, suffragists were not entirely silent on the question of representation, and their ponderings help to illuminate different ways of understanding the connections between group identity, political equality, and fair representation.

As a further caveat, I should clarify that I am not making any empirical claims about the relative preponderance of different themes of political equality in suffragist arguments. I think such a study would be valuable, but it extends beyond the scope of this project, whose purpose is to provide a preliminary interpretation of the substance of these arguments and their implications for our understandings of what fair representation requires.

In looking at the woman suffrage movement, I have tried to distill the many different arguments for women's political rights into a few prominent ways of conceiving "women" as a political group or class. How did women conceive their group identity, and what did they think was its political relevance? The suffragists, who generally were not intellectuals concerned with the internal coherence of their arguments, tended to mix divergent and even contradictory grounds in their arguments for the vote. Nonetheless, one can discern several distinct ways of conceiving women's political identity and role within the arguments for woman suffrage. First, a broad distinction may be drawn between claims for women as equal individuals and claims grounded in a view of women as a separate social group. Within the group-based claims, we may further distinguish several conceptions of women's identity as a social and political group. Interestingly, each of these group-based views asserts the importance of including what they all refer to as "woman's point of view" in politics. Each, however, understands the content of the point of view differently. Over all, then, I have discerned four different understandings of women's political identity in arguments for woman suffrage: (1) the individualistic, natural rights argument: women are equally human and so have standing to claim equal civil and political rights; (2) the view that women, as such, are naturally virtuous and morally superior to men; (3) the perception that women perform a distinctive social or functional role that has increasing relevance to politics; and (4) the belief that women's political identity arises out of their having been excluded from full participation in society and politics, with the result that existing laws and institutions are biased against women in ways that can only be undone through introducing women's distinctive experience into the political process. For each of these arguments, I have attempted to relate the view of women's identity as a group to a view of the fair political representation of women. How does the understanding of fair representation shift when women's group identity is differently conceived? How, if at all, do the resulting conceptions of fair representation differ from liberal representation?

The fourth argument for woman suffrage—that women have a distinctive voice that comes of their experience of marginalization—leads to a claim for women's *self*-representation in legislative bodies. It is not enough that women communicate their perspectives to men; a full respect for women's agency, and a full protection of their interests, requires that they act on their own behalf. Only through their legislative presence can women be sure that the "woman's point of view" on each policy issue is formulated and expressed. This argument enables us to fill in the first aspect of representation as mediation, the dynamics of legislative decision making, within a group-based theory of fair representation. For women's distinctive perspective to have any effect in shaping legislative outcomes, women's representatives must have the opportunity to express their views and be listened to receptively. Thus the process must be deliberative, rather than strategic; oriented toward reaching mutual understanding and agreement, rather than focused on a competition among interests. In the final section of the chapter I discuss the relationship between the defense of group representation and models of deliberative democracy, and the prospects for uniting them within a system of representative institutions.

I. Women's Claim to Individual Equality

In a clear and self-conscious echo of the natural rights language of the Declaration of Independence, the members of the first Women's Rights Convention in 1848 at Seneca Falls, New York, issued a Declaration of Sentiments:

> We hold these truths to be self-evident: that all men and women are created equal; that they are endowed by their Creator with certain inalienable rights; that among these are life, liberty, and the pursuit of happiness . . .
>
> The history of mankind is a history of repeated injuries and usurpations on the part of man toward woman, having in direct object the establishment of an absolute tyranny over her.[2]

Just as nature offers no ground for the authority of one class of men over another, the suffragists argued, it offers no excuse for the dominion of men over women. Women are fully equal to men in all the respects relevant to law and politics; there is no rational basis for denying women an equal right to self-government or for excluding them from full participation in politics.

"What necessary qualification fits men for the exercise of this sacred right which is not likewise possessed by women?" They are not less intelligent, as the statistics of educational institutions testified. Women are not less law-abiding, as is clear from the rolls of "churches, police courts and penitentiaries." Nor, despite the fact that they are barred from military service, are women any less patriotic than men: they fulfill their patriotic duty through philanthropic activities and reform movements rather than on the battlefield.[3]

In fact, suffragists argued, all the considerations that justified the American colonists' resistance to the Crown similarly supported women's claim to participate in the processes of self-government. What American could argue with the claim that there should be "no taxation without representation"?

> It is not enough for us that by your laws we are permitted to live and breathe, to claim the necessaries of life from our legal protectors—to pay the penalty of our crimes; we demand the full recognition of all our rights as citizens . . . We are persons; native, free-born citizens; property-holders, tax-payers; yet are we denied the exercise of our right to the elective franchise. We support ourselves, and, in part, your schools, colleges, churches, your poor-houses, jails, prisons, the army, the navy, the whole machinery of government, and yet we have no voice in your councils.[4]

Women's interest in an equal right to control their fate was just as profound as men's, and the denial of the franchise to women had resulted in legislation inflicting "injuries and usurpations" on women that were no less egregious than the "long train of abuses" that justified the Revolution. Following the Declaration of Independence in good form, the Declaration of Sentiments enumerates these injuries, which include the deprivation of the franchise and hence of political representation; discriminatory divorce, child custody, and property laws; exclusion from traditionally male occupations and professions; and unequal educational opportunities for women.[5]

Perhaps the most important benefit of republican government limited by a respect for individual rights is the sphere of freedom it preserves for individuals to lead a moral and worthwhile life according to their own lights. Following Ralph Waldo Emerson and John Stuart Mill more than Jefferson, some suffragist arguments for full political equality focused not on rights but on women's equal need—and responsibility—for a thorough-going self-development. This strand of suffragist individualism is epitomized by Elizabeth Cady Stanton's famous speech, "The Solitude of Self." From Emerson, Stanton took the notion of the radical independence of each individual, the exclusive responsibility for the fate of one's own soul, and hence the fundamental importance of the freedom to develop one's skills and judgment.

> The strongest reason for giving woman all the opportunities for higher education, for the full development of her faculties, her forces of mind and body; for giving her the most enlarged freedom of thought and action; a complete emancipation from all

forms of bondage, of custom, dependence, superstition; from all the crippling influences of fear—is the solitude and personal responsibility of her own individual life.[6]

From Mill, Stanton adopted the idea that the development of natural talents and capacities was essential not only for the individual's own happiness but also for the greater well-being of society as a whole. "We ask for the complete development of every individual, first, for his [sic] own benefit and happiness . . . [and second,] for the general good."[7] Together, these ideas lead to the conclusion that women have a claim not only to equal access to occupations and education but also to equal political rights, which are essential both as a means of expressing one's independent judgment and, when exercised, as one cause of self-development.[8] As one women's rights advocate put it, "The growing temper of the age is to 'let everybody into the game,' and this is not only good for the game but also for the players."[9]

Within this understanding of women's claims, the standard of political equality at which women should aim is that of a gender-blind Constitution and gender-blind laws. "Our demand is suffrage for women on the same terms as for men."[10] Since the natural basis of individual rights was the same for women as for men, there was no justification for any distinction between the sexes in the Constitution or in the law. "[M]ind recognizes no sex," Ernestine Rose argued against the language of the Fourteenth Amendment, and so "the term 'male,' as applied to human beings—to citizens—ought to be expunged from the constitution and laws as a last remnant of barbarism."[11] The goal of the women's rights movement was "to bury the black man and the woman in the citizen."[12]

In a manner strikingly similar to certain contemporary critiques of preferential legal treatment for women, some suffragists objected even to those laws that purported to protect women. To the common argument that male representatives already looked after women's legislative interests, Stanton retorted:

> [I]f, gentlemen, you take the ground that the sexes are alike, and, therefore, you are our faithful representatives—then why all these special laws for woman? Would not one code answer for all of like needs and wants? Christ's golden rule is better than all the special legislation that the ingenuity of man can devise . . . We ask no better laws than those you have made for yourselves.[13]

In fact, suffragists argued, the laws that men passed in the name of women's protection did not answer to any standard of women's well-being. Paternalistic arguments often turned on the view that women were far too delicate, and their interests far too sublime, for them to bother with the ugly business of politics. Again, Stanton expressed clearly suffragists' objection that the laws passed by existing legislatures clearly did not "shield [woman] by your protecting care from the rough winds of life." Rather, "[y]our laws degrade, rather than exalt women; your customs cripple, rather than free."[14] Moreover, however men tried to benefit women through political means, their efforts were illegitimate so long as they were undertaken without women's freely given consent. As Carrie Chapman Catt expressed it, "Male voters have never been named by any constitution or statute as the representatives of women; we therefore decline to accept them in that capacity."[15]

The predominance in suffragist arguments of these quintessentially liberal themes—the belief that individual equality and autonomy is the birthright of all human beings as such—suggests, correctly in my view, an easy harmony between suffragist individualism and the conception of fairness embedded in the liberal view of representation. Accordingly, women's status as a political group was viewed by many suffragists as provisional, something necessary for gaining the franchise for women but not likely to continue once these narrow political aims were won. Although, as Stanton argued, "[i]t is folly to say that women are not a class," this was only because it was *as* a class that women were excluded from full citizenship and equal membership in society.[16] As for interest groups within pluralist theory, women's solidarity is not an expression of an underlying social truth but is merely a strategic necessity if women's legal and political inequality is to be overcome.

Once the vote was won, women could be expected to vote as individuals, not as a bloc. Indeed, women should be encouraged to develop their capacity for independent political judgment, which is essential to a healthy democracy. Natural rights suffragists agreed with the notion, integral to the Jeffersonian tradition of American republicanism, that the moral, political, and economic independence of individual citizens was the bulwark of popular government. Similarly they shared the characteristic American antipathy to political classes of any sort, as is expressed clearly in an article about women's voting patterns in states where they had already received the franchise:

> No one wishes to see a solid labor vote, or a solid Catholic vote, or a solid native-American vote. When any sign of such massing appears, it is deprecated as the raising of a class standard, and so as a menace to democracy. . . . Women did not receive the vote because they were expected to use it differently from men. The use they might make of it was a subsidiary question. They received the vote because men came to feel that they were entitled to it, that for a democracy to refuse the franchise to any considerable body of its members who demanded it was undemocratic.[17]

The only interest women share is in eradicating gender-based discriminations in law and in society generally. Once these discriminations are overturned, women's political interests will be determined by other causes—the same ones that determine men's interests. For some suffragists, these causes sometimes did coincide with social class. Thus, as a Socialist, Jessie Ashley argued that the working class "subway girls" should join the "handsome ladies" who organized the suffrage parades: although "[o]nly the women of the working class are really oppressed, . . . it is not only the working class woman to whom injustice is done." But when it comes time to exercise the ballot they have won together, Ashley argued, women of different classes inevitably will vote differently.[18]

Individualist arguments for woman suffrage also seem logically connected to certain political strategies aimed at achieving political recognition and, ultimately, representation. First and foremost, the individualist argument suggests that the principles on which the vote was claimed had to be the central weapons in the suffragists' arsenal. These principles, supposedly self-evident, should themselves be sufficient basis for granting the vote to women. Indeed, although many other arguments were used to persuade power holders to give the vote to women—that a majority of women wanted it or, as I discuss below, that women's virtue would improve politics—some suffragists felt they should resist the temptation to resort to them, as they were not the real ground for woman suffrage and would distract from the real principles at stake. Anna Howard Shaw made the point quite forcefully:

Imagine saying to a man of 21, before allowing him to register for the first time:

> You must prove satisfactorily to a majority of your fellow citizens that a majority of the men who are 21, or will become 21, want the ballot; that all the men already enfranchised vote at every election and vote intelligently on all questions; that you, yourself, will use your ballot for useful reforms only, and that you, as well as other men to be enfranchised in the future, can not accomplish the same results without the vote; finally, that you and all future voters will not neglect either your business or your families by taking part in politics . . .

It seems to me very unfortunate that we suffragists should ever permit ourselves thus to over-qualify for the vote . . . We should say: The reason men are enfranchised is that, as citizens, they have a stake in the government. The reason women should be enfranchised is because, as citizens, they have a stake in the government. That is all there is to this question of woman suffrage.[19]

In addition to exercising the power of principled persuasion, suffragist strategies for gaining the franchise bore a strong similarity to the elemental forms of interest-group politics. If, as discussed in chapter 2, the normative force of interest groups' claims to political recognition arises from the combination of their numbers and the intensity of their preferences, then individualist suffragists were an interest group par excellence. The intensity of women's desire for the vote is reflected in the variety of moral arguments they articulated and the persistence with which they presented them. But one of the most effective of suffragist strategies for influencing legislatures had everything to do with mobilizing large numbers of voting and nonvoting citizens to support their cause. The nineteenth-century forerunner of interest-group strategies such as postcard mail-in campaigns was the petition, which suffragists, borrowing from the antislavery movement, tirelessly circulated. It was Susan B.

Anthony who raised the use of petitions to a political art by collecting 400,000 signatures on the first national petition for women's political rights.[20] Admittedly the dynamics of such activities diverged from the interest-group model because of the anomaly that women were a voteless pressure group; the power in their numbers was undoubtedly mitigated by this fact. Indeed, some legislators were unimpressed by the ability of women's rights advocates to muster large numbers of unenfranchised women behind their cause. A New York state legislator undiplomatically informed representatives of the Women's Trade Union League that "the 35,000 voteless women whom they represented naturally could not carry the same weight as thirty-five voting men."[21] In general, however, legislators must have been persuaded that an important social force was represented by the number of signatures on petitions, as it was an extremely effective strategy from the early stages of the women's rights movement, used initially to eliminate discrimination against women in civil law and later to gain the vote.

Those suffragists who addressed the issue were divided on the question of what would guarantee the fair political representation of women once they had the vote. As suggested above, implicit in the idea that women were not a permanent political class is the assumption that women will exercise the vote so as to put people in office who will preserve their diverse interests, and that those interests will not likely be defined along the lines of gender. Although some suffragists, discussed in greater detail below,[22] did argue that women themselves must be elected to office if women's interests were to be adequately represented, most suffragist leaders were silent on the subject or advocated the continuation of the movement's existing strategies for influencing male representatives. This stance was perfectly consistent with the premises of liberal representation, which would tend to regard the gender of elected officials as irrelevant to their ability to advance group interests. Rather, if women were an interest group, what mattered most for them was that elected representatives were aware that they controlled half the votes. Above all, women should persist in their lobbying and educational efforts to press elected officials of *either* sex to pursue policies beneficial to women.

II. "Woman's Point of View": The Distinctive Virtue of Womanhood

The idea that women's participation in politics should ultimately be motivated by concerns unrelated to gender was not shared by all suffragists throughout the movement, just as it is not shared by all contemporary feminists.[23] Indeed, the arguments for woman suffrage advanced by some suffragists were incompatible with the notion that women might vote or lead in ways that had nothing to do with the fact that they were women.[24] Although such arguments focus on different substantive reasons why women, *as* women, should participate in political life, they share a number of elements in common. In particular, they all emphasize that women's natural characteristics or distinctive skills give them something special to contribute to the public good, something that men are not capable of offering and that will improve the general well-being not only of women but of society as a whole.

A particularly common justification for woman suffrage was that women constituted a distinct moral force in society. The arguments rested on the claim that women had higher moral standards than men. Woman's greater virtue was said to stem in part from her natural role as mother, a role that required a nurturing capacity and consequently a gentler attitude toward humanity in general than was to be found among men. Alternatively, women's virtue seems to have been conceived in contrast to men's marked lack thereof, particularly in the area of sexual mores: whereas women were naturally faithful, men's nature had been corrupted, and it was women who bore the brunt of men's vice. Moreover, women were thought not to be susceptible to the many different temptations of vice. Finally, women were characterized as having a "natural intuition" for which men's rationality was a poor substitute when it came to moral matters.

Although these arguments were common throughout the women's rights movement of the nineteenth century, they had the greatest influence in the aftermath of Reconstruction. Not only did such themes resonate with those of the temperance movement, which intensified in the last two decades of the nineteenth century,[25] but they also provided a clear counterpoint to individualistic natural rights in the wake of the Reconstruction amendments to the Constitution. Suffragists were admonished during Reconstruction to acquiesce in the enfranchisement of the newly emancipated slaves without pressing any further constitutional demands on the country at a time when it was still reeling from the Civil War: this was "the Negro's hour," and women would have to wait. Hopes that woman suffrage could be defended from within the four corners of the Constitution were dashed by the introduction of the qualification *male* before the word *citizen* in the Fourteenth Amendment. Ellen Carol DuBois argues convincingly that having failed to win the franchise on grounds of *universal* rights, suffragists turned to arguments that asserted the equality of the *sexes* rather than reasserting the equality of individuals.[26] Despite the political appeal of these arguments and their resonance with popular views of women, ultimately they had a conservatizing effect on the suffrage movement.

The political uses of the virtue argument were of two general types. First, some women (and men) genuinely believed that women constituted a distinctive moral force in society because of their natural virtue. One way of understanding this belief is as an appropriation of a previously existing stereotype of women that was commonly used as a ground for their disempowerment. By actively affirming the stereotype one can turn it into an asset or point of honor, much as participants in the civil rights movement of the 1960s exorcised the negative connotations of the color black by proclaiming "Black is beautiful" and the gay rights movement adopted the pink triangle as a symbol of solidarity and pride. Rather than denying social difference or its significance for politics, it might be argued, women reasserted conventional gender distinctions in a positive cast as part of their claim to group recognition.

Second, some suffragists manipulated these arguments in a more direct fashion, deliberately catering to their audiences' prejudices in order to procure their own goals. If arguments for the vote are cast in terms of conventional distinctions between men and women, particularly when women are characterized by the passive virtues, political claims are likely to be received more sympathetically on the emotional level and viewed as less threatening on the rational level. Although it is difficult to locate evidence that demonstrates when stereotypes are being used in this way, the logic of it is apparent.[27]

In any event, arguments regarding the distinctive virtue of women often played out in both directions when it came to the question of suffrage: whereas some saw virtue as a justification for the role of women in the public sphere, others regarded virtue as a confirmation that women's place was in the domestic sphere but that they simply needed greater protection within that sphere. For the former, virtue provided a number of grounds for suffrage. Some suggested that women's suffering at the hands of immoral men was the female equivalent of military service and that women had paid for the right to vote in the currency of suffering. Others argued that the corruption that infected the American political system at the end of the century was a product of women's exclusion from politics. As one advocate of woman's suffrage explained the moral benefits of the vote for women,

> I am not one of those who think that the millennium will come soon after women get the vote, but I believe that women will take an unusual interest in the effort to clean up vicious conditions, because all down the ages women have paid the price of vice and crime.
>
> I do not believe that at heart a man is any worse than a woman, but all through the centuries he has been taught that he may do some things which a woman may not . . . *Public morals are corrupted because woman's point of view has no representation.*[28]

Because of their distinctive virtues, women would add a dimension sorely lacking in the presently corrupt public sphere. In particular, suffragists argued, women's virtue was strong enough to overcome the evils of liquor (and the power of the liquor interests), of the local political machines, of gambling, and of the sale of their "little sisters" into "white slavery." Jack London brings a number of these themes together in a style which, while flamboyant, is typical of the arguments of this type:

> I voted that women might vote because I knew that they, the wives and mothers of the race, would vote John Barleycorn out of existence and back into the historical limbo of our vanished customs of savagery. The women are the true conservators of the race. Men are the wastrels, the adventure lovers and gamblers, and in the end it is by their women that they are saved. The women know. They have paid an incalculable price of sweat and tears for man's use of alcohol. Ever zealous for the race, they will legislate for babes of boys yet to be born.[29]

By what process, on the virtue argument, would "woman's point of view" achieve representation in politics? First, women would use the ballot to elect morally upright men to office. In addition, women would continue to use their powers of gentle persuasion to induce legislators toward social and political reform. Suffragists of this type were the "moral prodders," who, in contrast to equal rights advocates, "felt that women might most effectively influence both legislators and voting public by taking humane, informed, and principled stands on issues, holding themselves aloof from the mundane trading of favors and compromise of principles required in partisan work."[30] Although a few argued that the contributions of womanly virtue to public affairs would be made manifest in their actual administration of public functions (particularly those relating to social reform), many suggested that for women themselves to hold public office would conflict with their peculiar virtues. Alice Stone Blackwell's comments that voting was "the quietest, easiest, most dignified and least conspicuous way of influencing public affairs" and that women's vote would "result in the election of better men to office" suggest that woman's virtuous and gentle nature does not permit her vigorous assertions into public affairs.[31]

Like Mill's hopes that plural voting or proportional representation would increase the influence of the "intelligent few" on public policy making,[32] the virtue argument for woman suffrage is not, strictly speaking, an argument for the recognition of specific group interests. Rather, in both cases, the political participation of the group in question is meant to have a salutary effect on the thoughtfulness and moral integrity of public deliberation. The influence of womanly virtue on politics constitutes "representation" only in the broadest sense of representation as "the making present *in some sense* of something which is nevertheless *not* present literally or in fact."[33] Neither the "intelligent few" nor virtuous women can make the claim that their representation is a matter of *fairness*; at most, it is a matter of prudence or practical advantage. In other words, although virtuous women or intelligent persons can argue that public decision makers would do well to heed their judgment, so long as they are not denied equal rights of citizenship they cannot claim that they are being treated *unfairly*, that the system of political representation fails to treat them as equal citizens. To the contrary, far from claiming an *equal* voice for women, the virtue-based argument, like Mill's argument for the "intelligent few," asserts that women should have a more powerful political influence than is given to the forces of vice. In short, although the virtue-based arguments may relate to an alternative theory of representation, such a theory's preoccupations would lie with governmental integrity and effectiveness more than with fairness per se.

III. The Functional Advantages of "Woman's Point of View"

Like the temperance movement, the rise of Progressivism at the turn of the century also had its effect on suffragist rhetoric. The themes of Progressive suffragists were similar in many ways to those of the virtue-based arguments for women's enfranchisement, insofar as they ascribed to women a distinctive interest in and talent for issues of social policy whose fulfillment would improve society as a whole. The differences, however, are at least as powerful as the similarities: whereas the virtue-based arguments emphasized women's natural attributes, the Progressive arguments stressed the increasing importance in urban politics of the social functions historically performed by women.

What I will call the "functionalist" argument for woman suffrage was most clearly and articulately expressed by social reformer Jane Addams, who presented a fairly sophisticated social theory about the appropriate role for women in politics. In her view, women's social functions are not necessarily determined by nature but have been strongly defined by custom. Women have historically held the immediate responsibility for providing most of the basic human needs: the bearing, rearing, and education of children; the production and preparation of food; the fabrication and care of clothing; the provision of primary health care; and so on. Traditionally women fulfilled these needs in the private sphere—indeed, within the household. But the modernization of social life, through both the rise of industry and urbanization, also occasioned a transformation of women's social role. Many of the tasks women formerly performed in their homes were now accomplished in large-scale manufacturing. In the process, many women themselves became wage earners in order to support their families.

At the same time, social and economic changes brought a concentration of the population in urban centers, a development that in itself created a great number of social problems and with them a set of new governmental responsibilities. Not coincidentally, many of these issues related to the provision of those basic human needs that were traditionally met by women in their private homes: child welfare and education, public health, food safety, and so on.

Together, social changes pointed toward women's increasing political role for a number of different reasons. First, economic changes had produced a new class of women—wage earners—whose interests clearly were not represented in political institutions. As one pro-suffrage commentator argued, even if one believed that male heads of families had no interests distinct from those of their female family members in farm or middle-class settings, the exclusion of women from most unions made clear that working women's interests were not represented by men.[34]

Second, Addams and others argued, social changes meant that women in general had a special interest in making sure these new challenges of social policy (frequently referred to as "civic housekeeping") were met. Because of women's experience in these areas they were particularly well equipped to assist in the formation of effective social policies:

> City housekeeping has failed partly because women, the traditional housekeepers, have not been consulted as to its multiform activities. The men have been carelessly indifferent to much of this civic housekeeping, as they have always been indifferent to the details of the household . . . The very multifariousness and complexity of a city government demand the help of minds accustomed to detail and a variety of work, to a sense of obligation for the health and welfare of young children and to a responsibility for the cleanliness and comfort of other people.[35]

Third, Addams perceived the social changes that brought women into the political sphere as parallel to those social and economic changes that had produced earlier extensions of the franchise. "[T]he phenomenal entrance of woman into governmental responsibilities . . . is co-incident with the consideration by governmental bodies of the basic human interests with which women have traditionally been concerned, quite as the membership of the middle class and that of the working class each in turn follow its own interests and became a part of representative government."[36] In other words, the politicization of the roles traditionally performed by women meant that women themselves had been transformed into political actors.

What is the nature of women's group identity on this functionalist view? First, women are not necessarily perceived as permanently or naturally different from men. Instead, socialized differences, which for most of history operated to exclude women from politics, had now become the very reason for their inclusion. On the other hand, there does seem to be an assumption that, at least for the foreseeable future, women's talents and perspectives, and particularly their concern over humanitarian issues, will remain substantially different from men's. Indeed, some have expressed the concern that the functionalist view radically undercut women's claims to political equality, as it makes women's political place contingent on historical developments rather than a matter of right. This raises the question whether, when social circumstances have changed once again, women's claim to a place in the public sphere will lose force.[37]

Within the functionalist framework, fair political representation for women must begin with woman suffrage, as the weight of women's votes would seem necessary for electing individuals to office who showed the appropriate concern for social issues. Addams and others frequently argued that women themselves should hold political office in order that "woman's point of view" would be a part of the solution of social problems: "Outside the use of the ballot, women have made effective their demands in two ways—one in organized groups of citizens watching the office-holder, and letting him know that he is being watched, offering suggestions, and endorsing the official who succeeded; the other as office-holders, actually doing the job *from the woman's point of view.*"[38]

Nonetheless it is questionable whether the fair representation of women actually depends on this second step. If the value of women's contribution to politics consists in their offering their insights into the problems of "civic housekeeping," then the representation of women could, it seems, be accomplished through the more limited means of soliciting their testimony at legislative hearings or else inviting their input on social policy. Unless the distinction between the sexes is drawn so radically as to signify that men *cannot* understand the new areas of governmental policy, the representation of "woman's point of view" could conceivably be accomplished without actually handing over more political *power* to women than is contained in the vote.

I have chosen to call this the "functionalist" view because it has a number of continuities with functional views of politics in general.[39] Like economic classes or sectors in those views, women are here regarded as a discrete social class that plays a distinctive role in the overall functioning of society as a whole, as an essential organ of the body politic. The claim of such a class to political representation is *not* a justice claim, not a claim that women have a right to a certain share of political power. Instead, it is an argument that the smooth functioning of society as a whole (whose promotion is the purpose of governmental activity) cannot be realized so long as any elemental social class is left out of the decision making, particularly when that class's labor is as socially necessary as women's domestic and industrial labor.

So understood, functionalist arguments for women's political participation and representation bear important similarities to Burke's corporate conception of society and the related idea of virtual representation.[40] For both, a group's legitimate claim to representation is based on two factors: first, that it bears interests which distinguish it from any other social group; second, that it is a substantial enough social interest that the cooperation of its members is essential to the order and flourishing of society as a whole. Moreover, in both views the significance of any particular group and its claim to political recognition are features of historical circumstance, not something established by an abstract theory of society or of rights. The central assumption for functionalist suffragists, as for Burke and contemporary neocorporatists, is that the social and economic actors whose cooperation is essential to stable economic production must have the opportunity to express their concerns and interests and to reconcile their demands with each other.[41] In contrast to some versions of corporatism, however, the functionalist argument for woman suffrage assumes that the interests that women would serve in their duties as "civic housekeepers" would be the common interests of *all* elements of society.

IV. Equality and "Woman's Point of View": Hearing Different Voices

In her important study Aileen Kraditor distinguishes two broad types of suffragist arguments. First, characteristic of the early movement was what Kraditor calls the "justice" argument. The themes in this argument are the same as those I have discussed as the "individualist" or natural rights defense of woman suffrage. In the later part of the movement, Kraditor argues, suffragists turned increasingly to arguments from "expedience" rather than justice, mostly as a response to changing political circumstances. "[T]he new era saw a change from the emphasis by suffragists on the ways in which women were the same as men and therefore had the *right* to vote, to a stress on the ways in which they differed from men, and therefore had the *duty* to contribute their special skills and experience to government."[42] Although Kraditor's account of the "expedience" argument emphasizes the themes I have described as "functionalist," Kraditor's distinction holds just as well for the virtue-based arguments: for both the virtue and functionalist arguments, the justification for women's participation in politics depends on what they have to contribute rather than on what is owed to them on the moral grounds of equality.

In general, Kraditor's distinction parallels a distinction in contemporary feminist debates regarding "equality" and "difference," debates that often focus on the question as to whether women should seek to be treated as equals (by which it is often assumed that they should receive the *same* treatment as men) or whether they should be treated differently. Many recent writers have observed that it is wrong to view equality and difference as dichotomous,[43] and I agree. However, it is important to note that for the suffragist arguments examined thus far, *arguments based on women's distinctiveness do not lay claim to justice or to any broad moral principle of equality.* Although the virtue and functionalist arguments may lay claim, as DuBois suggests, to an equality of the *sexes,* the justifications they offer for women's political participation are purely consequentialist. Women should be included in politics, on both views, because politics will be improved by it, not because justice requires it.

There is, however, a third variety of "point of view" arguments in the woman suffrage movement. Some suffragists rejected the notion that women's claim to political equality would be settled by the institution of equal political *rights* for women. Anne Martin, the strongest spokeswoman for this position, was highly critical of the Equal Rights Amendment advocated by the mainstream of the women's rights movement after suffrage was won, since it demonstrated that the National Women's Party and the League of Women Voters "apparently still believe that 'equality' can be legislated."[44] To the contrary, Martin and others argued, the genuine achievement of women's political equality required that women's voices and perspectives be balanced against men's within the legislative process itself:

> These laws were not enacted because men meant to be unjust or unkind to women, but because they looked at things simply from their own side of the question. That is human nature. If women alone had made the laws, no doubt the laws would be just as one-sided as they are now, only, in the opposite direction. As we need two eyes to get a correct perspective, *so we need both the masculine and the feminine points of view represented in legislation in order to get a just result.*[45]

Here, the claim that women's different point of view should be recognized was based unequivocally on grounds of equality rather than expedience; women's presence as lawmakers was necessary for a "just result." Moreover, the cause of contemporary unjust laws was not necessarily any hostile *intent* of men against women. Rather, injustice would result whenever *any* group was left out of the process because of a natural human tendency to see things only from one's own point of view. Interestingly, these suffragists drew a parallel between women's position and that of other excluded groups, since both suffered from the exclusion of their distinctive perspectives from the political process. Until a special Indian Affairs committee was formed in Congress, one suffragist stated, "nobody ever doubted for an instant that 'the only good Indian was a dead Indian.'" Women need similar institutional recognition in order to overturn the belief that "the only good woman is a voteless woman."[46] Similarly, Martin chastised the mainstream leadership for claiming to speak on behalf of other oppressed groups, for to do so effectively denied those groups their own voice. This tendency, she argued, was no different from the male paternalism that had historically been used to silence women:

> [T]hough our leaders protest against the passionate zeal with which men legislators regulate the affairs of women, they themselves are trying to do the same thing. By what right does either group [the Woman's Party or League of Women Voters] speak for women in industry, or women as a whole, in trying to get their respective programs through Congress? Their action is fully as autocratic as that of men legislators toward women, children, labor, negroes, Navajo Indians and other suppressed minorities. So long as our women leaders treat us all as wards or minors, there is no hope of really raising our status as a whole, no matter what laws they cajole out of male Legislatures.[47]

Underlying these arguments is the assumption that women's experience of social life, and hence their perspective on political concerns, was fundamentally different from men's. Women's lives were thoroughly structured by the fact that they were women; as Mary Ritter Beard remarked, "Women can't avoid being women whatever they do."[48] The fundamental difference between men's and women's perspectives meant that men simply were not capable of representing women:

> Man cannot represent woman. They differ in their nature and relations . . . The framers of all legal compacts are restricted to the masculine stand-point of observation, to the thought, feelings, and biases of man. The law then could give us no representation as woman, and therefore no impartial justice even if the present lawmakers were honestly intent upon this; for we can be represented only by our peers.[49]

Similarly, Harriet Burton Laidlaw argued that "insofar as women were like men they ought to have the same rights; insofar as they were different they must represent themselves."[50]

Moreover, at least in Martin's view, the sources of women's different experience are inextricably related to issues of equality. Martin argued that the greatest obstacle to women's social and political equality was their "inferiority complex," the internalized belief in their own inferiority to men.[51] This belief led women to underestimate their capacities and created a fear of asserting themselves in areas historically dominated by men. The ongoing reality of male domination of political, economic, and literary life reinforced women's inferiority complex and set up material obstacles to women's demonstration of their abilities.

As presented here, the obstacle to men's representation of women is an epistemological one: men lack the experience that women have, and consequently women's perceptions, concerns, and needs are inaccessible to them. Clearly one person cannot represent another if the representative does not understand the interests of the represented. Moreover, the distinctiveness of the different perspectives that arise from different social positions is inseparable from the issue of equality: representatives' own experience is partial, and so their judgments will naturally be biased toward those whose experience is similar to theirs. Even a well-meaning intention to be impartial is no protection against the inherent bias of experience. Thus "we can only be represented by our peers," and an equal representation for women must include women's peers—other women—among representatives.

From this perspective, women's political self-representation would advance the cause of women's equality in a number of ways. First, women's exercise of the vote and election to political office would overturn legislation contrary to women's interests. In this respect, the political implications of women's legislative voice were not radically different from those of the individualist arguments, except that it is conceivable that advocates of women's voice might sometimes favor laws that advanced women's interests without being gender-blind.

Further, an active participation in politics would lead women to overcome their fears and would give them substantive evidence to counteract their "inferiority complex." Moreover, electing women to Congress would "help release the creative energies of all women."[52] Again, this theme of self-development initially is similar to that in the individualistic argument for suffrage. Indeed, another of Martin's statements is barely distinguishable from Stanton's views in "The Solitude of Self": "One of the greatest hopes of the world lies in women finding themselves, and living their own lives as human beings, instead of living them vicariously, body and soul, through men."[53] The difference between the two views is not so much in their image of human flourishing and the importance of self-development therein, but on the height of the obstacles to women's development and, consequently, on the kinds of actions necessary to overcome those obstacles. Whereas individualist suffragists tended to believe that equal political rights for women were sufficient to remove the obstacles to women's development, Martin and others like her believed that equal rights were only the first step. The sources of inequality lay deep in the minds and practices of both men and women, so that equality could only be achieved by remaking social relations and social beliefs themselves:

> At bottom the struggle might almost be described as an effort to alter the tone of people's voices and the look in their eyes. . . . In some ways the change is too subtle for expression, but modern men and women recognize it, and know that in this spiritual emancipation lies the hope of finding answers to the more obvious problems of women's position.[54]

In Martin's view, the only sure way to working such deep attitudinal changes was for women to occupy all important social roles, and particularly that of representative.

Despite the deep-rootedness of women's inequality, there was nothing necessary about women's distinctive political perspective; in time, it could conceivably be overcome. In fact, Martin seemed to assume that if equality were aggressively pursued, the day would come when "we [shall] have, not a man-made or a woman-made world, but a *human* world," when "sex is put out of politics, and the world made human."[55] In the meantime, however, women must act in solidarity with one another if they were to have any hope of realizing the world Martin described; they must vote together on policies and work together to put women into elective office. Thinking along these lines, one commentator on the suffrage movement stated (albeit with poor predictive accuracy):

> For a long time the sex issue must be set; we cannot, for many generations, choose between Mrs. Brown and Mr. Smith in a manner as unsexed as we do between Mr. Brown and Mr. Smith. Women feel this sex difference still more than men; while a man may vote for a woman because he thinks her a good candidate in spite of being

a woman, for a long time many women will tend to vote for another woman as a demonstration of *esprit de corps*. That is unavoidable, because woman is still inferior in the state, and the persecuted must, in the words of Franklin, "hang together, or assuredly they shall hang separately."[56]

Within this view the failure to secure self-representation for women *would* result in the moral degradation of both individual women and the political system as a whole. But in contrast to the virtue or functionalist arguments, the cause of the degradation was a failure to live up to the nation's republican aspirations to freedom and equality rather than a failure measured by the standards of Victorian morality or social engineering. The republicanism envisioned by what I call voice suffragists, however, was distinctive in that it viewed the common good of society as a whole as constituted by the well-being of key social elements, and there was no doubt that women *were* key. The resulting vision is eloquently described in an article by Mary Putnam Jacobi, which merits lengthy quotation:

> In a democratic society, the government is the condensed expression of the collective activities of society. Of these activities it discharges the supreme function, the maintenance of justice. In doing so, it reflects and measures with considerable precision the moral sense of the community which chooses the government, elects its officials, prescribes their administration, and ratifies their laws.
>
> . . . [A]ccording to the democratic idea, all the recognized elements of the social organism are enabled, at least to a minimum degree, to secure representation of their thoughts, wills and respective situations in social institutions . . .
>
> . . . Exclusion of women from representation, after the democratic principle has been proclaimed, constitutes a contradiction of principle as positive as would the similar exclusion of any class of men [sic].[57]

As we have seen, the individualist argument for woman suffrage offered a familiar view of political equality and one that fits neatly into the scheme of liberal representation. These arguments for the franchise, grounded as they are in conceptions of individual equality and autonomy, place their advocates squarely within the mainstream of American political culture. Indeed, as I have noted already, clearly women's claims for individual equality were aimed fundamentally at establishing women's standing as full citizens rather than at securing the representation of any distinctively "female" political interests.[58] Individualist suffragists, who dominated the movement's leadership throughout its lifetime, neither demanded nor expected that gaining the franchise would produce substantively different political outcomes, except in areas in which women were not equal before the law.[59] Women did not constitute a long-term political "interest" that would seek or require representation over the long term. In pluralist terms, women were an interest group created by the "disturbance" of legal discrimination against them; once this disturbance was remedied, their mobilization as a group would no longer be needed. Although their exclusion from politics made women's rational trust in government impossible, their formal inclusion was all that was required to establish that trust. In short, the individualist argument for woman suffrage neither adds to liberal representation's understanding of fairness as a foundation of trust in government nor offers a critique of it.

The virtue and functionalist arguments, however, offer conceptions of effective representation and the common interest that are markedly different from those contained within liberal representation. In contrast to liberal representation's procedural conception of the definition of groups that are relevant for politics, both the virtue and functionalist views of women's political place offer a conception of politics in which women have a substantive contribution to make to the public good. Interesting as these arguments are, both express conceptions of the place of groups in politics familiar to us from chapter 1's review of prominent theories of representation: the virtue argument corresponds to Mill's argument for the representation of the class of the "intelligent few," and the functionalist argument corresponds to Burke's quasi-corporate view of virtual representation. Each argument presents an alternative to liberal representation that is intriguing in its own right. However, for the purposes of this project, the question is whether arguments for suffrage offer new insight into a conception of political *equality* that could inform a group-based conception of fair representation. Neither the virtue nor functionalist argument is based on claims for political equality as such, and so neither is ultimately helpful for this purpose.

The final class of suffragist argumentation, what I have called the "voice" argument, offers a claim for women's enfranchisement and representation that also rests on substantive rather than procedural grounds for women's political recognition. In contrast to the virtue and functionalist arguments, however, the voice argument is fundamentally an *equality* argument. Women not only need the franchise but also require representation to protect their distinctive substantive interests in politics. Women are not merely an interest group, mobilized solely for winning the franchise, but a group whose interests and identity are constituted by social processes that have long existed and will likely continue for a long time. Individual women's membership in this group is therefore involuntary, a matter of birth rather than choice. Clearly it is also dichotomous and immutable, which is why Mary Beard commented that "Women can't avoid being women whatever they do." Most important, women's rational trust in government is precluded not only by the current legal and constitutional discriminations against them but by men's incapacity to understand easily the substance of their political interests and concerns.

The voice argument for political equality thus acknowledges and comprehends the distinctive nature of group membership for historically marginalized groups. In the process it undergirds an argument for fair political representation that stands in marked contrast to liberal representation. Its defense of women's representation does bear certain similarities to Mill's claim that the permanent exclusion of any class of citizens undercuts their ability to trust in government; also evident is an element of the view shared by Mill and Burke that ultimately the citizens are the only reliable judges of their own suffering. But the voice argument adds an equality claim to each of these arguments, and one that resonates powerfully with recent pressures for an increased presence of marginalized ascriptive groups within legislative bodies: political equality for women depends not only on the *expression* of women's interests in legislative bodies but on their *self-representation*.

Although I believe that the voice argument for woman suffrage and women's political representation contains the seed of a coherent group-based theory of fair representation, it is not, as it stands, the complete articulation of an alternative to liberal representation. In order to understand more thoroughly its contribution to a critique of liberal representation, it is necessary to explore its implications for the complexities of representation as mediation. In the next section I argue that the voice argument is particularly helpful for understanding the consequences of a group-based view of political equality for the dynamics of legislative decision making. In contrast to liberal representation, a group-based theory of fair representation must favor a *deliberative and consensus-oriented* over a *competitive or bargaining* model of decision making.

V. Women's Voice and the Dynamics of Legislative Deliberation

The voice argument for women's political equality and political representation is essentially an *epistemological* argument: men lack deep knowledge of women's "thoughts, wills and respective situations," and so women must represent themselves. Although this epistemological point might appear to be resolvable through regular legislative consultations with women—perhaps by seeking out women's testimony within hearings—this solution would perpetuate the paternalism of men's relationship to women, and so would only tend to reinforce the social attitudes regarding women's helplessness and inferiority shared by both men and women. Moreover, without the power of the franchise and the power that comes with elective office, men will continue to turn a deaf ear to women's voices. Anna Howard Shaw, asking Woodrow Wilson who would speak for women if, lacking the vote, they could not join any political party, received the reply, "You speak very well for yourself." Shaw responded, "But not with authority."[60]

The argument for women's self-representation offers a critique of liberal representation whose implications are even more far-reaching than they may initially appear. Not only does the voice argument offer a substantive account of the reasons why equality might require women's legislative presence, but it also suggests that the process of legislative decision making must itself be transformed if the egalitarian promise of women's representation is to be fulfilled. If one goes so far as to say that justice requires the expression of the different experiential perspectives of different social groups, then one must go a step further to argue that justice requires that these different voices be *heard and responded to*, that they have an opportunity to affect legislative decisions. This is not to say that equality requires that the perspectives of some groups should be authoritative for the rest; quite the contrary, on this argument for women's rights the exclusive representation of the male perspective in politics has been precisely the problem, and it is not a problem that will be resolved by substituting women's perspective for men's. Rather, the claim that "woman's point of view" must be given a place in legislative decision making entails the further claim to a political process in which there is an exchange of perspectives, in which representatives of one distinctive point of view are able to communicate to others their understanding of what justice and public well-being require.

Consequently, the model of legislative decision making implicit in the voice argument for woman suffrage must be a *deliberative* or *discursive* model, in sharp contrast to the bargaining or competitive model contained within liberal representation. By a deliberative model of decision making I mean one in which participants aim at mutual agreement arrived at through a process of rational argumentation.[61] In contrast to a competitive or bargaining model of decision making, in which each actor trades off some of his or her aims in order to secure others, the actors in a deliberative process attempt to *justify* their preferences to the others. Participants in a deliberative process all share the aim of arriving at a decision based on reasons persuasive to all. Further, a deliberative process must presuppose that all participants share an interest in cooperation and stand as *equals* in that process. In other words, "the existing distribution of power and resources does not shape their chances to contribute to deliberation, nor does that distribution play an authoritative role in their deliberation."[62]

In the liberal conception of representation, the representative's knowledge of constituent interests is unproblematic; interests are generally conceived in material terms, or as clear and discrete preferences for some policies over others. Possessing the knowledge necessary for effective representation is a challenge only insofar as the *quantity* of knowledge required is so great. The representative must rely heavily on interest groups to supply the necessary information, but once they do so there is no cognitive barrier to his use or understanding of it.[63] There is no experiential barrier to the representative's understanding of constituent concerns, and so it is immaterial whether the representative is "like" his constituents. In fact, this set of assumptions is what makes descriptive representation appear ridiculous: it is absurd to say that I must be a farmer in order to understand that agricultural subsidies are in my farming constituency's interest. From this standpoint, the indignation expressed by critics of the notion that only women can represent women, or only Blacks can represent Blacks,[64] makes sense. "A politician need not himself be a member of the Chamber of Commerce of the United States to listen with respect to the testimony of a business leader who is pleading its case."[65] In the absence of any epistemological barriers to a representative's grasp of constituent interests, the activity required of the representative concerned to protect those interests is similarly unproblematic: knowing the range and intensity of constituent interests, the representative's task is to cultivate the relationships and make the bargains with other legislators that will win the package of policies which best satisfies those interests.[66]

In the voice model of legislative decision making, the representative's qualifications consist in a clear comprehension of the distinctive needs and concerns of his or her constituents, a comprehension that usually arises from the fact that the representative and his or her constituents are "similarly situated." This is not to say that a representative must be alike in every respect to his or her constituents, which *would* be an absurd requirement in that it would destroy the mediative distance between represented and representative, eliminating the dual exercise of agency that is integral to the activity of representation per se.[67] But for groups that have historically been excluded from politics, the representative must have some understanding of the ways in which the constituents' lives are shaped by that exclusion and by the privilege of others. The legislator's task is to communicate the constituents' distinctive perspective on matters of public policy, to clarify that the vantage point offered by privileged groups' social position is partial and incomplete, and that justice and the public interest look different when viewed from the group's "point of view." The legislative process should reflect the fact that, as Patricia Williams observes, "it really is possible to see things—even the most concrete things— simultaneously yet differently; and . . . seeing simultaneously yet differently is more easily done by two people than one."[68]

Williams continues this passage by saying that "one person can get the hang of [seeing things simultaneously yet differently] with time and effort," which points up another important feature of the dynamics of legislative decision making within the voice argument. Although it is true that individuals, left unchallenged, will perceive social and political affairs in a biased way, it is also true that they are capable of seeing things from another's point of view. Martha Minow's study of the treatment of social difference in American law reveals that even Supreme Court justices possess an impressive capacity to make the leap of perspective and see disputes from the viewpoint of marginalized groups—a capacity infrequently exercised, to be sure. Justice John Paul Stevens, criticizing a Texas city's refusal to grant a building permit for a home for the mentally retarded, took up the perspective of the mentally retarded in order to reach his judgment: "I cannot believe that a rational member of this disadvantaged class could ever approve of the discriminatory application of the city's ordinance in this case."[69]

In some ways, the "politics of perspective"[70] implicit in the voice argument has affinities with contemporary social contract theory as developed both by John Rawls and Thomas Scanlon, the core idea of which is that we gain great insight into the justice of a measure if we evaluate it from the perspective of disadvantaged members of society.[71] The key difference between contractualist views and the voice approach, however, is that whereas the former assumes that we, as individuals with rational agency, may rid ourselves of partiality by adopting the perspective of some abstract "other," in the voice approach we cannot presume to speak or reason as others would speak or reason for themselves, for we cannot escape the particularity of our own experience even through thought experiments. Seyla Benhabib's distinction between moral reasoning undertaken from the standpoint of a "generalized other" and from the standpoint of a "concrete other" is instructive here.[72] The former approach to moral reasoning, typified by the hypothetical choice situations like Rawls's original position, invites us to abstract from our particularity and reason according to what we have in common with an other. Benhabib argues that the standpoint of the concrete other forms the core of the "ethic of care" which Carol Gilligan found to be characteristic of women's moral reasoning.[73] Taking up this standpoint "requires us to view each and every rational being as an individual with a concrete history, identity and affective-emotional constitution."[74] Benhabib envisions a politics in which both kinds of moral standpoints can be played out, regulated by what she calls (drawing on the work of Jürgen Habermas) the communicative ethics of need interpretations. As its name suggests, this kind of political activity places dialogue among subjects at the center of political morality. The subject matter for discussion would be similar to that in other models of political discourse, including "[q]uestions of the most desirable and just political organization, as well as the distinction between justice and the good life, the public and the domestic."[75] In contrast to models of moral reasoning that rely exclusively on the standpoint of the "generalized other," however, a communicative ethic of need interpretations would include "the presumption . . . that these distinctions cannot be drawn in such a way as to privatize, hide and repress the experiences of those who have suffered under them, for only what all could consensually agree to be in the best interest of each could be accepted as the outcome of this dialogic process."[76]

Similarly, the process of legislative decision making within a group-based view of representation would have to include both kinds of position-taking: considerations of what citizens share and of the needs that distinguish some groups of citizens from others. Legislative discourse would have to respect the dignity shared by all individuals in virtue of their humanity, but it would also have to respond to the particular experiences of those whose needs were frustrated by false generalization. The difference between the view implicit in the voice argument and Benhabib's view of the communicative ethic is that, in the former, it is *not* the case that "all those affected are participants in [the] process."[77] Instead of the fully concrete other, the representative is present not in order that her *full* individuality be given recognition but that the elements of particularity which she shares with others like her, and which distinguish her and her constituents from others in a manner relevant to public policy, are recognized within legislative deliberations. The needs she articulates are not hers alone, but the needs shared by members of the group she represents. By articulating them, she invites other representatives to adopt the perspective of a member of her group, an other who is not fully concrete, not completely individualized, but who nonetheless has particular characteristics that are relevant to the dialogue but are not shared universally. In articulating the group's perspective on behalf of her constituents, the representative does not need to take up the standpoint of an other; the perspective is hers *immediately*, although it is not the full expression of her individuality.

These features of the self-representation of marginalized groups come through clearly in the remarks of women members of Congress. For many of them, their identity as women is critical to the performance of their responsibilities as representatives. Speaking of Democratic women in Congress on the issue of abortion, Senator Barbara Mikulski said, "We have a special obligation to the women of the United States to take up for them when they have been pushed out or left out."[78] Many of these representatives have a sense of solidarity based on gender identity. As Representative Maxine Waters put it, "I think there is a sisterhood that's born out of our common knowledge and experience with life."[79] Women legislators regard their personal experiences as immediately relevant to policy discussions. In the Senate's discussion of family leave policy, two women senators, Patty Murray and Diane Feinstein, related their experience of having to give up their jobs in order to give birth. Patty Murry said, "I am of the infamous sandwich generation, charged with caring for my own children and my parents at the same time . . . I personally understand the emotional consequences. I also know that when my family is safe and well cared for, I do a better job at work."[80] The relevance of personal experience was also apparent in the comments of African American Representative Carrie P. Meek of Florida on Social Security policy. Meek is a granddaughter of slaves and once worked as a domestic. Speaking of the House vote to require employers of domestic help to pay Social Security taxes on employees to whom they pay at least $1,800, Meek protested, "There are black and poor women who work every day for somebody different. They would never meet the threshold."[81] The novelty of such contributions, and their potential impact on policy, is not lost on observers. "They add a different voice, a perspective that senators in the past have absorbed, when they absorb it at all, from constituents and witnesses and sometimes from their wives."[82] The representatives are also conscious of the importance of women's legislative presence. "I want to say what my neighbor would say," Senator Murray commented, but "you have to be here to matter."[83]

The image of the legislature that emerges out of the voice argument is of a deliberative body, one in which deep differences in political perspective are gradually (if only partially) bridged through discussion aimed (to borrow Habermas's language) at reaching agreement. In contrast to the liberal model of legislative decision making, in which winning favored policies means playing the game of logrolling and pork barrels, trading favors and scoring points, the voice model envisions a process in which principled perspectives on public policy are exchanged and debated until some provisional agreement can be reached. It does not assume that there are no material conflicts of interest among groups but rather insists that the resolution of those conflicts should not be negotiated without the substantive input of all the groups affected by the decision, particularly those groups whose perspectives have been excluded in the past. Implicit in the voice model are rules regarding what kinds of reasons ought to count in the process of public decision making, but, in contrast to liberal principles of impartiality, those rules would not include the notion that public reasons should be unrelated to particular social positions.[84]

The image of the process of representation implicit in the voice argument for woman suffrage is similar in many respects to the "politics of difference" advocated by Iris Young. Young argues for the representation of oppressed groups as a necessary part of justice. Her view is particularly consonant with the voice argument insofar as she argues that

> because it assures a voice for the oppressed as well as the privileged, group representation better assures that all needs and interests in the public will be recognized in democratic deliberations. The privileged usually are not inclined to protect or advance the interests of the oppressed, *partly because their social position prevents them from understanding those interests*, and partly because to some degree their privilege depends on the continued oppression of others.[85]

Young also emphasizes that the needs of oppressed groups are best expressed by their own members and that a politics which incorporates group representation would encourage principled deliberation and produce policies that had been defended in terms of justice. Consequently, "[g]roup representation adds to [public] accountability because it serves as an antidote to self-deceiving self-interest masked as an impartial or general interest."[86]

Despite these important similarities between Young's view and the defense of group representation embedded in the voice argument, there are differences as well. First, whereas the voice argument supposes that differences in perspective are largely the *product* of women's subjection, and that we ought to aspire to a politics in which different perspectives are gradually dissolved by the dissolution of classes of privilege, Young argues that the justice in a "politics of difference" includes not only the public *recognition* of the importance of group differences but also the public *affirmation* of the value of particular group identities.[87] Young's view valorizes a pluralism of social groups as a source of an enriched politics and relates the diversity of group participation in politics to the formulation of policies wiser and more just than those formulated by a homogeneous body: "[G]roup representation promotes just outcomes because it maximizes the social knowledge expressed in discussion, and thus furthers practical wisdom."[88] Elsewhere, however, Young advances "a politics that asserts the positivity of group difference," which "asserts that oppressed groups have distinct cultures, experiences, and perspectives on social life with humanly positive meaning, some of which may even be superior to the culture and perspectives of mainstream society."[89]

Notwithstanding Young's argument, it is not the case that a view of group representation defended on grounds of *equality*, as is the voice view, carries with it an affirmation of group difference as valuable per se. Rather, the egalitarian concern with group difference stems directly from the connection between inequality and patterns of historical and ongoing group subordination, and is aimed at overcoming both. As I discuss in greater depth in chapter 6, although there are sources of group distinctiveness that are independent of the history of subordination, an equality-based defense of group representation is concerned only with the difference of perspective that is essential to overcoming social and political inequality. The representation of diversity may be desirable for other reasons, but those reasons tend to rest on consequentialist grounds rather than on arguments about justice.

VI. Group Representation and the Limits of the Deliberative Ideal

Notwithstanding the clear reasons why a group-based theory of fair representation must suppose a deliberative model of legislative decision making, there are good reasons to temper aspirations to deliberative democracy with a measure of both theoretical and pragmatic skepticism. As Anne Phillips has recently argued, ideas of group representation and deliberative democracy "move[] in close but uneasy association" with one another.[90] First, models of deliberative democracy tend to characterize it as a politics of the common good rather than of mere interest aggregation, and some state explicitly that expressions of self-interest should be barred from the public forum. But the aspiration to rise above interest politics may work against the effective representation of marginalized groups in several ways. Although the deliberative model anticipates that all participants in the deliberative process will be pressed by discussion to look beyond their particular interests in order to consider seriously the claims of others, marginalized groups' ability to advance the end of social and political equality depends on their capacity to advocate for their currently neglected interests within the deliberative process. To the extent that ideals of deliberative democracy contemplate ruling out expressions of self-interest altogether, they hamper marginalized group representatives' capacity to conform to the standards of public discourse while also effectively representing their constituents' perspectives and interests. Indeed, the status of marginalized groups *as* marginalized reflects, by definition, the fact that some of their fundamental interests are now systematically and unjustifiably neglected. Any discursive process in which that neglect can come to light must make space for the expression of group-specific interests.

At the same time, the hope contained within the voice argument is that an inclusive political discourse will produce a new recognition of shared interests among privileged and marginalized groups, including the recognition of a shared interest in justice.[91] Viewed in this way, concerns about the place of interest in a deliberative politics may lend more support to a critique of those models of deliberative democracy that disdain interest altogether than to a critique of marginalized group representation.

Other important critiques of deliberative democracy focus on the fact that it expresses an ideal of politics which places high moral demands on participants, precisely because, by requiring them to distance themselves from their narrow interests in order to arrive at a shared understanding of a common good, it displays a lack of realism concerning human psychology and motivation. As James Johnson has expressed it, deliberative democracy is utopian insofar as it makes "heroic assumptions about participants."[92] Yet if participants in deliberative democracy as normally described are "heroic," then it would seem that participants in a deliberative politics that included marginalized group perspectives would have to be divine.[93] Not only are representatives from privileged groups expected to listen attentively to others and be open to revising their understandings of their constituents' interests in the light of others' arguments—already an exacting standard; they are further expected to be willing to reconceive the status quo as unjustly privileging themselves and to relinquish that privilege in the interest of justice. Given the strength of human inclinations to perceive our own actions as just, this seems a great deal to ask of any political process.

In fact, I do not believe that the ideal of a deliberative politics of difference *is* naively utopian under all circumstances; the trick is to be more specific about the circumstances in which it is conceivable that privileged groups will relinquish some of their privilege in response to marginalized groups' claims of justice. What could possibly motivate a disposition in privileged groups to listen impartially to claims of marginalized groups in the manner I have described?

A glance at the historical record suggests two principal sources of the motivation of the powerful to heed the voices of those less powerful: (a) the desire to be just or at least to be able to justify one's position (both in the sense of one's beliefs and of one's social standing) to others;[94] and (b) the need to stem conflict in order to avoid its costs. Both can serve as motives to listen and try to understand a situation from the standpoint of another, even a less powerful other. If we look to the most profound historical moments of the inclusion of oppressed groups into democratic politics—including not only the Nineteenth Amendment but also the Civil Rights amendments, the Civil Rights Act, South African democracy, the inclusion of First Nations representatives in recent Canadian constitutional negotiations—we discover that all have a common thread: that a new responsiveness to oppressed groups arises with *both* a failure to be able to justify current practice *and* a social mobilization of the oppressed that threatens potentially high costs to privileged groups should they fail to resolve the conflicts.

What this suggests, however, is that the motive of a common good of justice and the motive of interest are in fact far more closely intertwined than prevailing models of deliberative democracy tend to admit. Models of deliberative democracy are imperfect tools for deepening our understanding or advancing the end of democratic egalitarianism so long as they assume a sharp disjuncture between a politics of interest and a politics of deliberation. Instead, this exploration suggests that we should conceive of politics as consisting of a continuum between perfect solidarity and the unbridled battle of interests. While the ideal of a perfectly deliberative legislature remains the appropriate aspiration of a conception of political representation that is just toward historically marginalized groups, we need not assume that we confront a dichotomous choice between a competitive (or adversarial) model of decision making and a deliberative (or consensual) one.[95] Rather, we should focus on fostering those conditions that will press legislative dynamics toward the latter and away from the former. In other words, while we may affirm a deliberative ideal of democratic politics, interest advocacy should retain an important place in our thinking about both theoretical models of political decision making and practical strategies for protecting marginalized groups.[96]

If we choose to think of politics and the possibilities for egalitarian deliberation in this way, I believe we will find that a concern for the capacity of political processes to approximate the deliberative ideal depends crucially on (a) social circumstances, particularly the degree to which marginalized groups are politically mobilized; and (b) the structure of political institutions. Both these factors can create pressures on privileged groups to cooperate in a deliberative mode with less privileged groups. The political mobilization of marginalized groups creates pressures in the manner I have described above. Political institutions can themselves create incentives for deliberation through decision rules that move in the direction of consensus or unanimity as a requirement of legitimate or binding political decisions (as in Calhoun's system of concurrent majorities or as in supermajority rules), as well as through norms of public discourse.[97] As Jon Elster has recently argued, the publicity of political argument can, by itself, have the effect of moderating the play of interests in political decision making even where interest is what motivates participants, a dynamic he describes as "the civilizing force of hypocrisy."[98]

In general, a discursive process that includes formerly marginalized groups might be expected to produce public policies that focus more on social welfare issues than does the current legislative agenda, since representatives of marginalized groups will work more than others to meet their groups' special needs. Some of these themes have emerged in current efforts to encourage greater numbers of women to run for elective office, efforts that were spurred on by the Senate Judiciary Committee's treatment of Anita Hill during the Supreme Court confirmation hearings for Clarence Thomas. Those hearings led many women to believe that issues of sexual harassment would have been taken more seriously by a committee that included women members. Several women candidates cited Hill's treatment during the hearings as the principal reason why they chose to run for the U.S. Senate in the 1992 race. Ruth Mandel explains the swell of support for women candidates as an expression of women's desire for someone who could "bring[] to the highest lawmaking body an experience which no one on the panel seemed to understand or have any sensitivity about."[99]

In fact, there is empirical evidence that the inclusion of members of historically disadvantaged groups in legislative bodies *by itself* shifts the dynamics of decision making toward a discursive, consensus-oriented model. Abigail Thernstrom's interviews with Black and White elected officials suggested that "governing bodies function differently when they are racially mixed, particularly where Blacks are new to politics and where racially insensitive language and discrimination in the provision of services are long-established political habits."[100] In another study, interviews of California city council members revealed that "the presence of minorities on councils was important for city politics even if it had not had an impact on policy." Not only did minority presence increase White members' sensitivity to minority concerns, but "[e]ven where minorities were not strongly incorporated, councilmembers talked about a new atmosphere and new pressure on the council once minorities were members. One official said, 'When minorities talk to the city council now, councilmembers nod their heads rather than yawn.'"[101] A Black commissioner from Muskegon County, Michigan, commented, "As long as one of us is in the room it makes all the difference . . . In all-white organizations and all-white homes they talk differently than when we are there."[102] Thus there is reason to believe that group representation, by itself, will tend to shift the dynamics of political decision making toward a more discursive model.

Another reason why the increased legislative presence of marginalized groups might encourage a move toward deliberation is that these groups favor process change as a matter of policy. In Sue Thomas's study of women legislators, she found that their actual manner of operating within legislatures differed little from that of men. Yet the survey data revealed that one reason why women legislators favored an increase in women's candidacies was that they believed the political process itself would change if more women were in office.[103] The *substance* of women's expectations about how the political process would change is particularly interesting. Thomas's interviews with women legislators revealed that they are likely to favor procedural change that would produce a more deliberative, consensus-oriented legislative process. With more women in legislatures, as one midwestern legislator argued, "[t]here would be more consensus politics. Women are better at consensus building."[104] Similarly, another study of state legislators found that women are more likely than men to favor an open process in which "all points of view can be aired and a consensus can be reached."[105] These findings and perceptions are interesting, and perhaps encouraging, insofar as they suggest that increasing the number of women in legislatures will make a direct contribution to the deliberativeness of decision making. At the same time, we should treat such conjectures cautiously, as they may contain essentialist undertones. In any event, it is important to note that the voice argument for a deliberative process of legislative decision making does not rest on any empirical claim that members of marginalized groups have a greater predilection for deliberation than others.

The voice argument for woman suffrage provides the elements of an equality-based argument for the presence of disadvantaged groups in legislative bodies. Furthermore, the answer it offers also fills in the first piece of the puzzle of representation as mediation, the mediation that occurs through the dynamics of legislative decision making. It does so in a way that clearly distinguishes a group-based view of fair representation from the liberal view, and provides substantive grounds that make sense of marginalized groups' desire for self-representation in a way the liberal theory cannot. Although, like liberal representation, the group-based view regards the justice of legislative policies as something that depends primarily on the fairness of the political process, the two conceptions are radically different in their estimations of what is required in order for that process to be judged as fair. Whereas the liberal view regards the legislative process as fair so long as legislators are duly elected within well-apportioned legislative districts, and so long as their political maneuverings are within the bounds of the law, the group-based view is more demanding. It requires that whatever the nature of the electoral system, women and other disadvantaged groups must be present as members in the legislative body. Moreover, it is not enough that the legislative process occurs within the bounds of the law; it must also involve the discursive exchange of the perspectives of all relevant social groups before a decision is reached. Finally, although the group-based view contains no independent standard for evaluating legislative decisions, it rests on the assumption that a process of this kind, grounded in a genuine commitment to equality, will produce policies that harmonize the competing interests of different social groups such that no group's interests are permanently frustrated.

5

Trust: The Racial Divide and Black Rights during Reconstruction

IN CHAPTER 1, I discussed the centrality of trust to theories of representation and their claims to define a legitimate order of government. As we have seen, the voice argument for woman suffrage, and its implications for the dynamics of legislative deliberation, offer important reasons why the institutions of liberal representation are incapable of fully supporting marginalized ascriptive groups' rational trust in government.

But Locke's characterization of the deepest foundation of political trust suggests that for some marginalized groups the obstacles to rational trust may be even greater than the voice argument reveals. Locke's profound insight was that in order for the people to have trust in their government, there must first be a solid social compact among them, a firm relationship of trust *among* citizens. By definition, marginalized ascriptive groups stand in an uncertain relationship to other citizens, one in which they can have little confidence that others take an interest in their well-being. What are the prospects for a scheme of fair and effective representation in a society divided along group lines? Does liberal representation answer to such circumstances?

Clearly in American society the deepest such division falls along the lines of race. Therefore, in order to develop an understanding of liberal representation's capacity (or incapacity) to sustain the rational trust of marginalized groups, we must examine the meaning of political equality, and its implications for political representation, for African Americans, the group that has been uniquely marginalized by the history of slavery. Like the previous chapter, this chapter seeks insight into the meaning of political equality for marginalized ascriptive groups by examining the rhetoric of equality at the time the group's inclusion into American politics was at stake. It explores the arguments for the franchise, for civil and political rights, and ultimately for political representation that were advanced by African Americans during Reconstruction after the Civil War.

What emerges from this inquiry is an account of the second dimension of representation as mediation within a group-based theory of fair representation, that is, an account of legislator-constituent relations. The repeated betrayal of marginalized group interests through history produces a profound—and often quite reasonable and understandable—distrust of privileged groups. This distrust extends to representatives from privileged groups who, while duly elected, may not be constrained to act on behalf of marginalized group interest: the electoral connection, designed to secure the accountability of legislators to constituents, fails in that design when it comes to weak groups. Whereas the voice argument for group representation focuses on the limitations of privileged groups' *capacity* to represent marginalized group interests, this chapter focuses on their *will* to do so. Because of the confluence of legislators' and constituents' interests when they are members of the same group, the self-representation of marginalized groups can help repair relations of trust between them and their representatives. And when the foundation of such trust is present, it improves the substance of the legislator-constituent relationship by encouraging undistorted and uninhibited communication.[1]

I. Reconstruction: From Slavery to Citizenship to Disfranchisement

The Black political experience during Reconstruction tells the story of trust given and trust betrayed, the story of the newly emancipated slaves' faith in the promise that "the right of citizens to vote shall not be abridged . . . on account of race, color, or previous condition of servitude,"[2] and of the failure of the federal government to enforce that right. When combined with the Fourteenth Amendment's commitment to due process and to the equal protection of the laws for all citizens, Blacks believed that the right to vote would secure their political equality with White citizens and make it possible for Blacks to overcome their degraded and subordinate status in American society. The Reconstruction amendments, together with the laws that anticipated and enforced them, held out the promise of political membership that was no longer conditional on the color of a person's skin, and, by and large, it was a promise Blacks accepted in good faith.

In fact, Blacks' initially overwhelming trust in the party responsible for these political reforms was not a demonstration of their credulity. Despite the failure of Presidential Reconstruction to protect freedmen's fundamental interests, by 1867 the Radical Republicans had control of Congress and extended suffrage to the freedmen. During Radical Reconstruction, there is no doubt that political and economic reforms in the South worked to improve Blacks' condition and resulted in a political system characterized by the greatest degree of racial equality in the nation's history, at least until recent years. "[I]f Reconstruction did not create an integrated society, it did establish a standard of equal citizenship and a recognition of blacks' right to a share of state services that differed sharply from the heritage of slavery and Presidential Reconstruction, and from the state-imposed segregation that lay in the future."[3]

Beginning around 1870, the very year the Fifteenth Amendment was ratified, the tide of Reconstruction turned. Southern Whites who had refused to vote in the federally sponsored elections held after the war returned to the polls. (In fact, Blacks' own sense of fairness contributed to this trend, as many voted against the disfranchisement of Confederate Whites.)[4] Consequently Republicans could not count on electoral victory based on the votes of Blacks, "scalawags," and "carpetbaggers" alone, so they began compromising their policies toward Blacks in order to recruit more southern White voters. Where Democrats retained legislative control, they developed increasingly creative means of depriving Blacks of the vote: the poll taxes, educational require-ments, and residency requirements that came to typify the Jim Crow South. At the same time, the late 1860s brought a dramatic rise in the incidence of violence against Blacks, much of it under the auspices of the Ku Klux Klan and much of it directed against Blacks who dared to vote Republican (or dared to vote at all). In the face of these strains the Radical Republicans lost their posi-tion of dominance in the party, and the Fifteenth Amendment was perhaps the last potent act of their rule. The early 1870s brought further causes of party fragmentation, including an economic depression. At the state level, where there were Republican majorities, Black officeholders initially benefited from the southern White reaction against the depression, which led some White Republicans to defect to the Democratic Party. But these gains were short-lived. As a second rash of violence and electoral intimidation against Blacks broke out in 1873–75, the Republican Congress failed adequately to enforce Black rights or to enact Charles Sumner's Civil Rights Bill.[5] The Demo-crats regained a majority in the House of Representatives in the elections of 1874. Republican President Hayes, narrowly elected in 1876, abandoned Re-construction altogether, withdrawing federal troops from the South. Before long the doors to Black political participation were slammed shut by the cam-paign of southern White violence and by legal restrictions, upheld by the Supreme Court, on their exercise of the franchise.

Black political rhetoric during Reconstruction is instructive for the insight it gives into the meaning of political equality, and its relationship to trust, for a group that had been so severely oppressed. As with the woman suffrage arguments, the Declaration's ideals of individual equality and government by consent are a dominant theme in early Black rhetoric, both in the free North before emancipation and among freedmen in the South in the years after emancipation. However, as Radical Reconstruction's extension of voting and office-holding rights gave way to Republican acquiescence in racist violence, Black rhetoric shifted away from the individualist rhetoric of the Declaration. Blacks' initial belief that their equal citizenship would be protected yielded to a profound distrust of Whites in general, a distrust that increasingly extended to their only political allies, the Republicans. Gradually, many Blacks reached the conclusion that a color-blind approach to political action would not suffice to protect the actual political rights of Blacks in the face of deep-seated White racism. Instead, Blacks argued in increasing numbers, the protection of their political interests would depend on Black cohesiveness and could no longer be entrusted to White Republicans. The implications for political representation were clear and were made explicit by Black leaders: Blacks' interests would not be heard if sounded through "white trumpets,"[6] expressed by White representatives. Thus Black rhetoric during Reconstruction traces a path from an individualistic and color-blind conception of political equality to a conception of equality that depends on the politicization of group identity and the representation of a group by its own members. In the process it reveals a great deal about the nature of the trust that exists between legislators and constituents, and about the different grounds of that trust within, on the one hand, the American scheme of liberal representation, and, on the other, for members of historically oppressed groups. To recall Hobbes, Black rhetoric demonstrates how, once their trust was betrayed, Black citizens felt they must "endeavour to provide" themselves the "Good" of representation "by other means."[7]

II. Early Rhetoric: The Declaration and Color-Blind Equality

The Declaration of Independence was the centerpiece of Black claims to citizenship, and particularly to the franchise, from the beginning of the free Black convention movement in the 1830s through Reconstruction.[8] Like the suffragists, Blacks presented their earliest arguments by following the form of the Declaration section for section, down to detailed lists of grievances. Before emancipation, free Blacks in the North demonstrated their dedication to the true principles of the Declaration by refusing to celebrate the Fourth of July; instead they gathered on the fifth to reflect on the document's unrealized promise, manifested both by slavery and by the denial of civil rights to free Blacks.[9] The intimate connection between the meaning of freedom and the legacy of the Declaration was also demonstrated by the Black community in Montgomery, Alabama, on New Year's Day, 1866, the third anniversary of the Emancipation Proclamation, where a large crowd of freedmen joined in a parade to celebrate *their* "independence day."[10] By the time of Reconstruction, one Black leader commented, "The colored people . . . had read the Declaration until it had become part of their natures."[11]

But the meaning the Declaration held for Blacks in their quest for political equality was not monolithic. Rather, they adopted and developed different strands of the document and constructed from those strands distinct rationales for their equality as citizens. Three themes in particular stand out in Black political argumentation during Reconstruction: the principle of equal natural rights grounded in the self-evident truth of the equality of all humans as such; taxation without representation (or, as Jefferson puts it, without consent); and the idea of independence itself, an idea that takes on a distinctive and telling significance for the newly emancipated and enfranchised citizens.

"We believe in the Declaration of Independence, that all men are born free and equal."[12] Presented with the truth, self-evident as the principles of the Declaration themselves, that Blacks were members of the human race, Whites would have to concede their obligation to extend equal political rights. The rights of life, liberty, and the pursuit of happiness, and of government by consent, were not limited to the White race by the Declaration; the founders "were wise enough, and careful enough . . . to rise above their prejudices, and, as if guided by an inspiration scarcely less than divine, gave to their children . . . a Declaration of Independence . . . without the stain of such an iniquity, that know[s] no white man, no black man; but embrace[s] in [its] God-like fold 'ALL MEN.'"[13] The logic is straightforward. "Am I a man? If I am such, I claim the rights of a man."[14]

Denying Blacks' full humanity was a common White strategy for defending slavery in the South and disenfranchisement in the North. Conversely, the continued denial of political rights could only be read as an implicit or explicit rejection of the essential human equality of Blacks and Whites. Emancipation, therefore, was not enough. As Judith Shklar argued, the idea of natural rights meant that nothing less than full citizenship was required to remove the stigma of Blacks' former enslavement.[15] Without the franchise, Black North Carolinian John P. Sampson argued in 1865, "liberty is a mockery." Voting was a right, and "no class of men can, *without insulting their own nature*, be content with any deprivation of their rights."[16]

Natural right provided one ground of Blacks' entitlement to the vote, but failing that there was another ground in Blacks' contributions to the support of the American regime. "Representation and taxation should go hand in hand; and it is diametrically opposed to Republican institutions to tax us . . ., and at the same time deny us the right of representation."[17] This comment, made at a preparatory meeting for a statewide freedmen's convention in North Carolina in 1865, seems peculiar as an argument for the freedmen's vote. Having recently themselves been the property of White masters, most were very far indeed from owning any taxable property.[18] In fact, even for those Blacks who were free before the war in both North and South, many of whom were taxed, the emphasis on the familiar slogan seems somehow misplaced: of all the grounds for the franchise, the issue of taxation is hardly the most compelling in the case of Blacks. The claim to representation was stronger than the ground of taxation. Their frequent reference to the phrase[19] illustrates the degree to which they located themselves within the American tradition, but it also suggests a deeper sense of entitlement—that if anyone could be said to have made a great sacrifice for the nation, clearly it was Blacks. Implicit in the cry, "no taxation without representation," was the assertion that a great part of the nation's wealth had been built by Black labor.

The connection between the issue of taxation and the broader claim that Blacks had made important contributions to the nation becomes clearer when one recognizes the frequent juxtaposition of this theme and that of Black military service.[20] Even before emancipation, significant numbers of Blacks volunteered in the Union Army to fight, as they saw it, to end slavery. By the end of the war more than 180,000 Blacks had fought for the Union, and approximately 68,000 of them had made "the ultimate sacrifice."[21] A national convention of Black soldiers and sailors meeting in Philadelphia in early 1867, "representing that class of people who were known as 'Black face, a loyal heart,'" requested the franchise in order to "lift us from the lap of hate and scorn" and to "place us on the footing of full citizenship." The nation would be preserved through their dedication as citizens as it had been through their dedication as soldiers. "Give us the ballot," they promised, "and the country is safe."[22] Just as earlier spokesmen had expressed their demand for suffrage in these terms, Richard H. Cain, a Black member of the U.S. House of Representatives, used them in 1874 to defend a civil rights act: "Inasmuch as we have toiled with you in building up this nation; inasmuch as we have suffered side by side with you in the war; inasmuch as we have together passed through affliction and pestilence, let there now be a fulfillment of the sublime thought of our fathers—let all men enjoy equal liberty and equal rights."[23] Whatever the aspect of equal citizenship claimed—whether the ballot, more effective representation, civil rights, or the equal provision of education for Blacks and Whites—Blacks had more than earned it through their contributions to the nation, and through their past suffering.

If natural rights and Blacks' contributions to American society constituted the primary ground for the vote, it was the Declaration's theme of independence that described Blacks' ideal for their exercise of the franchise. Given the history of slavery, the centrality of the idea of independence in Black thought is understandable, for perhaps the gravest challenge freedmen faced was in coming to terms with their past enforced *dependence* on Whites. If ever they were to attain genuine citizenship, they had to emancipate themselves from this element of their past. As T. Thomas Fortune expressed it, "To preach the independence of the colored man is to preach his Americanization."[24]

Independence described both the *goal* of Blacks' political rights and the *manner* in which those rights would be used. In contrast to some suffragists, Blacks who sought political rights wanted more than the affirmation of their essential human worth. They wanted to enter the political sphere as full participants and to use their votes to advance their political interests, particularly in the spheres of education, civil rights, and land reform. But at the same time the freedmen made it clear that while they demanded citizenship, and particularly the franchise, they were not asking for anything more. Blacks did not want special treatment or protection, only simple justice, an equal participation in the normal process of politics. Granted this, they would have the means necessary to protect their own interests and would no longer have to depend on the federal government. "[T]he ballot is the freedman's Moses," one White Republican declared;[25] nothing further was required to deliver Blacks from the degradation of slavery. The same view was expressed by a freedmen's convention in Virginia: "Fellow citizens, . . . we ask for no expensive aid from military forces, stationed throughout the South, overbearing State action, and rendering our government republican only in name; give us the suffrage, and you may rely upon us to secure justice for ourselves, and all Union men, and to keep the State forever in the Union."[26]

In particular, Blacks envisioned the suffrage as integrally connected to *economic* independence; at the same time, the vote was an essential tool toward that goal and was justified by Blacks' capacity for economic self-sufficiency. Relations of economic dependency had long been used as a justification for property qualifications for the franchise, and although Americans had abandoned property qualifications during the Jacksonian period, Blacks' lack of economic self-sufficiency immediately after emancipation was often used as an argument against giving them the vote.[27] Consequently Black leaders addressed arguments to White audiences about the need for Blacks to vote in order to remove the obstacles to economic advancement; at the same time, they exhorted Blacks to work hard so as to bring about that advancement.[28] Whether through elementary education, learning skilled trades, or acquiring small freehold farms, the principal economic goal of Blacks was to attain a source of livelihood that was not contingent on White beneficence or even on wages paid by Whites. It is not surprising that the early (but never fulfilled) promise of "forty acres and a mule" excited so much enthusiasm among freedmen,[29] for it would have been sufficient to enable freedmen to support themselves. Moreover, it was not a "handout," since "the land ought to belong to the man who (alone) *could work it*," and Blacks had been the ones to work southern land for centuries.[30] Frederick Douglass had, as usual, the most eloquent words to describe Blacks' desire for economic independence:

> Understand this, that independence is an essential condition of respectability. To be dependent, is to be degraded . . . We do not mean that we can become entirely independent of all men; that would be absurd and impossible, in the social state. But we mean that we must become equally independent with other members of the community . . . The fact is, we must not merely make the white man dependent upon us to shave him but to feed him; not merely . . . to black his boots, but to make them.[31]

Equally essential to Blacks' dignity was their independence in political matters; they could no more afford to be dependent on the political judgment of others than they could afford to depend on Whites for employment. An editorial in a Black-owned newspaper advised, "Be not the slave of authority; if you think anything of yourself, think for yourself."[32] The years after emancipation brought not only the freedmen's conventions but a variety of other independent Black organizations—including the Equal Rights Leagues, Black churches, and Black newspapers—aimed at defining Blacks' social and political priorities for themselves. As Leonard Sweet argues persuasively, institutional separatism did not signify a Black rejection of American culture and values but was in fact a powerful affirmation of Blacks' desire for inclusion. Black solidarity in these organizations was but a means of arriving at a vision of their citizenship independent of White influence.[33]

Just as the suffragists' adoption of the themes of the Declaration led to an ideal of gender-blind equality, the predominant conception of political equality expressed in early Black rhetoric during Reconstruction was that of color blindness. The vision of the American polity that informed the tradition of Black protest before the Civil War attained its fullest expression during Reconstruction, and it was captured in a phrase that for newly emancipated slaves had a magnificent ring: equality before the law without distinction of race or color. In the language of the founding instruments of the many Equal Rights Leagues that sprang up after the war, in the wording of civil rights bills, and in Black conventions' addresses to White citizens, these words appear again and again. "We claim exactly *the same rights, privileges and immunities as are enjoyed by white men*--we ask nothing more and will be content with nothing less."[34] "The object of the Association shall be to secure for every citizen, without regard to race, descent, or color, equal political rights."[35] "Distinction on account of race or color shall be prohibited and all classes of citizens, irrespective of race or color, shall enjoy all common, equal and political privileges."[36]

The idea that the burden of race would be removed from Blacks upon their entry into the political sphere was almost as important as emancipation itself. Like the abolition of slavery, the promise of formal legal equality signified a new age in the life of Black Americans. A Black teacher in the South, Robert G. Fitzgerald, wrote in his diary: "I heard a white man say, . . . today is the black man's day; tomorrow will be the white man's. I thought, poor man, those days of distinction between colors is about over in this (now) free country."[37] Equality before the law meant the elimination of color from the language of politics altogether, the abandonment of the idea that one race was entitled to any advantages over the other. In a speech at the Arkansas constitutional convention in 1868, William H. Grey added a touch of humor to the issue: "I do not desire to discuss the question of inferiority of races. Unpleasant truths must then be told; history tells us of your white ancestors who lived on the acorns which dropped from the oaks of Dodona, and then worshiped the tree as a God. . . . Justice should be like the Egyptian statue, blind and recognizing no color."[38]

Blacks did not leave their aspirations for legal and political equality in abstract terms; they were quite specific about those fields in which racial distinctions were most objectionable. First and foremost was the vote, the most important instrument for realizing their other political goals. Serving on juries, as well as the right to be tried by juries that included other Black citizens, were also high on the list of priorities. Because of Blacks' potent sense of the importance of education for their equal status as members of American society, and for their political development, equal access to schools was another central demand. (Interestingly, even during Reconstruction there was a debate within Black communities about whether Blacks would benefit most from separate or integrated schools.) Another civil right frequently asserted was that of equal access to public conveyances, a claim that has perplexed some observers of the period because the freedmen often lacked the financial resources to make use of public transportation.[39] In light of the importance of mobility as an emblem of their freedom, however, this claim makes a great deal of sense.[40]

Early in Reconstruction, some Black leaders were hesitant to claim equal access to political office with the same force with which they claimed other political rights. A certain ambivalence characterized the issue: on the one hand, some were uncertain about the propriety of Blacks' promoting themselves for public office so soon after they had been invited into the political community; on the other hand, they were not willing to entertain the suggestion that they had no right to do so.[41] As experience showed that White Republicans did not necessarily believe that the Black franchise entailed a right to hold office, however, Blacks became increasingly adamant that an equal opportunity to make the law, and to enforce it, was an essential element of equality *before* the law. At a Black political meeting in Savannah, James Sims stated the goal lucidly:

> Offices should be filled by both white and colored men who are capable of serving with honor. I would have white and colored aldermen and white and colored police men and the sooner people know it the better. Some people might be surprised to see white and colored men working shoulder to shoulder in the political field—I am not. I have children at school in Massachusetts and expect to see them in Congress some day.[42]

This ideal—that both the law and the actual institutions built on it should be blind to color—was also expressed as the principle of equal opportunity so familiar to us today. Blacks wished to make it clear that in pressing their demand for legal equality they were not asking for special privileges. Had the language of "reverse discrimination" emerged at that time, most Blacks would almost certainly have used it as the epitome of what they were *not* advocating. Instead, showing that they were well within the American tradition, Blacks adamantly rejected the notions of class legislation and privilege based on birth.[43] All they were asking, they said repeatedly, was an equal chance, a removal of the positive impediments that stood in the way of their political and social advancement. "What shall we do with the Negro?" Frederick Douglass, the premier defender of equal opportunity, had a simple answer: "Do nothing with us! . . . [I]f the Negro cannot stand on his own legs, let him fall . . . All I ask is, give him a chance to stand on his own legs! . . . If you see him on his way to school, let him alone, don't disturb him! . . . If you see him going to the ballot-box, let him alone, don't disturb him!"[44]

The fulfillment of the doctrine of color blindness would mean that political conflict would no longer be defined along the lines of race. More fundamentally, it would mean recognizing that there was no essential opposition of Black and White interests. "I regard the interests of the black man in this country as identical with the interests of the white man," Richard H. Cain stated in 1874.[45] Of course this does not suppose that political conflict would be eliminated altogether. Rather, Blacks would have the same diversity of interests as Whites, and their political action in the advancement of those interests would no longer be determined by their race.[46] The 1867 State Convention of the Colored Men of Alabama optimistically predicted its own extinction: "Hereafter, there will be no colored conventions in Alabama. Color will be regarded as an unnecessary prefix when bodies having political objects in view, or any other public bodies are to be designated."[47]

In the arena of partisan politics, the elimination of the "color line" would translate into a broader range of political options from which Blacks could choose. "[E]very American citizen should be safe and secure in the enjoyment of life, liberty, and property, it matters not what political party may be in control of the government," former congressman John R. Lynch argued. "This result will be an accomplished fact when the so-called race question is no longer in politics—when colored Americans, like other Americans, can affiliate with any party they want to without jeopardizing their civil and political rights."[48] Once genuine political equality was realized, Blacks simultaneously hoped and warned, Whites would no longer be able to assume their allegiance to the Republicans. One Black leader even stated explicitly what amounted to political heresy at the time—that Blacks might someday vote for the Democratic Party.[49]

As noted above, the principle of color-blind equality required that Blacks should have an equal opportunity to hold political office. Blacks assumed that in the normal course of events, and especially as the political education of Black citizens progressed, they would hold legislative seats. "Whilst we are not disposed to claim for ourselves more than we deserve, we cannot accept less without protest."[50] Indeed, to assume that Blacks would *not* hold office would be to admit either that the distribution of political talent was not equal across the races or that slavery had so sapped the race's political ability that they would have to content themselves with White leadership for the foreseeable future. Few Blacks were willing to allow either conclusion, although there were disputes over the degree to which Blacks could hope to hold office in proportion to their numbers in the electorate.[51]

What was clear, however, was that a racially neutral system of representation would *not* mean that Blacks could only be represented by members of their own race. For that matter, given the essential harmony of Black and White interests, there was no need to assume that Whites had to be represented by Whites. Robert Brown Elliott, a Black member of Congress from South Carolina, spoke pointedly against the disfranchisement of Confederate Whites, making clear that he felt a duty to protect the interests of both Whites and Blacks: "Sir, I speak not to-day in behalf of the colored loyalists of the South alone. I wish it to be distinctly understood that I represent here a constituency composed of men whose complexions are like those of gentlemen around me as well as men whose complexions are similar to my own."[52]

In the color-blind ideal of political representation, Blacks and Whites would vote for members of both races. Their votes would not be determined by candidates' positions on civil rights or racial equality, because these questions would be regarded as permanently settled. As Black editor T. Thomas Fortune expressed it after the failure of Reconstruction, "A government like ours is like unto a household. Difference of opinion on non-essentials is wholesome and natural, but upon the fundamental idea incorporated in the Declaration of Independence and re-affirmed in the Federal Constitution the utmost unanimity should prevail."[53] Blacks would engage in those healthy disagreements in the same degree as Whites and ultimately would reflect the same range of opinion as Whites on every political issue. Like Whites, they would have varying conceptions of the common good as well as differing economic interests, and these would form the foundation for their political choices in the electoral sphere. The representative's role would not be determined by race any more than the views of the electorate were determined by race; he or she[54] would act in legislative deliberations according to his or her view of the public interest or of the constituency's best interests.

In addition to its expression of faith in the sufficiency of a color-blind politics to protect Blacks' essential interests, Black Reconstruction rhetoric also reflected the two-sidedness of the trust of free government by offering evidence that the public interest would never be harmed through the exercise of Black political rights. This is among the messages conveyed in the above-mentioned statements that there was no difference between Black and White interests in politics. Blacks' worthiness of full political rights also stood behind the arguments for equal opportunity: given the chance, Blacks would prove themselves the equals of Whites and show that they deserved respect as well as rights.

> Our purpose is to remain in your midst an integral part of the body-politic. We are training our children to take our places when we are gone . . ., that they may thus be qualified to be useful citizens in their day and time . . . Deprive us of no rights belonging to us as citizens; give us an equal opportunity in life, then if we fail we will be content if driven to the wall.[55]

The sense that Blacks needed to prove their capacities and their respectability in order to be granted equal political rights caused Black leaders to point to Blacks' responsible exercise of political power wherever they had it. Theories about the degrading effect of slavery notwithstanding, Blacks *were* fit to participate in self-government. Many leaders emphasized the remarkable self-restraint with which Blacks greeted emancipation and the political rights extended to them. Alonzo Jacob Ransier, a Black member of the U.S. House of Representatives during Radical Reconstruction, observed that despite the "startling political fact" that four million Blacks were transformed into citizens in such a short period of time, this occurred peacefully.[56] In those states where free Blacks had had the franchise, leaders argued, they exercised it responsibly. Even more, Black leader William H. Grey asserted at a Black convention in Arkansas in 1865, "[w]e . . . have the satisfaction of knowing that, on several important elections, the Negro, standing firm to principle, has saved the people." He cited the example of New York, where "the Negro vote . . . saved the State to the Union party."[57]

One of the White Republican arguments against enfranchisement was that Blacks, out of loyalty to their former masters, would vote as they were told and consequently would undermine Republican strength in the South. Some Black communities answered this concern by organizing mock elections, complete with ward meetings, registration drives, and polling places, to coincide with regularly scheduled elections.[58] Even some southern Black city dwellers shared White Republican concern about the political judgment of rural "black belt" freedmen, whose access to political education was more limited than urban Blacks'. In Georgia, one such individual voiced his concern about the likely influence of "Mass William" and "Mass John" and proposed that the vote be withheld from rural freedmen for five years. He was quickly reassured by an older ex-slave about Blacks' determination to educate themselves regarding the use of their vote: "Every creature has got an instinct—the calf goes to the cow to suck, the bee to the hive. We's a poor humble degraded people but we know our friends. We'd walk fifteen miles in wartime to find out about the battle. We can walk fifteen miles and more to find out how to vote."[59]

Another strategy for demonstrating that Blacks ought to be entrusted with the vote was similar to one adopted by suffragists: both groups compared themselves favorably with those who already had the franchise.[60] Women, who were left out of the Fifteenth Amendment's expansion of the franchise, turned their ire on "ignorant ex-slaves." But Blacks themselves were not exempt from this temptation, and they indulged it surprisingly openly. Even prominent leaders such as Frederick Douglass engaged in verbal assaults on their enfranchised moral inferiors:

> [A] day's experience at the polls convinced me that the "body politic" is not more immaculate than many other bodies . . . I saw ignorance enter, unable to read the vote it cast . . . I saw Pat, fresh from the Emerald Isle, requiring two sober men to keep him on his legs, enter and deposit his vote for the Democratic candidate amid the loud hurrahs of his fellow-citizens.[61]

The leaders themselves constituted further evidence of the capacities of the Black race. Frequently Black leaders were spoken of as "representatives" of their race not because of any political activity on their part, but because their accomplishments were emblematic of Blacks' essential equality. In other words, they were *symbolically* representative of Black potential. An article in Frederick Douglass's *New National Era* commented on Hiram Revels's performance in the U.S. Senate from this point of view—albeit with only a lukewarm enthusiasm for what he had accomplished for Blacks. "Considering his brief stay and training he did well," the article conceded, although "[w]e could have wished for more activity in a virgin field for Negro talent." Still, "[t]he precedent itself was something. A Negro was occupying a seat in the United States Senate . . . as a representative figure of Negro interest, hope and possibility."[62]

III. The Sense of Betrayal and the Turn to Self-Representation

Ironically the doctrine of equality that Blacks believed in—and particularly the principle of formal political equality—was used by White Republicans to justify their abandonment of Reconstruction's protections for Black political rights. Congressman James A. Garfield, for example, declared that "[t]he Fifteenth Amendment . . . confers upon the African race the care of its own destiny. It places their fortunes in their own hands." The comments in an Illinois editorial reveal how short the step is from formal equality to the assumption that equal opportunity has been protected: "The negro is now a voter and a citizen . . . Let him hereafter take his chances in the battle of life."[63]

Once the idea of equal opportunity was widespread, and Whites could claim they had provided it by extending the franchise to Blacks, the door was open to the total abandonment of Blacks in their effort to develop their capacities as citizens and free members of society. It did not take long for this to occur: by 1871 many southern states had erected new barriers to Blacks' exercise of the franchise: poll taxes, residency requirements, literacy requirements, and registration procedures. Meanwhile the Ku Klux Klan launched a campaign of violence against any Black who attempted to vote Republican and against Whites who defended Blacks' right to vote, a strategy that was very effective in eliminating Republican control of southern legislatures. Although the federal government did implement congressional legislation against Ku Klux Klan violence, a second rash of electoral violence broke out between 1874 and 1876.[64] This time Congress failed to enact the Enforcement Act of 1875. Again, the decision not to enforce Black rights was justified in the language of laissez faire, so harmonious with the themes of equal opportunity: Blacks should free themselves of "the habit . . . [of relying] upon external aid."[65] As Reconstruction was about to collapse, Frederick Douglass expressed Blacks' sense of abandonment both poignantly and angrily: "When you turned us loose, you turned us loose to the sky, to the storm, to the whirlwind, and, worst of all, . . . to the wrath of our infuriated masters. The question now is, do you mean to make good to us the promises in your constitution?"[66]

The language of trust pervades the Black leadership's response to the Republican failure to enact the Civil Rights Bill and the Enforcement Act of 1875. While there was still some hope of their passage, one editorial stated, "We but call upon the Republican party to be *honest and faithful to its trust*, nothing else."[67] Some expressed anger that the Civil Rights Bill was "strangled by its pretended friends" even after Blacks had been "*true and faithful*" to the GOP.[68]

In the face of the Republican failure to protect Black interests, Blacks were especially resentful of the Republican leadership's expectation of their continued support. White Republicans frequently argued that Blacks should stand aside and let Whites run for public office in order to avoid alienating southern White voters. In 1871 Matthew Gaines, a former Black senator in the Texas state legislature, changed his attitude toward the Republican Party when its leadership abandoned him to back a conservative White for a seat in Congress. The candidate, Gaines said, was "no friend of blacks." Further, Gaines expressed his "special dislike for white Republicans 'who hardly spoke and won't shake hands. But just before election they will knock at your door.'"[69] Another newspaper editorial, written when the expiration of the Civil Rights Bill was imminent, expressed a similar resentment:

> The very men whom we had every reason to believe would aid in having this barbarous restriction removed . . . have boldly stood up in the halls of Congress and voted to have the abuse continued; and notwithstanding this fact, our suffrages are today being canvassed for the purpose of sending them back that they may be in place to practice the same outrage upon us in the next Congress.[70]

Increasingly the conclusion Black leaders drew from these trends was that they could not, after all, depend on Whites to represent them fairly.[71] Frederick Douglass, who has often been characterized as taking an accommodating attitude toward Whites, was suspicious of White Republican claims that the electoral strength of the party would be injured if Blacks insisted on promoting themselves for public office. Through this kind of intimidation, Douglass wrote, White Republicans "have in many instances prevented the representation of colored men in the Legislature, as that white Republican who would refuse to vote for a colored Republican, has that in him which prevents him from being able to represent fairly his black brother."[72] Before long he was sending an even stronger message:

> We hope that the colored people of the South will bear in mind that of the white members of Congress . . ., but a *very few* have opened their mouths in favor of the protection of the rights of their colored constituents on railroads, steamboats, in schools, hotels, and places of public amusement. . . . Colored voters of the South, you must not forget those who forget . . . your rights. You must teach them that they are mistaken in considering you mere voting machines, ready . . . to vote for any man calling himself a Republican.[73]

The move from betrayal to distrust had its next logical step in Blacks' arguments for greater political self-reliance, and in particular for Black self-representation. Occasionally Blacks had made claims for self-representation in the early years of Reconstruction, usually on grounds similar to those expressed in the voice argument for woman suffrage. Those arguments expounded the idea that Whites simply were unable to understand Black concerns and interests: it took the actual experience of oppression to be able to comprehend and express the needs of the Black community. Blacks had labored under "disadvantages which the white man is absolutely incapable of appreciating."[74] Objecting to the notion that "blacks still needed whites to act and think for them," a participant at one Black meeting in Alabama declared, "There is none but colored men that can truly sympathize with their race!"[75] And even if Whites did not need to sympathize with Blacks in order to represent their interests, they would still need to know what those interests were. Certainly they were not better situated to understand Black interests than were Blacks themselves. "Who can better know our interest than we do? Who is more competent to discern what is good for us than we are?" "There is no man in the world so perfectly identified with our own interest as to understand it better than we do ourselves."[76] Moreover, Blacks' capacity to articulate their political interests was no obstacle, as "[t]here is an eloquence in experience which can never be had elsewhere."[77]

Although these epistemological arguments are relevant to the nature of the trust that can exist between a Black constituency and a White representative, as discussed below,[78] they do not reflect the doubt and distrust of Whites that are expressed in later Reconstruction arguments for Black self-representation. In the latter arguments, quite apart from the question of whether Whites were cognitively well equipped to represent Blacks (the question that forms the central theme in woman suffrage arguments), it was clear that because they stopped short of addressing the fact of social prejudice, Whites *did not* represent Black interests. In reaction, "[m]any colored men are asking whether it is necessary for the colored voters of the country to form a new political alliance. The tardiness of the Republican party to accord full rights to colored citizens ... tends to strengthen the feeling that leads thinking colored men to cast about for better guarantees for their race."[79] In a protest against White Republican attempts to control the ticket in Louisiana, an editorial argued that Blacks should choose their own representatives. Even if White Republicans chose Black representatives, "the latter, if so selected [will not] express the sentiments of their race."[80] A San Francisco paper urged solidarity among the Black community there to "go for those who go for us."[81] Some arguments for Black self-representation were even less ambiguous:

> [W]e conscientiously believe[] the colored voters in this State are entitled to *personal—race*—representation in the National Legislature. That is, of the seven Congressmen sent by Louisiana to represent her people in the council of the country, the colored men, who compose by far the large majority of the voters in the Republican party, are entitled, by every honest consideration, to that choice as they themselves, unbiased, uninfluenced, and fairly dealt with, would unhesitatingly and overwhelmingly make. There is no question that, had such a latitude been allowed our people, the complexion of the Congressional delegation would have been different from what it is.[82]

When White Republicans criticized these views on the ground that Blacks were drawing a "color line" in politics, "black leaders responded that race, historically the 'cause of exclusion,' must now become a 'ground of recognition until the scales are once more balanced.'"[83]

Arguments that Blacks should take care not to vote for Republicans who fail to look after their interests seem initially to resonate with the individualistic theme of political independence discussed above. But whereas the earlier assertions of independence were made against Blacks' enforced dependency under slavery, and against a dependency on Whites in general, the later arguments are assertions of the need to resist an unreasonable loyalty to the Republican Party. In other words, while the emphasis on independence in the early rhetoric focuses on the connection between independence and human dignity, the theme of independence that emerges in the waning years of Reconstruction is of the sort Hobbes mentioned: when we can no longer trust others to provide us with a benefit, it is only rational to provide it for ourselves, in a manner independent of their agency.

IV. Trust and the American Scheme of Liberal Representation

Within the American scheme of representation, the emphasis on trust may appear misplaced: the entire American constitutional framework is constructed on the premise that trust and the virtue which justifies it are usually at a premium in human society and ought not to be relied on in the search for stable and legitimate government. Actually, even Locke agreed on the importance of economizing trust in the design of political institutions, but it was Madison who thought that institutions could be designed so as to substitute governors' interest for their virtue and yet maintain institutions that would advance the public good.[84] In the Madisonian scheme, trust as a *cognitive* state, as a well-founded belief that political institutions will not abuse the public interest, supplanted the Lockean idea of trust as a moral relationship.

In this section I discuss the central features of Madison's substitution, examine the reasons why his arrangements were insufficient to warrant freedmen's trust in their representatives, and attempt to show what this failure reveals about the legislator-constituency relationship in a theory of representation concerned with the political equality of historically oppressed groups.

Madison's approach to constitutional design consists in separating the legitimacy of representative government from the virtue of the governors, the rationality of trusting a *system* of government from the rationality of trust in its particular agents. As in every other aspect of his constitutional thought, Madison's principal concern in designing the institutions and relationships of political representation is to compensate for the fact that "[e]nlightened statesmen will not always be at the helm."[85] Madison does include in his definition of the "competent legislator" the moral virtue of "upright intention" as well as the intellectual virtues of "sound judgment" and "a certain degree of knowledge."[86] However, he clearly does not expect that all members will live up to these standards. Why, then, should the people entrust their interests to a body comprised of men who are likely to be less than fully competent? First, the harm that can be done by the House is limited by the powers of both the Senate and other branches of government. "With less power, therefore, to abuse, the federal representatives can be less tempted on one side, and will be doubly watched on the other."[87]

But in addition to this general argument regarding the protections against abuses of the public good by the House as a body, Madison offers a number of reasons why the individual representatives, even in the absence of an "upright intention" to pursue the common good, will be constrained to act in accordance with that good: "If we consider the situation of the men on whom the free suffrages of their fellow-citizens may confer the representative trust, we shall find it involving every security which can be devised or desired for their fidelity to their constituents."[88] Bowing toward the judgment of the citizenry, Madison begins by saying that their evaluation of candidates as worthy of election is likely to have some basis in the candidates' actual character. Further, having been given the compliment of election, representatives' natural gratitude will tend to incline them benevolently toward their constituents' welfare. But we need not rely on these benign motivations, particularly given that the person who seeks office has already demonstrated a personal desire for the "honors and distinctions" popular government affords. For such ambitious characters, the satisfaction of their "pride and vanity" is secure only to the extent that they "preserv[e] the favor" rather than "subver[t] the authority" of the people. Thus the kind of person who is likely to seek office in the first place is also likely to seek reelection, and the frequent election of House members means that "they will be compelled to anticipate the moment when their power is to cease" and push them to take actions that will lead the people to a renewal of their "trust."[89]

Perhaps the most important reason why representatives will be constrained to legislate in the public interest is that "*they can make no law which will not have its full operation on themselves and their friends,* as well as on the great mass of the society."[90] Madison notes that the principle that the legislative branch should be subject to its own laws "has always been deemed one of the strongest bonds by which human policy can connect the rulers and the people together."[91] Finally, Madison argues, the House will not escape the effects of their own laws through class legislation that favors them or any other social class, as it will be prevented by the constitutional system of checks and balances and by natural principles of constitutional and just law, but, "above all," by the spirit of liberty that "actuates the people of America."[92] Again, as in Locke's framework, the final guarantee that government will be faithful lies in the hands of the people themselves, their unwillingness to tolerate any laws incompatible with liberty.[93]

Thus, in Madison's theory, two pillars substitute for a moral relationship of trust between legislator and constituent: the system of electoral accountability and the fact that legislators and their class allies are themselves subject to the laws they make. Why did both these protections fail Blacks during Reconstruction?

Electoral accountability is taken as a substitute for a relation of trust between legislator and constituent for two reasons. First, the representative is presumed to desire reelection so that he or she will act in the interests of constituents in order to gain it. This creates reasonable grounds for the constituents to have confidence that the *individual representative* will promote their well-being. Second, if the representative fails to protect constituent interests, there is a sufficient choice among alternative candidates to allow constituents to elect one who will likely do a better job. Consequently, even if constituents' confidence in their representative is disappointed, they still have grounds for faith in the electoral *system* taken as a whole. Indeed, as I suggested in the discussion of trust in chapter 1, these two aspects of the institutionalization of trust are mutually reinforcing: if individual representatives are likely to act in constituents' interests, there is reason to believe that the system as a whole will advance a common interest or public good;[94] moreover, if the electoral system generates, as it is expected to, a healthy political competition, then this will motivate representatives to act in their constituents' interest or face removal from office.[95] For Blacks during Reconstruction, a crucial ingredient of electoral accountability was missing, since the electoral system's competitiveness was far from healthy. Blacks who were dissatisfied with the performance of their representatives could not count on the availability of alternative candidates who would do a better job of looking after their interests. Clearly, given southern Democrats' commitment to White supremacy, any Democratic candidate was worse than even the least conscientious Republican candidate. In effect, Blacks had no rational choice but to vote Republican, and this reality was not lost on the Republican leadership. Indeed, it was the unavailability of any reasonable alternative that made the Republican betrayal of Blacks as painful as it was, since it created the feeling that Blacks were once again dependent on the good will and beneficence of Whites. Blacks' only alternative was to form a third party, an option some considered but most rejected as infeasible. The lack of any reasonable alternative to the Republican Party also contributed to Blacks' lack of control over the selection of Republican candidates for office: once the disqualifications for Confederate voters were removed, White Republicans insisted on running candidates who would attract White votes needed to maintain a strong Republican presence in southern legislatures and congressional delegations. Usually, such candidates were neither Black nor aggressive in promoting Blacks' civil rights. The cumulative effect of these factors meant that White Republicans could be assured of Black votes regardless of their activism on Black political rights. Acting in the interest of the Blacks they represented, and in a manner responsive to them, was not a necessary concomitant of being elected by them so long as the available alternatives were worse.[96]

Given this scenario, it is not surprising that the second pillar of the Madisonian scheme, that the representative is subject to the laws he or she participates in making, was not an effective safeguard for Blacks represented by White Republicans. This second protection assumes a broad similarity between the representative's interests and those of the people. But whereas Blacks' interest in the protection of their civil and political rights was as profound as an interest can be, White Republicans' interest in Black rights was limited to their implications for Blacks' electoral support of the party in the South. Certainly White Republicans' own rights did not depend on the passage of legislation such as Sumner's Civil Rights Bill and the Enforcement Act of 1875; there was a radical discontinuity of interest between Blacks and Whites on this score. In the absence of a community of interest between representative and represented, a representative from a privileged group will not be affected by legislation in the same way as members of a disadvantaged group. In some ways, this reflects the argument made in the preceding chapter on the theme of "voice," which made the case that a representative who lacks the experience of the effect of the laws on a particular group thereby lacks the knowledge necessary to legislate in the interests of that group. But as the case of Reconstruction makes clear, the problem of trust need not rest on such subtle grounds: White Republicans did not need the experience of a lynching to know that their Black constituents had an interest in being protected from violence.

In a way, this flaw in the substitution of interest for trust is indirectly acknowledged by both Madison and his twentieth-century counterparts, particularly Robert Dahl. For Madison, the ultimate security against Congress's enactment of class legislation rests with "the people," whose love of liberty will not allow them to tolerate class legislation. But Madison's faith in the people depends on his ability to speak of them univocally, as "*the* people," undivided by any single interest that will lead a majority to favor legislation which would advance their class interests. As I noted in chapter 2, Dahl acknowledges that the system of interest representation works in accordance with political equality only where there are no deep social cleavages that define permanent minorities. Translated into Lockean terms, the substitution of interest for a moral relationship of trust between rulers and ruled, between representative and constituent, is adequate *only when we presuppose a relation of trust among the people themselves*, a social contract completed by the mutual recognition of the equal membership of all its members. Despite the supposition within Madisonian and pluralist theory that society is prior to the Constitution, both fail to take into account the deep divisions within society itself. For Madison, the failure consisted in not recognizing the cleavage between North and South; for Dahl and other pluralists, the failure was not considering the consequences for political representation of the division between Blacks and Whites and, to a lesser degree, between men and women and between Whites and other racial minorities. Americans in the founding period prided themselves on having had, in contrast to the British, "an opportunity of forming a compact *betwixt themselves*; from which alone, their rulers derive all their authority to govern."[97] But Americans generally have not attended to the partiality of that compact, the fact that it did not bridge some deep divisions in American society and that it left some groups out altogether.

What this shows is that the sufficiency of constitutional arrangements depends on the social conditions that lie behind them and that it is difficult, if not impossible, to define constitutional schemes that replace social relations of trust.[98] On the other hand, again using Locke as our guide, the requirements for social trust, while demanding, do not insist on a thorough-going mutual respect. In Locke's social compact, clearly individuals will not regard one another as moral equals. Some will be more industrious and rational than others and, accordingly, will have accumulated a greater store of property; they will rightly regard themselves as superior in some sense. But there is one dimension of equality that is essential: all must acknowledge that others have rights which they are morally bound to respect, even in the face of disagreement over where the boundaries between individuals' rights fall. Without this, there is nothing to prevent citizens from willfully invading the rights of others so long as the opportunity exists to do so with impunity. For those who do not recognize others' claim to rights as legitimate, participation in political society involves no relinquishment of the prerogative to act on the basis of interest rather than obligation. For those whose rights are not respected by others, the ability to trust in government is limited to government's ability and willingness to enforce their rights *against* those others. In the absence of such a government, however, these people do not have recourse to the action on which both Locke and Madison relied: they cannot join with the rest of "the people" because they are not acknowledged by the rest as part of the people.

From this standpoint, it is abundantly clear that Blacks' inclusion in the American body politic was profoundly flawed in precisely these terms. Less than six years before emancipation, the Supreme Court had declared that Blacks as such had no "political rights which the dominant race might not withhold or grant at their pleasure."[99] Only four years before emancipation, Stephen Douglas won his senatorial race against Lincoln largely on the platform of that decision, on the assertion that "this Government was made on the white basis[,] . . . for the benefit of white men and their posterity for ever, and I am in favor of confining citizenship to white men . . . instead of conferring it upon negroes, Indians, and other inferior races."[100] In an environment where a great many, perhaps even a majority, of Whites shared sentiments similar to those of Justice Taney and Stephen Douglas, the extension of citizenship to Blacks was bound to be incomplete. At a minimum, it is inconceivable that full citizenship would be effective without a simultaneous and concerted effort on the part of the Republican Party and the federal government to begin remaking the social relations between the races. Radical Reconstruction began making progress in this direction, particularly insofar as it moved toward an improvement in Blacks' social position, for example, through some of the land reform measures pursued by the federal government and by Black-controlled legislatures. But sustaining progress of this type required a leadership and resolve greater than Republicans were prepared to offer.

Given a deeply divided society, how could the self-representation to which Blacks began to turn at the end of Reconstruction possibly restore Blacks' reasons for political trust? On the level of the relationship between legislator and constituent, the answer is clear: at least when it comes to the interests that divided Blacks from Whites, Black voters could depend on Black representatives to act in accordance with their well-being, for the representatives' own essential interests were equally at stake. In fact, Thomas Holt's study of the behavior of the Black leadership in the South Carolina legislature during Reconstruction reveals that although they were divided along class lines on some issues of social policy, they acted in solidarity on questions of civil and political rights.[101]

More recently, both scholarly and journalistic evidence shows that Black representatives demonstrate a strong tendency to support the policy issues that most concern Black voters, particularly issues of social policy.[102] Notwithstanding Carol Swain's argument that White representatives can represent Black interests (which I do not deny), her empirical evidence establishes clearly that African American representatives reliably rank high on indexes of support for both civil rights and welfare policy. Black representatives ranked higher on these indexes than did White representatives, even when White representatives were elected from districts with a majority or a large minority of Black voters, and even when the Black representatives were elected from majority-White districts.[103] In the first session of the 103rd Congress, African American members voted as a bloc on key votes. The evidence on the level of local decision-making bodies is similar. On Chicago's city council, African American and Latino aldermen were "nearly three times more supportive of minority and poor interests than their white counterparts."[104] While there is diversity within the ranks of Black legislators, there is a strong empirical basis for the claim that they are, on average, more reliable advocates for the interests of African Americans than are White representatives.[105]

The claim that the self-representation of marginalized groups justifies group members' trust in their representatives finds further support in the research on women legislators. Sue Thomas's important study includes the finding that whereas only 33 percent of male state legislators think that representing women is very important, 57 percent of women legislators think so.[106] Women legislators expressed a special pride in their accomplishments on issues concerning women and children much more frequently than did male legislators.[107] Although women's legislative interests extend across the whole range of policy areas, there is a clear gender gap in legislative priorities. In particular, women's legislative priorities more frequently focus on issues concerning women and children than do men's.[108] Women legislators, on average, do have policy priorities different from men's and act as aggressive advocates for them.[109] Indeed, these recent studies show that as women's legislative presence increases, so does the level of energy they invest in women's issues.[110]

Claims that members of marginalized groups are better representatives for those groups than are nonmembers, however, must address a number of objections. First, partisan differences clearly exist among women, legislators, and voters alike, just as differences exist among African Americans and Latinos (as well as any other group one might name). Some women are pro-choice; others are antiabortion. Moreover, the mere fact that there is a patterned difference between the legislative priorities of Black and White legislators, or of male and female legislators, does not by itself demonstrate that the marginalized group representatives do a better job of representing their groups' interests and concerns than do representatives from privileged groups. In other words, it may be that these legislators constitute a political elite whose priorities do not accurately reflect the priorities of their constituents; it is possible, for example, that female legislators are simply more liberal than women in general.[111] To be more certain of the relationship between the legislative presence of marginalized groups and the legislative protection of their interests (or, as some express it, between descriptive representation and substantive representation), we require further empirical comparisons of the political attitudes of marginalized groups within the electorate and those of the groups' political elites. But the fact of differences within marginalized groups, by itself, would seem to undercut claims for their legislative presence. Given such differences, what remains of the "group" that can be represented?

The diversity of issue positions within social groups has led Iris Young to distinguish what she calls "social perspective" from both "interests" and "opinions." Although members of marginalized groups may define their interests differently and may hold a variety of opinions on social and political issues, Young argues, they nonetheless share a perspective on social and political life because they are similarly situated in relation to other groups.[112] I find this argument helpful and generally persuasive. It helps to explain the fact that, despite partisan differences among women legislators, they nonetheless share similar legislative priorities. The content of their positions on welfare policy, women's issues, or children's issues may be different, but women of both parties give a higher priority to these issues than do their male colleagues. Similarly, notwithstanding differences of race and class, survey research shows that the gender gap on policy issues in the general population parallels the differences between men's and women's priorities within legislatures. In 1992, for example, women's top three policy priorities were health care, flextime, and equal pay for equal work, precisely the sorts of policies for which women legislators tend to be more aggressive advocates than men.[113]

My only disagreement with Young here concerns the suggestion that "perspectives" and "interests" can be neatly separated. My understanding of the relationship between perspectives and interests is rather that a group's shared perspective helps to define the boundaries within which different interpretations of interest are possible. It is not enough to say that women share a social perspective that leads them to regard policies affecting women and children as especially important. More than this, women whose positions on those policies differ would nonetheless be likely to agree that the interests of women are insufficiently attended to if those policies are left off the legislative agenda. The historic neglect of the perspectives of marginalized groups has resulted in a narrowing of the range of policy alternatives that legislatures consider in addition to shaping the content of legislation in a manner that overlooks or actively harms marginalized group interests. That members of those groups may interpret their interests differently does not mean there are no identifiable group interests at all, as I suspect Young would agree.

These studies and arguments help to support the claim that, *on average*, representatives from marginalized groups are more reliable advocates for those groups than are representatives from privileged groups. Thus even if we follow Madison and seek to economize trust, self-representation for marginalized groups helps to restore the relation of rational trust between legislator and constituent that has been damaged by the history of inequality. In part, the restoration of trust through marginalized group representation arises from the simple claim that these groups will have a greater number of advocates in the legislature, and so a better chance of affecting the legislative agenda. Jane Mansbridge has made the additional (and very important) argument that strengthening the trust of marginalized groups in their representatives improves the quality of representation by facilitating communication between legislators and constituents. Because of the distrust that follows naturally from the history of oppression, citizens from marginalized groups are likely to be wary of representatives who are not group members, even when those representatives are in fact sympathetic to the group's interests. As a consequence of the group members' wariness, they are less likely to contact representatives from privileged groups in the first place. Thus African American citizens are less likely to contact their district's representative if the individual is White than if he or she is Black.[114] Even when contact does occur, communication may be distorted by the lack of trust between representative and constituents. Mansbridge relates the story of the relationship between women activists for the Equal Rights Amendment (ERA) and Senator Birch Bayh, who acted as their mentor and advocate. But when Bayh proposed a change of wording to the amendment, arguing that it would then be more likely to be passed, the ERA activists suspected him of trying to diminish its force. Their suspicions arose in part from his assignment of an insensitive staffer to the issue, one who had labeled ERA supporters as "hysterical." Had the relationship between the senator and the activists been characterized by a greater degree of mutual trust, which Mansbridge argues it almost certainly would have been if Bayh had been a progressive female legislator (who would be unlikely to appoint an insensitive staffer to such an important issue), women would now be protected by an ERA. "[T]he deeper the communicative chasm between a dominant and a subordinate group," Mansbridge concludes, "the more descriptive representation is needed . . . to bridge that chasm."[115] This suggests that the self-representation of marginalized groups may generate a spiral of trust: as more representatives are elected who share a group's identity and whom group members feel they can trust, communication between the group and elected officials will improve, which will produce a more effective advocacy for group interests by sympathetic representatives, which will improve the chances for passage of legislation that protects group interests, which will itself generate greater system-level trust in government on the part of marginalized groups.

For a minority group, however, the relationship of trust between citizens and government is not so easily restored by self-representation, at least in a system where majority rule determines the outcome of votes in the legislative assembly. The attempt to promote a minority group's political equality through increasing its representation in a legislative body collapses at the moment the vote is taken, at least where deep conflicts of interest divide the majority from the minority. Nonetheless, most theorists of legislative decision making assume that representatives of different interests will have some effect on one another's thinking, and if that assumption is correct there is reason to believe that the self-representation of a marginalized group will have some effect on legislative outcomes.[116] As we saw in chapter 4, there is some empirical basis for believing that the introduction of larger numbers of women and minority members into legislative bodies will enhance the deliberative features of legislative decision making; it is also possible to redesign institutions so as to create incentives for deliberation and increase the clout of minority legislators.[117] For marginalized groups' trust in their representatives to translate into a broader trust in government, changes along these lines must occur.

As I have noted elsewhere, that a particular representative comes from a marginalized group is clearly no guarantee that he or she will advocate for the group's interests as most of its members understand them. Trust in a representative is not justified by his or her mere similarity to oneself. In addition, there must be mechanisms of accountability to bind the representative to constituents' interests, as I discuss in greater depth in chapter 7. The relationship of trust between citizens from marginalized groups and representatives who are also group members is not automatic; it is secured particularly through representatives' electoral accountability to a constituency defined around marginalized group identity. For these reasons, majority-minority districts are among the best means for enhancing the trust in government of disadvantaged minorities within a single-member district system of elections. The account offered here explains why members of marginalized groups are *justified* in believing that members of their own groups, on average, are likely to be more trustworthy representatives than are nonmembers. Not only are group members more likely to understand group members' interests, as in the voice argument, but because they are group members the legislation they help to frame and pass will likely affect them just as it affects their constituents. As in the Madisonian model, marginalized group representatives' own interests as citizens bind them to the interests of their constituents. The same is not necessarily true for representatives from privileged groups. Thus self-representation for marginalized groups does not supplant the Madisonian foundation of trust, as naive accounts of descriptive representation presume, but rather supplements it.

The failure of trust between marginalized and privileged groups operates at several levels. At the level of legislator-constituent relations, it takes the form of group members' inability to trust their representatives to advocate for their interests. At the level of the political system, it consists in marginalized citizens' inability to trust that their government will enact and pursue policies that give at least some weight to their interests. At the level of society, it consists in a general distrust between individuals who belong to marginalized groups and those who are relatively privileged. The capacity for the self-representation of marginalized groups to repair these failures of trust diminishes as we move from the first level to the third. Because of the commonality of interest and perspective between marginalized group members and the representatives who come from those groups, self-representation almost automatically increases trust. For marginalized groups' legislative presence to improve groups' trust in the political system, it must translate into legislative attention to the distinctive needs that they have, needs which are rooted in the history of their disadvantage. These are the kinds of needs that can, as Michael Ignatieff points out, be articulated as rights and asserted *against* the collectivity: rights to an equal education, to adequate child care, to freedom from sexual harassment, to decent housing, to freedom from crime-ridden neighborhoods. Ignatieff argues that another kind of need exists that is not so easily articulated in terms of rights: the need *for* the collectivity, for membership, for recognition, for respect from its other members.[118] The legislative presence of marginalized groups can offer *symbolic* affirmation of a group's place in the life of the body politic and its members' capacity to perform important public roles, and such symbolism is especially important for groups with a history of marginalization.[119] But enhancing representation for members of historically disadvantaged groups will not, by itself, supply this latter need. It will not, by itself, repair the social compact by bringing them into it; that would require direct efforts to bridge the divide within civil society.[120] Yet it is possible that the representation of these groups, and the building of relationships within the decision-making body, might provide a starting point for relationships of trust across group boundaries. These are the needs that must be met if we are to achieve trust at the broadest level of society. In any event I think Calhoun's insight was correct, that in the *absence* of institutions which encourage the building of trust across deep social divides, there is *no* hope they will be bridged.

The cycle of trust and betrayal through which Blacks traveled during Reconstruction is typical of the experience of Blacks—and of other severely oppressed groups—throughout history. It reveals an alternation of the desire for inclusion and the impulse to separatism that emerges in response to the actions of the dominant elements of society: the desire for inclusion is prompted by actions which give hope that meaningful inclusion is possible, and the impulse to separatism is brought on by actions which disappoint that hope. Frederick Douglass had his counterpoint in Henry M. Turner, who led the emigration movement in the 1880s; in the civil rights movement of the 1950s and 1960s, Martin Luther King, Jr., and the Southern Christian Leadership

Conference were followed by Malcolm X and the Black Power movement. The cycles of trust and betrayal, inclusion and separation, "hope and independence,"[121] seem likely to be repeated so long as the groups long excluded from full membership, and still suffering the effects of that exclusion, lack an effective political voice.

6

Memory: The Claims of History in Group Recognition

IN THE PRECEDING chapters on the themes of voice and trust in group-based claims to fair representation, I attempted to clarify why members of historically marginalized ascriptive groups might have a strong interest in being represented by other members of those groups, and to show that that interest is integrally connected to a group-based understanding of political equality. But, in itself, groups' interest in representation, even if undergirded by the groups' own understandings of what equality requires, does not answer the question of why the broader community (including relatively privileged groups) should recognize that claim as compelling. That a particular group lacks a political voice or a solid foundation of trust with elected representatives is not, in itself, enough to establish that it is *owed* a voice. As we saw in chapter 4, neither the demonstration that society is group-structured nor the claim of a group to separate representation is necessarily a sufficient ground for defining political constituencies along group lines. Rather, the definition of the groups that ought to be recognized in a scheme of representation has both an empirical side (that these groups *do* constitute discrete communities of interest capable of being represented) and a normative side (that the recognition of these groups within the process of political representation is an essential element of a common good).[1]

This chapter's main purpose is to offer a schema for identifying groups that have a strong claim to special recognition within political institutions, and a particularly strong claim to be represented by their own members in legislative bodies. In other words, whereas the two preceding chapters established equality-based arguments for a revised conception of two aspects of representation as mediation—legislator-constituency relations and the dynamics of legislative decision making—it is not yet clear what theory of social groups is entailed by a group-based view of fair representation. How are we to distinguish the groups with a strong moral claim to representation from those without such a claim?

The groups that merit representation, I propose, are characterized by two attributes: their contemporary inequality as compared to other social groups and a history of discrimination and oppression. Because of the connection between contemporary inequality and past discrimination, considerations of justice provide the strongest grounds for the special recognition of certain social groups. This connection, once explicated, confirms the intuition that a *contemporary* injustice is committed when historically marginalized groups are underrepresented in politics.[2] For members of these groups, political equality cannot be realized without the recognition that there is a causal connection between their history of oppression and their current lower-than-average status in society and politics. As I noted in the introduction, the causal connection between the history of marginalization and contemporary inequality reproduces both cultural and material injustice. The negative social meanings that members of dominant groups ascribe to marginalized groups have functioned to legitimize marginalization; the subordinate social position of marginalized groups in turn reinforces the negative social meanings that others attach to them. Both dynamics reproduce patterns of cultural and material inequality over time. Finally, history is an important element of marginalized group identity because part of what defines a group as marginalized is its position of structural inequality. We cannot have confidence that every pattern of inequality that follows the lines of identifiable social groups is structural (i.e., reproduced even in the absence of intentional and overt discrimination) unless it is reproduced over time. The deeper the historical pattern of inequality, the clearer its systemic character and its injustice.

In short, the link to history is not, as some argue in defense of affirmative action programs, that these groups are owed compensation for past iniquities and past inequities. Rather, my position is that the claims of marginalized ascriptive groups to special representation in politics are legitimized by a clear and strong connection between *present* inequality and the kinds of past discrimination that were sanctioned by dominant social groups and often enforced by the state.

I have used the terms *memory* and *history* to signify that there are two aspects to the relevance of the past for contemporary equality among citizens. "Memory" highlights the *subjective* side of a history of discrimination, the meaning the past has for members of those groups who were the targets of discrimination and oppression. On this side, the connection between the history of discrimination and contemporary inequality consists in group members' internalization of, or struggles against, the negative social meanings that have historically been attached to their group by dominant groups—the meaning that generally provided the rationalization for discrimination and oppression. "History" designates the *objective* side of discrimination and oppression, the *evidence* provided by law, documents, and other generally accepted sources that the discrimination actually occurred. It further refers to the empirical evidence by which contemporary patterns of group-structured inequality can be connected with the history of discrimination. Such history is objective in the sense that it relies on the kinds of evidence that are broadly accepted in our social and political culture. Thus the objective side of group definition and identification makes a direct appeal to a notion of shared public reason, a reason in which empirical evidence, while always contestable, is accepted, in principle, as a valid basis for public decisions.

Understanding group-based claims to political recognition in this way provides us with an answer to each of the major liberal objections to group representation. Moreover, and in a way that is exceedingly important for a group-based theory of fair representation, it provides criteria for assessing the relative merits of different groups' claims for recognition. The latter is particularly important insofar as even the most compelling of recent arguments for group representation do not establish reasons for assessing competing group claims.

The chapter proceeds in five sections. First, I present an overview of the principal critiques of group representation that follow from liberal representation. Second, I offer an account of what I am calling "memory," the subjective side of the identity of historically marginalized groups. The third section articulates the objective side of these groups' identities, the "history" of their oppression and of the links between that oppression and contemporary inequality. Fourth, I show why these two aspects of group identity demonstrate the strength of some groups' *equality-based* claims to special recognition in public life, and particularly in institutions of political representation. The final section explains how this defense of group representation answers each of the liberal objections. It also summarizes an important difference between my defense of group representation and other recent arguments, and shows how the concepts of "memory" and "history" can facilitate judgments about the claims to representation of marginalized groups other than women and African Americans.

I. Critiques of Group Representation

Recall that liberal representation is constituted by two strands of argument about equality and fairness in representative democracy. The first strand is the idea of "one person, one vote," the Supreme Court standard of representational fairness as *equal* representation, developed since legislative districting was first deemed justiciable in the early 1960s. Here, the standard of fairness is that of individual equality: each person's vote should have the same effective weight as every other person's vote, and consequently legislative districts must be of roughly equal size. Further, legislative districts must not be gerrymandered so as to favor the electoral majority, and certainly must not be drawn so as to diminish the representation of racial or ethnic minorities. So long as these principles are observed, any outcome of a free and open election—and so any representational effect—is procedurally fair, "whatever it is."[3] The second strand is expressed in the theory of interest-group pluralism. In simplified form, the pluralist view of fair representation as *equitable* representation rests on the free mobilization and organization of individuals who share particular interests. Individuals secure the representation of their interests in public policy decisions by organizing pressure groups to influence policy makers. Successful candidacies and policy outcomes are conceived as the product of the energy expended by various groups, and are fair so long as individuals have equal freedom and opportunity to organize. Taken together, these two strands constitute a wholly coherent theory of fair representation that observes liberalism's commitments to individual equality and to individuals' autonomy in identifying and acting on their political interests and preferences.

It is possible to identify four distinct arguments against group representation that flow from the liberal understanding of fair representation:

Autonomy

Recognizing a group as having a special claim to representation, perhaps through practices such as race-conscious districting, does violence to the autonomy of individuals within that group to identify and act on their political interests. Group representation only makes sense on the assumption that social groups are internally homogeneous, that group characteristics identify the communities of interest relevant for politics. But this is clearly false: obviously not all women are pro-choice, for example, and not all Blacks favor redistributive programs. Yet group representation assumes that an individual member of a recognized group has a set of interests that are determined by membership in that group, and so fails to respect individuals' capacities to reach independent judgments about their good. As Abigail Thernstrom sums it up, "democratic choice and democratic institutions require a fluidity and freedom that are at odds with the concept of labeling citizens for political purposes on the basis of race or ethnicity."[4]

Individual Equality

Group-based representation fails to treat individuals equally if and when it guarantees seats to certain groups rather than distributing seats on the basis of a competitive electoral process in which each person has an equally weighted vote. But even when a legislative districting scheme does weight each person's vote equally, it fails to conform to liberal standards of equality insofar as it is aimed at increasing the representation of some groups rather than others, as in cases of race-conscious districting. Such practices reaffirm and ossify distinctions among classes of citizens rather than conforming to the liberal ideal of difference-blind equality.[5] Moreover, any attempt to increase the representation of particular ascriptive groups in representative institutions will, directly or indirectly, involve a decision to reduce the representation of some other group. Clearly such a decision involves conferring public benefits on the basis of attributes that are, as Rawls puts it, "arbitrary from a moral perspective,"[6] and so should not affect citizens' standing in public life.

Responsibility

Singling out specific groups as deserving of special political recognition encourages a "victim mentality" among the groups in question.[7] In so doing it actively discourages groups from undertaking the kind of political organization that *would* result in—and legitimize—the recognition of their interests in politics. Thus granting special recognition to particular groups actually undercuts their political agency and prevents them from taking responsibility for their own political future. Such "victim" claims are particularly pernicious when based on a history of past discrimination rather than on evidence of contemporary discrimination, as is so often the case in arguments for "affirmative gerrymandering." A history of discrimination does nothing to justify affirmative action policies of any kind because such policies tend to benefit people who were not themselves victims of discrimination,[8] while imposing burdens on others who never discriminated against members of ascriptive groups and so should not be held responsible for patterns of past discrimination.[9] Instead of policies aimed at enhancing the representation of historically disadvantaged groups, justice demands the redress of discrimination on a case-by-case basis.[10]

Stability

In addition to the above arguments, which follow from traditional liberal commitments to equality and autonomy, some critics of group representation present a fourth argument. This argument, based on considerations of political stability and "governability," is not distinctively liberal but is often made in conjunction with the liberal arguments against group representation. Its proponents contend that the very diversity and number of groups that might make claims based on past discrimination is likely to strain government's capacity to cope with the competing demands. This view lies at the heart of worries about the "balkanizing" effects of group recognition.[11] As Nathan Glazer observes,

> Each group stands in a different position: the amount of prejudice and discrimination inflicted, whether by law or custom, has varied enormously from group to group

and over time, and we have an extraordinary breadth of experience ranging from the relatively mild mistreatment of Southern and Eastern European groups to the harsh enslavement and systematic segregation of blacks.[12]

The multifariousness of group experiences, especially when combined with the fact that some group memberships are overlapping (one may be both a woman and Black, both disabled and Native American), leads to a potentially endless multiplication of group claims, all justified on the basis of a history of discrimination. If entitlements to scarce social goods are based on membership in these groups, some critics feel, the demand on public resources will tend to strain institutions' capacity to fulfill their primary functions. The Supreme Court's majority opinion in *City of Richmond v. J. A. Croson Co.* made the point perfectly clear: "To accept Richmond's claim that past societal discrimination alone can serve as the basis for rigid racial preferences would be to open the door to competing claims for 'remedial relief' for every disadvantaged group."[13]

Any defense of group representation that seeks to preserve a democratic commitment to the principles of individual equality and autonomy must, I think, be able to answer these concerns. I believe that the following argument, based on a two-sided, subjective and objective, definition of groups, is equal to that task.

II. Memory

We all experience, at some time in our lives, the sense of wrong that comes of others' failure or refusal to understand our point of view, the denial of an opportunity to make ourselves understood. But for members of marginalized groups, the injury caused by voicelessness is magnified because the refusal of others to hear attaches not to them as individuals in particular circumstances but to attributes they did not choose to bear and cannot control. Action based on prejudices and stereotypes about such involuntary traits is an affront to a person's agency, and frequently operates to suppress that agency by denying its existence. Being treated on the basis of characteristics given by birth or fate creates a connection between the individual bearer of those characteristics and others who share them. From the standpoint of individuals who act on the basis of such traits, all those bearing the traits are interchangeable; an injury to one could as easily have been an injury to any other person sharing those characteristics.[14]

But the interconnection between individual members of marginalized ascriptive groups extends across time as well as space, for each instance of an action based on group stereotypes or prejudice carries with it the whole history of the cultural and social meaning of group attributes. Christopher Nolan, a remarkable young Irish writer left mute and paralyzed by cerebral palsy, writes in his autobiography of his connectedness to the generations of disabled who never gained a voice: "Century upon century saw crass crippled man dashed, branded and treated as dross in a world offended by their appearance, and cracked asunder in their belittlement by having to resemble venial human specimens offering nothing and pondering less in their life of mindless normality."[15] Nolan writes with a sensibility that he does so not on his own behalf alone but as a representative and liberator of others whose intelligence is masked by disability and denied by the able-bodied world. His reach extends not only outward, to his voiceless contemporaries, but also backward, into the history of suffering of others like himself. By writing of his own experience, "he was resurrecting them and schooling their bones, asleep so very long, to come with him and bear witness that crones caused their banishment."[16]

In these brief passages Nolan offers us a glimpse of the sense of collective memory that is often shared by members of historically marginalized ascriptive groups. He suggests the connection between the history of the attitudes of the able-bodied toward the disabled, their entrenchment in, and re-creation through, social practices, so that the experience of the disabled today is continuous with the history of the broader society's treatment of them. Moreover, he asserts that it is precisely the power of privileged groups to define certain characteristics as "different" that is the defining element of ascriptive group membership: a negative social meaning is *ascribed* to those characteristics by persons who do not possess them, and that negative meaning makes the traits a justification for the subordinate status of those who do possess them. In this role, dominant groups are Nolan's "crones" who judge the disabled as "offering nothing and pondering less."

Members of marginalized ascriptive groups carry the burden of their history with them in their day-to-day lives. The history of discrimination is a residue deposited within and among the structures of social life, in a manner frequently invisible to members of privileged groups and independent of any intention on their part to perpetuate discrimination (though obviously intentional discrimination is not a thing of the past). For the physically disabled, stairs in public buildings are among the more obvious and concrete social structures that re-create group marginalization; without discriminatory intent they effectively exclude persons in wheelchairs. Other emblems of marginalization are more subtle reminders to individuals of the past subordination of others like themselves. Such reminders, which Shelby Steele, turning to literary theory, identifies as the "objective correlatives" of historic oppression,[17] may be as rare and discrete as a Confederate flag or a cry of "YAA-HOO!" in the woods;[18] or they may be as diffuse and familiar as Black janitors with White supervisors. Steele observes that "Blacks grow up in America surrounded by correlatives to their collective pain," and that "our memory of oppression has such power, magnitude, depth and nuance that it constantly drains our best resources."[19]

The sense that members of ascriptive groups are simultaneously connected with their history of marginalization and with the experience of other group members is painfully apparent in Blacks' experience of the verdict in the Rodney King police brutality case. Speaking of the videotape of King's beating, Brad Shore, who teaches anthropology at Emory University, commented: "Watching these images on TV resonates in lots of ways. . . . To blacks, there's no doubt they have multiple significance. One of the images that would be called to mind would be the Ku Klux Klan, the entire history of a circle of whites beating a black man, and a circle of whites wearing uniforms is not so different from a circle of men wearing hoods."[20] A Black college senior stated that the King verdict "sends a very scary message to me . . . I can be driving my car and fitting a description. I try to respect cops as much as I can [but] I'm very scared that something like this could happen to me."[21] Another student asked, "What assurances can you give me that what happened to Rodney King won't happen to my kids?"[22]

As these examples show, the history of subordination is an inescapable feature of contemporary society for members of ascriptive groups because it permeates social life. American culture reflects the history of discrimination not only through the "objective correlatives" noted by Steele but also because the negative images connected with ascriptive group traits are built into everyday language. W.E.B. DuBois pointed out the moral meanings that have been attributed to different colors in our culture and that attach as tenaciously to the color of a person's skin: "Everything great, good, efficient, fair, and honorable is 'white'; everything mean, bad, blundering, cheating, and dishonorable is 'yellow'; a bad taste is 'brown'; and the devil is 'black.'"[23] Iris Young summarizes cultural images of women that prevailed in the last century: "As a group women are physically delicate and weak due to the specific constitution of their bodies, the operation of their reproductive and sexual parts. Because of their ovaries and uterus women are subject to madness, irrationality, and childlike stupidity, and they have greater tendencies toward sexual licentiousness than men."[24] For any particular marginalized ascriptive group, a cultural history could be written of the negative images that have been associated with ascribed characteristics, the circumstances under which those images or labels gained currency, and the mutations they have undergone over time.[25]

The negative images attached to ascriptive groups contribute to individuals' contemporary experience of social subordination in several ways. First, as Kenneth Clark's famous psychological experiments showed to the Supreme Court's satisfaction in *Brown v. Board of Education*, negative stereotypes are internalized by group members themselves so that racial discrimination, including segregation, "generates a feeling of inferiority as to their status in the community that may affect their hearts and minds in a way unlikely ever to be undone."[26] Shelby Steele explains this phenomenon from the standpoint of a member of an ascriptive group: "You cannot be raised in a culture that was for centuries committed to the notion of your inferiority and not have some doubt in this regard."[27] As psychological research on "learned helplessness" suggests, individuals who attribute their failure to achieve their goals to circumstances beyond their control eventually cease trying. Negative stereotypes about ascriptive groups offer a ready-made set of such circumstances and create the expectation of failure.[28] Thus the prevalence of negative images of ascriptive groups within the culture undercuts individuals' sense of agency, and these images themselves are connected with the history of discrimination against those groups because they so often served as the public rationalizations for discrimination.[29]

Second, as a number of feminist theorists have recently argued,[30] these images have so permeated social and cultural life that members of relatively privileged groups often engage in their use and reinforcement even without being aware they are doing so. On the other hand, members of the ascriptive groups to which the images attach are often painfully aware of others' use of them, which is understandable given the consequences for their own power to be heard and understood. Moreover, to the extent that the images undercut marginalized group members' social status, their use, even if unintentional, serves to reinforce the advantage of historically privileged groups and further decreases their propensity to perceive that stereotypes *are* being used. Simone Weil captures this dynamic when she writes:

> Someone who does not see a pane of glass does not know that he does not see it. Someone who, being placed differently, does see it, does not know the other does not see it.
>
> When our will finds expression outside ourselves in actions performed by others, we do not waste our time and our power of attention in examining whether they have consented to this.[31]

This dual perception of negative group images, one from within marginalized ascriptive groups and one from without, further reinforces the sense of voicelessness of individual members of those groups, for to protest the images will be perceived by members of relatively privileged groups as a protest against the air, utterly insubstantial. The individual is driven back, again, to the continuity between the history of discrimination, the images used to justify it, and the contemporary experience of marginalization or inequality that results from the persistence of those images in contemporary culture.

For these reasons, membership in an ascriptive group is often deeply constitutive of the individual's identity and shapes his or her sense of agency in profound ways. This is true in ways similar to Michael Sandel's characterization of familial and community bonds and attachments,[32] and to Will

Kymlicka's characterization of membership in a cultural community. Echoing Steele's comment quoted above, Kymlicka states, "Someone's upbringing isn't something that can just be erased; it is, and will remain, a constitutive part of who that person is. Cultural membership affects our very sense of personal identity and capacity."[33] However, the consequences for individual identity and agency of membership in a marginalized ascriptive group are somewhat different from membership in nonmarginalized groups or cultural communities: whereas the meaning of membership in the latter is defined from *within* the group's or culture's own history and values, the meaning of membership in a marginalized group is also (and sometimes only) defined from *without*. For marginalized groups, the meaning of membership for individual identity is too often not so much something to be celebrated and discovered, as in Sandel's characterization of the situated subject,[34] but, above all, something to be borne. Patricia Williams, a brilliant and successful African American legal scholar, was questioned by a White man whether she "'really identified as black'": "I was acutely aware that the choice of identifying as black (as opposed to white?) was hardly mine; that as long as I am identified as black by the majority of others, my own identifying as black will almost surely follow as a simple fact of human interdependency."[35]

It would be wrong to suggest that group membership is *only* a burden and never something to be celebrated.[36] Like cultural membership as Kymlicka describes it, membership in marginalized ascriptive groups may serve as the "context of choice" which "provid[es] meaningful options for us, and aid[s] our ability to judge for ourselves the value of our life-plans."[37] Frequently membership in an ascriptive group, like membership in an ethnos or nation, is "an important and constitutive element of personal identity," and choosing to identify with one's group is a perfectly rational and reasonable step to take.[38] But for groups with a history of discrimination, the context of choice that membership provides may not be a primary good, as Kymlicka argues for cultural membership, for several reasons: it may be sharply limited by prejudice, the options it provides may be few or undesirable, and the value of the life-plans it offers for judgment may be scant. Kymlicka connects individual equality to membership in a cultural minority by pointing to the ways minority status threatens a community's capacity to sustain its *internally defined* identity. While I find his argument compelling, it does not tell the whole story of the link between individual equality and group identity for marginalized ascriptive groups where individual equality (understood in part in terms of what Rawls identifies as "perhaps the most important primary good," self-respect)[39] is affected by the *externally imposed* identity defined by the historical and cultural meanings of ascriptive characteristics. As Hannah Arendt explains, when others impose an identity on a person, "one can resist only in terms of the identity that is under attack. Those who reject such identification

on the part of a hostile world may feel wonderfully superior to the world, but
their superiority is then truly no longer of this world; it is the superiority of a
more or less well-equipped cloud-cuckoo-land."[40]

So far, I have considered the reasons why individual identity for the member of a marginalized ascriptive group is inextricable from the identity attached to ascriptive characteristics by nonmembers and by the deep-rooted
history of those meanings within the broader culture. When ascriptive group
identities become politicized, they take on an additional dimension of meaning for groups as communities or organizations, as their leaders and membership locate their contemporary claims against the background of the history of
discrimination against them. Just as individuals cannot make sense of their
own cultural experience without reference to ascribed group identities and
their history, the collective claims of historically marginalized groups, at least
to them, are only intelligible within the framework of the group's past relationship with relatively privileged elements of society. This is true, I think, of
all marginalized ascriptive groups when they mobilize around group identity,
although in different ways and to different degrees. Collective memory is especially potent for the two marginalized ascriptive groups that persistently occupy the lowest social positions in the United States: Native Americans and
African Americans. Stephen Cornell argues, "[F]or Indians, . . . [the] sense of
history is rooted here, in this land, in the geography of their present. Most
forms of Indian political action are explicitly grounded in a consciousness of
that history and, more often than not, are articulated in explicitly historical
terms."[41]

As a number of observers of the politics of marginalized groups have noted,
there is a paradoxical character to the emergence of a self-understanding that
can inform their political claims. To the extent that group political action
arises out of the need to resist the burdensome identities imposed by the
dominant culture, a collective sense of identity and a collective memory may
surface as a *response* to discriminatory treatment, creating a solidarity and
group self-consciousness that would not otherwise exist. As we saw in chapter
4, this sense exists at least as far back as the woman suffrage movement: some
suffragists understood women's group identity as a product of the fact that it
was as women that they were excluded from politics. Once women enjoyed
full political equality, some argued, the need to act as a group would sub-
side.[42] Similarly, many Black political leaders during Reconstruction were vo-
ciferous advocates of the idea of color-blind equality until it became clear that
White Republicans were not willing to protect Blacks' political rights, and it
was this that caused Black leaders to turn toward Black political solidarity as
their only source of political hope. This dynamic has changed very little in the
twentieth century and shapes the emergence of new ascriptive group identities
in politics as much as it has in the past. Writing on the gay liberation movement, Stephen Epstein notes that even gays who believe that no essential dif-

ference in sexuality divides homosexuals and heterosexuals must re-create the distinction in order to protest it by organizing around gay identity.[43]

A further paradox in the emergence of an ascriptive group identity that informs political action is that although the history of oppression is palpable in the everyday lives of individuals, the development of an understanding of the meaning of that history for contemporary political action may entail a good deal of work. We saw above that cultural meanings of ascriptive group identity are burdensome to individual members of ascriptive groups without necessarily being visible to others. These meanings tend to place a burden of responsibility on individual members: either they accept the images of their inferiority and internalize them or they attempt to disprove them through the demonstration of their stereotype-defying ability. The process of organizing politically around group identity is one of appropriating the meaning of that identity so as to ease the burden individuals must bear. Collective memory is brought out of silent shadows and into the light of open discussion of shared experience. In contrast to individual remembering, in which group members are the passive recipients of the cultural meanings of race, gender, and so on, political remembering involves collective agency. Native American peoples, for example, have a strong oral tradition through which they pass down the history of their life on the land, of the treaties they entered, and of the betrayal and destruction they suffered at White hands.[44] Without the preservation of this history, and the exercise of this particular form of collective agency, marginalized groups might lack confidence in their standing to make claims against the broader political community. They would lose the sense of dignity without which it is difficult to lay claim to an entitlement to be treated as equals. In other words, the articulation of a shared history is an important part of the formation of a group consciousness that includes "an awareness of group oppression, an analysis of the sources of that oppression, and a willingness to take collective action."[45]

III. History

From the standpoint of the subjective experience of members of marginalized ascriptive groups, the memory of past oppression is inseparable from the claim to contemporary equality. As we have seen, memory stands in a paradoxical relation to equality. It may weaken individuals' capability of asserting their equality by reinforcing a negative self-image; at the same time, however, memory may strengthen groups' collective agency by providing an explanation for their current unequal status, an explanation that counters negative stereotypes.

This subjective experience, however, does not explain how memory relates to the kinds of claims to recognition that should be regarded as valid within the public sphere. What could these subjective meanings of ascriptive group membership possibly have to do with the question of what society owes them? This question is particularly vexing because of the very subjectivity of memory: that individuals on their own or collectively in groups *experience* a sense of injury does not mean they have been injured in a way that warrants public redress, particularly when the injury is unintended. The moral uncertainty that can surround group claims based on subjective experience renders those claims vulnerable to dismissal by persons disinclined to respect them. Such was the vulnerability exploited so egregiously by the Supreme Court's majority opinion in *Plessy v. Ferguson*, which argued that if Blacks felt that the segregation of train cars was a badge of inferiority, it was "solely because the colored race chooses to put that construction upon it."[46]

Even those who are sympathetic to the idea that the suffering are the only ones equipped to name their pain are forced to the conclusion that we cannot make the subjective experience of injury the basis for political action.[47] Locke has taught us well that we are seldom good judges in our own cases, and our experience of injustice is not always synonymous with its actuality. In fact, as Steele and others have noted, the claim to innocence that accompanies the cry of victimization is in itself a form of political power.[48] This should arouse our suspicion. Indeed, such suspicion is reflected in the theories of representation of both J. S. Mill and Burke, both of whom develop schemes of representation in which legislators could *heed* the cry of suffering groups without actually ceding any final *power* to the sufferers.[49]

But the existence of distinct social groups defined by a history of oppression, and of continuities between past oppression and contemporary inequality, is not confined within the minds of group members. In addition to the subjective side of group identity, there is a multifaceted *objective* side. By "objective" I mean that both the existence of distinct marginalized groups and the connection between current group-structured inequality and a history of oppression can be confirmed by evidence that cannot easily be dismissed as existing solely in the minds of group members. This evidence is constituted by phenomena (written laws, historical accounts based on documentary and other conventionally accepted sources, statistical studies, etc.) that are generally accepted as valid in American society. In short, I will argue, the Supreme Court's statement in *Croson* that "claims of past wrongs" are "inherently unmeasurable" is absurd.[50]

Any account of the connection between past discrimination and contemporary inequality must begin with the evidence of the past discrimination itself. For some marginalized ascriptive groups, that evidence is all too easy to assemble: the history of the exclusion of Blacks, women, and Native Americans from the Constitution's embrace is well established. For each of these groups, as for others, one can trace a history of legal discrimination, ranging from exclusion from full citizenship, to failure to protect constitutionally defined civil and political rights, to innumerable legally enforced restrictions on access to both public and private facilities, to discriminatory hiring, to discriminatory treatment in bids for government contracts, and so forth.

It is equally clear where an account of the connection between past and present inequality must *end*: with the establishment that historically oppressed groups do not enjoy full social and political equality in the present. Again, a quick study of widely available statistical evidence provides a stark account of the group structure of social and political inequality in the United States, at least for some groups. In 1994 women who had attended four years of high school earned 69 percent of what men earned with the same educational level; college-educated women earned 64 percent of college-educated men's earnings.[51]

The unemployment rate for Blacks in 1995 was 10.4 percent compared to 4.9 percent for Whites; the unemployment rate for Black youths aged sixteen to nineteen was 35.7 percent compared to 14.5 percent for White youths; for Hispanics, the overall rate of unemployment was 9.3 percent; for Hispanic youths, it was 24.1 percent.[52] At the time of the 1990 decennial census 27.2 percent of Native American families lived below the poverty line. The same year the rate was 7.8 percent for Whites and 27.8 percent for Blacks. Current figures are much the same: in 1995 only 9.4 percent of White families, compared to 31.3 percent of African American families, lived in official poverty.[53]

Political inequality is, of course, much more difficult to measure than economic inequality; obviously the central purpose of this project as a whole is to ascertain the different ways political equality might be affected by the level of women's and minority groups' presence in legislative bodies. Whatever their ultimate significance from the standpoint of equality, however, the numbers are clear. Despite their recent electoral gains, women remain vastly underrepresented compared to men. In 1995 women held forty-seven, or 10.8 percent, of the seats in the U.S. House of Representatives; they also held a record number of Senate seats, for a total of eight.[54] At the local level women are doing better: as of 1992, 23.7 percent of local government officials were women. Women do better at the state level, where they hold 14 percent of elective offices and 17 percent of legislative seats.[55] As a consequence of race-conscious districting, African Americans now hold 9.2 percent of seats in the House of Representatives, closer to a proportional share of congressional seats than they have ever had. As I discussed in chapter 3, those recent gains are currently unstable. Meanwhile Blacks, with only one seat, remain seriously underrepresented in the Senate. It is at the local level that Blacks remain most egregiously underrepresented, occupying only 2.3 percent of local government seats.[56] Hispanics hold seventeen seats (4 percent) in the U.S. House (and none in the Senate)[57] but comprise 7 percent of the voting-age population.

Difficult though it is to establish an objective connection between past op-pression and present inequality through historical and sociological research, it is not, as the *Croson* Court stated, impossible. Carefully crafted historical studies attempt to retrace the path groups have traveled from a past of state-enforced discrimination to a present characterized by inequality which per-sists despite the courts' strict scrutiny of all but difference-blind laws and policies.

Although it is far beyond this project's scope to detail the historical roots of contemporary inequality, there are historical studies that do just that. In *The Declining Significance of Race*,[58] for example, William Julius Wilson offers a persuasive argument showing the processes by which economic transforma-tions, combined with patterns of violence, social prejudice, and legal discrim-ination against Blacks, produced concentrated Black populations in poor urban centers, where both the debilitating effects of poverty and the absence of well-paying jobs perpetuate a Black underclass. In other words, the oppres-sion of Blacks under slavery is continuous with the social and economic forces that produced an urban underclass. Thus, in Wilson's analysis, the history of slavery and of state-sanctioned discrimination against Blacks is an *indispens-able* component of any plausible explanation of the existence of a Black under-class. As Wilson puts it in a more recent book, "no serious student of American race relations can deny the relationship between the disproportionate concen-tration of blacks in impoverished urban ghettos and historic racial subjugation in American society."[59] Similar histories can be told for other marginalized ascriptive groups.[60]

Histories such as these tell the story of how *structural inequalities* are pro-duced over time and how social institutions can reproduce existing inequali-ties across time, across generations, even within a legal environment where the principle of color-blind equality reigns. Although we certainly have not eradi-cated all intentional discrimination against historically oppressed groups, its more overt forms have generally been replaced with more insidious ones. Nu-merous scholars have observed, however, that actions and policies can easily have a discriminatory effect without any discriminatory intent at all. Most obvious are policies aimed at equal opportunity that reproduce relations of inequality because they fail to "correct for systematic inequalities that exist in resources, access to information and general political knowledge, all of which predetermine the ability of different groups to participate effectively."[61] Robert Hill, in an excellent overview of the forms of structural discrimination, singles out what he calls "past-in-present" discrimination, particularly in such areas as education and health care, where "racially 'neutral' practices in an institutional area . . . have differential negative impact on minorities because of past inten-tional discrimination in the same institutional area."[62] Other processes that reproduce inequality from one period to another, or from one social sphere to another, include "side-effect" discrimination (where the links between social spheres mean that discrimination or inequality in one sphere will appear as inequality in another).[63] Hill names another dynamic the "Matthew effect," the process by which the rich get richer and the poor get poorer. For example, scholars whose work has been funded in the past are more likely to receive funding in the future.[64] The incumbency effect in electoral politics is another important example of the "Matthew effect." These and similar dynamics preserve the status quo of group-structured inequality by preventing substantial redistributions of resources and by creating the perception that existing inequalities are stable or legitimate or both.[65]

In fact, as we saw in chapter 3, *Croson* notwithstanding, the notion that a history of discrimination gives a group a special claim to recognition is not altogether foreign to American political culture. The "totality of circumstances" analysis that is embedded in voting rights jurisprudence and legislative history effectively acknowledges that a history of discrimination has ongoing implications for political equality. Further, such acknowledgment has not been restricted to cases involving legislative districting. In *Gaston County v. United States*,[66] for example, the Supreme Court overturned a Virginia literacy requirement for voter registration, not because it had discriminatory *intent* but because it would have a discriminatory *effect* on Blacks. The Court's reasoning was that the history of school segregation, which provided Blacks with an inferior education, meant that a literacy requirement for the vote would inevitably function disproportionately to exclude Blacks from the polls. Even if discrimination was not consciously intended, the Court judged that a literacy test clearly constituted discrimination at one remove. Group claims based on memory and history have a logic similar to that of the Court in *Gaston County*. They do not rest on the accusation that inequality is a product of intentional discrimination; rather, they assert that inequality is reproduced out of past discrimination through a variety of processes, sometimes at many removes. In fact, it may be reasonable to ask whether any reasonable conception of fairness could sanction polices and institutions that systematically reproduce relations of social inequality among groups from which individuals have no escape. As Judith Shklar expresses this intuition,

> [W]hen we can alleviate suffering, whatever its causes, it is passively unjust to stand by and do nothing. *It is not the origin of the injury*, but the possibility of preventing and reducing its costs, that allows us to judge whether there was or was not unjustifiable passivity in the face of disaster.[67]

But marginalized groups' claims to recognition are even more powerful than this, and less vulnerable to the charge that some relations of inequality are perfectly consistent with fairness and do not command a remedy. Marginalized groups' principal objection is not only that certain processes reproduce inequality over time. Rather, their claims to recognition hinge specifically on the history of discrimination against them, because the connection between history and contemporary inequality inflicts a dual injury: (1) it reinforces and re-creates the groups' subordinate social status, but (2) at the same time, it leaves unbroken the connection between the groups' inequality and the stereotypes that historically were used to justify that inequality. History-based inequality makes it difficult for individual members to escape from their subordinate social position by translating past patterns of inequality into contemporary ones both *materially* (by translating, for example, educational inequality into unequal voting power, as in *Gaston*) and *psychologically* (by reinforcing the suggestion that inequality is the consequence of inferiority). Left unaddressed, the historical reproduction of inequality is self-reinforcing not only because of institutional dynamics; it also strikes a blow at individuals' self-esteem, which diminishes their agency to escape subordinate social roles.

IV. Memory, History, and Group Representation

Together, the memory and history that link past discrimination with contemporary equality operate to create distinct worlds along group lines. The relation between past and present may be stronger or more clearly drawn for some groups than for others; it is clearest, perhaps, for Blacks and Native Americans. Marginalized groups are divided from relatively privileged groups by social experience, by the opportunities available to them, by their very perception of social relations. A recent study comparing Black and White views of racial inequality, for example, shows that "it is hardly an overstatement to say that blacks and whites inhabit two different perceptual worlds. Whites simply do not acknowledge the persisting prejudice and discrimination that are so obvious to blacks."[68] Moreover, this division, and the material and political inequality that sustains it, can be traced back to systematic, state-supported discrimination, reproduced across time through both intentional and unintentional actions. It is true that the divisions are not total, that the groups themselves are divided by cross-cutting memberships in marginalized ascriptive groups (as well as by class), a fact that has undeniable moral implications. But to the extent that discrete social groups *are* constituted in this two-sided way, subjectively by memory and objectively by history, a clear basis for distinguishing groups for purposes of political representation exists.[69]

By understanding social groups and group-structured inequality through this complex of concepts and processes, we can move toward an appreciation of the deep connection between individual political equality and group membership. Because of the impact of group inequality on individuals' opportunities, self-esteem, and sense of their own agency to define and pursue a life worth living, political systems that overlook patterns of structural inequality will never treat members of marginalized groups as equals. To the extent that a commitment to political equality is a defining attribute of a liberal democratic society, there is a collective responsibility to dismantle the processes that reproduce the inequality generated by the state's support of past discrimination. Until such dismantling has occurred, procedural conceptions of fairness, whether in competition for employment, education, or political representation, will function to reproduce inequality at the same time as they mask it.

As we have seen in the preceding chapters, these considerations produce two strong arguments for the idea that the fair representation of the interests shared by members of marginalized groups depends on the representation of those groups by their own members. The first argument is that structural inequalities will remain unredressed so long as the voices of marginalized groups are left out of public deliberations. Essentially this argument is about the *epistemic* requirements of effective representation; it rests on the claim that since members of privileged groups lack the experience of marginalization, they often lack an understanding of what marginalized groups' interests *are* in particular policy areas. The representative who acts as an advocate for women's interests must have some understanding of the ways women's lives are shaped by the privilege of men. The most effective starting point for that knowledge is the representative's own experience of exclusion and subordination. Her task as a legislator is to articulate, in women's distinctive "voice," her constituents' particular perspectives on matters of public policy, to clarify that the vantage point offered by men's social position is partial and incomplete, and that justice and the public interest look different when seen (as suffragists so often put it) "from woman's point of view." Only in a legislative process that includes the open exchange of different groups' perspectives on what equality requires can there be much hope that some disadvantaged groups' interests will not be systematically thwarted.

But the deep social divisions that separate marginalized ascriptive groups from the rest of society produce radically different *interests* among social groups, as well as different *perspectives* on the requirements of equality. This conflict of interests leads to a second important argument for group representation, one grounded in the notion of *trust*. Even in a system such as ours, which economizes trust, there is still a claim to legitimacy which rests on the belief that citizens can trust government not to act in a manner that permanently violates their essential interests. One of the pillars of such trust is the notion that legislators will not pass legislation which will harm citizens' essential interests, because in a republican government the legislators are themselves subject to the laws. But this argument collapses in a society deeply divided along group lines. Because of the structural inequalities discussed above, laws promulgated by male legislators, for example, are likely to affect the interests of most men in a manner markedly different from the ways they affect the interests of women. Laws regarding maternity benefits or sexual harassment are a good example of this sort of difference of interest. Given deep divisions of interest among groups, then, in an important sense legislators from dominant groups are *not* subject to the laws they pass, and this undercuts marginalized groups' reasons for trusting government to look after their essential interests. In fact, despite the economy of trust, a markedly unequal distribution of rational trust exists between historically marginalized and relatively privileged groups, at least so long as the latter hold a far more than proportional share of the legislative seats.

From this standpoint, political representation is an especially appropriate forum for eradicating structural inequality. The process of dismantling broad structural inequalities can only take place (a) *discursively*, through an exchange of perspectives on the causes of contemporary inequality, and (b) *recursively*, through a movement back and forth between the fact of group-structured inequality and an equality-driven inquiry into its causes. It seems reasonable to suppose that these dynamics can find an institutional home only within bodies in which decision making proceeds through joint deliberation. While official institutions of political representation are not the only bodies in which such processes can ameliorate group-structured inequality, surely they are important ones.

A view of society in which membership in historically disadvantaged groups gives rise to an equality-based claim to representation contains an image of a common good constituted by a shared responsibility for ameliorating inequality—a responsibility that stands independent of any attendant allegations of blame. The relationship among social groups is not one of moral inferiority or superiority; it is not disclosed by comparisons of relative guilt for a history of disadvantage, nor is it measured by the relative strength of group members' work ethic. Rather, implicit in a group-based view of political equality and fair representation is the premise that just social cooperation must be ever vigilant of the degree to which its benefits are delivered differentially to different social groups. In the language of social contract theory à la Thomas Scanlon, a scheme of social cooperation is just only so long as it is based on principles that no one could reasonably reject.[70] As we have seen, however, from the standpoint of marginalized ascriptive groups, any scheme of social cooperation based on principles alone is not likely to survive the standard of reasonable rejection; because of the myriad and subtle ways in which ostensibly fair principles and procedures can reproduce structural inequalities, only a constant reevaluation of the structural consequences of principled institutions and actions can produce genuine fairness. This reevaluation must take place in the context of a political process that includes the voices and perspectives of groups left at the bottom of the distribution of the benefits of social cooperation; only from their perspectives are the mechanisms that reproduce inequality apparent. As Patricia Williams puts it: "Justice is a continual balancing of competing visions, plural viewpoints, shifting histories, interests, and allegiances. To acknowledge that level of complexity is to require, to seek, and to value a multiplicity of knowledge systems, in pursuit of a more complete sense of the world in which we all live."[71]

As I suggested above, in the liberal view of representation the groups that merit representation are identified procedurally: if a sufficient number of individuals feel sufficiently strongly about a political issue to mobilize around it, and if the pressures they exert on governmental officials are not counterbalanced by the conflicting pressures exerted by other groups, they have a strong claim to the recognition they will receive in an open political system. From the standpoint of historically marginalized groups, the pluralist view of group definition is flawed in two ways. First, because of the ongoing effects of past discrimination, these groups face special obstacles to mobilization that other groups do not face. Most clearly, they have fewer financial resources to spend on lobbying and other forms of interest group activity. Second, and more fundamentally, even if these obstacles to equal opportunities for mobilization could be overcome, representation would still be unfair if legislative assemblies did not contain some threshold number of the members of these groups.[72] The reason for this is that structural inequalities rooted in discrimination affect not only individuals' full participation in the electoral process but their freedom to participate as equals in all social institutions. Groups have a claim to representation because explaining these dynamics in the process of policy making provides their members with an important source of hope for achieving full participation in society as a whole.

Because of the close connection between a view of the group structure of society and an understanding of the common good, these differences in group theory parallel differences between a liberal conception of the common good and that embedded in a group-based theory of fair representation. In the liberal view the common good is again defined procedurally, as the outcome of the fair competition of competing interests and a tallying of individuals' equally weighted preferences.[73] So long as no one's preferences are weighted more heavily than another's in the tallying up, the common good is achieved. There is no independent standard of the common good against which legislative programs can be evaluated.

In the group-based view of political equality, our social life is too deeply structured by the history of state-supported inequality to sustain a purely procedural view of the common good. The conception of the common good toward which public policy should aim must incorporate a conscious focus on the good of groups whose good has been systematically overlooked in the past. Their well-being provides an independent standard of the common good against which the effects of legislative policies can be judged: to the extent that these groups are systematically disadvantaged within the existing scheme of social cooperation, we have failed to realize the common good. In both views the notion of the common good is inseparable from the realization of genuine political equality, but the requirements of the group-based view of equality include a constant evaluation of the impact of government policies on the well-being of marginalized groups.

V. Responses to Liberal Critiques of Group Representation

Most of the answers to the liberal critiques of group representation outlined above will be self-evident by now. But for the sake of clarity, let me respond to each in turn:

Autonomy

Nothing in the argument I have presented contradicts the principle that individuals' public identity should be determined by their own judgments regarding their political interests and concerns. I do think that the concern for autonomy would be a valid objection to institutional schemes in which legislative seats were specifically set aside for certain groups, if members of those groups had no other channels for expressing their political preferences. This would be the case, for example, if seats were designated for Black representatives, and Black citizens were allowed to vote only for candidates for those seats. For this reason I am suspicious of any designation of legislative seats for groups in which there is not a consensus on virtually all matters of public policy, and I know of no such groups.[74]

This problem falls away in an approach to group definition that rests on both memory and history. A strong group-based claim to representation rests crucially on the existence of individuals who express a shared "memory" or lay claim to a collective group identity. The subjective aspect of group definition responds to the intuition that recognition should not be extended to a group that lacks a sense of shared identity. Indeed, it would be ridiculous to regard a person as a representative of a class of citizens who did not believe themselves to *be* a class. The constitution of a group from the subjective, or "memory," side is an expression of agency for both the individual group members and the group's representative, who presents the relevant aspects of group identity to other participants in the public sphere.

Individual Equality

As should be abundantly clear from the above argument, a group-based conception of fair representation turns on the claim that prevailing conceptions of difference-blind equality are wrong-headed in that they fail to recognize that treating persons as equals may often require a positive attention to their membership in certain kinds of social groups. Although it may be true that recognizing social difference reinforces the popular impression that deep divisions exist between social groups, this is perfectly appropriate insofar as those impressions are empirically accurate. The inegalitarian consequences of social difference do not disappear simply because we choose not to recognize them. To the contrary, ignoring social difference will only serve to perpetuate group-structured inequality. Finally, it may be the case that recognizing one group's claim to social resources or to legislative seats will mean denying another group's claim, but we have no reason to believe that no principled criteria exist by which judgments of that sort can be made.

Responsibility

As I have already suggested, a history-based argument for group representation does *not* regard special protections for certain groups as *compensation* for past discrimination. A collective responsibility to recognize certain groups' claims to recognition arises out of a commitment to *contemporary* equality, not a desire to acknowledge guilt for past wrongs. Although it is true that members of privileged groups benefit from the dynamics of structural inequality that are rooted in a history of discrimination, they are no more morally responsible for *causing* their advantage than members of disadvantaged groups are responsible for causing their disadvantage. The justification for redressing group-structured inequality is not only that the circumstances which cause some to be better off than others have nothing to do with effort or ability, but that they are "arbitrary from a moral point of view." In addition, since those inequalities are continuous with a past that was clearly *unjust*, they are themselves unjust. Time does not heal the wounds of injustice when it leaves in place the institutions and practices that embody that injustice.

Stability

The two-sided approach to group identification also answers the argument that the recognition of any group-based claims will lead to a multiplication of an unmanageable number of such claims, indistinguishable from one another on grounds of justice. Again, the groups that have the strongest claims to recognition are those that have a strong sense of collective memory and collective agency, *and* whose contemporary inequality is clearly connected with a history of discrimination. Given these criteria, it is not the case that we cannot make judgments about the relative strength of different groups' claims to recognition, as indeed I believe we do all the time. Implicit in the antigroup argument about stability is, I think, a fear that recognizing any group's claims as valid will convey the message that marginalized groups' interpretations of the causes of inequality would somehow be privileged, unchallengeable by those who were not members of those groups. But arguments about the existence of structural inequalities must be made to, and accepted by, others, based on evidence they could reasonably accept. Although members of marginalized groups have a strong claim to be *heard* and taken seriously in the public sphere, and (given the existence of radical inequality) many of their claims against the rest of society are likely to be valid, this does not mean that their voices are the final authority on what justice requires.

Clearly the problem of distinguishing the groups that merit special recognition from those that do not is exceedingly difficult from both a theoretical and practical perspective. Any judgment that a group's justice-claims are unwarranted is likely to produce a strong sense of injustice among the group's members. Moreover, the power to make such judgments, whether exercised by political theorists or legislative assemblies, is always susceptible to misuse because of the partiality of human judgment.[75] But political representation is a scarce good, and it is impossible to speak of just or fair representation without addressing the principle by which it should be distributed. This is one of the few points on which I disagree with Iris Young's defense of group representation.[76] In the argument I have presented, the differences in perspective that give rise to strong moral claims are largely the *product* of groups' subjection; we ought to aspire toward (though we will never reach) a politics in which the differences of perspective caused by oppression are gradually dissolved by the dissolution of classes of privilege. Although some sources of group distinctiveness are independent of the history of subordination, an equality-based defense of group representation is concerned only with the difference of perspective that is essential to overcoming social and political inequality. The representation of diversity may well be desirable for other reasons, but these reasons have little to do with justice. To put it somewhat differently, an egalitarian approach to marginalized ascriptive groups should seek to make them less *ascriptive*, to make membership in them a matter of choice rather than something imposed on the individual by others.[77] Whether it requires the preservation and affirmation of the content of group identities is not, in my view, a question one can answer as a matter of general principle; it is likely to vary from group to group, from context to context. Finally, from a practical point of view, the defense of group representation on grounds of diversity does not, in itself, help us to address the problem of adjudicating among groups' conflicting claims to the scarce resource of political representation.[78]

In essence, my disagreement with Young arises from the fact that assessing the fairness of a system of political representation must always involve an assessment of *institutions* of representation. If we aim at reconciling the values of individual equality and autonomy with a recognition of the ways in which group membership structures life-chances, we must attend to the ways in which different institutional solutions satisfy some values and thwart others. Although other defenses of group representation provide a strong justification for promoting it, they have not done so in a way that answers the institutional problems of seat allocation. The problem with a defense of group representation grounded in the value of diversity is that it is inherently incapable of providing criteria for solving this institutional problem. As I argue in the next chapter, I believe the approach to group identification that I have offered leads us to some clear criteria for making judgments about the relative merits of different institutional solutions to the problems of group representation.

My main purpose in offering the two-sided definition of marginalized groups developed in this chapter is to meet the practical political challenge of distinguishing stronger from weaker group claims to special recognition in the sphere of political representation. By considering the extent to which groups meet the joint criteria of "memory" and "history," it is possible, at least in principle, to reach judgments about where particular groups stand in a hierarchy of claims. I have argued that African Americans and women have very strong claims to special efforts to enhance their political representation because of the depth of the history of discrimination against them and the patterns of structural inequality that continue to marginalize their members, and because there has also been significant political mobilization around these identities. Both the "objective" and "subjective" sources of group identity are strong for these two groups. I do not mean to suggest, however, that these are the only groups for which strong claims can be made. The historical case for the claims of Mexican Americans has already been made in the "totality of circumstances" analyses of voting rights jurisprudence, particularly in California and Texas. The claims of other groups might be equally strong. Gays and lesbians, for example, might have a strong prima facie case for self-representation, since they have faced a deep history of state-sponsored discrimination that continues to reproduce systemic biases against them in numerous areas of the law—not to mention the current trends toward *contemporary* state-sponsored discrimination against them. Similar points could be made about persons with disabilities. These reflections are not decisive, however, since defensible judgments about group claims must always be grounded in careful historical analysis that considers both aspects of a group's identity.[79] A history of state-sponsored discrimination and contemporary patterns of inequality are both important; but so is the interpretation that group members give to these phenomena. In particular, a group's claim to recognition in the sphere of political representation depends critically on whether some substantial portion of its members have developed a sense of shared political identity.[80] As I noted above, without such a shared identity, it is impossible to identify the shared interests for which they should hold representatives accountable. Without a subjective sense of shared political interests, representatives have nothing to represent and constituents have no developed agency to exercise.

Without engaging in the historical analysis I have undertaken with respect to women and African Americans, I would be irresponsible to articulate judgments about the relative strength of other groups' claims to political representation. At the same time, it might be useful to consider some of the issues that other groups' claims might raise, as it suggests the ways in which "memory" and "history" provide tools for political judgment in other cases. Consider first the case of Native Americans. I suggested earlier that African Americans and Native Americans are the groups that most easily meet the criteria of "memory" and "history," as both groups have been subjected to extreme forms of state-sponsored domination and continue to suffer from stark patterns of economic and social inequality. But the case of Native Americans does not necessarily yield a strong claim to legislative representation, as we discover by examining the content of their subjective sense of group identity. As Will Kymlicka has argued forcefully, native peoples in North America, in contrast to women and African Americans, have not, for the most part, defined their claims against the majority as claims to *inclusion* on the basis of equal citizenship but rather as claims to *exclusion* from the political authority of the majority culture. While they do claim special group recognition, they claim it in the form of rights of self-government, not political representation in shared legislative institutions. Indeed, Kymlicka argues, "the logical consequence of self-government is reduced representation, not increased representation. The right to self-government is a right against the authority of the federal government, not a right to share in the exercise of that authority."[81] It seems likely that the just treatment of Native Americans and other colonized peoples requires some combination of rights of self-government and rights of self-representation. But Kymlicka's arguments indicate that the subjective self-understanding of Native Americans does not readily conform to the model of political inclusion through political representation which I have defended in this book. Even for groups whose "memory" and "history" create strong grounds of special recognition, then, it does not follow automatically that self-representation is the form that recognition should take. An argument for the self-representation of Native Americans in legislative bodies would have to be grounded in a historical inquiry aimed at illuminating the nature of the ethical relationship between conquering and colonized peoples, a project that extends far beyond what I have undertaken here.[82]

For some groups, claims to self-representation might be tempered by the fact that they possess some but not all the relevant forms of group identity. Some groups—for example, Irish Catholics—have historically been subject to state-supported discrimination but are not currently the focus of negative ascriptive meanings nor disadvantaged by patterns of structural inequality. Although some forms of group recognition might be appropriate for them, such as public acknowledgments of the injustice of past state actions against them, their claims to special measures for their self-representation in legislative bodies would not be strong. Other groups might have a strong subjective sense of their marginalization and might even be right to think that they are marginalized in the sense that negative meanings are attached to their group by the majority. It has been suggested to me that evangelical Christians, for example, should qualify as a marginalized group.[83] Yet if such groups do not also occupy a position of structural disadvantage, my argument for legislative self-representation would not apply to them.[84]

A more difficult challenge is posed by groups that have been victimized by state-sponsored discrimination and continue to be marginalized by systemic biases against them but that lack the subjective sense of group identity necessary to sustain a relationship of accountability between representative and constituents. In the United States class constitutes a group of this sort. The state-sponsored maintenance of structures of class-based inequality has been a fundamental presupposition of liberal democratic order. Economic policy, whether Keynesian or monetarist, accepts as a given the existence of capital and labor and makes choices about how to manage the relations between them.[85] Being born into poverty makes it likely that one will be poor as an adult. Negative social meanings undoubtedly attach to being poor and reinforce the lack of self-esteem that combines with other structural forces to keep people in poverty. Yet class membership in the United States clearly does not function as a source of subjective identity for individuals to nearly the same degree as sex, race, or ethnicity, even while it may determine our life-chances more thoroughly than any of those identities.[86] Despite the merits on objective grounds for recognizing class difference as especially relevant for fair political representation, the *subjective* side of class identity is relatively weak. In the absence of social dynamics that produce both a heightened subjective salience for class and better prospects for social and political mobilization around class identity, it is hard to make the case for special solicitude for the increased self-representation of the poor and working class as such. To do so in the absence of subjective group identity would be to advocate vanguardism, the definition of the interests of the class independent of the self-understandings of its members. This I take to be deeply problematic from the standpoint of democratic accountability and individual autonomy. The case of class thus illustrates that claims for the legislative self-representation of a marginalized group do not follow immediately from claims of social injustice.

Nonetheless, there may be some ground for believing that the institutional changes which would facilitate representation for marginalized groups with a strong sense of subjective identity might encourage other marginalized groups, including the poor, to develop a sense of the political relevance of their marginalization. In the next chapter I argue for electoral reform in the direction of proportional and semi-proportional representation. There are good reasons to think that such electoral changes would yield a more fluid politics which, by creating new opportunities for representation, might also create new incentives for the political mobilization of hitherto passive marginalized groups.

I stated above that the criteria of "memory" and "history" are intended as tools to facilitate our political judgments about the relative strength of group claims to self-representation. As a final note I should emphasize that judgments of this sort are political not only in the sense that they concern a shared political life and shared political institutions but also in the sense that they are judgments we must reach through deliberation with others. Claims to special recognition always appeal to other political agents, justified through reasons we hope they will accept. Ultimately this is the most important reason why I do not claim decisive authority for the judgments I express here concerning the relative strength of groups' claims to representation: those judgments are nothing more nor less than my contribution to an ongoing political deliberation about fair representation.

7

The Institutions of Fair Representation

GIVEN THE theoretical defense of a group-based conception of fair representation, what are the desiderata of a system of political representation? That we may think there is an equality-based imperative to enhance marginalized group representation does not, by itself, resolve many questions about how best to design institutions of representation; nor does it tell us how to reconcile the goals of group representation with other important or indispensable goals of a system of political representation. As everywhere in politics, the devil is in the details. Most fundamentally, I am concerned to identify institutional arrangements that can accommodate the strongest claims to group representation without violating the principles of individual autonomy and individual equality—the values usually presented as the strongest arguments against group rights or group recognition of any sort. In addition, institutions of representation will, ideally, satisfy a range of other dimensions of good government in addition to satisfying criteria of fair representation, including political stability (an institutional system's propensity to produce smooth, law-governed transitions of political leadership); the requirements of publicity (the ease of citizens' comprehension of political processes); and the compatibility of representative institutions with the prevailing political culture.

The purpose of this discussion is to relate the theoretical defense of group representation to practical means of bringing it about. Other discussions of group representation have tended to conflate the former with the latter, identifying group representation with specific institutions that bring it about.[1] In her earlier discussions of the political representation of women and ethnic minorities, for example, Anne Phillips's critique of such institutional devices as consociational democracy and party quotas seemed to undermine her willingness to defend the positive merits, from the standpoint of democratic equality, of efforts to enhance the legislative presence of marginalized groups.[2] Abigail Thernstrom and Carol Swain have tended to identify any attempt to increase the legislative presence of racial minorities with race-conscious districting.[3] Such conflations lead us to criticize the particular institutional form of group representation, and then to mistake our criticism of the institutions for criticisms of the principle itself. But it is crucial to separate the two steps of an inquiry into group representation, that is, to separate the normative defense from the institutional design that will translate it into practice. That some institutional forms of group representation are not morally acceptable does not mean the concept itself is flawed.

At the same time, the theoretical defense of group representation is not complete without some discussion of institutions, for if there is *no* morally acceptable scheme of institutions that can embody the normative ideal, it means the normative argument can function only as a critique of existing practice, not as an aid to the creative rethinking of our political possibilities.[4] My aim, then, is to explore the different institutional means for embodying the three different aspects of representation as mediation that a group-based theory of fair representation entails. In the course of this exploration, it should become clear (if it is not clear already) that not every institutional means for enhancing the legislative presence of historically marginalized groups is consonant with the aspirations I have articulated in the previous chapters, nor with the aspiration to reconcile a group-based theory of fair representation with the democratic commitment to individual equality and freedom. Neither is there a *single* attractive institutional scheme for enhancing the legislative presence of women and minorities. As we shall see, a number of institutions fit the bill, more or less. Thus there are more means to group representation than are morally praiseworthy and more than one morally praiseworthy means.

In identifying the desiderata of fair institutions of representation, it is helpful to return to the notion, presented in chapter 1, that we best understand political representation as a set of processes and institutions that mediate between the individual citizen and political outcomes in at least three ways: by the way an electoral system aggregates voters for the purpose of defining the constituencies that merit political representation; through the structure and closeness of legislator-constituency relations; and through the dynamics of legislative decision making. The following discussion addresses the institutional concerns that attach to each dimension of representation as mediation.

I should note that although my inquiry to this point has been mainly focused on the American context, I have not limited myself to that context in considering institutional alternatives. Not only do I look beyond electoral systems based on territorial districts, but I have also explored, in a preliminary way, some of the implications of differences between parliamentary and presidential systems of government for measures aimed at enhancing accountability and deliberation. Some of the institutional alternatives I explore (such as party-list proportional representation) are much less feasible within the context of American political culture than they are in other societies. I have nonetheless included them here for two reasons. First, although the normative defense of group representation arises out of an analysis of American patterns of inequality, my general conclusions about representational fairness for marginalized groups may be valid in other contexts as well. Second, limiting the scope of the study to the most familiar and acceptable institutional alternatives would have been less likely to suggest the full range of political possibilities for enhancing fair representation for marginalized groups.

I. Defining Constituencies

The theoretical defense of marginalized group representation clearly implies that a crucial test of a system of representation is whether it secures some threshold level of representation for marginalized groups that have both an objective experience of historical oppression and contemporary inequality as well as a subjective sense that they constitute a group with shared political interests. But these criteria underdetermine the shape a system of representative institutions will take. We also need criteria for determining the basis for aggregating nonmarginalized citizens into representable constituencies. Moreover, some methods of ensuring marginalized group representation are fundamentally incompatible with the principles of individual equality and individual autonomy; others give rise to consequences that are undesirable from the standpoint of other important values of a political system, such as citizens' ease of understanding or their propensity to produce stable governments. The following evaluates alternative means of increasing the presence of representatives from marginalized groups within legislative bodies by defining political constituencies around group identity.

Race-Conscious Districting

Until recently the practice of race-conscious districting (also known as creating "majority-minority" districts) has been the principal means of increasing the electoral influence of racial and ethnic minorities. As discussed in chapter 3, the practice has two sources: first, as a remedy in minority vote-dilution cases (brought under Section 2 of the Voting Rights Act or the Fourteenth Amendment); and, second, in "covered" jurisdictions, as a strategy for meeting the preclearance requirements of Section 5 of the Voting Rights Act. The current wisdom is that in order to be confident of a minority group's capacity to elect the representative of its choice, districts must be drawn so that minority voters comprise at least 65 percent of the district.[5]

Race-conscious districting has undoubtedly been an effective means of enhancing minority legislative presence. The round of redistricting that followed the 1990 census doubled the number of majority-minority congressional districts and yielded a 50 percent increase in the number of African American members (from twenty-six to thirty-nine) of the House of Representatives and a 38 percent increase in the number of Latino members (from thirteen to eighteen).[6] The creation of majority-minority districts has also produced a substantial increase in the number of minority legislators at the state level, though not quite as marked as the increases at the federal level.[7] Compared to single-member districts drawn without regard to race and to multimember districts, race-conscious districting clearly does a better job of bringing minority representatives to office.

As I have discussed in chapter 2, the most serious critique of race-conscious districting is that it places the state in the role of labeling and separating citizens according to race, doing grave injustice to the principle of individual autonomy. As Justice Kennedy expressed this view in his opinion for the majority in *Miller v. Johnson,* "When the State assigns voters on the basis of race, it engages in the offensive and demeaning assumption that voters of a particular race, because of their race, 'think alike, share the same political interests, and will prefer the same candidates at the polls.'"[8]

But race-conscious districting is not nearly so morally objectionable as its critics make out. Certainly it preserves individual equality in the form of "one person, one vote" as well as any other districting scheme. The charge that it violates individual autonomy by grouping individuals according to ascriptive characteristics that they may or may not affirm as an important source of identity would have more merit were it not that the practice is only defended where there are preexisting patterns of racial bloc voting—i.e., where voters have already identified themselves as divided along racial lines.[9]

Even if demonstrated patterns of bloc voting overcome the challenge to group-conscious districting from the principle of individual autonomy, however, the practice has important limitations as a tool for advancing representational fairness as I have outlined it. Among the most obvious weaknesses of the practice is that it is only capable of enhancing the representation of geographically concentrated groups. Because many ethnic and racial minorities are geographically dispersed, there is a systemic limit to the capacity of group-conscious districting to approach proportionality. Thus before *Shaw* and *Miller* the capacity of race-conscious districting to yield increases in minority office holding was reaching its theoretical limit at the level of national institutions (though not at state and local levels).

Other disadvantages of group-conscious districting are endemic to single-member district plurality systems as such. In her study of representatives' behavior in their home districts, Carol Swain criticizes race-conscious districting on the ground that the "electoral security that benefits representatives from historically black districts can have a negative effect on the caliber of their representation."[10] However, Swain criticizes safe districts only in the case of Black representatives; she neither studies the relative responsiveness of White candidates from safe districts nor follows the line of her critique to a more general condemnation of single-member plurality district systems, which have always contained safe seats and which generally advantage incumbents in electoral competitions. As I discuss at greater length below, fair representation depends crucially on representatives' accountability to their constituents. To the extent that it diminishes representatives' need to consult closely with constituents, geographic districting per se—including race-conscious districting—undercuts one of the components of fair representation.

As Lani Guinier and others have argued forcefully, a further weakness of single-member plurality district electoral systems is that it "wastes" votes. "Districting," she argues, "breeds gerrymandering as a means of allocating group benefits; the operative principle is deciding whose votes get wasted."[11] Because these are winner-take-all systems, in which candidates need only receive a bare majority to be elected, only the votes that constitute that majority are effective in placing a representative in office. Citizens who vote for the losing candidate "waste" their votes insofar as their vote contributed nothing to the election of a representative. Because they are unable to identify a member of the legislative assembly for whom they voted, they are likely to feel altogether unrepresented, notwithstanding the theoretical obligation of the member from their district to attend to their interests. Even members of the victorious majority have "wasted" their vote insofar as only the votes needed to constitute a majority were effective in electing the representative. This is a source of particular concern in majority-minority districts, which, as I have noted above, are usually drawn to ensure supermajorities of 65 percent. Members of the minority community whose votes were in surplus of the number needed to elect a representative of the minority group's choice might have been included in a neighboring district where they may have been able to influence the election's outcome, thus securing additional clout in the legislative body for the minority community. As I discuss further below, systems of proportional and semi-proportional representation "waste" a much smaller percentage of citizens' votes than do single-member district systems.[12]

Finally, in the current context of two-party politics in the United States, it is a commonplace that gains for minority legislators, almost all of whom are Democrats, yield net gains in legislative seats for the Republican Party. This occurs because majority-minority districts concentrate Democratic voters in a single district rather than creating smaller, racially diverse Democratic majorities in several districts. While Black Democrats have tended to favor race-conscious districting despite this consequence, it is undeniable that their legislative agenda—as well as the power of the Congressional Black Caucus—have suffered within the Republican-led Congress.[13]

Plurality Multimember Districts or At-Large Systems

Multimember districts that follow a majoritarian principle (rather than a scheme of proportional or semi-proportional representation) are one of the most common causes of minority vote dilution.[14] Nonetheless I mention them here because the empirical evidence clearly indicates that women candidates tend to be more successful in multimember than in single-member districts. Even in plurality systems, multimember districts result in the election of greater numbers of women than do single-member districts.[15] In the United States, for example, states with multimember districts elected an average of 21.8 percent women legislators, whereas states with single-member districts averaged only 12.4 percent. Moreover, both African American and White Anglo women tend to be more successful in multimember than in single-member districts, a tendency that appears to hold for other minority women as well.[16] The scholarly consensus is that this difference occurs because multimember districts create an incentive for parties to run women candidates. One male political leader in a single-member district system commented, "The only time to run a woman . . . is when things look so bad that your only chance is to do something dramatic."[17] When a party can run only one candidate, choosing a woman often carries a perceived risk that voters will prefer a male opponent regardless of their partisan preferences. In multimember district systems, however, parties must run several candidates, so their *failure* to present women candidates may be risky insofar as it may communicate a bias against women.[18] At the same time, women and minorities both fare better in proportional representation systems than in plurality systems, even when the latter use multimember districts. From the standpoint of enhancing the legislative presence of marginalized groups in general, there is no advantage to plurality multimember districts over proportional and semi-proportional representation systems. Indeed, one would regard plurality multimember districts as desirable only if one were concerned about political stability in the face of deep social divisions. Because multimember plurality districts exaggerate majority voter strength even more powerfully than do single-member districts, they are more likely to create a legislature with a strong majority party.

Reserved Seats

Several electoral systems set aside legislative seats for groups that historically have been denied significant representation. In New Zealand the Maori Representation Act of 1867 divided the country into four electoral districts and gave Maori males the right to elect one representative from each district to Parliament.[19] In 1993, however, New Zealanders voted in a national referendum to adopt a mixed-member proportional representation system. The new system will be used in the next general election.

While guaranteeing some Maori representation, the four Maori seats always constituted a substantial underrepresentation of Maoris, a situation that only became starker as the number of general seats increased while the number of reserved Maori seats stayed the same. Thus while they hold four of ninety-five seats in Parliament, Maoris constitute 20 percent of the population.[20] Maori voters may choose whether to be listed on the Maori register of voters or on the general register; they are not required by law to vote according to their ethnic identity, and they may switch from one roll to the other every five years, at census time. In addition, Maori candidates may choose to run for general seats, and they have had some electoral success in such competitions.

Few New Zealanders appear enthusiastic about reserved seats under the current system. A substantial majority of Pakeha (White) New Zealanders oppose separate Maori representation, some on the grounds that separate representation is fundamentally racist and paternalistic.[21] Others argue that the system prevents Maoris from having effective political clout by ghettoizing Maori representatives within Parliament and also leaves non-Maori representatives feeling that they are not responsible for protecting Maori interests.[22] As one community leader put it:

> The Maori have no real political role and influence. They have no political voice. Their representation in the polity, the four Maori seats, is token, chiefly for show. On any Maori issue, we are totally at the mercy of the Pakeha. They constitute the majority and they run the whole show. Our situation is not very different from that of the colonised peoples all over the world . . . And the tragedy for us is that ours is not even seen by the world as a colonial condition.[23]

At the same time, Maoris have been reluctant to give up the reserved seats, as they provide at least some legislative presence for their interests and symbolically represent Maoris' status as a distinct people within New Zealand.[24]

The new mixed-member proportional representation system, modeled on the German system, increases the total number of seats in Parliament from 99 to 120, and the reserved Maori seats from 4 to 5. As in the current system, the Maori seats will be filled from a separate register of voters, but individual Maoris have the option to vote from the general instead of the Maori roll. In contrast to the current system, the reserved Maori seats will henceforth depend on the number of people of Maori descent who opt to register as Maoris, and Maori districts will be redrawn following each census.[25]

The state of Maine also has reserved seats in its legislature for native peoples. Both the Penobscot and Passamaquoddy tribes have the right to elect a representative to the legislature. The representatives so elected are, however, nonvoting members of the legislature, since voters from these communities are also eligible to vote in general elections for a voting representative. However, the two Indian representatives have all the other privileges of members of the state assembly, including voting within committees. The Canadian province of New Brunswick is considering the adoption of a plan for Aboriginal representation on the model of Maine.[26]

Although the two reserved seats reflect a much closer proportionality to the population of native people in the state of Maine than do the four Maori seats in New Zealand, the power of the Indian representatives to have an impact on legislation is limited because theirs are nonvoting seats. The representatives do provide some constituency service for their communities and are able to raise issues of concern to their communities within the legislature, but their influence is clearly limited.

In its final report in 1991 Canada's Royal Commission on Electoral Reform proposed the creation of Aboriginal constituencies within the framework of the existing single-member district electoral system. Following the New Zealand model, the Commission proposed that Aboriginal voters have the option to register in special constituencies or to vote with the general, non-Aboriginal population.[27] As in the New Zealand system following its recent electoral reform, Aboriginal seats would be apportioned according to the number of voters who registered in the special polls rather than a set number of reserved seats being guaranteed. Thus they would not be numerically over- or underrepresented relative to non-Aboriginal constituencies; the number of citizens constituting a riding would be the same for Aboriginals and for non-Aboriginals.[28] These seats would come out of the total number of seats apportioned to the province in which the special Aboriginal riding was created, and the members elected to fill them would have full voting rights in Parliament. The Commission emphasized that nothing about separate Aboriginal representation should be regarded as prejudicial to Aboriginal communities' other political objectives, including self-government. According to the report, there was strong support for special Aboriginal constituencies among Aboriginal communities across Canada.[29]

Finally, in Taiwan women are guaranteed representation under a system of reserved seats. Different districts are used for different types of elections: in some elections, women are guaranteed a seat in districts in which there are four or more seats; in other elections, district magnitude must be at least seven in order for women to be guaranteed a seat; in still other elections, the threshold is ten seats. Overall, the system of reserved seats results in legislative bodies in which women constitute 10 percent of the membership.[30] Recently women have had some success in winning seats beyond the guaranteed number. Some favor eliminating the system of guaranteed representation for women, arguing that it functions as a quota and limits the number of women elected.[31]

The most obvious objection to a constitution that reserves seats for any ascriptive group is that it employs the power of the law to impose a group identity on individuals, and consequently violates the principle of individual autonomy. However, none of the schemes of guaranteed representation described above actually functions to deny individual members of marginalized ascriptive groups the freedom to decide whether their ascriptive group identity is the one they wish to express in electoral politics. In the case of the reserved Maori seats and the proposed Aboriginal seats in Canada, individuals have the choice to use their vote as an expression of ethnic identity and interest or to join the general electorate. Of course reserving seats for a group does presuppose that it constitutes a more powerful identity for its members than do other group identities that might provide the basis for constituency definition. In particular, the creation of special constituencies for Aboriginal communities would likely lead to the election of representatives who are already relatively powerful within those communities, a tendency that may suppress the influence of Aboriginal women.[32] Because the electoral devices for special constituencies are no different from those that prevail in other districts, this danger does not loom as large for institutions of guaranteed representation.

Another concern that reserved seats raise is that by constitutionalizing group identity they ossify lines of group cleavage and permanently entrench intergroup conflict. This is the concern of balkanization, a charge that critics assert against many different forms of group recognition. What such critics generally fail to acknowledge, however, is that the intergroup conflicts for which guaranteed representation is a partial remedy are already prominent and, for all practical purposes, are permanent features of the political landscape. Recognizing the existence of divergent group interests does not, in itself, create the difference between groups. Nor do the divergent perspectives and interests to which group representation give expression necessarily produce irresolvable political conflict. Indeed, in cases where they do so, the minority status of these groups will ensure that their interests are not the ones that prevail. Rather, the hope is that by having the opportunity to express their distinctive interests, marginalized group representatives may be able either to negotiate with other representatives to identify policy alternatives that serve all citizens' interests in a more equitable manner or to identify compromise positions whose costs are acceptable to the majority.

The threat of balkanization is one we must take seriously. As we saw in chapter 1, a theorist of representation must decide whether the public interest is best served by giving expression to the group cleavages that structure social life, as in Mill's theory, or by suppressing group differences, as in Madisonian theory. Some sources of political conflict are so deep, divisive, and destabilizing that the polity can ill afford to give them easy expression. The experience of the real Balkans makes clear that the suppression of group difference, even at the cost of some freedom, is preferable to the anarchy and mutual destruction that can arise when intergroup conflict is unleashed.[33] Consequently mechanisms of guaranteed representation are perhaps more likely to be acceptable to the majority in the case of Aboriginal peoples, whose numbers are relatively small and whose claims, though often substantial, can be absorbed without devastating consequences for the majority population.[34]

Reserving legislative seats for marginalized groups seems most appropriate in the following settings: first, within single-member district electoral systems that provide no other opportunity for a group's self-representation and, second, in systems where a minority's interests are starkly different from those of the majority but its numbers are so small that it would not otherwise have any legislative representation. Because reserved seats necessarily constitutionalize group identity, they are consistent with principles of individual autonomy only where there is a high degree of internal group cohesion or where, as with the Maori, individuals have a choice to be identified either as a group member or as an ordinary citizen. In addition, entrenching a group identity in the constitution would seem to be a mistaken strategy unless the differences between the group in question and the rest of society were generally regarded as permanent. Not surprisingly, the proposals for reserved seats that find most support are those connected to Aboriginal identities.

Intraparty Quotas

Anne Phillips's work on women's representation has focused on the strategy pursued within Nordic systems of party quotas for women candidates.[35] This strategy has clear advantages as far as getting women elected to office, as the record of those countries makes clear, but it has disadvantages as well. First, it does not provide any direct mechanisms of accountability to the constituency that women candidates purportedly represent, i.e., women. If the initiative to run women candidates comes from the party leadership, then women so elected will owe their first allegiance to their parties and will necessarily pursue the agenda of women's distinct concerns or interests only where it coincides with or complements the party's stated agenda.

The prospects of this strategy, in any event, are much greater in a parliamentary system based on proportional representation than in an electoral system with single-member districts. In the latter, party organizations at the district level will have a great deal of control over the party's nominees and may resist women's and minorities' candidacies as electorally risky. Moreover, only in a parliamentary system is there likely to be sufficient party cohesion to discipline members to accept quotas.[36] This point raises a number of questions about the relative merits of parliamentary and presidential systems of government for marginalized group representation, and I can address them only tentatively here. Within a system of party government and strict party discipline, legislators are accountable directly to their party leadership and only indirectly to constituents. In such circumstances, women representatives' ability to represent women's distinctive interests and perspectives would seem to depend on the openness of party leadership and their power within the party caucus. Parliamentary assemblies may have important advantages over congressional assemblies when it comes to deliberation. The traditions, in parliamentary assemblies, of party discipline, loyal opposition, and ministerial responsibility combine to encourage the expression of principled disagreement, in contrast to the evasion of responsibility for policy decisions that tends to characterize debate in the United States Congress. Nonetheless, within a system of party discipline, individual representatives are not completely free to alter their public political judgments in response to arguments from other representatives; nor are they free to express views that stand in tension with the party platform. Whether they are in government or in opposition, therefore, it would seem that women representatives' hopes for influencing policy will depend on their power to expand the range of discourse *within* the parties rather than on deliberative exchanges at the parliamentary level.[37]

Consociational Democracy

Systems of consociational democracy guarantee representation for minorities by formally entrenching their place in government office. They have evolved in countries characterized by deep ethno-linguistic divisions to secure political stability by guaranteeing the influence of all major national groups in government decisions; thus the classic examples of consociational democracy are Belgium, Switzerland, and the Netherlands. The characteristic features of consociational democracy, as Arend Lijphart identified them in his influential study, are fourfold: (1) government by a "grand coalition" of elites from all the major segments or sections of the society; (2) a mutual veto or (borrowing Calhoun's phrase and concept) rule of "concurrent majorities";[38] (3) proportionality in legislative and bureaucratic office holding; and (4) internal autonomy for the major social segments.[39] Like Calhoun's system, consociational democracy—both in theory and practice—is designed to compel cooperation between two or more national blocs with fundamentally different character and interests through institutions that roughly balance their political power. Such systems have a further similarity with Calhoun's in that they are powerfully elite-driven systems: accommodation among the elites (who are, in these systems, popularly elected by their respective populations) is what determines policy outcomes, with little or no direct dependence on mass public opinion.

In her earlier work Anne Phillips argued in favor of consociational democracy as a model for enhancing the representation of women in legislative bodies. She found it an attractive solution insofar as it simultaneously gives institutional recognition to the existence of deep and important group differences without reducing *all* politics to those differences. Thus while it secures the proportional representation of subnational groupings in legislatures, it leaves a wide space for the expression of differences internal to those groupings through partisan competition.[40]

Phillips did acknowledge important weaknesses in consociationalism. As she noted, one of its problems is that it entrenches group cleavages in circumstances where one wishes they will eventually disappear, as she discusses in the case of Nigeria. Where it is consciously introduced as a device for resolving intergroup conflict, it may have the tendency to give smaller groups a stake in special group recognition, with the consequence that it can further balkanize a country. There is also the troubling question of who will have the power to decide which groups will be included in the consociational arrangements. It seems likely that this power will be wielded by those groups that are already relatively powerful compared to other groups that may have an equally defensible moral claim to inclusion, so that the resulting institutions may contribute little to the political equality of the historically marginalized groups about which we should be most concerned.

In addition to these weaknesses, consociational democracy suffers from a number of other deficiencies. First, it is a solution to intergroup conflict that is only likely to be successful in countries where (a) there are few (two or three) relevant social cleavages (otherwise accommodation would require negotiations among too many different parties); (b) the minority bloc or blocs are sufficiently large to threaten the majority's fundamental interests should it refuse to cooperate politically (that is, there is some rough balance of bargaining power);[41] and (c) the blocs are sufficiently internally homogeneous to provide clear outcomes as to each bloc's leadership and to keep clear boundaries between social segments; where cleavages exist within segments, contests over leadership might make it difficult for the other bloc's leadership to know whom to negotiate with.

Second, consociational democracy stands in direct tension with the notion of shared citizenship and with the principle of the equality of individual citizens. Because citizens elect leaders from within their blocs, there are few institutional processes in which they participate jointly with citizens from other blocs. In effect, then, their citizenship is not something they enjoy as individuals; rather, they are incorporated into citizenship by way of their membership in their subnational grouping. This violates the principle of the equality of citizens insofar as the influence of a citizen from the minority group is likely to be proportionately greater than that of a citizen from the majority.[42] It also stands in tension with the principle of individual autonomy, as citizens have no choice but to vote according to their group identity and have been legally allocated to political jurisdictions on the basis of that identity. Even if, as Phillips emphasized, they may still have the opportunity to express other dimensions of their political identity through partisan affiliation, they do not have the option of abandoning their group identity as irrelevant should they so wish.

This is not to say that consociational democracy is an illegitimate system for countries where it has evolved. Historical circumstances may exist in which group conflict is so intense that a consociational solution offers the best prospect for a peaceful and balanced negotiation of differences. In the absence of a sense of shared citizenship through which intergroup differences can be negotiated, consociationalism may be the only alternative to destructive competition. But it does have important disadvantages, particularly in circumstances where constructing a shared political community offers the greatest potential rewards to all concerned. Most important, it shares with Calhoun's system of concurrent majorities the flaw that it ossifies a particular social cleavage at the constitutional level, and consequently inhibits the emergence of other forms of intergroup conflict. Thus consociationalism is not a solution to the problems of chronic marginalization; as currently practiced, it privileges ethno-linguistic differences above differences of gender or class.

Proportional Representation

What remain are procedural approaches to constituency definition that rely on self-defined constituencies, that is, proportional and semi-proportional representation systems. Advocates for marginalized group representation increasingly view such systems as the most promising direction of institutional reform.[43]

Varieties of proportional representation systems abound, and each can be blended in various ways with aspects of territorial districts. All proportional representation systems share a number of features, however. First, whether they aggregate voter preferences along the lines of partisan difference or by some other criterion, they all seek to secure representation for citizens roughly proportionate to their share of the voting population. As one scholar puts it, "Any true PR method will always produce perfect proportionality (a complete correspondence between vote and seat shares) when this can be achieved."[44] Second, all systems of proportional representation allow individuals to form *self-defined constituencies*. In contrast to systems of territorial representation, in which one's membership in a particular constituency is the accident of the districting authority's decision to draw a district's boundary in one place rather than another, in a system of proportional representation one chooses not only who one's representative will be but also the other citizens with whom one wishes to form a representable constituency. In party-list systems of proportional representation, that choice takes the form of identification with one party rather than another; in other forms of proportional representation, such as the single transferable vote system, constituencies may form around individual candidates rather than around parties.

The principal types of proportional and semi-proportional representation (hereafter referred to as "PR" and "semi-PR," respectively) are party-list PR, the single transferable vote (STV), cumulative voting, and limited voting:[45]

PARTY LIST PR

In these systems parties win seats in proportion to the number of votes cast for them. In some systems the allocation of seats is subject to a threshold; Germany's system defines a threshold of 5 percent, for example. In party-list systems, lists of candidates may either be closed or open. In the former, the party fixes the order in which candidates will be assigned seats. In open list systems, voters may indicate some preference among candidates.[46] In virtually all party-list PR systems, however, parties maintain substantial control over which candidates will be offered; while voters may be able to influence which candidates on a list are elected, the parties themselves, more than the candidates, are the focus of electoral choice.

SINGLE TRANSFERABLE VOTE (STV)

Also known as "preferential voting," the STV system allocates one vote to each citizen.[47] However, each voter may register a preference order of candidates. A candidate wins a seat when he or she attains the necessary quota of votes: $(v / s + 1) + 1$, where v is the total number of votes cast and s is the number of seats to be filled. This method almost always results in a surplus of votes, since a candidate is unlikely to receive exactly the quota of votes. An elected candidate's surplus votes are reallocated among the remaining candidates according to a weighted average of the second preferences indicated on the ballots; the process is then repeated until all the seats are filled.[48]

CUMULATIVE AND LIMITED VOTING

Cumulative voting systems give each voter as many votes as there are seats to be filled. A voter may allocate these votes among candidates in any way he or she wishes, "spending" them all on one candidate or spreading them among several candidates. In contrast to STV systems, which permit voters only to register ordinal preferences, cumulative voting also allows voters to register the intensity of their preferences (their cardinal preferences). Limited voting works on the same principle as cumulative voting in that voters receive multiple votes which they may "spend" in any way they like, with the difference that voters have fewer votes than there are candidates. This has the effect of raising the threshold of representation (the percentage of votes a candidate must receive in order to win a legislative seat).[49] Both cumulative and limited voting are likely to secure representation for the largest minority party (in contrast to a single-member district system, which will secure representation for the minority party only when it can win a majority within individual districts).[50]

MIXED SYSTEMS

Any of these methods of PR and semi-PR may be blended with geographic systems of representation to create modified or mixed PR systems. Perhaps the best-known mixed system is Germany's additional member system, in which half the candidates are elected through party-list PR and the other half as individual candidates in single-member geographic districts. After the district-based candidates are elected, the remaining half of the seats are allocated to the parties in proportion to the votes they received on the PR half of the ballot.[51] Another approach to mixing elements of PR with territorial representation is to use one of these methods within multimember districts that are smaller than the entire jurisdiction. In fact, with the exception of Israel, in which the entire country constitutes a single electoral district, all existing systems are "mixed" in this sense.

Taken together, PR systems produce electoral outcomes which, relative to "first-past-the-post" single-member plurality systems, enhance the legislative presence not only of minority political parties but also of women[52] and ethnic minorities.[53] A study of the electoral success of women in twenty-seven democracies showed that even after the record numbers of women elected to Congress in the 1992 elections, the United States still ranked only seventeenth. (Before those elections it had ranked twenty-third.) Of the sixteen countries with higher rates of female representation, thirteen, or 81 percent, use some form of proportional representation. Even at its high point, the number of female representatives in the House of Representatives was 11 percent, compared to an average of 24 percent in PR countries.[54] Perhaps the clearest evidence for the importance of PR devices in the election of women comes from countries that combine single-member geographic districts with PR. In the 1983 elections in Germany, for example, the single-member district ballot elected only 4 percent women, whereas the PR ballot elected 16 percent women.[55] In both Australia and Japan the lower houses use single-member district elections, whereas the upper houses use PR. In both countries the upper houses elect three to ten times as many women as the lower houses.[56] These findings tend to support the claim, asserted by Pippa Norris, that the electoral system is the *most* important variable determining women's electoral success.[57]

The advantages of PR systems for ethnic and racial minorities are equally clear. Indeed, it was precisely to secure the representation of ethnic and religious minorities that PR was first introduced in many European countries.[58] The historical record of experimentation with semi-PR in the United States also reveals its success in enhancing the legislative presence of racial and ethnic as well as partisan minorities.[59] More recently, more than fifty local governments in the United States have instituted cumulative voting schemes,[60] at least eight of which have been part of the settlement of minority vote dilution lawsuits.[61] These schemes have been quite successful in electing minority candidates where such candidates previously had been excluded from electoral office and have also benefited Native Americans, Latinos, and African Americans.[62]

As I have discussed above, some of women's relative success in PR systems is a consequence of the fact that they use multimember rather than single-member districts (SMDs) and thereby create incentives for parties to include women on their slates of candidates. Another important determinant of the electoral prospects of historically disadvantaged groups is the size, or "magnitude," of multimember electoral districts, that is, the number of legislators elected from each. Although disadvantaged groups seem to reap some benefits from PR devices even when district magnitudes are as low as two,[63] some research indicates that women's rate of election increases directly with increases in district magnitude.[64] It is a general law of PR systems that the larger the district, the greater the proportionality of electoral outcomes; this law applies to women and ethnic or racial minorities as stringently as to partisan minorities.

Institutions of PR and semi-PR overcome all the usual objections to group representation. Such systems have the advantage of preserving individual *equality* virtually perfectly: every citizen receives a vote or votes that have the same weight as any other citizen's. Arguably PR systems also treat citizens more *equitably* than do single-member plurality systems, since those who support minority parties or candidates are still able to achieve some legislative representation.[65] As Lani Guinier argues, the aspiration to equity seems better served in systems of "winner-take-only-some" than in "winner-take-all" systems.[66] Although one might agree with Charles Beitz when he argues that proportional representation is not an *imperative* of the principle of political equality in any general sense, the moral case for PR is strong for historically marginalized groups whose prospects of electoral success would otherwise be poor.[67]

Another argument in favor of STV, cumulative voting, and limited voting systems is that they permit citizens to indicate the order or intensity of their preferences at the same time that they preserve the equal weight or value of individual citizens' votes. Finally, because they aggregate citizens into constituencies according to citizens' own judgments about what their defining political interests are, they face none of the ethical challenges that can be launched against race-conscious districting. Both features render these forms of PR better approximations of the ideals of procedural fairness than single-member district systems can ever be.

Advocates of PR also claim further democratic advantages of PR compared to single-member district systems. There is empirical evidence that voter participation is higher in PR than in SMD systems.[68] At least since John Stuart Mill, defenders of PR have argued that it contributes to a sense of citizen efficacy because it "wastes" many fewer votes than do SMD systems. In other words, in PR systems a much higher percentage of citizens' votes actually contribute to the election of a representative, so that more citizens are able to identify a representative whom they have had some role in electing. In the American context, a decided advantage of PR and semi-PR mechanisms over existing SMD elections is that once district magnitude is two or more, gerry-mandering becomes virtually impossible.[69]

Familiar objections to PR do not appear decisive when we take all the available evidence into account. Perhaps the most common and disturbing are references to the political instability that results from the multiplication of political parties and the difficulty of forming a majority government in parliamentary systems. Weimar Germany, Israel, and Italy are the most frequently cited cases. Some of this instability is caused by the emergence of small "fringe" parties whose influence in the coalition-building process becomes exaggerated and results in policies that the vast majority of voters would not endorse, as in the case of Israel's ultra-religious parties. However, Israel has a uniquely low threshold of representation in which only 1 percent of the vote is required to win a seat. Instituting a higher threshold would greatly reduce this tendency. The problem of weak coalitions is more difficult to solve, as the case of Italy demonstrates. Systems afflicted with these disadvantages of PR are the exception rather than the rule, however. Recent empirical work shows that coalition governments are, on average, no more unstable than single-party governments.[70] Moreover, most critiques of PR concern its disadvantages within parliamentary systems, where a government's authority to govern is dependent on its ability to command a legislative majority. If we return our focus to the American system, where legislative and executive powers are independently elected, these problems cannot arise. Indeed, even Maurice Duverger, who was generally opposed to PR because of the problems of accountability that result from the obstacles to electing a clear governing party, believed that PR would be salutary in the United States at both the national and state levels.[71]

At the same time, if we are especially concerned with the American case, not all PR systems are equally attractive candidates for political reform. Party-list PR is not a strong candidate for reform, since the United States lacks a tradition of partisan diversity. More to the point, for a group-based theory of fair representation, the differences at issue are not best understood as ideological differences, the sort best reflected in party-list PR. Although the differences between parties of the left and those of the right may have some bearing on the political identifications of members of historically marginalized groups, ideological differences within those groups might prevent the emergence of group-based parties as such. If that were the case, the introduction of party-list PR would do little to increase marginalized group representation. Because voters choose parties and leave it to party elites to determine the order in which candidates will be elected, party-list systems in themselves place no particular pressure on elites to include women and minorities on their slates. Israel's poor record of electing women to public office is a case in point. In order to make a difference in the representation of women and other marginalized groups, party-list systems must include strong movements *within* the parties on behalf of these groups' equal representation. As Anne Phillips has detailed, such mobilization was a critical factor in the emergence of party quotas for women in Nordic party-list PR systems.[72]

Another problem with party-list PR, from which other systems may also suffer but to a lesser degree, is the advantage that already established parties would have over new parties. This advantage would constitute a systemic barrier to marginalized group representation. Because both the single transferable vote and cumulative voting are candidate-focused rather than party-focused systems, they are likely to allow a better chance of success for candidates who are not aligned with a political party or who represent a party new to the electoral scene.[73]

This brings up a more general reservation I have about PR systems, one that other advocates of group representation have not generally taken up. Institutions of PR and semi-PR are *procedural* solutions to inequities in *substantive* outcomes and, as such, may not be adequate to overcome structural barriers to marginalized group representation. Under any of these systems, it is still quite conceivable that even where group-structured interests exist, some groups will be better positioned to translate those interests into electoral results than will others. In other words, it is quite possible that the structural barriers that tend to reproduce group-structured inequalities in the socioeconomic spheres will also function in the political sphere under systems of PR or semi-PR. To complicate matters further, it is likely that some of these barriers may not be apparent to anyone until after new electoral structures are in place. For this reason we should be skeptical that any difference-blind procedural solution, without some attention to its consequences for the legislative presence of marginalized groups, will suffice to secure fair representation for those groups.

With the exception of PR, all the foregoing institutional strategies for enhancing the legislative presence of marginalized groups are results-oriented rather than procedural. All the strategies—race-conscious districting, reserved seats, and consociational democracy—begin with the supposition that the representation of certain groups is a desirable goal, and they all directly intercede in the electoral process to guarantee the representation of those groups. I have attempted to show that the strongest objection against such substantive approaches to representational equity—that it undercuts the principle of individual autonomy by labeling citizens according to their group membership—is not as decisive as it initially appears. Yet I share with critics of such strategies a belief that procedural solutions to the problems of inequality are preferable insofar as they leave open a greater space for citizen's self-definition of their political identities and interests. The challenge, then, is to identify electoral institutions that take care not to reproduce the structural inequalities that characterize historically marginalized groups' social position, but at the same time secure individuals a full measure of freedom to define their own political identities.

II. Dynamics of Legislative Decision Making

As I argued in chapter 3, a group-based conception of fair representation leads us to reconceive the ideal of legislative decision making as a deliberative rather than a conflictual, competitive process. On the competitive model, representatives act as aggressive advocates for the interests of their constituents against the interests that compete with them. They are not concerned to identify common ground among groups with conflicting interests but instead seek to maximize the fulfillment of the interests they represent, without much regard for the costs to others. In this model of politics, especially in its most aggressive forms, historically marginalized groups are virtually certain to lose the political competition. As legislative minorities who do not control the most powerful positions within the legislature, they lack sufficient clout to secure their constituents' interests.

In a deliberative model of legislative decision making, representatives aim at reaching agreement through exchanging different perspectives on the common interest and the place of particular interests within it. Only in such a process will the distinctive perspectives of historically marginalized groups have a deeply transformative effect on the political agenda and offer the prospect of redesigning public policies in ways that will have the long-term effect of ameliorating group-structured inequality. This was the thrust of chapter 4's theme of "voice": that the mere presence of marginalized group perspectives within the legislature can have its most profound effect on public policy only if representatives from relatively privileged groups are open to reconceiving the public interest in response to the light such perspectives shed on social and political problems.

As an ethic of legislative behavior, the deliberative model is extremely demanding. Not only does it require legislators to take a much broader view of the public interest by recognizing the place of marginalized groups within the "public," but it also requires that they develop their capacity to listen in a spirit of impartiality to points of view that may be starkly alien to them and that challenge the justice of their own social positions.[74] Consequently, as critics of deliberative democracy have argued, the deliberative model runs the risk of being naively utopian. As Anne Phillips argues, "deliberative democrats sometimes seem to inhabit a world of romanticized dreams."[75]

Nonetheless, the arguments in chapter 3 also made clear that it is not possible to maintain a perfectly sharp distinction between a deliberative politics in which marginalized group differences play an important role and a politics in which group interests are in play. This is true on the theoretical level insofar as differences between groups' interests are directly relevant to arguments concerning unjust structural inequalities. But it becomes even clearer as we move from theoretical ideals of the decision-making process to a discussion of the institutional means for approximating those ideals. When we consider the structure of institutions whose purpose is to encourage deliberation, such as juries, we see that what encourages decision makers to engage in deliberation aimed at reaching agreement is a combination of incentives (making their interests in cooperation greater than their interests in conflict), institutional norms (some kinds of arguments are valid, others are not),[76] and the relative position of the parties (the more equal in power, the greater the likelihood they will deliberate). In other words, institutions that foster deliberation use a mix of appeals to higher principles and reliance on parties' narrow self-interests. Consequently it is as imprudent to be too pessimistic about the capacity of human beings to put aside partial and selfish interests in the name of a shared interest in justice as it is to be overly optimistic. As Jane Mansbridge has argued persuasively, while self-interest powerfully shapes political action, it does not, as a matter of empirical fact, utterly displace motives of the common good.[77] History provides numerous examples of moments when the bearers of power relinquished that power, but they have seldom done so without the pressure of mass social movements. Social upheaval provides an occasion and an incentive for privileged groups to reconsider whether their power is just, and may help to open their minds to the perspectives of others.

Clearly, though, if one is interested in securing a place for marginalized groups within legislatures that will last longer than a brief historical moment, and so have some prospect of changing political agendas over the long term, one cannot rely on the good will of representatives of privileged groups. Moreover, it is utopian to suggest that deliberation has the capacity to eliminate conflicts of interest altogether. Knight and Johnson are doubtless correct that the best we can hope for is that a more deliberative model of legislative decision making would reduce the *scope* of conflict and produce agreement on the dimensions of disagreement, the substance of the conflicts that continue to divide groups from one another.[78]

In thinking about the institutional desiderata of a group-based theory of fair representation, then, we should avoid excesses of both optimism and pessimism about the prospects for a deliberative model of legislative decision making. Moreover, because deliberation will not in itself eliminate conflicts of interest, we ought to conceptualize the difference between competitive and deliberative models of decision making as a continuum, not a dichotomy.[79] Thus the task of institutional design aimed at fair group representation is to focus on institutional changes that would have the effect of moving representatives away from competition and toward deliberation, without the expectation that we can ever achieve a "pure" form of deliberative decision making.

As I have discussed briefly above,[80] one hope is that the mere presence of representatives from historically marginalized groups will produce changes in legislative dynamics. There are two reasons why the increased representation of these groups might have such an effect. First, the novelty of marginalized group perspectives may, by itself, strike representatives from privileged groups sufficiently powerfully that they change their understanding of social issues and revise their policy positions accordingly. Although such a change is unlikely, it is not unthinkable, particularly when representatives from privileged groups are already sympathetically disposed toward the claims of marginalized groups. Whether this is a plausible source of political change depends on the empirical reality of legislators' reactions to the presence of representatives from marginalized groups, a reality that, to my knowledge, has not been studied. Even if the presence of new group perspectives does have such an effect, however, it is likely to be a time-bound effect, greater when such representatives first appear on the scene and diminishing as their perspectives become more familiar.

Second, and more plausibly over the long run, an increase in the number of representatives from historically marginalized groups will enable those groups to form coalitions with one another and with blocs of progressive legislators in order to advance their policy agendas.[81] To the extent that such legislative alliances hold up, relatively powerful legislative blocs will occasionally have to negotiate with marginalized group representatives in order to secure their legislative agendas. While this sort of bargaining and log-rolling would not entail the same sort of change in understanding and in political preferences that the deliberative model supposes, it would move legislative decision making in that direction by forcing relatively privileged legislators to take marginalized group interests and perspectives into account as they formulated their policy agendas.

The notion that an increase in numbers increases minority legislators' political clout is clearly borne out by the experience of the Congressional Black Caucus in the 103rd Congress following the 1992 elections. In those elections the number of Black members of the House of Representatives swelled from twenty-five to thirty-nine, largely as a consequence of legislative redistricting. The membership of the Caucus grew from twenty-six to forty. To the extent that they could act solidaristically, they constituted a voting bloc that President Clinton and his party's leadership could not afford to ignore in their attempts to advance the Democratic legislative agenda. The Caucus exercised its clout on a number of important bills, including one on deficit reduction and one on a line-item veto, as well as on foreign policy matters (particularly U.S. policy toward Haiti).[82] It is important to note that the influence of the

Caucus depended a great deal on the confluence of events that produced a Democratic House and a Democratic President; since the 1994 elections produced a Republican majority in the House, the Caucus's influence on the legislative agenda has dropped precipitously.[83]

Notwithstanding the importance of numbers, there are more direct institutional means of pressing legislative decision making toward deliberation and consensus. Indeed, we know this from our study of John Calhoun, whose method of concurrent majorities (in the form of bloc vetoes) was designed precisely to encourage compromise and agreement between the two great sections of the United States. Calhoun was deeply impressed by the unanimity requirement for jury verdicts and its propensity to encourage deliberation among jurors:

> Under its potent influence, the jurors take their seats with the disposition to give a fair and impartial hearing to the arguments on both sides . . . —not as disputants, but calmly to hear the opinions of each other, and to compare and weigh the arguments on which they are founded—and, finally, to adopt that which, on the whole, is thought to be true. Under the influence of this *disposition to harmonize*, one after another falls into the same opinion, until unanimity is obtained.[84]

Calhoun believed that a decision rule that created an "urgent necessity" of agreement could encourage deliberation and compromise among representatives of different collective interests just as it could encourage deliberation among jurors. Although the connection to Calhoun is generally recognized only by their critics,[85] recent advocates of marginalized group representation have also recognized the possibilities of decision rules that encourage deliberation between representatives of privileged and marginalized groups.

In *Justice and the Politics of Difference*, Iris Young argues for a scheme of group representation that would include a "group veto power regarding specific policies that affect a group directly, such as reproductive rights policy for women."[86] Although she does not directly connect such a group veto power to the encouragement of deliberation between privileged and marginalized group representatives, her notion of group representation does include a responsibility on the part of decision makers to show that "their deliberations have taken group perspectives into consideration."[87] It seems reasonable to assume that the sort of group veto Young proposes would mean not only that policies affecting marginalized groups could not be enacted without their consent but also that the threat of veto would encourage decision makers to consult with group representatives in advance of their decisions. Similarly Lani Guinier has proposed schemes of cumulative voting within legislative bodies. In her scheme, legislative proposals of particular interest to minorities would be clustered, and each legislator would receive a "budget" of votes which he or she could "spend" on the different proposals according to the intensity of the policies' effects on constituency interests. Just as cumulative voting in the electoral sphere enables electoral minorities to secure representation by registering both the direction and intensity of their preferences,[88] cumulative voting in the legislative sphere would enable legislative minorities to forgo a vote on certain issues in order to secure some of their highest legislative priorities.[89]

Both these proposals suffer from important weaknesses. Young's proposal of group vetoes immediately raises the question of who would be invested with the power to exercise the group veto. Since marginalized groups in the electorate are not internally homogeneous, and since the idea of group representation necessarily aspires to more than one legislator from such groups, it is likely that intra-group disagreements will arise with respect to the exercise of such a veto. Who would have the power to decide which issues affected a group's "fundamental interests"? There is also the difficulty of deciding which issues groups would have the power to veto. How would a minority group persuade the majority to grant it a veto over some issues? I have further concerns about the impact of such a power on the dynamics of legislative decision making, as it could have the effect of leading relatively privileged representatives to pursue their policy agendas through legislative means that skirt the substantive areas over which groups have veto power rather than encouraging deliberation among groups. Finally, one might question whether any sort of special power at the legislative level, possessed by some groups and not by others, is consistent with the principle of democratic equality. Young's group veto appears open to the criticism that it simply shifts political privilege from some groups to others.

Guinier's proposal for cumulative voting within legislative bodies has similar defects, including the question of who would have the power to decide which pieces of legislation would be bundled with each other, how many votes legislators could exercise in a given vote, and other issues that would profoundly affect the ability of legislative minorities to affect policy outcomes. In addition, however, Guinier's scheme would likely diminish rather than enhance the deliberative potential of legislatures, as it would force legislators to consider policies as clusters when their view of the public interest might lead them to consider them individually. It would therefore bind their hands in an arbitrary manner, potentially sacrificing a more broadly beneficial set of policies to the interests of minority influence. By relating special decision rules to specific policy areas, both Young's and Guinier's proposals seem to me to constrain the political freedom of the legislature to design creative and innovative policies, and this does not seem to me a promising strategy for democratic change.

Other devices of legislative decision making, however, may be manipulated in ways that enhance the power of marginalized groups within the legislature without prejudicing the policy agenda. Supermajority rules, which Guinier also advocates,[90] are probably the most versatile of these tools. Because they do not give special powers to any identifiable group, or link the exercise of such powers to particular group interests, they do not run afoul of the principles of either legislative or individual autonomy. Instead, by requiring more than a simple majority in order to pass legislation, supermajority rules would increase the power of legislative minorities as coalition partners, and so enhance the incentives of more powerful legislative blocs to give some place to marginalized group interests in their policy agendas. Such rules have a disadvantage, however, in that they make it more difficult for legislatures to pass *any* legislative program and might lead to legislative paralysis. Such paralysis would almost certainly not favor the interests of marginalized groups, as it would tend to perpetuate the status quo. A supermajority requirement could be restricted to especially important legislative items, such as the budget and appropriations bills authorizing expenditures above a certain amount. Such restrictions might enhance the legislative clout of marginalized group representatives in general by creating incentives among legislative majorities to bargain on a broader array of legislative policies.

In thinking about the dynamics of legislative decision making, it is also important to consider the relationship between the number of marginalized group representatives and the legislative effect we seek. Several theorists have observed that the numerical representation of marginalized groups in strict proportion to their presence in the population may be either more or less than is needed to secure policy changes that protect group interests. As Young argues, for large groups, such as women, strict proportionality may be more than they need; for small minorities, such as Native Americans, proportionality would yield so few seats as to render the group inaudible.[91] Will Kymlicka notes, however, that different kinds of decision-making processes have implications for different levels of group representation. "The more consensual the process," he argues, "the more threshold representation may be sufficient."[92] There is a limit to this logic, however, for I would not want to go so far as to claim that in a perfectly deliberative body a single representative would be sufficient to secure the needs and interests of a marginalized group.[93] Because of the internal diversity of these groups, a plurality of representatives would be more likely to achieve a fuller understanding within decision-making bodies of group members' distinctive experience of various policies. With that caveat, Kymlicka's point is persuasive: the more competitive (and less deliberative) a decision-making body, the larger the number of marginalized group representatives needed to secure the group's basic interests. In a more competitive, majoritarian model, the more representatives a group can send to the legislature, the better it will be able to secure its interests.

In sum, these institutional considerations suggest two distinct ways in which increasing the power of legislative minorities—whether through an increase in their numbers or through devices that prevent numerical differences from translating directly into differences of power—can work to enhance the political equality of marginalized groups. First, by increasing incentives and opportunities for a deliberative politics in which the distinctive perspectives of marginalized groups can play a substantive role in policy formation, such changes can contribute to a transformative politics that aims to dismantle structural or systemic discrimination. As Lani Guinier puts it, the aim is an "interactive, deliberate legislative decisionmaking process that compensates for the way prejudice and 'neutral' decisional rules encourage unfair political competition, grant the majority disproportionate power, and distort or marginalize the perspective of minority group representatives."[94] Second, even where this deliberative process remains beyond the reach of political actors, mechanisms that enhance the relative power of legislative minorities can at least ensure that they have a greater capacity to protect some of their most important interests. In other words, even without a transformation of the self-understandings of privileged groups, an enhanced legislative voice can serve the end of equity.

One possible objection to mechanisms that increase the power of legislative minorities, such as supermajority requirements, is that they might be as effective in advancing the political aims of dangerous minorities as well as the marginalized groups we are concerned to protect. The focus in the foregoing discussion has been on procedural devices rather than on group-specific ones on the ground that the former can more easily avoid the dangers of group essentialism. But such tools may be wielded by any hands; what would prevent radical political groups on the right or the left from using these procedural mechanisms for pernicious ends? We should remember that Calhoun's devices, so similar to the ones discussed here, were designed to enhance the legislative power of the slaveholding South.

This is a troubling point, but there are at least two responses to it. First, the power of legislative minorities depends both on the size of the majority required for binding decisions and on the number of representatives a group is able to elect. Very small fringe groups could be prevented from doing much legislative harm either by increasing the threshold of representation (e.g., by decreasing district magnitude or, as in Germany, setting a relatively high official threshold of representation) or by decreasing the size of the supermajority required for the passage of legislation. Second, the full range of constitutionally protected rights and checks and balances would remain in place as protections against legislative excesses.

III. Legislator-Constituent Relations

Just as the mere presence of marginalized group representatives in legislative bodies does not guarantee that they will be able to effect policy changes which serve the interests of their constituents, neither does it guarantee that those interests will be adequately represented and defended. This is a point on which scholars who are clearly hostile to the concept of group representation and those who are generally sympathetic to it converge.[95] These observations stand as a reminder that one of the principal weaknesses of the idea of descriptive representation is that it leaves unspecified the proper relationship between legislators and their constituents.

I have already emphasized that the group-based theory of fair representation includes a conception of legislator-constituency relations that respects both the distinctive agency of the representer (including, among other things, his or her skills as an advocate, orator, and negotiator) and the agency of the represented (including especially the insight citizens from marginalized groups have into the causes of, and the likely effectiveness of alternative remedies to, their conditions of marginalization). I have argued that an important part of the agency of representatives from marginalized groups rests on the fact that they share the experience, and therefore the insight, of their constituents. Because of this commonality, there are good reasons why citizens from marginalized groups are likely to prefer a representative from their own ranks over one from a relatively privileged group. But critics of descriptive representation are right to worry that a shared group identity is not, in itself, sufficient to secure effective representation. This is true in part because of the internal diversity of all social groups: no person can claim, solely on the basis of his or her ascriptive characteristics, to represent all who share those characteristics. Further, representatives, once elected, are members of a political elite whose activities and preoccupations are necessarily removed somewhat from the preoccupations of any particular constituency. The fact of election itself places a distance between representative and constituents and underscores the differences between them. It was for this reason that Anti-Federalists were so concerned to bind representatives to their constituents by a strict delegate model of representation and by the frequency of elections.[96]

The Anti-Federalists' institutional solutions to the problems of accountability are not especially helpful to the group-based theory of fair representation defended here. A strict delegate model of representation is incompatible with the idea of a deliberative assembly. Genuine deliberation requires an openness to changing one's judgment about an issue in the light of others' arguments, whereas the delegate model requires the representative's dogged and unyielding pursuit of constituent interests. Neither are short terms of election an attractive option in times when campaigns already absorb so much of incumbents' time and money.

In her recent discussion of marginalized group representation, Anne Phillips focuses considerable attention on the relationship between deliberative models of legislative decision making and the problem of representatives' accountability to constituents. She is deeply ambivalent about the idea of deliberation because the deliberative role requires that representatives have some degree of freedom to modify their positions in response to others' arguments.

The source of her ambivalence is that such freedom appears to stand at odds with the notion that representatives are present in legislative bodies not to advance their own conceptions of the common good but to protect their constituents' fundamental interests. On her understanding of accountability, representatives ought to stand unwaveringly by the interests of their constituents. This means they ought to stand by their commitments during the election, for it was because of the convergence of those commitments with their constituents' understandings of their own needs, concerns, and interests that they were elected in the first place. This would seem to leave little room for maneuvering within a deliberative legislative process, as there is no way for representatives constantly to recur to constituents for guidance on policy issues as those issues unfold in the course of legislative discussion. At the same time, Phillips regretfully concludes that "there is no combination of reforms that can deliver express and prior commitments on every issue that will come to matter."[97]

Phillips argues that it is precisely because of the inescapable if partial autonomy of representatives that the presence of marginalized groups in legislative bodies is so important. "Representatives *do* have autonomy, which is why it matters who those representatives are."[98] If mechanisms of accountability were sufficiently strict—that is, if representatives could be given binding instructions on every issue relevant to constituents—then it would not matter who represented the interests of marginalized groups. But because representatives must have some freedom of judgment in the legislative process, it becomes all the more important that they share the experience of their constituents. "[I]t is in those spaces where we have to rely on representatives exercising their own judgement that it can most matter who the representatives are."[99]

This conclusion has its own troubles for Phillips, however, as it rests on substituting the shared experience of representatives and constituents for the institutional mechanisms that make representatives accountable to constituents. Yet shared experience can function as such a substitute for accountability only where we suppose there is some essential identity between all members of a marginalized group. Phillips, for good reason, does not wish to make any such claims of essential identity; she recognizes that it is entirely possible that the election of women will not automatically result in the protection of women's interests.[100] Phillips's reasoning leads her to a conundrum which she is unable to resolve: The representation of marginalized groups cannot depend exclusively on the presence of their members in legislative bodies because we cannot assume an essential identity between group members as such. Yet strict mechanisms of accountability are not a feasible means of keeping marginalized group representatives true to their groups' interests, both because she believes it unlikely that legislative constituencies will be organized along group lines (at least in the case of women)[101] and because representatives must have some degree of autonomy in order to function as members of a legislature in which some deliberation takes place. Thus Phillips is caught: either she must insist on mechanisms of strict accountability, which themselves render the identity of representatives irrelevant; or she must implicitly rely on essentialist claims about group identity, which are philosophically and sociologically unsustainable. Her arguments do not resolve this dilemma. She simply concludes that "[r]epresentation has to include both accountability and relative autonomy, otherwise we are reduced to mere aggregation of initial preference and interest."[102]

This conclusion is doubtless correct, but Phillips has not explained how it resolves the conundrum to which her arguments lead her. Nor can she, I believe, because of several problematic moves in her argument. The most important of these is her tendency to identify representatives' accountability with a strict delegate model of political representation.[103] In other words, she tends to assume that representatives' performance of their duty depends on their strict adherence either to the direct instructions of their constituents or to the legislative agenda they identified during their campaigns. But as Phillips suspects, such a model of representation is incoherent. Indeed, it is incoherent not only within a defense of marginalized group representation that focuses on the importance of groups' presence within legislative bodies, as Phillips explicitly recognizes, but within *any* plausible account of the processes of political representation. The latter point is well established by Hanna Pitkin's discussion of the delegate-trustee debate within theories of political representation. As Pitkin argues, *neither* a pure model of delegation *nor* a pure model of trusteeship captures the necessary character of political representation. Representation as such must account for the presence within the political process of both the agency of the represented (which a pure trustee model obliterates) and the agency of the representer (which a pure delegate model obliterates).[104] Consequently our understanding of the accountability of representatives to their constituents must include not only their accountability for the interests and concerns their constituents express by electing them but also for their exercise of the power of independent judgment which inevitably attends their role as representatives. As I have discussed in chapter 5, the latter forms of accountability (or responsibility) are secured within the Madisonian scheme of representation (which supposes a considerable degree of representatives' autonomy from constituent commands) by two means: (a) the fact that representatives are themselves bound by the legislative decisions they make; and (b) the fact that they are dependent, for reelection and for the approbation that politicians universally seek, on constituents' judgment that they have executed their trust well.

A complete defense of marginalized group representation, then, must demonstrate how the agency of the representative is shaped by his or her membership in a historically marginalized group, for this is what determines the

representative's capacity to make the sort of contributions to legislative deliberations that can produce more responsive and egalitarian policy outcomes. I
have presented an argument laying out the relationship between marginalized
group identity and the agency of the representative in chapter 4. That argument supports Phillips's conclusion that marginalized group representatives'
contributions depend on the shared experience of representative and constituents, but it contradicts her belief that claims of shared experience necessarily
rest on essentialist assumptions. It is true that whether or not a system of
political representation for historically marginalized groups incorporates
essentialist assumptions depends on whether or not it establishes independent
mechanisms of accountability between those groups and the representatives
who share their identities. Critics of descriptive representation are correct
when they argue that we cannot assume that a female representative automatically represents the self-identified interests of women or that an African
American representative represents the self-identified interests of Blacks. We
need, in addition, institutions that allow marginalized groups to mobilize
around group identity in order to elect representatives of their choice and that
make the representatives so elected directly accountable to their constituents
for their legislative actions. I have addressed some of the alternative electoral
devices for allowing groups to mobilize in these ways in the foregoing section
on constituency definition.

A concern for legislators' accountability leads us to focus now on institutional devices that facilitate communication between representatives and
constituents. The first question we must ask is whether the conventional
mechanisms of accountability are insufficient. Although critics of descriptive
representation remark that mere descriptive similarity does not guarantee genuine representativeness, they often fail to address the question of how descriptively representative legislators will come to occupy their seats. Assuming they
have been elected to office through devices similar to the methods by which
other representatives are chosen, the problem of accountability is neither
more nor less vexing for representatives from marginalized groups than for
any other representative.[105] As discussed in chapter 5, elections are meant to
secure the accountability and responsibility of representatives by appealing to
their desire for reelection and public esteem. In this light, increasing the competitiveness of an electoral system is an important element of political accountability. Term limits and other electoral reforms that diminish the incumbency advantage, which currently characterize American politics, would
therefore appear to support the conception of representational fairness advanced here.

While contested elections are an essential part of a responsible system of
political representation, they are a blunt instrument for achieving the sort of
accountability the group-based theory of representation presupposes. In the
view I have defended, the representative's accountability requires a movement

back and forth between consultations with constituents and deliberations with other legislators. Indeed, it makes sense to characterize the role of the representative as requiring deliberation on two levels. Within the legislature, she must attempt to persuade other representatives to reconceive the public interest in a way that takes account of the perspectives and interests of her constituents. But because deliberation requires that she also be open to revising her judgments in the light of others' arguments, in those cases where her judgments on the merits of an issue have changed or she has judged that her constituents' best interests lie in trading off certain claims in order to secure others, she must also engage in a project of persuading her constituents of the reasons for her judgments. At the same time, she must be open to the possibility that because of the pressures of legislative deliberation and its distance from the lives of her constituents, she should further revise her judgments in the light of her discussions with them.

Given the large size of constituencies within representative democracies, such an intimate model of legislator-constituency relations may seem unrealistic. Yet recent innovations in political life and communications technology render it more feasible than one might suppose. Journalistic evidence suggests that electoral candidates and representatives are increasingly turning to "town hall meetings" to establish and maintain contact with citizens.[106] Such meetings have featured prominently in the last presidential campaign and were used as well in the latest round of constitutional negotiations in Canada.[107] It is not difficult to imagine a representative constituting panels of citizens who are themselves "representative" of the most important differences within her constituency and engaging in deliberative consultations with them. Such consultations could be focused on a particular policy issue,[108] or they might just be held periodically to enable a sense of changing constituency concerns to emerge through discussion.

Another means of maintaining close contact with constituents would be to create electronic focus groups by selecting a discrete number of citizens, taking care to include among them individuals who represent significant differences within the community, and soliciting their regular participation in an electronic dialogue on the Internet. Although this would not be a substitute for the face-to-face deliberation of town hall meetings, it is a form of consultation and deliberation that has other advantages. It also is a relatively low-cost form of participation for citizens, as they could participate in electronic conversations at times that were convenient for them and without having to travel far from home. This would depend on providing easy access to the Internet to citizens who did not already have it, perhaps through local public libraries or community centers. It would also require careful efforts to prevent a bias in favor of those who have easier access to computer services and networks.

These suggestions are contemporary versions of Jefferson's proposal to "divide the counties into wards"; they provide citizens with the opportunity to engage directly in the political process, but in ways that do not demand so much of citizens' time and energies that they are unsustainable. They are similar to proposals for "strong democracy" insofar as they focus on the importance of eliciting citizens' own judgments about politics within institutions that foster democratic deliberation,[109] but they moderate the ambitions of "strong democracy" by locating such practices within a scheme of political representation. They neither presuppose nor demand that a substantial proportion of citizens engage actively in political discourse, which I believe is an unrealistic expectation. At the same time, because they would involve soliciting the participation of citizens who themselves represent significant differences within the community, they run fewer risks than "strong democracy" of privileging those who, because of the advantages they have enjoyed relative to other citizens, are more competent participants in public discussion. It is this feature that connects such mechanisms of democratic accountability directly to the aim of representing historically marginalized groups.

IV. Summary: Sketch of a Fair System of Political Representation

I am reluctant to be too specific in describing the sorts of electoral institutions that could balance the claims of proceduralism and those of substantive equality, the claims of individual equality and autonomy and those of justice toward marginalized groups. Political theorists may risk certain hazards in proposing institutional reforms. In particular, as I discussed at the beginning of this chapter, there is the risk that specific suggestions concerning institutions may be confused with theoretical claims and that criticisms aimed at the former might be taken as criticisms of the latter. In addition, no set of suggestions is likely to exhaust the possibilities for institutional change. Yet without being specific, it is impossible to ascertain whether the reconciliation of diverse political goods lies within the realm of practical possibility. The purpose of the following institutional suggestions, then, is not to propose a program of political reform but to indulge in the sort of imaginative construction that can assist us in assessing the plausibility of theoretical claims about group representation, particularly the claim that we can affirm a notion of group representation without doing violence to the principles of individual equality and individual autonomy. With those caveats, what might a fairer system of political representation look like?

Inspired by Charles Beitz's notion of complex proceduralism,[110] my approach to the institutional challenges of group representation attempts to steer a course between procedural and substantive interpretations of political equality.[111] It preserves the idea that procedural solutions to political conflicts have a double advantage: first, if properly constructed, they do not bias outcomes in favor of some participants over others; second, by giving individuals an equally weighted role in influencing political outcomes, they preserve the principle of individual equality. Yet my approach guards against the dangers of difference-blind proceduralism—principally the danger that even reformed procedures will function to advantage already privileged groups, often in unforeseen ways—by building into electoral systems a recursive process in which electoral changes can be reviewed with an eye toward their effectiveness at achieving marginalized group representation in those places where there is clear evidence that group members have chosen, or would choose if they could, to mobilize around group identity. In other words, while I do not support institutional changes that will *guarantee* proportional representation for marginalized groups no matter what, I do think we would probably need some outcome-conscious review process aimed at identifying structural barriers that prevent marginalized groups from achieving electoral success where they have the political will to do so. The presumption would be that such a process could rely on further procedural changes, without introducing substantive preferences for any group or groups into electoral institutions.

To begin with, a fairer scheme of representation would include some mechanisms of proportional representation. In the American case, devices such as the cumulative vote and the single transferable vote, as candidate-based rather than party-based systems, would appear more desirable than the alternatives, since the dimensions of diversity we wish to express are not the sort best expressed through the ideological agendas of political parties. Moreover, the deliberation we seek within legislative bodies is not compatible with the party discipline or party government that party-list PR implies. Devices of semi-PR should be implemented within districts whose magnitude is as close to seven as circumstances allow, since it is at that point that the maximum benefits of PR for women and minority representation begin to be realized. Of course larger district magnitudes would be possible at state and local levels than at the national level of government. At the same time, however, it would be desirable to maintain some geographic basis of constituency definition, both as a matter of cultural continuity with the tradition of geographic representation (a Burkean gesture) and because of the importance to many citizens of constituent service as a form of political representation. Finally, maintaining some geographic basis of representation is important for the purpose of maintaining clear and close communication between representatives and constituents, and for constituting "town hall" meetings and focus groups within constituencies.

On top of these structures, a group-based system of fair representation might replace existing districting commissions with electoral commissions comprised of leaders from the principal salient groups in the jurisdiction. Such commissions would include a good balance of the sexes, to be sure, but would also include representatives of significant racial and ethnic minorities. The commissions' tasks would be parallel to that of existing districting commissions, in the sense that they would have oversight for electoral system changes and would evaluate changes with an eye toward enhanced representation of groups at issue. Changes could also be reviewable, as they are now, by courts and federal agencies.

Guaranteeing some form of group representation on the electoral commissions might seem to stand in tension with the principle of autonomy insofar as it does entrench group identity in legal-institutional arrangements. However, these commissions' decisions would in fact be far less determinative of ultimate electoral outcomes than are existing districting bodies. Currently, districting agencies draw single-member districts with full knowledge of the distribution of demographic and political groups within states, and consequently with full consciousness of the consequences of their decisions for electoral outcomes. This knowledge is precisely what makes possible the practices of race-conscious districting and incumbency protection through the creation of "safe" seats. While the electoral commissions I am proposing here would have full access to the same kinds of information, their capacity to determine the electoral fate of individual candidates would be sharply diminished because they would be working with multimember districts, which do not easily lend themselves to gerrymandering of any form.

That historically marginalized groups would have direct representation on these commissions appears less controversial when we recognize that several states already secure the representation of substantive communities of interest through their districting rules and on their reapportionment commissions. In Hawaii, for example, the districting guidelines include the requirement that, "[w]here practicable, submergence of an area in a larger district wherein substantially different socio-economic interests predominate shall be avoided."[112] The Colorado Reapportionment Commission, comprised of eleven members, is required by law to include at least one member who lives west of the continental divide.[113] For electoral commissions to execute their responsibilities fairly and impartially, and to prevent current office holders from manipulating electoral laws to their own advantage, it would be extremely important for them to be independent of legislative bodies and for their decisions to have binding authority.[114]

Within legislatures, institutional changes should aim at pressing representatives away from strategic exchanges and toward deliberative ones. For the reasons articulated in the discussion of the dynamics of legislative decision making,[115] I do not believe that proposals such as Lani Guinier's for cumulative voting within legislatures, or Iris Young's for group vetoes, offer desirable solutions to the challenge of enhancing marginalized group representatives' effectiveness within legislative bodies. Supermajority requirements on issues of particular urgency (such as government budgets) seem more likely to increase incentives for deliberation without prejudging policy questions and unduly limiting representatives' agency to innovate.

Finally, to secure the accountability of representatives to their constituents, institutional changes should encourage electoral competitiveness. In addition, there is ample room within representative institutions for experimentation with different mechanisms of legislator-constituency communication, from "town meetings" inspired by past democratic practices to the creative use of new communications technologies.

The immediate prospects for massive institutional change on any of these levels are quite slim, insofar as those who currently hold power within electoral institutions have strong incentives to maintain the status quo. At the same time, there are growing pressures for institutional change in the name of democratic responsiveness. In the American context, these pressures take the general form of a rhetoric of disdain for "insider" politicians, partisan dealignment and the growth of third-party movements, the press for term limits, and popular support for limits on campaign spending. But there are also pressures for change that are more immediately connected to the representation of historically marginalized groups. Since the beginning of this decade, we have seen both an increase in the use of semi-proportional representation schemes as ways of addressing the problem of minority vote dilution and an increase in support for the spread of such measures. The Center for Voting and Democracy, a Washington-based lobby and public education group that advocates PR in the United States, has a growing membership and sponsors who are prominent in both academic and political circles. Representative Cynthia McKinney of Georgia has recently proposed legislation to enable the use of multimember districts with semi-proportional representation devices in congressional elections.[116] Eleanor Smeal, former president of the National Organization for Women and currently head of the Fund for the Feminist Majority, has expressed support for proportional representation.[117] Thus despite the trend of Supreme Court decisions away from race-conscious districting, not all the current political forces oppose representational fairness for historically marginalized groups.

Above all, these reflections lead to the conclusion that we do not yet know what institutional changes would most effectively increase representational fairness; they are, rather, an invitation for institutional experimentation. I am a believer in the notion that one of the advantages of American-style federalism is that it offers multiple laboratories for democracy at the various levels of government. At a more general level, complex constitutional government means that we can realize a multiplicity of political values—including both stability and responsiveness—by layering different institutions upon one another. Indeed, one of the strongest arguments in favor of the idea of the complexity of fair representation is that it enables us to see that no one dimension of representation needs to do all the work. Representation is not only about electoral processes any more than it is exclusively about legislative decision making or legislator-constituency relations. Each of these dimensions of representation is itself open to multiple interpretations, and changes in each will produce different interactions with other aspects of representative government. The complexity of representation offers many different points of possible institutional intervention by which we can strive to enhance representational fairness. As such, it allows great scope for a pragmatic sensibility, which has ever been a central feature of constitutionalism.

Conclusion

Descriptive Representation with a Difference

Plessy v. Ferguson was among the first official responses to the problem of how to construe the civil and political equality of a group that is not regarded by more powerful groups as deserving of equality. The answer it offered was something like this: It cannot be the business of the public sphere to attend to dominant social attitudes toward groups. Treating people as equals means only that their group traits must not be used to deny them the legal rights enjoyed by others. Certainly the law is powerless to enforce social attitudes, and it neither can nor should guarantee that members of some groups be regarded as equals by members of other groups. If those who make the law believe that some public interest will be served by protecting the dominant group from contact with other groups, there is nothing to prevent them from doing so, as long as they do not deprive the subordinate group of any constitutionally declared rights.

Justice Harlan's dissent, which has become the standard of equality that has governed the American political scene at least since the 1960s, was that while it may be true that one cannot legislate mutual respect between groups, one can at least prevent dominant groups from enacting their prejudices into law. We must begin with the presumption that citizens *ought* to regard one another as equals, regardless of racial or other differences, and we must not give the sanction of law to their decision to do otherwise. Since most legal distinctions of race, and many legal distinctions of gender, are motivated by attitudes of social prejudice, we must subject them to particularly close scrutiny wherever they occur. The presumption must be that justice is blind with respect to morally arbitrary differences among persons and that of all differences those given by birth are the most arbitrary.

The response of historically marginalized groups, as revealed in the arguments examined here, runs along these lines: The difference-blind view of equality articulates a noble aspiration, one with which we generally agree. The problem arises when it is put into practice in a society that has long been structured by our oppression, for it cannot address the myriad ways in which that history of oppression has become embedded in the very structure of our society. Difference-blind equality assumes that so long as no attention is paid to social difference, it will have no effect. In fact, as long as we pay no attention to difference, we will never overcome the inequalities that difference has been used to justify. Inequality that follows the lines of social difference means, perhaps paradoxically, that difference can only stop mattering when we have effectively addressed the deep and subtle ways in which it does matter.

The project of addressing the ways in which difference matters is one that depends crucially on institutions of political representation. Although it is possible that a vision of equality which is responsive to social difference can be pursued through the judicial system, as Martha Minow advocates,[1] it is only in institutions of representation that the experience of group member-ship can be brought to bear on public policy in a manner that gives full credit to the agency of group members themselves. In particular, it is only through institutions of representation that members of marginalized groups may offer their distinctive perspectives on public matters in a manner that does not regularly reaffirm and re-create the option of members of privileged groups to allow them a voice or not. Once groups' claims to representation are estab-lished on grounds of equality that are powerful even when viewed from within the liberal political tradition, the question as to whether they shall be heard becomes a matter not of choice but of right.

Of course the crucial question is whether the view of equality on which group claims rest *can* be viewed as convincing within the liberal tradition. In principle, I believe it can, for both visions of equality share a fundamental commitment to the dignity of the individual, to individual freedom in formu-lating a plan of life in accordance with a self-affirmed conception of the good, and to individuals' emancipation from unchosen and avoidable constraints on that freedom. The difficulty is that liberal equality, in aiming at a distribution of social resources that is, as Ronald Dworkin puts it, "ambition-sensitive and endowment-insensitive,"[2] tends not to be sensitive enough to the "endow-ment" (or, in Michael Sandel's language, the "encumbrance")[3] bestowed by history on members of marginalized groups. It is difficult to overemphasize the importance of history in the group-based view of political equality or the degree to which liberal views of equality are inattentive to the role of history in the reproduction of inequality. Indeed, if a group-based view of representa-tion is most aptly characterized in terms of the ways memory shapes it, the liberal alternative might best be described as afflicted with amnesia. As a gen-eral matter, liberal views of equality and fairness are profoundly ahistorical.[4]

This is a theme in liberal theory too complex to examine in detail here. But I do not believe that a group-based and history-based approach to equality is fundamentally incompatible with the liberal commitment to individual auton-omy and individual equality. Indeed, I think it offers a reconceptualization of autonomy that contributes more than it takes away from liberal views of fair-ness. Although a liberal theory may be theoretically coherent without attend-ing to history because it tends to reside in the realm of ideal theory and perfect compliance, the assumptions of ideal theory and perfect compliance render the step toward the meaning of equality in contemporary society a treacherous one to make. In particular, I think that the bridge most often used between ideal theory and practical liberal ethics—proceduralism—is where we should focus our attention if we are concerned to reconcile liberalism's aspirations with the actual experience of historically marginalized groups. In short, the democratic aspirations of liberalism are incompatible with the theoretical neatness that characterizes the move from a commitment to autonomy and equality to a universalistic characterization of the individual and to difference-blind procedural conceptions of fairness.

Liberal wariness of group-based claims to recognition arises from a suspicion that such claims make groups' moral status prior to individuals' moral status and will result in the denial of individual equality and autonomy in the name of group equality. Instead, I would argue that the social and political equality of individuals is mediated by their membership in groups because of the ways in which group membership shapes their life-chances and their self-esteem. For some citizens the social meaning of group membership is perhaps the strongest determinant of the social bases of self-respect that Rawls characterizes as the most important primary good.[5] It is only when we assume that politics is about the competition for scarce resources rather than a negotiation of the fair terms of cooperation that group recognition appears to threaten individual equality.

The vision of fair representation that takes the group-based conception of equality seriously might best be described as "descriptive representation with a difference." Like the "mirror" views of representation discussed in chapter 1, the group-based view insists that no system of representation is fair in which legislative assemblies fail to reflect the characteristics of the body of citizens. But whereas other views of descriptive representation fail the test of theoretical coherence because they fail to account for the egalitarian and representational values of a descriptively representative body, the group theory of representation developed here can meet that test. Like the liberal theory of representation, it offers an image of a unified process of representation that begins with a conception of the individual and ends with a standard for evaluating the fairness of legislative outcomes.

In the group-based theory of fair representation, individuals are construed as moral equals whose identities and interests are nonetheless partially constituted by their membership in social groups, groups that stand in relations of power and subordination to one another and whose power relations have a long-standing history. These groups define an essential dimension along which political representation must take place if individuals' equal standing as members of the political community is to be realized. For it is only from the standpoint of membership in particular groups that the diverse meanings of equality in different policy arenas can be articulated. In the process of legislative decision making, no group's perspective is authoritative. Rather, that process involves a discourse among competing understandings of what justice requires in a particular policy domain, and the discourse is aimed at reaching a normative agreement regarding what it would be reasonable for all to accept.

The identification of the groups that should be included in such deliberations is not left to their own discretion, nor to the discretion of the privileged groups in society. Rather, they are defined in a two-sided fashion, which reflects a respect *both* for the status of individual members of disadvantaged groups as (in Rawls's language) "self-originating sources of valid claims"[6] and for the need for agreement within the political sphere about what constitutes a valid claim—that is, what justifies a claim for recognition. The first is provided by the "subjective" side of group identification, the memory of group subordination that operates as a continuing obstacle to individuals' capacity to pursue a life in accordance with their conceptions of the good. The second is the "objective" side of group identification, the history of marginalization that charts a path from past discrimination to contemporary inequality and so demonstrates that inequality is the product of an "endowment" rather than a lack of "ambition."

In a group-based theory of fair representation, the relationship between legislator and constituent is one of trust that comes of shared experience. It is, however, a relationship in which the distinctive agency of the represented and that of the representative are preserved. The agency of the represented is not limited (as, for example, in Burke's view) to the brute expression of suffering but rather includes the notion that the experience of subordination brings with it an understanding of social conditions that is substantively relevant to policy making. The experience of oppression brings not only a knowledge of the sources of inequality but also a power of judgment regarding the likely effectiveness of alternative approaches to ameliorate that inequality. Although constituents' judgments, like all human judgments, are fallible, they are grounded in an intimate familiarity with their groups' social conditions and with the psychological effects of those conditions on group members. That understanding may not be *sufficient* to guarantee effective policies to address a group's problems, but, in the group-based view, it is at least very likely to generate such policies. In this view the representative's agency is not, as in liberal representation or the theories of Burke, Madison, and Calhoun, of an entirely different species from that of the represented. Rather, the group-based theory of fair representation extends the notion, expressed by Mill, that the representative shares his or her constituents' experience, and consequently shares the cognitive agency that arises out of that experience.[7] In addition to this form of agency, the representative is likely to have some exceptional abilities, such as the leadership skills necessary to encourage group consensus, and the oratorical skills necessary to communicate the group's perspective within the legislative assembly. But the agency the representative shares with the represented is an *essential* part of the agency that makes the representative an effective and trustworthy advocate. No matter how skilled at coalition building, no matter how effective at speech making, a representative who lacks an understanding of the experience of oppression will not be able to explain why some policies reinforce the constituency's experience of subordination while others alleviate it. Whereas representatives who are not group members may, with focused effort, attain such an understanding, those who are group members are likely to possess it immediately, as an outgrowth of their own experience.

When it comes to evaluating legislative outcomes, the group-based view of fair representation shares some features with liberal representation. It is, in a way, a process-based view of equality, in that political equality consists fundamentally in sustaining discursive practices and processes in which the previously silenced groups have a voice. Thus no policy can be judged fair if the process that produced it excluded a marginalized group that is affected by it. In addition, however, there is a results-oriented component to the evaluation of policies in that no policy, no matter how it was arrived at, can be considered fair which systematically reproduces the inequality of historically marginalized groups. As I argued in chapter 5, the process of decision making is thus simultaneously discursive and recursive, as decision-making bodies must reevaluate even their own policies from the standpoint of whether they tend to ameliorate or to re-create relations of inequality between groups.

Some readers may be slightly perplexed about the relationship between liberalism and the account of fair representation I have offered here. I have presented my defense of group representation as a critique of what I have called "liberal representation," but I have also been concerned to show why committed liberals may embrace forms of group recognition and group representation without any pangs of conscience. Because liberalism has not historically attended to questions of identity, the liberal tradition is limited in the extent to which it can provide argumentative resources for political claims that are grounded in group-based identities. In order to construct an argument for group representation one has to reach outside that tradition. Yet liberalism is perhaps the most commodious of ideologies; it is capable of accepting myriad adherents into its fold. So long as one stands beside the principles of individual equality and individual autonomy, as I do, one can find a place under liberalism's umbrella. Moreover, some of the most important recent work in political theory has been focused precisely on finding space within liberalism for the politics of identity.[8] So while I have offered a critique of the understanding of representation that flows most immediately from the liberal tradition, I certainly do not wish to cast myself as anti-liberal.

Stuart Hampshire has written: "There is a sense in which justice, both procedural and substantial, can be called a negative virtue, whether it is applied to individuals or to institutions or to policies. . . . One has to ask, in a Hobbesian spirit, what it prevents rather than what it engenders."[9] A negative view of justice is a common feature of liberal theories[10] and one that my understanding of fair representation shares. It is a negative view not because it endorses a minimalist account of the state, nor because it rests on a conception of negative rights as the foundation of a just regime; it does neither. Rather, it is a negative view of justice because it begins not with a substantive ideal of the just society but with a concern for redressing the palpable injustices of our current practices and institutions.[11] Within the view I have offered, the activity of representing marginalized groups consists above all in the effort to redesign those structures of social and political life that reliably and arbitrarily reproduce inequality along group lines. Although I affirm an ideal of society in which diversity can flourish without bringing domination in tow, rather than a society in which group-based identities have been overcome, my defense of group representation does not turn on this choice.

Intergroup conflict is a permanent feature of politics, and no scheme of institutions can avoid that inevitability. Yet institutions of representation are among our most important tools for managing conflict so that it does not destroy the environment in which we may pursue our other worthy goals. More than that, the practices and institutions of representation have the potential to transform conflict into a resource for social and political justice. Whether we employ them to that end is a matter of political choice. In fact, it is a species of the more general choice whether to acknowledge the existence of unjust group-structured inequality and whether to attempt to redress it—whether, in Judith Shklar's terms, to be actively just or passively unjust. It is no solution to argue that for the sake of social stability we must avoid giving recognition to claims grounded in group identity. As Shklar wrote: "We often choose peace over justice, to be sure, but they are not the same. To confuse them is simply to invite passive injustice."[12] In any case, there is little reason to think that recognizing group difference will have the destabilizing consequences its critics prophesy. To the contrary, history suggests that prolonged injustice, left to simmer unattended beneath the surface, will eventually erupt in unpredictable and potentially destructive ways. Burke, our adopted friend of group recognition, had it right when he argued that a concern both for justice and for peace dictate efforts to ameliorate the injuries of exclusion. "Our measures," he tells us, "*must be healing.*"[13] Although representation for marginalized groups is not in itself a cure for injustice, there is good reason to believe it is at least a healing measure.

Notes

Introduction
Voice, Trust, and Memory

1. The increase in minority representation following the 1992 elections is directly traceable to an increase in the number of "majority-minority" legislative districts, i.e., districts in which African Americans or Latinos constitute a majority of the voting-age population. Changes in voting rights law during the 1980s had encouraged states to draw majority-minority districts wherever minority populations' geographic concentration would allow, so long as doing so would not give minorities more than proportional representation in legislatures. But it was not until the 1990 census, and the legislative reapportionments and redistrictings which followed from it, that the legal changes of the preceding decade had their full effect on the redistricting process. Thus the 1992 elections were the first elections in which the "quiet revolution" of race-conscious districting had a large impact on the legislative presence of minorities. For a comprehensive study of the sources and consequences of race-conscious districting, see Chandler Davidson and Bernard Grofman, eds., *Quiet Revolution in the South: The Impact of the Voting Rights Act, 1965–1990* (Princeton, NJ: Princeton University Press, 1994).

2. 509 U.S. 630 (1993).

3. In the U.S. House of Representatives, the number of women jumped from twenty-nine to forty-eight; after the elections, there were six rather than only two female senators. *Congressional Quarterly Almanac: 103rd Congress, 1st Session, 1993* (Washington, D.C.: Congressional Quarterly, 1994), p. 16. In a June by-election Kay Bailey Hutchinson's victory raised the number of female senators to seven.

4. Women constituted 22 percent of the new congressional representatives who were elected in 1992 but made up 41 percent (seven of seventeen) of the freshmen who lost their seats in 1994. *Congressional Quarterly Weekly Report*, 7 November 1992 (supplement), pp. 7–10; 12 November 1994, p. 3234. Despite these losses, enough women won other seats to maintain the total number of female representatives at forty-nine.

5. See, e.g., Wilma Rule, "Women's Underrepresentation and Electoral Systems," *PS: Political Science and Politics* 27 (4) (1994), pp. 689–92.

6. Iris Marion Young, *Justice and the Politics of Difference* (Princeton, NJ: Princeton University Press, 1990), pp. 185–91; Anne Phillips, *Engendering Democracy* (University Park, PA: Pennsylvania State University Press, 1991), pp. 60–91; Phillips, *Democracy and Difference* (University Park, PA: Pennsylvania State University Press, 1993), pp. 90–102; Phillips, *The Politics of Presence* (Oxford: Clarendon, 1995); Lani Guinier, *The Tyranny of the Majority: Fundamental Fairness in Representative Democracy* (New York: Free Press, 1994).

7. Iris Young's discussion of the concept of a social group is especially instructive and has had a powerful influence on my own thinking about marginalized groups. *Justice and the Politics of Difference*, pp. 42–48.

8. See especially Guinier, "The Triumph of Tokenism," in *The Tyranny of the Majority*, pp. 56–58; and Phillips, *The Politics of Presence*, pp. 156–60.

9. Iris Young and Lani Guinier have been especially attentive to this problem: Young proposes group vetoes and Guinier proposes schemes of "cumulative voting" within legislatures. Young, *Justice and the Politics of Difference*, p. 184; Guinier, "No Two Seats: The Elusive Quest for Political Equality," in *The Tyranny of the Majority*, pp. 107–8. Both devices would certainly enhance the legislative clout of marginalized group representatives. As I discuss in some detail in chapter 7, however, both techniques run afoul of the notion that we should avoid essentializing group identity. See chapter 7, section II, below.

10. See John Rawls, *A Theory of Justice* (Cambridge: Harvard University Press, 1971), p. 85.

11. I reserve the term *fair representation* for the most general normative characterization of a view of representation. Thus liberal representation, the group-based theory I offer here, and the theories of Burke, Madison, Calhoun, and Mill are all theories of "fair representation."

12. Young, *Justice and the Politics of Difference*, p. 5.

13. Judith N. Shklar, *The Faces of Injustice* (New Haven: Yale University Press, 1990), p. 126.

14. Jane M. Mansbridge, *Beyond Adversary Democracy* (New York: Basic Books, 1980), p. xii.

15. I borrow the concept of "presumptive injustice" from Ian Shapiro. Shapiro argues that a commitment to democratic justice requires a suspicion of hierarchy wherever it occurs and a challenge to those who support or benefit from hierarchies to justify them. The presumptive injustice of hierarchy is, in Shapiro's view, rebuttable: there are circumstances in which other social and political interests outweigh the democratic interest in equality, and perhaps even serve it. *Democracy's Place* (Ithaca: Cornell University Press, 1996), p. 126. My argument is more focused but similar in form: I wish to argue that patterns of structural inequality along the lines of historically marginalized groups are intrinsically suspect, even though it might turn out that some patterns of group-structural inequality do not offend justice. It is conceivable, for example, that differences in culture may overlap with marginalized group identity in ways that yield voluntary choices for ways of life that are less remunerative than those pursued by relatively privileged groups, and that the differences in remuneration are not a product of the privileged group's historically greater power. It is difficult to think of any noncontroversial examples of such choices, but there is no reason in principle to suppose that they do not exist.

16. See, e.g., George A. Theodorson and Achilles G. Theodorson, eds., *A Modern Dictionary of Sociology* (New York: Thomas Y. Crowell, 1969), pp. 17, 353, 416; Gordon Marshall, ed., *The Concise Oxford Dictionary of Sociology* (New York: Oxford University Press, 1994), pp. 19, 510.

17. Nancy Fraser, *Justice Interruptus: Critical Reflections on the "Postsocialist" Condition* (New York: Routledge, 1997), chapter 1.

18. Ibid., p. 15.

19. Even this interest might not be shared by every member of the group, since some individuals may be able to use the group's marginalization for personal advantage. For example, it is not difficult to imagine individual members of a marginalized group who allow themselves to be used as tokens by organizations that wish to convey an image of tolerance without actually changing practices that disadvantage group members gener-

ally. But it is difficult to conceive of reasons why the existence of such individuals should affect our judgments about the moral claims of those group members who do share an interest in overcoming marginalization.

20. Max Black, "The Elusiveness of Sets," in *Caveats and Critiques: Philosophical Essays in Language, Logic, and Art* (Ithaca: Cornell University Press, 1975), p. 88.

21. Rawls, *A Theory of Justice*, p. 86.

22. For further discussion, see Charles R. Beitz, *Political Equality: An Essay in Democratic Theory* (Princeton, NJ: Princeton University Press, 1989), pp. 75–77.

23. Rawls, *A Theory of Justice*, p. 87.

24. See Beitz, *Political Equality*, pp. 94–96. Beitz notes that this symbolic or expressive function, while valuable, is not sufficient to justify a procedural regime or to reject procedural inequalities that do not reinforce objectionable inequalities elsewhere in society.

25. For an elaboration of the relationship between substantive and procedural principles in Beitz's view, see especially *Political Equality*, pp. 109–17.

26. Imperfect procedural fairness also stands in contrast to perfect procedural fairness, which articulates a standard and a procedure that will *always* realize it. Rawls believes that in the real world there are very few examples of perfect procedural fairness. *A Theory of Justice*, p. 85.

27. For a related discussion, see Beitz, *Political Equality*, pp. 47–48.

28. Certainly there are features of criminal procedure that embody these principles, including the various rights of criminal defendants and the structure of the adversary trial process.

29. Cf. Shapiro, *Democracy's Place*, pp. 123, 126.

30. As Joseph Carens and I have suggested in "Muslim Minorities in Liberal Democracies: The Politics of Misrecognition," in *The Challenge of Diversity: Integration and Pluralism in Societies of Immigration*, ed. Rainer Bauböck, Agnes Heller, and Aristide R. Zolberg (Aldershot: Avebury, 1996).

Chapter 1
Representation as Mediation

1. Hanna F. Pitkin, *The Concept of Representation* (Berkeley: University of California Press, 1967), p. 209.

2. It is true that all government institutions may be regarded as representative institutions in one way or another. Indeed, many of the institutions of civil society are also sites of representation to which my arguments in this book may be relevant. However, this study is concerned primarily with legislative representation, and the ways in which other institutions can be representative are beyond its scope.

3. See Pitkin, *Concept of Representation*, chapter 7, for a detailed discussion of this controversy.

4. For further discussion, see chapter 4, section V, below. It is worth noting that political parties tend to cut across these different aspects of representation as mediation and to resolve many of the questions internal to each aspect. A strong party system, for example, both limits the responsibility of a representative to his or her district and dictates the dynamics of legislative decision making.

5. A possible exception is constituency service, which some regard as a form of political representation (though it is not *legislative* representation, as it takes place outside the hall of the legislative assembly).

6. 478 U.S. 109, 167 (1986) (concurring in part and dissenting in part).

7. See, e.g., the discussion in Arend Lijphart, *Democracies: Patterns of Majoritarian and Consensus Government in Twenty-One Countries* (New Haven: Yale University Press, 1984), chapter 9, and sources cited.

8. Ibid., pp. 147–49.

9. See the discussion in ibid., pp. 107–8.

10. See, e.g., Charles R. Beitz, *Political Equality: An Essay in Democratic Theory* (Princeton, NJ: Princeton University Press, 1989), p. 12; Cass Sunstein, "Beyond the Republican Revival," *Yale Law Journal* 97 (8) (1988), p. 1543.

11. Notably Keith Bybee, whose book *Mistaken Identity: The Supreme Court and the Politics of Minority Representation* (Princeton, NJ: Princeton University Press, 1998) focuses specifically on the ways in which citizens' political identities are forged within processes of political deliberation over the shape of representative institutions.

12. 377 U.S. 533, 562 (1964).

13. *An Inquiry into the Principles and Policy of the Government of the United States* (New Haven: [1814] 1950), quoted in Gordon S. Wood, *The Creation of the American Republic, 1776–1787* (New York: W. W. Norton, 1969), p. 590.

14. "Towns and counties, it may be presumed, are represented when the human beings who inhabit them are represented." John Stuart Mill, *Considerations on Representative Government*, ed. Currin V. Shields (Indianapolis: Bobbs-Merrill, [1861] 1958), p. 119.

15. See, e.g., Heinz Eulau and Paul D. Karps, "The Puzzle of Representation: Specifying the Components of Responsiveness," in *The Politics of Representation: Continuities in Theory and Research*, ed. Heinz Eulau and John C. Wahlke (Beverly Hills: Sage, 1978), pp. 55–71; Bruce Cain, John Ferejohn, and Morris Fiorina, *The Personal Vote: Constituency Service and Electoral Independence* (Cambridge: Harvard University Press, 1987).

16. See Pitkin, *Concept of Representation*, p. 87; A. H. Birch, *Representation* (New York: Praeger, 1971), pp. 54–59.

17. Speech to Convention of the State of New York on the Adoption of the Federal Constitution, 21 June 1788, reprinted in Herbert J. Storing, ed., *The Anti-Federalist* (Chicago: University of Chicago Press, 1985), p. 340.

18. Letter to John Penn, in *Works*, vol. 4 (Boston: Little, 1856), p. 205; cf. p. 195.

19. Pitkin, *Concept of Representation*, p. 87.

20. Quoted in Storing, *The Anti-Federalist*, p. 358 n. 23.

21. Quoted in Birch, *Representation*, pp. 58–59.

22. In particular, as Heinz Eulau notes, the fact of the election of the representative always already distinguishes him or her from the represented in an important way. "Changing Views of Representation," in Eulau and Wahlke, *The Politics of Representation*, p. 51.

23. Pitkin, *Concept of Representation*, pp. 64–65.

24. I discuss the importance of trust in political representation in section III of this chapter.

25. "Human Nature," in *The Moral and Political Works of Thomas Hobbes of Malmesbury* (London, 1750), quoted in John Dunn, "Trust and Political Agency," in *Trust: Making and Breaking Cooperative Relations*, ed. Diego Gambetta (Oxford: Basil Blackwell, 1988), p. 74.

26. Dunn, "Trust and Political Agency," pp. 74–75. Allan Silver makes a similar point regarding the making of compacts: "Trust is both central to this process and enhanced by it." "'Trust' in Social and Political Theory," in *The Challenge of Social Control: Citizenship and Institution Building in Modern Society*, ed. Gerald D. Suttles and Mayer N. Zald (Norwood, NJ: Ablex, 1985), p. 57.

27. See, e.g., Pitkin, *Concept of Representation*, p. 128.

28. See also the discussion in ibid., pp. 128–29.

29. Mill, *Considerations on Representative Government*, pp. 154–56. It is worth noting, however, that Mill's usage stretches the concept, for the franchise is not an agency *transferred* or *delegated* from one subject to another. Rather, having the franchise signifies that one possesses the agency that is relevant for political action in the first place.

30. John Locke, *Two Treatises of Government* 2, sec. 149, ed. Peter Laslett (Cambridge: Cambridge University Press, 1988), p. 367.

31. For a discussion of this distinction, see Peter Laslett's introduction to ibid., p. 114.

32. Judith N. Shklar, *Ordinary Vices* (Cambridge: Harvard University Press, 1984), p. 184.

33. "Thoughts on the Cause of the Present Discontents," in *The Works of the Right Hon. Edmund Burke*, 4th ed., vol. 1 (Boston: Little, Brown, 1871; 12 vols.), p. 503. Unless otherwise noted, all references to Burke's writings and speeches are to this edition of his collected works.

34. Speech to the Electors of Bristol, in *Works*, vol. 2, p. 96 (emphasis in original).

35. Pitkin, *Concept of Representation*, p. 174; see also Samuel H. Beer, "The Representation of Interests in British Government: Historical Background," *American Political Science Review* 51 (3) (1957), pp. 614–19.

36. I make this argument in detail in "Burkean 'Descriptions' and Political Representation: A Reappraisal," *Canadian Journal of Political Science* 29 (1) (1996), pp. 23–45.

37. Letter to Sir Hercules Langrishe (1792), in *Works*, vol. 4, p. 293.

38. Letter to the Chairman of the Buckinghamshire Meeting (on parliamentary reform) (13 April 1780), in *Works*, vol. 6, p. 296.

39. Letter to Sir Hercules Langrishe, p. 293 (emphasis added).

40. Ibid., p. 253 (emphasis in original).

41. Speech on a Motion Made in the House of Commons . . . for a Committee to Inquire into the State of the Representation (1782), in *Works*, vol. 7, p. 95.

42. Arguing against the forceful suppression of Ireland on grounds that it would destroy the prosperity that gives Britain an interest in Ireland, Burke said, "either, in order to limit her, we *must restrain* ourselves, or we must fall into that shocking conclusion that we are to keep our yet remaining dependency under a general and indiscriminate restraint for the mere purpose of oppression." Letter to Samuel Span, in *Burke's Politics: Selected Writings and Speeches on Reform, Revolution and War*, ed. Ross J. S. Hoffman and Paul Levack (New York: Knopf, 1959), p. 125.

43. Speech on Conciliation with America (1775), in *Works*, vol. 2, p. 140.

44. "Thoughts on the Cause of the Present Discontents," p. 492.

45. As Pitkin puts it, the discovery of the national interests "presupposes the partic-ipation of representatives of every interest so that all considerations will be brought to bear." *Concept of Representation*, p. 187.

46. Speech on a Motion Made in the House of Commons . . . for a Committee to Inquire into the State of the Representation, p. 96.

47. Locke, *Second Treatise*, sec. 225, p. 415.

48. *The Federalist Papers*, ed. Clinton Rossiter (New York: New American Library, 1961), No. 10, p. 79.

49. In this Madison differs considerably from Alexander Hamilton, whose descrip-tion of the "natural aristocracy" resonates with Burke's characterization of the internal hierarchical structure of different elements of the nation. For example, Hamilton sug-gests that the commercial interest comprehends not only merchants but also mechanics and manufacturers. The latter, he argues, "will always be inclined . . . to give their votes to merchants. . . . They know that the merchant is their natural patron and friend; and they are aware that however great the confidence they may justly feel in their own good sense, their interests can be more effectually promoted by the merchants [whose] . . . wit and superior acquirements . . . render them more equal to a contest . . . [in] the public councils." *Federalist* 35, pp. 214–15.

50. *Federalist* 10, p. 79.

51. See Jennifer Nedelsky, *Private Property and the Limits of American Constitutional-ism* (Chicago: University of Chicago Press, 1990), pp. 186 et seq. for a detailed and persuasive argument on this point.

52. *Federalist* 10, p. 84.

53. Ibid., p. 83.

54. Wood, *The Creation of the American Republic 1776–1787*, p. 411.

55. Nedelsky, *Private Property and the Limits of American Constiutionalism*, p. 159.

56. *A Disquisition on Government, and Selections from the Discourse* (New York: Liberal Arts Press, [1850] 1953), p. 5.

57. Ibid., p. 20.

58. Ibid., p. 53.

59. Ibid., pp. 50–53.

60. Richard Hofstadter, "John C. Calhoun: The Marx of the Master Class," in *The American Political Tradition* (New York: Vintage, 1948), pp. 89–90.

61. Speech on the Reception of Abolition Petitions, reprinted in *Union and Liberty: the Political Philosophy of John C. Calhoun*, ed. Ross M. Lence (Indianapolis: Liberty Fund, [1837] 1992), p. 474.

62. The relationship between racial division and the failure of political trust is ex-plored in chapter 4.

63. *A Discourse on the Constitution and Government of the United States*, in Lence, *Union and Liberty*, p. 274.

64. In chapter 7, I address the challenge of defining political institutions that en-hance minority representation and minority clout within legislative bodies without os-sifying social cleavage by embedding group identities within a constitution.

65. Mill, *Considerations on Representative Government*, p. 86.

66. Ibid., p. 94.

67. Ibid.

68. Although not necessarily against the interests of "property" per se. Rather, Mill thinks it plausible that a working-class majority would legislate raises in wages, regulation of work conditions, and protection from foreign competition, all of which might, over the long run, "relax[] industry and activity, and diminish[] encouragement to savings." Ibid., p. 95.

69. Mill, *Considerations on Representative Government*, p. 47. Note the similarity to Burke's suggestion, discussed above, that it is important to attend to soundings of social discontent because they may signal an immanent withdrawal of social cooperation, which is usually destructive of the general welfare of society.

70. As Dennis Thompson demonstrates, the contrast between these two rationales for participation reflects the two distinct functions of good government that inform every aspect of Mill's theory: government must both *protect* citizens from abuses of power and *educate* them to realize their fullest moral and intellectual capacities. *John Stuart Mill and Representative Government* (Princeton, NJ: Princeton University Press, 1976), p. 9 and passim.

71. Note that these considerations relate to the fourth aspect of representation as mediation, discussed above in section 1.

72. J. S. Mill, "Recent Writers on Reform," in *Essays on Politics and Culture*, ed. Gertrude Himmelfarb (Gloucester, MA: Peter Smith, [1859] 1973), p. 360.

73. Ibid., p. 107.

74. Under the Hare system, a seat is allocated to each candidate who wins a quota of first-choice votes, where the quota is defined by the number of electors divided by the number of seats to be filled. If more than a quota of first-choice votes are given to a single candidate, the surplus votes are reallocated among the remaining candidates. This process of vote redistribution continues until all the seats are filled. As with other proportional representation systems, the Hare system makes it likely that virtually every voter will have played a part in electing a representative, and each can point to at least one elected representative for whom he or she voted. For a more detailed discussion of the Hare and other schemes of proportional representation, see Douglas Rae, *The Political Consequences of Electoral Laws* (New Haven: Yale University Press, 1967), pp. 40–46.

75. Mill, *Considerations on Representative Government*, p. 125.

76. Ibid., p. 120; see also pp. 111–12, 123. In chapter 7, I favor strategies for enhancing marginalized group representation that would, like Mill's system, permit the voluntary formation of constituencies. For a discussion of the harmony between Mill's view and what I call "liberal representation," see chapter 2, section II.

77. Ibid., pp. 116–17.

78. Ibid., pp. 82–83.

79. Thompson, *John Stuart Mill and Representative Government*, p. 25.

80. As Hanna Pitkin notes, the activity of the political representative must therefore consist of something more than merely giving information about constituent views. *Concept of Representation*, p. 63.

81. Mill, *Considerations on Representative Government*, p. 45.

82. Ibid., p. 83.

83. Ibid., p. 79.

84. For a detailed discussion of the qualities of the competent minority, see Thompson, *John Stuart Mill and Representative Government*, pp. 77–87.

85. Ibid., pp. 123, 118.

86. In fact, in a different section of *Considerations on Representative Government*, pp. 139–40, Mill proposes that this group be given plural votes. This proposal seems to be an alternative to proportional representation rather than a device to be instituted in conjunction with it. As Dennis Thompson notes, however, Mill became increasingly ambivalent about plural voting because of the tendency to identify it with the representation of property rather than of intelligence or competence. Thompson, *John Stuart Mill and Representative Government*, pp. 99–101.

87. See the discussion in Thompson, *John Stuart Mill and Representative Government*, pp. 80–82.

88. Mill, *Considerations on Representative Government*, p. 101.

89. As the temperance example cited above illustrates, Mill thought it important that this activity of political self-definition occur even if some citizens made poor judgments about what their political interests were. This commitment to the public affirmation of citizens' own definitions of their political concerns is also reflected in Mill's view that representatives ought to present constituents' fundamental or "life-blood" beliefs even if those beliefs were false. "Such convictions," he wrote, "are entitled to influence in virtue of their mere existence, and not solely in that of the probability of their being grounded in truth. A people cannot be well-governed in opposition to their primary notions of right, even though these may be in some points erroneous." Ibid., p. 183.

90. See the discussion in Thompson, *John Stuart Mill and Representative Government*, pp. 112–17.

91. I am grateful to David Welch for suggesting this metaphor.

92. These concerns are especially prominent in chapter 4.

93. Calhoun's insights are particularly relevant to the discussions in chapters 5 and 7.

94. See especially chapter 6.

95. See especially chapter 7.

96. I discuss the problem of balkanization further in chapter 7, section I. For an insightful and thought-provoking reflection on conservatives' use of the language of balkanization, see Pamela S. Karlan, "Our Separatism? Voting Rights as an American Nationalities Policy," *University of Chicago Legal Forum* (1995), pp. 83–109.

97. This is true even of systems of proportional representation. For example, party-list systems of proportional representation tend to favor ideological groupings, whereas gender- or race-based group differences might find more expression in candidate-focused schemes of proportional representation such as cumulative voting. These issues are discussed in detail in chapter 7.

98. It is important to note that although there is some connection between involuntary and immutable group membership, the two are not identical: membership in a group may be involuntary without being immutable (as in the given example of legal residence) or, less probably, immutable without being involuntary (as might be the case, for example, for "out" gays and lesbians).

99. Burke, *Reflections on the Revolution in France*, ed. Thomas H. D. Mahoney (Indianapolis: Bobbs-Merrill, 1955), pp. 50, 57–58.

100. See, e.g., ibid., p. 179.

Chapter 2
Liberal Equality and Liberal Representation

1. J. R. Pole, *The Pursuit of Equality in American History* (Berkeley: University of California Press, 1978), p. 1.

2. John Rawls, *A Theory of Justice* (Cambridge: Harvard University Press, 1971), p. 511. See also, e.g., Ronald Dworkin, *Taking Rights Seriously* (Cambridge: Harvard University Press, 1978), pp. 180–83, on the "equal concern and respect" that is owed to all persons as such.

3. See Amy Gutmann's *Liberal Equality* (Cambridge: Cambridge University Press, 1980), where she distinguishes eudaemonist from rationalist groundings of liberal equality. The former emphasize humans' capacity for pleasure and pain (i.e., their status as feeling beings), whereas the latter emphasize humans' endowment with a capacity for rationality and moral judgment (i.e., their status as thinking beings).

4. Rawls, *A Theory of Justice*, p. 74.

5. *Plessy v. Ferguson*, 163 U.S. 537, 559 (1896) (Justice Harlan, dissenting).

6. There are occasional exceptions to this rule, as for example when a legislature wishes to confer some special benefit on a disadvantaged group. However, such laws must be justified by a "rational state policy" and are subject to strict judicial scrutiny when they affect "discrete and insular minorities," as the Supreme Court suggested in the now famous footnote 4 in *United States v. Carolene Products Co.*, 304 U.S. 144 (1938).

7. Not all social goods are scarce. Fundamental civil rights and liberties, for example, can be extended to all citizens without imposing any material cost. Few people any longer suggest that they should not be so distributed. The disputes begin at the points where abundant goods (such as the right to vote) blur into scarce goods (like the power to secure one's political will).

8. Will Kymlicka, *Contemporary Political Philosophy* (Oxford: Oxford University Press, 1990), p. 56.

9. Rawls, *A Theory of Justice*, p. 73. Rawls calls this the principle of "fair equality of opportunity." I should note, though, that in Rawls's view this doctrine does not go far enough in the direction of equality. The problem with equal opportunity is that it does not acknowledge that even natural talents and abilities, as well as the psychological or familial circumstances that produce the motivation to develop those abilities, are "morally arbitrary" insofar as they are not subject to individuals' control. They, like race and sex, are accidents of birth. This observation leads Rawls to articulate a further principle of democratic equality, the difference principle, which compensates for inequalities of natural talent by requiring that the least advantaged members of society receive the greatest benefits from any social inequality. See pp. 75–83.

10. Ibid., p. 86.

11. Ibid., p. 87 (emphasis added).

12. The psychology of procedural approaches is worth noting here. Because its outcomes are fair by definition, proceduralism takes the responsibility for outcomes out of the hands of any particular group or individual. In this way, procedural solutions such as equal opportunity entail a relinquishment of control over a situation, so that there is a strange similarity between saying, "May God's will be done" and "Let the market

decide" or "May the best man win." Each of these statements suggests a situation in which the loser has no claim against anyone, no grounds to complain about the outcome. This suggests that when we adopt procedural solutions there is some danger that we may be abandoning our responsibility for the inequalities they produce.

13. Allison M. Jaggar, "Sexual Difference and Sexual Equality," in *Theoretical Perspectives on Sexual Difference*, ed. Deborah L. Rhode (New Haven: Yale University Press, 1990), p. 242.

14. This is no imaginary example and is particularly striking when poverty overlaps with minority race or ethnicity. Fetal alcohol syndrome, just one among many examples, occurs at a much higher rate among Native Americans below the poverty line than among the rest of the population. See Michael Dorris, *The Broken Cord* (New York: Harper and Row, 1989).

15. Brian Barry, "Equal Opportunity and Moral Arbitrariness," in *Equal Opportunity*, ed. Norman E. Bowie (Boulder, CO: Westview, 1988), p. 33.

16. Rawls, *A Theory of Justice*, p. 85.

17. As Douglas Rae has phrased it, "The choice of criteria in a society . . . will be *neutral only if every pair of subjects are identically talented or stand in a relation of generalized superiority-inferiority on all criteria.* Under *any* other circumstance, the selection of criteria is itself an act of unequal allocation, favoring some people over others." Douglas Rae, *Equalities* (Cambridge: Harvard University Press, 1981), p. 71 (emphasis in original).

18. Young, *Justice and the Politics of Difference* (Princeton, NJ: Princeton University Press, 1990), p. 116. This is what Catharine MacKinnon seems to have in mind when she writes, "The differences attributed to sex are the lines inequality draws, not the basis for those lines. . . . Differences are inequality's post hoc excuse." "Legal Perspectives on Sexual Difference," in *Theoretical Perspectives on Sexual Difference*, ed. Deborah L. Rhode (New Haven: Yale University Press, 1990), p. 213.

19. Deborah L. Rhode, "Definitions of Difference," in *Theoretical Perspectives on Sexual Difference*, p. 208 (citing *General Electric Co. v. Gilbert*, 429 U.S. 125 (1976)).

20. MacKinnon, "Legal Perspectives on Sexual Difference," p. 217.

21. In his dissenting opinion in *Baker v. Carr*, Justice Frankfurter noted egregious examples of malapportionment. In New Jersey, which had a county-based system for electing state senators, the smallest county had 35,000 residents whereas the largest had 905,000. In Minnesota the smallest district for state representatives had 7,290 inhabitants and the largest had 107,246. In California the ratio of populations in the smallest and largest Senate districts was 1 to 297. 369 U.S. 186, 321–22 (1962).

22. The doctrine was first announced in *Gray v. Sanders*, which stated: "The conception of political equality from the Declaration of Independence, to Lincoln's Gettysburg Address, to the Fifteenth, Seventeenth and Nineteenth Amendments can mean only one thing—one person, one vote." 372 U.S. 368, 381 (1962).

23. 376 U.S. 1 (1964).

24. 377 U.S. 533 (1964).

25. *Wesberry v. Sanders*, 376 U.S., at 8 (emphasis added).

26. "The fact that an individual lives here or there is not a legitimate reason for overweighting or diluting the efficacy of his vote." *Reynolds*, 567. Note the similarity between this notion and the doctrine of liberal neutrality addressed in the above discussion of equal opportunity. Just as factors such as race and sex are "morally arbitrary" characteristics that ought not to be considered in the allocation of social goods, place of

residence is here regarded as a morally arbitrary factor that ought not to determine the weight of one's vote.

27. Ibid., p. 555.

28. In fact, the Court recognized, some such constraints were important to curb the potential for partisan gerrymanders. Ibid., pp. 578–79.

29. *Kirkpatrick v. Preisler*, 394 U.S. 526, 537 (1969).

30. *Reynolds*, pp. 623–24.

31. Arthur F. Bentley, *The Process of Government* (Cambridge: Harvard University Press, [1908] 1967), p. 269.

32. David B. Truman, *The Governmental Process* (New York: Knopf, 1953); Robert A. Dahl, *A Preface to Democratic Theory* (Chicago: University of Chicago Press, 1956).

33. It seems fair to say that until recently interest-group pluralism was the central paradigm of American politics, in Thomas Kuhn's sense of a "paradigm" as "an accepted model or pattern" that "define[s] the legitimate problems and methods of a research field." *The Structure of Scientific Revolutions* (Chicago: University of Chicago Press, 1970), pp. 22, 10. In recent years the pluralist model has been revised by the "new institutionalism," which (among other things) challenges the pluralist notion that the formation of interest groups is exogenous to the political process and that political institutions themselves make no substantive contribution to policy outcomes. James G. March and Johan P. Olsen, *Rediscovering Institutions* (New York: Free Press, 1989), pp. 18, 162–66. Despite the modifications of institutional approaches, the pluralist understandings of the process of representation—and particularly of the nature of the interest groups that secure representation—remain relatively unchanged in the respects relevant for this analysis, as is reflected in the approaches of recent work on interest groups. See, e.g., John R. Wright, "Contributions, Lobbying, and Committee Voting in the U.S. House of Representatives," *American Political Science Review* 84 (2) (1990), pp. 417–38; Richard L. Hall and Frank W. Wayman, "Buying Time: Moneyed Interests and the Mobilization of Bias in Congressional Committees," *American Political Science Review* 84 (3) (1990), pp. 797–820.

34. David Truman distinguishes "categoric" groups, in which people simply share a characteristic, from "interactive" groups, in which the members have some relationship to one another. *The Governmental Process*, pp. 23–24.

35. Ibid., p. 33.

36. See, e.g., ibid., p. 37 ("even a temporarily viable legislative decision usually must involve the adjustment and compromise of interests. Even where virtual unanimity prevails in the legislature, the process of reconciling conflicting interests must have taken place"); Robert A. Dahl and Charles E. Lindblom, *Politics, Economics, and Welfare: Planning and Politico-Economic Systems Resolved into Basic Social Sciences* (New York: Harper Torchbooks, 1953), p. 309 ("From what we have said it is clear that a considerable measure of bargaining is an inherent aspect of polyarchy. For the resolution of group conflict and the search for agreement is largely carried on by bargaining").

37. "The economic pressure groups really become an occupational parliament of the American people, more truly representative than the Congress elected by territorial divisions." John R. Commons, *The Economics of Collective Action* (New York: Macmillan, 1950), p. 33.

38. E. E. Schattschneider's critique of interest-group pluralism characterizes the pluralist view in this way: "It is hard to imagine a more effective way of saying that

Congress has no mind or force of its own or that Congress is unable to invoke new forces that might alter the equation. Actually the outcome of political conflict is not like the 'resultant' of opposing forces in physics." E. E. Schattschneider, *The Semisovereign People* (Hinsdale, IL.: Dryden, 1975), pp. 37–38. Insofar as Schattschneider claims that pluralists overlook the contributions of legislators and institutional norms to political outcomes, however, this is something of a caricature of pluralist thought, as I discuss below.

39. Dahl, *Preface to Democratic Theory*, pp.131–32.

40. Truman defines the "rules of the game" as "those interests or expectations that are so widely held in the society and are so reflected in the behavior of almost all citizens that they are, so to speak, taken for granted." *The Governmental Process*, p. 512. Cf. Dahl, *Preface to Democratic Theory*, p. 132: "In a sense, what we ordinarily describe as democratic 'politics' is merely the chaff. It is the surface manifestation, representing superficial conflicts. Prior to politics, beneath it, enveloping it, restricting it, condition-ing it, is the underlying consensus on policy that usually exists in the society among a predominant portion of the politically active members. Without such a consensus no democratic society would long survive." More recently, however, Dahl has argued that the existence of an underlying consensus on core policy questions is an "illusion." To the contrary, he now argues, conflict over fundamentals of public policy is inevitable in any large modern democracy, and we should not hope to discover or to create an underlying consensus. *Dilemmas of Pluralist Democracy: Autonomy vs. Control* (New Haven: Yale University Press, 1982), pp. 186–88.

41. Truman, *The Governmental Process*, p. 511.

42. I address this weakness in section IV, below.

43. As Dahl puts it, "[a] central guiding thread of American constitutional develop-ment has been the evolution of a political system in which all the active and legitimate groups in the population can make themselves heard at some crucial stage in the pro-cess of decision." *Preface to Democratic Theory*, p. 137.

44. Alfred DeGrazia, *Public and Republic* (New York: Knopf, 1951), pp. 169–70 (quoting T. V. Smith). Dahl and Lindblom express this in less colorful language: "[S]o long as the opportunity for political action is kept open to the greater number, such policies will be determined within broad and often vague limits set by widely shared norms and the expectations of policy makers that they will activate the greater number against them whenever, in placating minorities, they exceed the boundaries set by the highly ranked, intense, and stable preferences of the greater number." *Politics, Econom-ics, and Welfare*, p. 314.

45. Dahl examines this problem in democratic theory at length in *Preface to Demo-cratic Theory*, chapter 4.

46. That financial contributions are among the indicators of the intensity of citizen preferences points to an obvious critique of interest-group pluralism, i.e., that the op-portunities for political influence are not equal for rich and poor. I address this and other critiques in section IV, below.

47. Dahl, *Preface to Democratic Theory*, p. 134. Moreover, no matter what the inten-sity with which a minority asserts claims on public policy, the activities of minority interest groups will not overpower any intense majority preference. Here, too, the sys-tem is self-correcting, as the general public will let legislators know when they have violated the "rules of the game" or other stable preferences, either through electoral

mechanisms or through public outcry. See, e.g., Dahl and Lindblom, *Politics, Economics, and Welfare,* p. 516; Truman, *The Governmental Process,* pp. 348–50.

48. Rawls, *A Theory of Justice,* p. 85.

49. See, e.g., Truman, *The Governmental Process,* p. 510.

50. As Dahl lays out in his *Preface to Democratic Theory,* pluralism produces stability only in societies where there are no conflicts that deeply and permanently divide a large segment of the population against another large population group. No amount of interest-group activity, for example, could have prevented the U.S. Civil War because of the nature of the political cleavage between North and South, a cleavage that encompassed important differences of economic as well as social and political interests. See chapter 4.

51. "Representation in Political Theory and in Law," *Ethics* 91 (3) (1981), pp. 396–98.

52. Ibid., pp. 398–99. Rogowski distinguishes two forms of equal representation: "equally weighted representation" (meaning that each individual's preferences "count" as much as any other's in the election of representatives) and "equally powerful representation" (individuals' preferences are equally satisfied by legislative outcomes). As he notes, the former notion of equal representation is what the principle of "one person, one vote" expresses; it is also the same as what Jonathan Still refers to as "equal shares" in "Political Equality and Election Systems," *Ethics* 91 (3) (1981), pp. 378–79.

53. See, e.g., Gordon E. Baker, *The Reapportionment Revolution: Representation, Political Power, and the Supreme Court* (New York: Random House, 1966), pp. 16–17; Lani Guinier, "Groups, Representation, and Race Conscious Districting: A Case of the Emperor's Clothes," in *The Tyranny of the Majority* (New York: Free Press, 1994), pp. 127–29, and sources cited. For a discussion of the corporate character of towns in the early colonial view of representation, see J. R. Pole, *Political Representation in England and the Origins of the American Republic* (New York: St. Martin's, 1966), pp. 38–54.

54. See the discussion in chapter 1, section I.

55. *The Reapportionment Revolution,* p. 102. Baker himself, however, was an advocate of "one person, one vote" as a requirement of democratic equality, and he was critical of the notion that geography is the best proxy for socially relevant interests.

56. See, e.g., Baker, *The Reapportionment Revolution,* pp. 15–18. In her intriguing study of representation in the early American republic, Rosemarie Zagarri suggests that this normative conclusion—that geography is a proxy for socially relevant interests—is itself the product of a historical evolution from "spatial" to "demographic" understandings of representation. In the former view, *places* are what should receive political representation; in the latter, shared *interests* should be represented. The transformation from the former to the latter in American political discourse can be traced, Zagarri argues, in the constitutional debates over representation between the small states, which favored spatial concepts of representation, and the large states, which favored the demographic model. Ultimately the demographic view came to take over political discourse completely. Rosemarie Zagarri, *The Politics of Size: Representation in the United States, 1776–1850* (Ithaca: Cornell University Press, 1987).

57. See the discussion in section II, above.

58. See, e.g., *Mahan v. Howell,* 410 U.S. 315 (1973) (involving a plan for state legislative districts) and *Abate v. Mundt,* 403 U.S. 182 (1975) (involving a districting plan for a county board of supervisors). For a related discussion, see also Bernard Grofman,

"Criteria for Redistricting: A Social Science Perspective," in *UCLA Law Review* 33 (1) (1985), pp. 86–88.

59. Guinier, "Groups, Representation, and Race-Conscious Districting," p. 129.

60. For further discussion of the voluntary formation of constituencies, see chapter 1, section VII (discussing John Stuart Mill's advocacy of proportional representation on the ground that it permits the voluntary formation of constituencies) and chapter 7, section I (discussing the propensity of contemporary versions of proportional representation to allow self-defined constituencies to emerge around marginalized group identities).

61. Cf. John Stuart Mill, *Considerations on Representative Government*, ed. Currin V. Shields (Indianapolis: Bobbs-Merrill, 1958), pp. 111–12, 123.

62. Douglas Rae, *The Political Consequences of Electoral Laws* (New Haven: Yale University Press, 1971), pp. 88–92; Douglas Amy, *Real Choices/New Voices: The Case for Proportional Representation in the United States* (New York: Columbia University Press, 1993), pp. 82–86.

63. Maurice Duverger, "Duverger's Law: Forty Years Later," in *Electoral Laws and Their Political Consequences*, ed. Bernard Grofman and Arend Lijphart (New York: Agathon, 1986), p. 70.

64. See, e.g., Amy, *Real Choices/New Voices*, p. 34. Charles Beitz disagrees. See *Political Equality* (Princeton, NJ: Princeton University Press, 1989), pp. 132–40. Amy also points out that single-member district systems are also more likely than systems of proportional representation to produce "manufactured majorities" (i.e., legislative majorities that actually won only a plurality of the popular vote) and can even produce minority rule. Amy, *Real Choices/New Voices*, pp. 33–36.

65. See, e.g., the discussion in Mark E. Rush, *Does Redistricting Make a Difference? Partisan Representation and Electoral Behavior* (Baltimore, MD: The Johns Hopkins University Press, 1993), p. 29.

66. Arguably they support some. Among traditional districting standards are requirements for district compactness and contiguity, which some argue facilitate stronger communications between legislators and constituents by shortening the distances representatives must travel to various parts of their districts. Further, some scholars believe that traditional districting practices, taken together, frustrate attempts at gerrymandering. As Bernard Grofman argues, however, there are good reasons to be skeptical of both claims. See "Criteria for Redistricting: A Social Science Perspective," pp. 88–90, and sources cited.

67. See especially Maurice Duverger, *Political Parties*, trans. Barbara and Robert North (London: Methuen, 1954), pp. 245–55.

68. See the discussion in Beitz, *Political Equality*, p. 130 n. 14, and accompanying text; Amy, *Real Choices/New Voices*, pp. 157–60.

69. A widely noted example of this phenomenon is the success of the National Rifle Association in preventing serious gun control legislation, despite the fact that a majority of voters favor gun control.

70. Beitz, *Political Equality*, p. 135.

71. Pamela Karlan, "Maps and Misreadings: The Role of Geographic Compactness in Racial Vote Dilution Litigation," in *Harvard Civil Rights-Civil Liberties Law Review* 24 (1) (1989), pp. 241–48; Lani Guinier, "No Two Seats: The Elusive Quest for Political Equality," in *The Tyranny of the Majority*, pp. 107–8. I discuss these legislative strategies in greater detail in chapter 7, pp. 224–27.

72. Robert Dixon, *Democratic Representation: Reapportionment in Law and Politics* (New York: Oxford University Press, 1968), p. 462.

73. Beitz, *Political Equality*, p. 149.

74. Schattschneider, *The Semisovereign People*, pp. 34–35. I should also note another important internal critique of pluralist theory, i.e., Mancur Olson's *The Logic of Collective Action* (Cambridge: Harvard University Press, 1971). There, Olson demonstrates that the problem of free-ridership creates a greater obstacle to the organization of large groups than of small groups. Interesting as his argument is, its relevance to this project is tangential.

75. Robert A. Dahl, "Polyarchy, Pluralism, and Scale," *Scandinavian Political Studies* 78 (4) (1984), p. 235. See also Dahl, *Dilemmas of Pluralist Democracy*, pp. 46–47; and Dahl, *After the Revolution? Authority in a Good Society* (New Haven: Yale University Press, 1970), pp. 105–15.

76. See, e.g., Robert A. Dahl, *Democracy and Its Critics* (New Haven: Yale University Press, 1989), p. 323 and chapter 23.

77. Dahl, "Polyarchy, Pluralism, and Scale," p. 238.

78. See also Jane J. Mansbridge, "Living with Conflict: Representation in the Theory of Adversary Democracy," *Ethics* 91 (3) (1981), p. 471: "But when cross-cutting cleavages are not the norm, permanent minorities . . . can find their interests stripped of almost all protection." Similarly Lani Guinier invokes a Madisonian concern to prevent the "tyranny of the majority" by ensuring that shifting majorities, rather than "permanent and homogeneous" majorities, rule. See, e.g., *The Tyranny of the Majority*, pp. 4, 78. The difference between her critique and others' is that she emphasizes the homogeneity of the ruling majority rather than the permanence and cohesiveness of the dominated minority. Neither characterization is perfectly accurate: the critical question concerns the permanence of the *cleavage* between majority and minority, and the permanence of the numerical imbalance between them. Whether the two blocs are perfectly internally cohesive is much less important.

79. See, e.g., Derrick Bell, *And We Are Not Saved: The Elusive Quest for Racial Justice* (New York: Basic Books, 1987), p. 97, in the voice of the fictitious Geneva Crenshaw: the Madisonian solution to majority tyranny is "a persuasive approach if coalition building occurs freely across racial lines, but [not] when blacks are consistently excluded from the coalition-building process."

80. See, e.g., Dahl, *Democracy and Its Critics*, pp. 254–60; Dahl, *Dilemmas of Pluralist Democracy*, pp. 99–100.

81. Dahl, *Dilemmas of Pluralist Democracy*, pp. 89–94.

82. I discuss such institutions in chapter 7.

83. Albert P. Weale, "Representation, Individualism, and Collectivism," *Ethics* 91 (3) (1981), p. 463.

84. Young, *Justice and the Politics of Difference*, p. 185.

85. Swain, *Black Faces, Black Interests* (Cambridge: Harvard University Press, 1993), pp. 207–9; Swain, "Black Majority Districts: A Bad Idea," *New York Times*, 3 June 1993, p. A23; Abigail Thernstrom, "Redistricting, in Black and White: By Any Name, It's a Quota," *New York Times*, 7 December 1994, p. A23.

86. Carol Swain, "Some Consequences of the Voting Rights Act," in *Controversies in Minority Voting: The Voting Rights Act in Perspective*, ed. Bernard Grofman and Chandler Davidson (Washington, D.C.: Brookings Institution, 1992), p. 294.

87. See especially Chandler Davidson and Bernard Grofman, eds., *Quiet Revolution in the South: The Impact of the Voting Rights Act, 1965–1990* (Princeton, NJ: Princeton University Press, 1994).

88. Bernard Grofman, "*Shaw v. Reno* and the Future of Voting Rights," *PS: Political Science and Politics* 28 (1) (1995), p. 27.

89. Abigail Thernstrom, *Whose Votes Count? Affirmative Action and Minority Voting Rights* (Cambridge: Harvard University Press, 1987), p. 234.

90. Ibid., p. 5.

91. Cf. the discussion in chapter 1, pp. 78, 83–84.

92. As Thernstrom puts it, if communities are thought to benefit from the presence of Blacks on decision-making bodies, "that is an argument not for federal intervention but for black political organization." *Whose Votes Count?*, p. 240.

93. See, e.g., ibid., pp. 154, 187–88, 205, 239–40; Swain, *Black Faces, Black Interests*, pp. 211–16.

94. Thernstrom, *Whose Votes Count?*, p. 109. Thernstrom does not indicate the senator's race, although her distinction in this paragraph between "lawmakers," on the one hand, and "blacks and Hispanics," on the other, seems to warrant the inference that the senator was White.

95. Ibid., p. 90 (emphasis added).

96. 430 U.S. 144, 186 (1977) (Burger, dissenting) (emphasis added). This view is not exclusive to conservatives, as reflected by the fact that liberal Justice William Brennan expressed a similar concern in a separate opinion in the same case: "even a benign policy of assignment by race is viewed as unjust by many in our society, especially by those individuals who are adversely affected by a given classification." 430 U.S., p. 174.

97. Thernstrom, *Whose Votes Count?*, p. 124. It is important to note, as in fact some of Thernstrom's critics have noted, that her book does not offer a systematic defense of her thesis that group-conscious districting contradicts fundamental principles of fairness. See, e.g., Harvard Sitkoff's review in the *American Historical Review* 94 (1) (1989), p. 242. However, this failure does not mean that no such defense is available, as the foregoing has attempted to show. In fact, the principles of liberal representation are implicit in many of Thernstrom's arguments and assumptions, and, as we have seen, it is a fully coherent theory of representation. What remains for Thernstrom's critics is to demonstrate the weaknesses of the theory of representation which she implicitly affirms. Such a demonstration is one aim of this book.

98. See the discussion in chapter 6, sections III and IV.

99. Senate Judicary Committee, *Voting Rights Act Amendments of 1982*, 97th Cong., 2d sess., S. Rept. 97–417, p. 34, reprinted in *United States Code Congressional and Administrative News 1982*, vol. 2 (St. Paul, MN: West, 1982), p. 212.

100. See the discussion in chapter 1, section VIII.

Chapter 3
The Supreme Court, Voting Rights, and Representation

1. Different scholars have characterized the inconsistencies in the Supreme Court's voting rights jurisprudence somewhat differently. Samuel Issacharoff, for example, distinguishes a process-based or pluralist theory of voting rights from a "historically and

sociologically specific" theory. Whereas the former recognizes the general ill of majority faction, the latter regards with "special urgency" the need to remedy majority dominance over historically disadvantaged groups. "Polarized Voting and the Political Process: The Transformation of Voting Rights Jurisprudence," *Michigan Law Review* 90 (7) (1992), pp. 1833–91. Lani Guinier's critique of geographic districting turns on a distinction between the theoretical grounds of territorial representation discussed in the last chapter, in which geography is treated as a proxy for the interests that should receive political expression in the process of representation, and a more direct acknowledgment that political representation gives expression to group interests. Lani Guinier, "Groups, Representation, and Race Conscious Districting: A Case of the Emperor's Clothes," in *The Tyranny of the Majority: Fundamental Fairness in Representative Democracy* (New York: Free Press, 1994), pp. 199–256; and "No Two Seats: The Elusive Quest for Political Equality," in *The Tyranny of the Majority*, pp. 71–118. Pamela Karlan's interpretation of voting rights jurisprudence distinguishes a strand of territorial representation from a strand of what she calls the "civic inclusion" model of voting and representation, in which the emphasis is on the need to include members of historically disadvantaged groups as full citizens in the political process. See Karlan, "Maps and Misreadings: The Role of Geographic Compactness in Racial Vote Dilution Litigation," *Harvard Civil Rights-Civil Liberties Law Review* 24 (1) (1989), pp. 173–248; and Karlan, "The Rights to Vote: Some Pessimism about Formalism," *Texas Law Review* 71 (7) (1993), pp. 1705–40. Richard Pildes and Richard Niemi have characterized the recent shift in voting rights jurisprudence as a product of the collision of two "tectonic plates" of representation theory which have been present in the jurisprudence all along, that of geographic representation and interest representation. Richard H. Pildes and Richard G. Niemi, "Expressive Harms, 'Bizarre Districts,' and Voting Rights: Evaluating Election-District Appearances after *Shaw v. Reno*," *Michigan Law Review* 92 (3) (1993), pp. 483–587. For other criticisms of voting rights jurisprudence, see Mark E. Rush, "In Search of a Coherent Theory of Voting Rights: Challenges to the Supreme Court's Vision of Fair and Effective Representation," *Review of Politics* 56 (3) (1994), pp. 503–23.

2. The principal cases are *Shaw v. Reno*, 509 U.S. 630 (1993); *Miller v. Johnson*, 115 S. Ct. 2475 (1995); *Bush v. Vera*, 116 S. Ct. 1941 (1996); and *Shaw v. Hunt*, 116 S. Ct. 1894 (1996).

3. The more radical explanation for the popular legitimacy of these decisions, which I regard as highly plausible, is the extent to which American public culture is shaped by racism. See especially Kimberlé Crenshaw, "Race, Reform, and Retrenchment: Transformation and Legitimation in Antidiscrimination Law," *Harvard Law Review* 101 (7) (1988), pp. 1331–87.

4. See, e.g., Nancy L. Schwartz, *The Blue Guitar: Political Representation and Community* (Chicago: University of Chicago Press, 1988), chapter 3 (pp. 39–56); Bernard Grofman, Lisa Handley, and Richard G. Niemi, *Minority Representation and the Quest for Voting Equality* (New York: Cambridge University Press, 1992), chapters 1–3; Issacharoff, "Polarized Voting and the Political Process," pp. 1838–59; Mark E. Rush, "The Supreme Court's Approach to Gerrymandering and Representation," *Journal of Law and Politics* 6 (4) (1990), pp. 683–722; Keith Bybee, *Mistaken Identity: The Supreme Court and the Politics of Minority Representation* (Princeton, NJ: Princeton University Press, 1998), chapters 4 and 5.

5. The Voting Rights Act of 1965 was crafted in response to the violent southern White reaction to the civil rights movement during and after Freedom Summer, and resulted from Lyndon Johnson's command to his attorney general to fashion the "goddamnedest toughest" voting rights law possible. Chandler Davidson, "The Voting Rights Act: A Brief History," in *Controversies in Minority Voting: The Voting Rights Act in Perspective*, ed. Bernard Grofman and Chandler Davidson (Washington, D.C.: Brookings Institution, 1992), p. 17. Framed as an act to enforce the Fifteenth Amendment's prohibition on state practices that "den[y] or abridge[] the right of any citizen of the United States to vote on account of race, color, or previous condition of servitude," the Voting Rights Act secured African Americans' access to the ballot by prohibiting a variety of practices (literacy tests, poll taxes, etc.) that had been implemented following Reconstruction to disenfranchise Blacks. Section 5 of the Act also required federal preclearance of changes in voting procedures in states and local jurisdictions with histories of discriminatory voting practices ("covered" jurisdictions). This "first generation" of voting rights for African Americans, guaranteeing access to the voting box, was extended to language minorities as well after 1975.

6. These efforts included two principal strategies: gerrymandering electoral districts so as to divide or overconcentrate minority populations and minimize minority communities' capacity to elect representatives; and switching from single-member electoral districts to multimember or at-large systems in which minority populations' votes would be swamped by White votes. (Among minority vote dilution initiates, the shorthand terms for these techniques are "cracking" [dividing], "packing" [overconcentrating], and "stacking" [submerging in a multimember district].) The use of multimember districts was often accompanied by "anti-single-shot-voting" requirements, which prevented minorities from enhancing the value of their votes by choosing only their preferred candidate on a multicandidate ballot. See chapter 5 for an overview of the history of African American voting rights during Reconstruction.

7. Davidson, "The Voting Rights Act: A Brief History," p. 24. Richard Engstrom defines vote dilution slightly differently, as "the practice of reducing the potential effectiveness of a group's voting strength by limiting its ability to translate that strength into the control of (or at least influence with) elected public officials." Richard L. Engstrom, "Racial Discrimination in the Electoral Process: The Voting Rights Act and the Vote Dilution Issue," in *Party Politics in the South*, ed. Robert Steed, Laurence Moreland, and Ted Baker (New York: Praeger, 1980), p. 197.

8. Lani Guinier elaborates the distinction between the "first generation" and "second generation" of voting rights in "The Triumph of Tokenism," in *The Tyranny of the Majority*, pp. 49–50.

9. The vote dilution cases had been foreshadowed by *Gomillion v. Lightfoot*, the first racial gerrymandering case overturned by the Court, 364 U.S. 339 (1960). In that case, White officials in Tuskegee, Alabama, redrew the city's boundaries so as to place African American neighborhoods outside the city limits and effectively deny African Americans a voice on the city council. Although the Court treated the case as a denial of the right to vote under the Fifteenth Amendment rather than a denial of equal protection under the Fourteenth Amendment, the logic of its argument that racial gerrymandering of this sort is impermissible is wholly consistent with the pluralist ethos and informs the Court's decisions in later vote dilution cases.

Until the 1982 amendments to the Voting Rights Act, minority vote dilution cases were decided on Fourteenth Amendment (equal protection) grounds. After those amendments they have been decided on statutory grounds, following the principle that courts should decide cases on constitutional grounds only where statutory bases for decision are unavailable.

10. 393 U.S. 544 (1969).

11. Davidson, "The Voting Rights Act," pp. 28–29.

12. 403 U.S. 124, 149 (1971).

13. 412 U.S. 755, 766 (1973).

14. *Zimmer v. McKeithen*, 485 F. 2d 1297, 1305 (5th Cir. 1973).

15. *City of Mobile v. Bolden*, 446 U.S. 55 (1980).

16. For a helpful overview, see Grofman, Handley, and Niemi, *Minority Representation and the Quest for Voting Equality*, pp. 35–37.

17. In addition to amending Section 2, Congress extended the temporary provisions of the Act for another twenty-five years.

18. The standards they sought to entrench were drawn directly from the decisions in *White* and *Zimmer*, discussed above in n. 14.

19. 42 U.S.C. § 1973. Shortly after the passage of the 1982 amendments, the Court decided a Fourteenth Amendment vote dilution case, *Rogers v. Lodge*, 458 U.S. 613 (1982). There, they relaxed *Mobile*'s "smoking gun" standard of discriminatory intent to allow, as circumstantial evidence of such intent, the presence of the *Zimmer* factors. However, the Court did not overrule *Mobile*, with the consequence that there is technically a divergence between the standard for unconstitutional vote dilution (discriminatory intent) and the Section 2 standard (discriminatory effect). This divergence has no practical effect so long as the Court continues to accept the constitutionality of Section 2, because of the legal principle that, where possible, cases should be decided on statutory rather than constitutional grounds. See Grofman, Handley, and Niemi, *Minority Representation and the Quest for Voting Equality*, pp. 41–42.

20. 478 U.S. 30 (1986).

21. All these factors were listed as relevant to a Section 2 violation in the Senate Report of the 1982 amendments to the Voting Rights Act. Senate Judiciary Committee, *Voting Rights Act Amendments of 1982*, 97th Cong., 2d sess., S. Rept. 97–417, pp. 28–29, reprinted in *United States Code Congressional and Administrative News 1982*, vol. 2 (St. Paul, MN: West, 1982), pp. 205–7.

22. 478 U.S., at 50–51.

23. Ibid., p. 51.

24. The test leaves unanswered the question as to whether the test is a necessary or sufficient condition for establishing a Section 2 claim. The lower courts have answered this question in different and conflicting ways: some hold that plaintiffs must satisfy both the three-pronged test and a "totality of circumstances" inquiry guided by the criteria laid out in the Senate Report of the 1982 amendments; others maintain that meeting the test is sufficient to satisfy a Section 2 challenge; still others contend that meeting the test is not necessary if a "totality of circumstances" inquiry supports the challenge. There is also a question as to whether a showing of racially polarized voting is sufficient even when the first prong of the test has not been met, on the argument that a geographically concentrated minority group might be able to secure representative

responsiveness by constituting a strong swing vote in a district, even where they are not numerous enough to constitute an electoral majority. See Grofman, Handley, and Niemi, *Minority Representation and the Quest for Voting Equality*, pp. 54–60.

25. Laughlin McDonald, "The 1982 Amendments of Section 2 and Minority Representation," in Grofman and Davidson, *Controversies in Minority Voting*, p. 70.

26. See ibid., pp. 74–77; see also Grofman, Handley, and Niemi, *Minority Representation and the Quest for Voting Equality*, p. 134 ("the simple truth is that at the congressional and state legislative level, at least in the South, Blacks are very unlikely to be elected from any districts that are not majority minority"); Issacharoff, "Polarized Voting and the Political Process," p. 1855 ("racial bloc voting is the single most salient feature of contemporary political life in this country").

27. In *Johnson v. DeGrandy*, 114 S. Ct. 2647 (1994), the Court held explicitly that the maximization of majority-minority districts was not required by Section 2.

28. 478 U.S., at 102 (emphasis in original) (Justice O'Connor, concurring).

29. Such a residential pattern underlay some of the districts overturned in the Court's recent decision in *Bush v. Vera*, 116 S. Ct. 1941 (1996). See also Timothy G. O'Rourke, "The 1982 Amendments and the Voting Rights Paradox," in Grofman and Davidson, *Controversies in Minority Voting*, pp. 104–5.

30. "If, because of the dispersion of the minority population, a reasonably compact majority-minority district cannot be created, 2 does not require a majority-minority district." *Bush v. Vera*, 116 S. Ct., at 1961. (O'Connor's opinion for the plurality). As I explain in greater detail below, however, the recent decisions leave uncertain what the new standards for permissible majority-minority districts are.

31. 478 U.S. 109 (1986).

32. Ibid., p. 124.

33. Ibid., p. 125.

34. The standard of group cohesiveness is its proclivity to vote as a bloc, a principle articulated by Justice Stevens in his concurrence in *City of Mobile v. Bolden*: "The mere fact that a number of citizens share a common ethnic, racial, or religious background does not create the need for protection against gerrymandering. It is only when their common interests are strong enough to be manifested in political action that the need arises. For the political strength of a group is not a function of its ethnic, racial, or religious composition; rather, it is a function of numbers—specifically the number of persons who will vote in the same way." 446 U.S. 55, at 88 (1980) (Stevens, concurring).

35. This case was brought by Indiana Democrats, who garnered almost 52 percent of the popular vote for the House but won only 43 percent of its seats. Their challenge to the gerrymandered plan was not sustained.

36. 478 U.S., at 110.

37. John Hart Ely, *Democracy and Distrust: A Theory of Judicial Review* (Cambridge: Harvard University Press, 1980), p. 103.

38. In making this claim I part company with Mark Rush, who perceives the reapportionment decisions as a strand of jurisprudence that is analytically distinct from vote dilution and gerrymandering jurisprudence. Mark E. Rush, "Gerrymandering: Out of the Political Thicket and into the Quagmire," *PS: Political Science and Politics* 27 (4) (1994), pp. 682–85.

39. In his opinion for the Court in *Reynolds*, Chief Justice Warren remarked, "Our constitutional system amply provides for the protection of minorities by means other

than giving them majority control of state legislatures. And the democratic ideals of equality and majority rule, which have served this Nation so well in the past, are hardly of any less significance for the present and the future." 377 U.S. 533, at 566.

40. Ibid., pp. 560–61.

41. Karlan, "The Rights to Vote," p. 1718.

42. *The Reapportionment Revolution: Representation, Political Power, and the Supreme Court* (New York: Random House, 1966), p. 109.

43. In fact, a sense of the unfairness of an electoral system's tendency to dilute a group of voters' electoral strength is present even in *Reynolds*, where Chief Justice Warren wrote that "if a State should provide that the votes of citizens in one part of the State should be given two times, or five times, or 10 times the weight of votes of citizens in another part of the State, it could hardly be contended that the right to vote of those residing in the disfavored areas had not been *effectively diluted*." 377 U.S., at 562 (emphasis added).

44. 379 U.S. 433, 439 (1965).

45. Ely, *Democracy and Distrust*, pp. 140–41.

46. 446 U.S., at 113 (Justice Marshall, dissenting) (emphasis added).

47. *Karcher v. Daggett*, 462 U.S. 725, 748 (1983) (Justice Stevens, concurring) (emphasis added).

48. Ely uses the language of market correction explicitly in laying out his theory of judicial review. *Democracy and Distrust*, pp. 102–3.

49. 403 U.S., at 154–55.

50. *Holder v. Hall*, 114 S. Ct. 2581, 2596 (1994) (Justice Thomas, concurring).

51. Samuel Issacharoff, "Judging Politics: The Elusive Quest for Judicial Review of Political Fairness," *Texas Law Review* 71 (7) (1993), p. 1682 (emphasis added).

52. 478 U.S., at 132.

53. Some have suggested that one way out of these difficulties is to turn to randomized computer districting, as discussed above in chapter 2, section III. Even if random districting is not practical as an actual substitute for current districting practices, it might at least provide a standard against which to judge a districting scheme. The chronic underrepresentation of an identifiable group relative to the average representation it would receive from a repeated series of random districting could be taken as evidence of impermissible vote dilution. See, e.g., the discussion in Charles R. Beitz, *Political Equality: An Essay in Democratic Theory* (Princeton, NJ: Princeton University Press, 1989), p. 148; and Issacharoff, "Judging Politics," pp. 1695–1702. This is an appealing strategy, but it is subject to important limitations. First, there is some question as to whether current computer technology is sufficiently developed to make fully computerized districting possible. Ibid., pp. 1698–99. More to the point, the courts have generally allowed state districting bodies to consider partisan factors such as incumbent protection and the preservation of "communities of interest" in designing their districting plans, arguing that these embody "legitimate state purposes." Even if one puts aside the many reasons for doubting the defensibility of these factors' role in districting, clearly giving them a role renders useless any standard of fairness based on random districting.

54. 478 U.S., at 139. An interesting parallel can be made here to interest-group pluralism, which acknowledges the unfairness of pluralism's potential to shut out "permanent minorities" but does not offer clear standards for judging patterns of marginali-

zation that fall short of permanent exclusion. Both in its theory of interest groups and its account of fair representation, pluralist proceduralism does not admit of subtle judgments of unfair bias.

55. Mark E. Rush, *Does Redistricting Make a Difference? Partisan Representation and Electoral Behavior* (Baltimore, MD: The Johns Hopkins University Press, 1993), pp. 127–28.

56. 430 U.S. 144 (1977).

57. See the discussion in chapter 2, section IV.

58. As Rush himself suggests when he distinguishes partisan identity from racial group identity. *Does Redistricting Make a Difference?*, pp. 41–42.

59. In such cases as *White v. Regester*, 412 U.S. 755 (1973).

60. In the Voting Rights Act preclearance provisions.

61. For a discussion of the relationship between minority representation and past housing discrimination, see Karlan, "Maps and Misreadings," pp. 177–79; and Guinier, "Groups, Representation, and Race-Conscious Districting," in *The Tyranny of the Majority*, p. 141.

62. Issacharoff, "Polarized Voting and the Political Process," p. 1872.

63. See, e.g., *Wygant v. Jackson Board of Education*, 476 U.S. 267, 276–77 (1986): "Societal discrimination, without more, is too amorphous a basis for imposing a racially classified remedy . . . [A] public employer . . . must ensure that, before it embarks on an affirmative-action program, it has convincing evidence that remedial action is warranted. That is, it must have sufficient evidence to justify the conclusion that there has been prior discrimination."

64. For an interesting analysis of American judicial interpretations of equal opportunity and affirmative action, and a comparison with Canadian treatments of the same questions, see Sandra J. Clancy, "Imagining Affirmative Action and Equal Opportunity: American Failures, Canadian Challenges." Ph.D. diss., University of Toronto, 1997.

65. 509 U.S., at 642.

66. In so doing the Court distinguished the case from *United Jewish Organizations of Williamsburgh v. Carey*, in which a divided Court had held that minority-majority districts are not subject to constitutional scrutiny unless they dilute majority voting strength.

67. 509 U.S., at 647.

68. Ibid., p. 648.

69. 509 U.S., at 658.

70. Following the 1990 census Georgia gained an eleventh congressional seat, and accordingly redistricted. The state's population is 27 percent African American. Its previous districting plan, containing ten districts, had included one that was majority-Black. In its new plan, the state legislature drew a second majority-Black district. A third district was a "minority-influence" district, that is, one in which African Americans were not a majority of the voting-age population but constituted a sufficiently large bloc (35 percent) that they could act as a swing vote in elections. The Department of Justice twice refused Section 5 preclearance on the ground that the state had failed to "recognize" minority populations, and it implied that the state could have done so by drawing a third majority-minority district. Using districting plans provided by the Justice Department, the legislature finally submitted a districting plan with three majority-Black districts and received preclearance. As the Court noted, all three districts elected Afri-

can American candidates in the 1992 elections. After the decision in *Shaw*, five White voters challenged the plan as an unconstitutional racial gerrymander. The district court upheld their challenge, and the Supreme Court (divided as in *Shaw*) affirmed. The most important of the factual differences between *Shaw* and *Miller* was that the plaintiffs in the latter case did not make any allegations about the "bizarreness" of the majority-minority districts' shape.

71. 115 S. Ct., at 2486.

72. Without directly stating that the Department of Justice's preclearance authority under Section 5 does not authorize it to enforce Section 2 against covered jurisdictions, the Court thus hinted at such a conclusion. In the 1996 Term the Court made this conclusion explicit in *Reno v. Bossier Parish School Board*, 117 S. Ct. 1491 (1997). The Justice Department may no longer evaluate a districting scheme's propensity to dilute minority voting strength unless there is reason to believe that such a tendency will produce *retrogressive* effects.

73. The most sensible account of the right to the appearance of a color-blind electoral process is presented in Pildes and Niemi's article, "Expressive Harms," which is a noble attempt to discover the logic of the *Shaw* decision and its implications for race-conscious districting. While Pildes and Niemi acknowledge that the doctrine they propose is not immune to criticism (including the objection that it contains a racial bias against minorities), it does at least propose a reasoned justification for the decision and a manageable *Shaw* standard for the lower courts to apply.

The doctrine they propose is one of "expressive harm," whose core idea is that the legitimacy of state institutions is undermined by the *appearance* of a constitutional flaw. The constitutional flaw in question, they argue, is not that a law has either an unconstitutional purpose or an unconstitutional effect, as would be the case if the Court had held that race-conscious districting per se were unconstitutional (as, resisting the urgings of Justices Scalia and Thomas, it explicitly did not do). Instead, the constitutional flaw that must be at issue in *Shaw* is that the state appeared to engage in "value reductionism," that is, it appeared to subordinate a multiplicity of important constitutional values to a single value. According to this interpretation of *Shaw*, "what distinguishes 'bizarre' race-conscious districts is the signal they send out that, to government officials, race has become paramount and dwarfed all other, traditionally relevant criteria" for districting. "Expressive Harms," p. 501. In other words, the harm in *Shaw* is not that the state actually relied on racial considerations to the exclusion of all others but that it *appeared* to do so. The significance of the "bizarre" shape of District 12 was not that it violated any independent constitutional standard of compactness but that it created the *appearance* that the state relied excessively on race in drawing its boundaries (even if, in fact, the state did not *actually* do so). In short, Pildes and Niemi argue, *Shaw* can only mean that even where majority-minority districts do not inflict any real, material harm on citizens, they might inflict the "expressive harm" of an apparently illegitimate state decision-making process. "Public policies can violate the Constitution not only because they bring about concrete costs, but because the very meaning they convey demonstrates inappropriate respect for relevant public values. On this unusual conception of constitutional harm, when a governmental action expresses disrespect for such values, it can violate the Constitution." Ibid., p. 507.

Whether the Court will adopt this interpretation of *Shaw* remains uncertain. Clearly the holding in *Miller* that district shape is relevant only as evidence of the "predominance" of race in districting decisions, and is not of the essence of an unconstitutional racial gerrymander, suggests that the "expressive harm" reading of *Shaw* is too generous to majority-minority districts. In her plurality opinion in *Bush*, however, Justice O'Connor explicitly embraced Pildes and Niemi's interpretation of *Shaw*. In addition, her separate concurrence in *Bush* articulates criteria for race-conscious districting that flow directly from the "expressive harm" interpretation: that a state may draw majority-minority districts without incurring strict scrutiny if it does so in order to avoid minority vote dilution (in accordance with Section 2 of the Voting Rights Act), if it has "a strong basis in evidence" that the *Gingles* criteria are met, 116 S. Ct., at 1970, and if the districts it creates do not "subordinate traditional districting criteria to the use of race for its own sake." 116 S. Ct., at 1969. Since Justice O'Connor appears convinced of the constitutionality of Section 2, her vote stands in the way of Justices Scalia's and Thomas's view that race-conscious districting should be ruled unconstitutional per se. Thus, for the time being at least, the Pildes-Niemi reading of *Shaw* seems likely to govern future voting rights adjudication.

74. See the discussion in chapter 2, section IV.

75. Recall the discussion in chapter 1, section VIII.

76. For a general discussion, see Pamela Karlan's excellent article, "Our Separatism? Voting Rights as an American Nationalities Policy," *University of Chicago Legal Forum* (1995), pp. 83–109.

77. 509 U.S., at 647.

78. 512 U.S., at 905.

79. See, e.g., *Shaw I*, 509 U.S., at 658.

80. 115 S. Ct., at 2487.

81. See Issacharoff, "Judging Politics," pp. 1643–1703, for a discussion of the challenges of defining a genuinely neutral districting process.

82. Discussed above at p. 86.

83. See, e.g., *Miller*, 115 S. Ct., at 2491 (requiring "a strong basis in evidence of the harm being remedied" rather than a generalized history of discrimination); *Bush v. Vera*, 116 S. Ct., at 1961; *Shaw II*, 116 S. Ct., at 1902–3 (citing *City of Richmond v. J.A. Croson Co.*, 488 U.S. 469, 499 [1989]) ("A State's interest in remedying the effects of past or present racial discrimination may in the proper case justify a government's use of racial distinctions . . . For that interest to rise to the level of a compelling state interest, it must satisfy two conditions. First, the discrimination must be '"identified discrimination."' . . . A generalized assertion of past discrimination in a particular industry or region is not adequate because it 'provides no guidance for a legislative body to determine the precise scope of the injury it seeks to remedy.'").

84. *Shaw II*, 116 S. Ct., at 1903 n. 5 (citing *Wygant v. Jackson Bd. of Education*, 476 U.S. 267 [1986]).

85. See especially Justice Thomas's concurrence in *Bush*, joined by Justice Scalia.

86. "*Whether or not* in some cases compliance with the Voting Rights Act, standing alone, can provide a compelling interest independent of any interest in remedying past discrimination, it cannot do so here." 115 S. Ct., at 2490–91 (emphasis added).

87. *Shaw II*, 116 S. Ct., at 1921 (Justice Stevens, dissenting).

88. This second point is central to Pamela Karlan's "civic inclusion" model of voting rights jurisprudence in "Maps and Misreadings."

89. See the discussion in the introduction, section IV.

90. *City of Richmond v. J. A. Croson Co.*, 488 U.S. 469 (1989); and *Adarand Constructors, Inc. v. Pena*, 115 S. Ct. 2097 (1995).

91. For the argument that the Justice Department has pursued a "max-black" policy, see Justice Kennedy's opinion in *Miller v. Johnson*, 115 S. Ct., at 2492–93 and the accompanying note. For the argument that there is no such policy, see Bernard Grofman, "*Shaw v. Reno* and the Future of Voting Rights," *PS: Political Science and Politics* 28 (1) (1995), p. 33. See also Timothy O'Rourke, "The 1982 Amendments and the Voting Rights Paradox," p. 104: "[T]he operative standard is a qualified proportional representation," that is, drawing minority districts where population distributions permit, to the point of proportionality.

92. Richard Briffault makes an argument along these lines in "Race and Representation after *Miller v. Johnson*," *University of Chicago Legal Forum* (1995), p. 77.

93. This view is expressed, with respect to race, in Gary King, John Bruce, and Andrew Gelman, "Racial Fairness in Legislative Redistricting," in *Classifying by Race*, ed. Paul E. Peterson (Princeton, NJ: Princeton University Press, 1995), pp. 85–110; and, with respect to both ethnicity and gender, in Anne Phillips, *Democracy and Difference* (University Park, PA: Pennsylvania State University Press, 1993), p. 99 ("If there were no substantial obstacles in the way of equal participation, then those active in politics would be randomly distributed according to their ethnicity or gender").

94. This is the reason for one of my rare—but in this case quite substantial—disagreements with Lani Guinier. Her conception of interest representation leads her to advocate systems of proportional representation whose underlying view of fairness is essentially proceduralist. One of the consequences of Guinier's proceduralism is that she cannot offer any substantive standard of fairness against which to judge electoral outcomes, and she can offer no reasons for special solicitude for historically marginalized groups as compared to any other kind of interest group. I anticipate that Guinier would be troubled if her scheme of cumulative voting were adopted and, as a result, historically marginalized groups remained chronically underrepresented; but there is nothing in her theoretical account either to explain or justify the dissatisfaction she might feel in such circumstances. For further discussion of the limits of pure proceduralism, see chapter 7, section I.

95. 116 S. Ct., at 2010.

96. See the discussion above, at p. 80.

97. Issacharoff, "Polarized Voting and the Political Process," p. 1872.

98. David B. Truman, *The Governmental Process* (New York: Knopf, 1953), p. 511.

99. See, e.g., ibid., p. 162: "Changes in the personnel of these groups, changes in their patterns, and the like, will constantly create mild or strong disturbances; individuals consequently may increase or decrease their activity in existing groups, enter new associations, or drop out of current ones. Both individuals and groups, therefore, are constantly in the process of readjustment."

100. "[W]hile membership in a racial group is an immutable characteristic, voters can—and often do—move from one party to the other or support candidates from both parties." *Bandemer*, 478 U.S. at 156 (Justice O'Connor, concurring).

101. Iris Marion Young, *Justice and the Politics of Difference* (Princeton, NJ: Princeton University Press, 1990), p. 46.

102. These issues are discussed in greater depth in chapter 6.

103. 509 U.S. 630 (1993).

104. For one account of the Court's role as the exemplar of public reason, see John Rawls, *Political Liberalism* (New York: Columbia University Press, 1993), pp. 231–40.

105. 116 S. Ct. 1894 (1996).

106. 115 S. Ct. 2475 (1995).

107. 116 S. Ct., at 1903.

108. *Thornburg v. Gingles*, 478 U.S. 30 (1986), discussed in chapter 3, section I.

109. 116 S. Ct. 1941 (1996).

110. 116 S. Ct., at 1961.

111. Lani Guinier, "Groups, Representation, and Race Conscious Districting: A Case of the Emperor's Clothes," in *The Tyranny of the Majority: Fundamental Fairness in Representative Democracy* (New York: Free Press, 1994), p. 266 n. 11.

112. In *Bush*, 116 S. Ct., at 1954, Justice O'Connor cites the authority of *Karcher v. Daggett*, 462 U.S. 725, 740 (1983) and *White v. Weiser*, 412 U.S. 783, 797 (1973) to sustain the assertion that incumbency protection is a legitimate state purpose. Neither of these cases, however, offers any substantive justification for regarding it as such. Rather, both simply list incumbency protection among the legislative considerations to which courts should defer.

113. *Bush v. Vera*, 116 S. Ct., at 1992 (Justice Stevens, dissenting).

114. The record in *Bush* clearly established that "majority-white Texas districts have never elected a minority to either the State Senate or the United States Congress." 116 S. Ct., at 1992 (1996) (Justice Stevens, dissenting) (citing Brief for Petitioners in No. 94-806, p. 53). The plurality opinion explicitly assumed (though "without deciding") that there was a strong basis in evidence for a finding that the racial polarization prongs of the *Gingles* test were met. 116 S. Ct., at 1961. Similarly the record in *Miller* also establishes clear patterns of racially polarized voting. Brief for the United States (No. 94-631), pp. 37–38, and notes 19–20 (23 February 1995); Brief for Appellants (No. 94-797), pp. 6–9 (21 February 1995).

115. 115 S. Ct., at 2504.

116. Ibid., p. 2497 (emphasis in original).

117. For a helpful discussion, see Richard H. Pildes and Richard G. Niemi, "Expressive Harms, 'Bizarre Districts,' and Voting Rights: Evaluating Election-District Appearances after *Shaw v. Reno*," *Michigan Law Review* 92 (3) (1993), pp. 577–78: "Th[e] different treatment of race and other interests may be a basis for criticizing *Shaw*, but it is the sine qua non of the decision."

118. 116 S. Ct., at 1952, citing Pildes and Niemi, "Expressive Harms," Table 6, pp. 571–73, and Table 3, p. 565.

119. See Pildes and Niemi, "Expressive Harms," p. 567.

120. The Florida district is Congressional District 22. See Pildes and Niemi, Figure 3(F), p. 548, and Table 3, p. 565. Justice Stevens protests in his dissent in *Shaw II*, "I [do not] see how our constitutional tradition can countenance the suggestion that a State may draw unsightly lines to favor farmers or city dwellers, but not to create districts that benefit the very group whose history inspired the Amendment that the Voting Rights Act was designed to implement." 116 S. Ct., at 1922.

121. Pildes and Niemi, "Expressive Harms," p. 578.

122. In her comparison of race, class, education, ideology, gender, age, union membership, and region as determinants of party identification, Katherine Tate concludes that "race identification appears to be the major component of Black partisanship today.

Middle-class Blacks and working class and poor Blacks are all equally likely to identify with the Democratic party." Tate, *From Protest to Politics: The New Black Voters in American Elections* (Cambridge: Harvard University Press, 1993), p. 65.

123. 116 S. Ct., at 2008 (Justice Souter, dissenting).

124. For further discussion, see Pildes and Niemi, "Expressive Harms," pp. 516–18.

125. 116 S. Ct., at 1983–84 (Justice Stevens, dissenting).

126. See Pamela S. Karlan and Daryl J. Levinson, "Why Voting is Different," *California Law Review* 84 (4) (1996), especially pp. 1220–27.

127. Two decisions in the 1996 Term, handed down as I completed the final changes to the manuscript of this book, continue these trends. In the first, *Reno v. Bossier Parish School Board*, 117 S. Ct. 1491 (1997), the Court decided that the Department of Justice is not authorized by the Voting Rights Act to enforce Section 2's provisions against minority vote dilution, and so may not deny preclearance to districting schemes that dilute minority voting strength unless those schemes also produce a *retrogression* in minority representation as defined by Section 5. Yet in *Abrams v. Johnson*, 117 S. Ct. 1925 (1997), the Court tightened its definition of retrogression. That case presented the aftermath of the Court's 1995 decision in *Miller v. Johnson*, in which it overturned a Georgia congressional districting plan that contained three majority-Black districts. Although the state legislature had, in 1991, drawn up a plan with two majority-Black districts, it failed to agree on an alternative to the plan overturned in *Miller*. The federal district court drew up a plan containing only one majority-minority district, which the Supreme Court upheld in this decision. According to the Court's decision, the 1991 plan with two districts was not an appropriate legal benchmark because no election had ever been held under it; consequently the district court's plan was not retrogressive even though it had fewer majority-minority districts than a previously approved plan.

Chapter 4
Voice: Woman Suffrage and the Representation of "Woman's Point of View"

1. See Judith N. Shklar, *American Citizenship: The Quest for Inclusion* (Cambridge: Harvard University Press, 1991), pp. 57–61; Walter Lippmann, "The Vote as a Symbol," *The New Republic*, 9 October 1915, p. 4. For a discussion of the contemporary symbolic importance of legislative presence, see Anne Phillips, *The Politics of Presence* (Oxford: Oxford University Press, 1995), pp. 39–40.

2. Elizabeth Cady Stanton, Susan B. Anthony, and Matilda Joslyn Gage, *The History of Woman Suffrage*, vol. 1 (Salem, NH: Ayer, 1985), p. 70.

3. Call to Convention for the National American Woman Suffrage Association, 1902, in *History of Woman Suffrage*, vol. 5, p. 23.

4. Elizabeth Cady Stanton, Address to the New York State Legislature (1854), in Stanton, Anthony, and Gage, *The History of Woman Suffrage*, vol. 1, p. 595. The mention of "native, free-born citizens" relates to one of the darker aspects of some suffragists' arguments: that it was wrong for the White, native-born, educated women to be denied the vote when "ignorant" Black and immigrant men were granted it—women suffered a great indignity, they felt, at being ruled by their social inferiors. Later, some suffragists used this view strategically to assure Southerners that woman suffrage, particularly if

supplemented by an educational requirement for the vote, would guarantee White supremacy in the post-Fifteenth Amendment South. See, e.g., Aileen S. Kraditor, *The Ideas of the Woman Suffrage Movement, 1890–1920* (New York: W. W. Norton, 1981), pp. 137–38.

5. Stanton, Anthony, and Gage, *History of Woman Suffrage*, vol. 1, pp. 70–71.

6. Elizabeth Cady Stanton, "The Solitude of Self," reprinted in *Elizabeth Cady Stanton/Susan B. Anthony: Correspondence, Writings, Speeches*, ed. Ellen Carol DuBois (New York: Schocken, 1981), p. 247.

7. Ibid., p. 248. See also, e.g., Fannie Catherine Boies, "Democracy and Woman Suffrage," *The New Republic*, 27 October 1917, p. 357: "A community is unable to reach its highest development when one-half of its members are denied an active part in all the forces which make for its welfare. As the community gives to each individual woman the opportunity to develop all that is best and highest in her, so in turn will the community be benefitted."

8. See, e.g., Wendell Phillips's address to the seventh National Woman's Rights Convention in November 1856: "I would have it constantly kept before the public, that we do not seek to prop up woman; we only ask for her space to let her grow . . . I say the very first claim, the middle and last claim of all our Conventions should be the ballot . . . not for any intrinsic value in the ballot, but because it throws upon woman herself the responsibility of her position. Man never grew to his stature until he was provoked to it by the pressure and weight of responsibility; and I take it woman will grow up the same way." Stanton, Anthony, and Gage, *History of Woman Suffrage*, vol. 1, pp. 640–41.

9. Walter E. Weyl, "Working for the Inevitable," *The New Republic*, 9 October 1915, p. 16.

10. Anna Howard Shaw, "Equal Suffrage—A Problem of Political Justice," *Annals of the American Academy of Political and Social Science* 56 (November 1914), p. 94.

11. Stanton, Anthony, and Gage, *History of Woman Suffrage*, vol. 2, p. 356, quoted in Ellen Carol DuBois, "Outgrowing the Compact of the Fathers: Equal Rights, Woman Suffrage, and the United States Constitution, 1820–1878," *Journal of American History* 74 (3) (1987), p. 846.

12. DuBois, "Outgrowing the Compact of the Fathers," p. 846, paraphrasing Stanton, Anthony, and Gage, *History of Woman Suffrage*, vol. 2, p. 186 ("Here black men and women are buried in the citizen").

13. Address to the New York Legislature (1854), quoted in Stanton, Anthony, and Gage, *History of Woman Suffrage*, vol. 1, p. 604. It is worth noting that the issue of gender-based distinctions in law later became a point of contention in both the woman suffrage movement and the campaign for an Equal Rights Amendment in the 1920s. See Nancy Cott, *The Grounding of Modern Feminism* (New Haven: Yale University Press, 1987), chapter 4. The central question was—and remains—whether women should accept legislative protections, particularly in the workplace, or whether *any* gender-based distinctions in law perpetuate a separate and necessarily unequal status for women.

14. Stanton, Address to the New York Legislature (1867), quoted in Stanton, Anthony, and Gage, *History of Woman Suffrage*, vol. 2, p. 273.

15. *Address to the Congress of the United States* (New York: National Woman Suffrage, n.d. [1918?]), p. 15.

16. Stanton continued: "so long as there is any difference in the code of laws for men and women, any discrimination in the customs of society, giving advantages to men over women." Quoted in Zillah R. Eisenstein, *The Radical Future of Liberal Feminism* (Boston: Northeastern University Press, 1986), p. 156.

17. "Women as Voters," *The Nation*, 29 November 1917, p. 587.

18. Kraditor, *Ideas of the Woman Suffrage Movement*, p. 157.

19. Shaw, "Equal Suffrage," p. 96.

20. Eleanor Flexner, *Century of Struggle: The Women's Rights Movement in the United States* (Cambridge, MA: Belknap, 1975), pp. 85–86, 111.

21. Mary R. Beard, "The Legislative Influence of Unenfranchised Women," *Annals of the American Academy of Political and Social Science* 56 (November) (1914), p. 60.

22. See section IV, below.

23. Indeed, some of the differences among contemporary feminists bear a striking resemblance to differences within the suffrage movement. The liberal feminism of Susan Moller Okin, for example, may reasonably be read as an extension of the democratic individualism of the Declaration of Sentiments. And the virtue suffragists have much in common with feminists who argue that women are bearers of a distinctive mode of reasoning, or "maternal thinking" feminists.

24. The case can be made that there was actually a transition from the early suffragist movement's focus on natural rights-based arguments for women's equality to arguments for political rights that were grounded in women's *differences* from men. Ellen Carol DuBois, for example, argues that one such shift took place after the disappointment of the Reconstruction amendments, which introduced the word *male* into the eligibility criteria for voting and other political and civil rights. Dubois argues that considerations of logical consistency played a role in this shift: "The demand for woman suffrage, in that it claimed the vote for women as women, permitted the cultivation of sex-consciousness far more than had the equal rights and universal suffrage approach." "Outgrowing the Compact of the Fathers," p. 851. Although my purpose here is not to give a historical account of the changes in suffragist rhetoric over the course of the movement or to locate the themes discussed here within a broader view of the movement as a whole, it seems fair to say that the four themes emerged more or less sequentially over the life of the movement. However, it is also true that none of the later themes ever replaced or even severely displaced the preceding ones, and the insistence on women's natural equality with men held a central place in suffragist rhetoric throughout.

25. The women leaders of the temperance movement had a sometimes uneasy alliance with the leaders of the woman suffrage movement. Flexner, *Century of Struggle*, pp. 189–90. The virtue-based arguments for women's political rights provided the stablest common ground between the two movements.

26. DuBois, "Outgrowing the Compact of the Fathers."

27. See also the discussion in Kraditor, *Ideas of the Woman Suffrage Movement*, pp. 45–46.

28. Remarks of Dr. Katharine Bement Davis, chief of Parole Commission, New York City, at the National American Woman Suffrage Association Convention of 1916. Quoted in Stanton, Anthony, and Gage, *History of Woman Suffrage*, vol. 5, pp. 499–500 (emphasis added).

29. Quoted in Ella Seass Stewart, "Woman Suffrage and the Liquor Traffic," *Annals of the American Academy of Political and Social Science* 56 (November 1914), p. 147. See also, e.g., Fannie Catherine Boies, "Democracy and Woman Suffrage," *The New Republic*, 27 October 1917, p. 357: "It is undoubtedly true that women have higher ideals and higher moral standards than men. There are fewer criminals among women than among men, and the majority of women believe in the single standard of morality . . . If they had the power which the ballot would give them, . . . [p]olitical life would be lifted to a higher plane, and the moral standards of the entire community would be raised. These higher standards of morality and higher ideals would finally become embodied in the law, since the law is the result of the corporate will of the people expressed by means of the ballot."

30. Nancy F. Cott, "Women and the Ballot," *Reviews in American History* 15 (2) (1987), p. 295. The distinction between "moral prodders" and "equal righters" is introduced by Felice D. Gordon in *After Winning: The Legacy of the New Jersey Suffragists, 1920–1947* (New Brunswick, NJ: Rutgers University Press, 1986), pp. 4, 32.

31. "Twelve Reasons Why Women Want to Vote," *The Woman's Journal*, 6 May 1893, p. 143.

32. See the discussion in chapter 1, section VII.

33. Hanna Pitkin, *The Concept of Representation* (Berkeley: University of California Press, 1967), pp. 8–9 (emphasis in original).

34. "In an industrial state women have an economic interest that does not find expression in the vote of the male family representative. This economic interest is prevailingly a labor interest, but it is not such as to find adequate expression in the male labor vote . . . The situation is clearly one demanding direct political representation for women." Alvin S. Johnson, "The Effect on Labor," *The New Republic*, 9 October 1915, p. 15.

35. Jane Addams, Address to the National American Woman Suffrage Association Convention of 1906, quoted in Stanton, Anthony, and Gage, *History of Woman Suffrage*, vol. 5, p. 178. See also, e.g., Neva R. Deardorff, "Women in Municipal Activities," *Annals of the American Academy of Political and Social Science* 56 (November) (1914), p. 75: "Although there are many things that women cannot do, there are many that they can do equally as well as men, and there are a few which only they can do. And while it is true that it is largely as a result of the demands of the women citizens that much of this social service has been assumed, once assumed, it is practically impossible to carry it on without women."

36. Jane Addams, "The Larger Aspects of the Woman's Movement," *Annals of the American Academy of Political and Social Science* 56 (November 1914), p. 2.

37. Kraditor, *Ideas of the Woman Suffrage Movement*, pp. 71–72; see also Anna Howard Shaw's arguments against consequentialist justifications for the franchise in "Equal Suffrage."

38. Deardorff, "Women in Municipal Activities," pp. 72–73 (emphasis added).

39. For an analysis and critique of functionalism, see A. James Gregor, "Political Science and the Uses of Functional Analysis," *American Political Science Review* 62 (2) (1968), pp. 425–39.

40. See the discussion in chapter 1, section IV.

41. For a clear and concise discussion of corporatist theories, see Alan Cawson, *Corporatism and Political Theory* (Oxford: Basil Blackwell, 1986). See especially the definition of corporate groups in terms of their function, pp. 37–39.

42. Kraditor, *Ideas of the Woman Suffrage Movement*, p. 66 and chapter 3.

43. See, e.g., Young, *Justice and the Politics of Difference*, pp. 163–68; Karen Offen, "Reply to DuBois," *Signs: Journal of Women in Culture and Society* 15 (1) (1989), p. 201.

44. "Political Methods of American and British Feminists," *Current History* 20 (3) (1924), p. 400.

45. Alice Stone Blackwell, "Twelve Reasons Why Women Want to Vote," p. 143 (emphasis added). Martin practiced what she preached and was the first woman to run for the United States Senate. She ran unsuccessfully as an independent candidate in Nevada after women won the franchise there, in both 1918 and 1920.

46. Stanton, Anthony, and Gage, *History of Woman Suffrage*, vol. 5, p. 385. As discussed below, however, the equality-based "point of view" argument could not have been satisfied by the creation of institutions whose function was limited to advisory roles; it was essential that women themselves be among elected officials.

47. Anne Martin, "Political Methods of American and British Feminists," p. 400.

48. Quoted in Cott, *The Grounding of Modern Feminism*, p. 5.

49. Statement of the Reverend Antoinette L. Brown at the Syracuse National Convention, 1852, quoted in Stanton, Anthony, and Gage, *History of Woman Suffrage*, vol. 1, p. 524.

50. Kraditor, *Ideas of the Woman Suffrage Movement*, p. 111; the remarks of Frances Squire Potter, quoted in Stanton, Anthony, and Gage, *History of Woman Suffrage*, vol. 5, p. 228, are also illuminating:

Louis XIV said an infamous thing when he declared: "I am the State," but he announced his position frankly. He was an autocrat and he said so. It was a more honest . . . position than that of a majority of voters in our country today. Can it help but confuse and deteriorate one sex, trained to believe and call itself living in a democracy, to say silently year by year at the polls, "I am the State?" Can it help but confuse and deteriorate the other sex, similarly trained to acquiescence year after year in a national misrepresentation and a personal no-representation?

See also comments of Shaw, "Equal Suffrage," p. 292 ("[N]o class nor all classes of men are capable of representing any class or all classes of women").

51. "Woman's Inferiority Complex," *The New Republic*, 20 July 1921, p. 210.

52. Quoted in Kathryn Anderson, "Anne Martin and the Dream of Political Equality for Women," *Journal of the West* 27 (2) (1988), p. 30.

53. Quoted in ibid., p. 32.

54. Lippmann, "The Vote as a Symbol," p. 5.

55. Martin, "Woman's Inferiority Complex," p. 210. See also Cott, *The Grounding of Modern Feminism*, pp. 113–14.

56. W. L. George, "Woman in Politics," *Harper's*, June 1919, p. 87. See also Cott, *The Grounding of Modern Feminism*, pp. 107–8. Although a minority of woman leaders of this period pushed for the election of women to political office, particularly on the state or national level, others did use the strategy of temporary solidarity for the purpose of eventual individual freedom. One clear case of this was Alice Paul's leadership of the Congressional Union and the National Woman's Party between 1914 and 1916. There, the strategy was to hold the Democratic Party responsible for its failure to endorse woman suffrage by mobilizing woman voters in suffrage states against Democratic candidates, regardless of their genuine political leanings or individual candidates' positions on

woman suffrage. The strategy, while interesting, met with dubious success. See Flexner, *Century of Struggle*, p. 276; Kraditor, *Ideas of the Woman Suffrage Movement*, pp. 233–37.

57. "The Status and Future of the Woman Suffrage Movement," 1902, Mary Putnam Jacobi Papers, Schlesinger Library, Radcliffe College (used with permission).

58. See the discussion at in section I, above.

59. The historical fact is that woman suffrage has had little impact on the contours of American politics. Disappointing though this was for those who hoped that suffrage would revolutionize politics, it is not particularly surprising given that the dominant conceptions of women's political equality challenged none of the fundamental assumptions of mainstream political institutions. In the absence of a stronger challenge, those institutions were fully as capable of absorbing women's participation in politics as they were of absorbing immigrants.

60. Karlyn Kohrs Campbell, *Man Cannot Speak for Her: A Critical Study of Early Feminist Rhetoric*, vol. 1 (New York: Greenwood, 1989), pp. 173–74.

61. For a more detailed discussion of democratic deliberation, see Bernard Manin, "On Legitimacy and Political Deliberation," *Political Theory* 15 (3) (1987), pp. 338–68; and Joshua Cohen, "Deliberation and Democratic Legitimacy," in *The Good Polity: Normative Analysis of the State*, ed. Alan Hamlin and Philip Pettit (Oxford: Basil Blackwell, 1989), pp. 17–34.

62. Cohen, "Deliberation and Democratic Legitimacy," p. 23. Charles Larmore offers a stronger interpretation of the standard equality that must inform genuine deliberation. Not only must differences in power play no role in individuals' opportunity to contribute to the conversation, but participants ought to regard one another with equal respect, that is, as having a "capacity for working out a coherent view of the world" and the valid claim to demand rational justifications of our actions. *Patterns of Moral Complexity* (Cambridge: Cambridge University Press, 1987), p. 64.

63. See David B. Truman, *The Governmental Process* (New York: Knopf, 1953), pp. 333–34. The representative needs both the "specialized information" provided by interest groups and the "political knowledge" of which political forces stand behind different policy positions.

64. See, e.g., Abigail Thernstrom, *Whose Votes Count? Affirmative Action and Minority Voting Rights* (Cambridge: Harvard University Press, 1987), p. 235.

65. Truman, *The Governmental Process*, p. 339.

66. See ibid., pp. 343–45. David Mayhew's *Congress: The Electoral Connection* (New Haven: Yale University Press, 1974) (especially part 2) provides the now classic account of legislators' techniques for securing these optimizing packages, where optimality is construed in terms of the package most conducive to a member's reelection.

67. See Pitkin, *The Concept of Representation*, p. 209, and the discussion in chapter 1, section I, above.

68. *The Alchemy of Race and Rights* (Cambridge: Harvard University Press, 1991), pp. 149–50.

69. *Making All the Difference: Inclusion, Exclusion, and American Law* (Ithaca: Cornell University Press, 1990), p. 101, quoting Stevens's separate opinion in *City of Cleburne v. Cleburne Living Center, Inc.*, 473 U.S. 432 (1985).

70. Interestingly, the visual metaphor of perspective thoroughly permeates discussions of marginalized group representation, particularly discussions of women's representation. We have seen already that suffragists often framed their claims in terms of

"woman's point of view." Constance Morella, Republican co-chair of the bipartisan Women's Caucus, recently commented that "there are times when I think the women's perspective should shine through some legislation, or we lose opportunities." Linda Feldmann, "When Republican Women in House Talk, Gingrich is among the First to Listen," *Christian Science Monitor*, 30 March 1995, p. 18. In the theoretical literature Iris Young has recently defended claims for social group representation on grounds of their distinctive "perspective," where "perspective" is distinguished from "interests" and "opinions." "Deferring Group Representation," in *NOMOS 39: Ethnicity and Group Rights*, ed. Will Kymlicka and Ian Shapiro (New York: New York University Press, 1997). For further discussion of Young's argument, see chapter 5, section IV.

71. John Rawls, *A Theory of Justice* (Cambridge: Harvard University Press, 1971), pp. 150–53; Thomas M. Scanlon, "Contractualism and Utilitarianism," in *Utilitarianism and Beyond*, ed. Amartya Sen and Bernard Williams, (Cambridge: Cambridge University Press, 1982), p. 117.

72. "The Generalized and the Concrete Other: The Kohlberg-Gilligan Controversy in Feminist Theory," in *Feminism as Critique: On the Politics of Gender*, ed. Seyla Benhabib and Drucilla Cornell (Minneapolis: University of Minnesota Press, 1987).

73. Carol Gilligan, *In a Different Voice: Psychological Theory and Women's Development* (Cambridge: Harvard University Press, 1982).

74. Benhabib, "The Generalized and the Concrete Other," p. 87.

75. Ibid., p. 93.

76. Ibid.

77. Ibid.

78. Kevin Merida, "Democratic Women in Senate Vow to Fight Abortion Curbs," *Washington Post*, 22 July 1993, p. A15.

79. Kevin Merida, "'Sisterhood' of the Hill 'Shaking Up the Place,'" *Washington Post*, 2 August 1993, p. A10.

80. Adam Clymer, "Voices of New Women Resound in the Senate," *New York Times*, 11 February 1993, p. A28.

81. Merida, "'Sisterhood' of the Hill," p. A10.

82. Clymer, "Voices of New Women Resound in the Senate," p. A28.

83. Ibid.

84. The model of public deliberation presented by Amy Gutmann and Dennis Thompson offers one intriguing portrait of a public discourse that is compatible with the voice model. "Moral Conflict and Political Consensus," *Ethics* 101 (1) (1990), pp. 64–88. See also their *Democracy and Disagreement* (Cambridge: Harvard University Press, 1996).

85. Young, *Justice and the Politics of Difference*, p. 185 (emphasis added).

86. Ibid.

87. See, e.g., ibid., p. 191. The tendency to collapse recognition and affirmation in some defenses of group-based claims is part of what leads Charles Taylor to do the same in his more critical assessment of such claims. "The Politics of Recognition," in *Multiculturalism: Examining the Politics of Recognition*, ed. Amy Gutmann (Princeton, NJ: Princeton University Press, 1994).

88. Young, *Justice and the Politics of Difference*, p. 186. But note that this characterization tends to elide the distinction between functionalist and egalitarian defenses of group representation. See the discussion in section IV, above.

89. Young, *Justice and the Politics of Difference*, p. 166.

90. Anne Phillips, *The Politics of Presence* (Oxford: Oxford University Press, 1995), p. 145. For a related discussion, see Iris M. Young, "Justice and Communicative Democracy," in *Radical Philosophy: Tradition, Counter-Tradition, Politics*, ed. Roger S. Gottlieb (Philadelphia: Temple University Press, 1993), pp. 123–43.

91. In this respect it is quite closely related to the arguments of Edmund Burke, who saw the ends of justice and the interests of cooperation as mutually reinforcing. See the discussion in chapter 1, section IV.

92. James Johnson, "Arguing for Deliberation: Some Skeptical Considerations," Department of Political Science, University of Rochester, 1995, photocopy, pp. 25–26.

93. Cf. Rousseau's description of democracy: "If there were a people of gods, it would govern itself democratically. So perfect a government is not suited to men." *Social Contract*, Book 3, chapter 4, in *Rousseau's Political Writings*, ed. Alan Ritter (New York: W. W. Norton, 1988), p. 126.

94. Cf. Scanlon, "Contractualism and Utilitarianism."

95. Indeed, as Jane Mansbridge has suggested, communicating and advocating for interests may itself be an important component of a deliberative process, a necessary step along the way of identifying both the possibilities for and the limits of agreement on public policy issues. Jane J. Mansbridge, "The Rise and Fall of Self-Interest in the Explanation of Political Life," in *Beyond Self-Interest*, ed. Jane J. Mansbridge (Chicago: University of Chicago Press, 1990), p. 22. See also her essay, "A Deliberative Theory of Interest Representation," in *The Politics of Interests: Interest Groups Transformed*, ed. Mark P. Petracca (Boulder, CO: Westview, 1992), pp. 32–57, where she argues that interest-group mobilization contributes information and multiple perspectives to political deliberation. While I am sympathetic to the latter view, it does not offer an answer to the permanent underrepresentation of the interests and perspectives of historically marginalized groups.

96. For a helpful discussion, see David M. Estlund, "Who's Afraid of Deliberative Democracy? On the Strategic/Deliberative Dichotomy in Recent Constitutional Jurisprudence," in *Texas Law Review* 71 (7) (1993), p. 1474: "Even for a theorist who advocates a deliberative model of legitimacy, it may be entirely consistent to recommend strategic, nondeliberative political activity for certain individuals or groups as a reponse to largely strategic action in the rest of the population . . . Certainly, legitimacy is not enhanced by the existence of suckers."

97. I discuss institutional changes that would encourage deliberation at greater length in chapter 7.

98. Jon Elster, "Strategic Uses of Argument," in *Barriers to Conflict Resolution*, ed. Kenneth J. Arrow et al. (New York: W. W. Norton, 1995), p. 250.

99. Mike Feinsilber, "Women Turn Anger into Political Sword," *Toronto Globe and Mail*, 28 April 1992, p. A8. Among the women candidates are Lynn Yeakel of Pennsylvania, Carol Moseley Braun of Illinois, and Jean Lloyd-Jones of Iowa.

100. Thernstrom, *Whose Votes Count?*, p. 239.

101. Rufus P. Browning, Dale Rogers Marshall, and David H. Tabb, *Protest Is Not Enough: The Struggle of Blacks and Hispanics for Equality in Urban Politics* (Berkeley: University of California Press, 1984), p. 141.

102. Juan Williams, "From Caucus to Coalition: Can the Black Freshman Class in Congress Shape the Clinton Program?" *Washington Post*, 10 January 1993, p. C2.

103. Sue Thomas, *How Women Legislate* (New York: Oxford University Press, 1994), p. 107.

104. Ibid., p. 110.

105. Debra L. Dodson and Susan J. Carroll, *Reshaping the Agenda: Women in State Legislatures* (New Brunswick, NJ: Center for the American Woman and Politics, 1991), p. 79.

Chapter 5
Trust: The Racial Divide and Black Rights during Reconstruction

1. I am indebted to Jane Mansbridge for helping to clarify the connection between descriptive representation and communication. For her discussion, see "In Defense of 'Descriptive' Representation," paper presented at the annual meeting of the American Political Science Association, San Francisco, 29 August–1 September 1996, especially pp. 12–14.

2. U.S. Constitution, amend. 15.

3. Eric Foner, *Reconstruction: America's Unfinished Revolution, 1863–1877* (New York: Harper and Row, 1988), p. 372. This chapter relies heavily on Foner's work for its broader view of Reconstruction politics.

4. See, e.g., E. Foner, *Reconstruction*, p. 324.

5. The Civil Rights Bill died in 1874, but by the summer of 1873 the lack of Republican resolve to enact it was clear, as it had been the subject of fruitless debate during the previous session of Congress.

6. The phrase is that of Rev. Henry McNeal Turner, who was elected to the Georgia state legislature in 1868. The Democratic-controlled body refused to seat duly elected Black senators and representatives on the ground that the Constitution did not guarantee them the right to hold political office. Turner's response was memorable: "[W]e are told that if black men want to speak, they must speak through white trumpets; if black men want their sentiments expressed, they must be adulterated and sent through white messengers, who will quibble and equivocate and evade as rapidly as the pendulum of a clock." Reprinted in *The Voice of Black America: Major Speeches by Negroes in the United States, 1797–1971*, ed. Philip S. Foner (New York: Simon and Schuster, 1972), p. 360.

7. "*Trust* is a Passion proceeding from the *Belief of him* from whom we *expect* or *hope* for Good, so *free* from *Doubt* that upon the same we pursue no other Way to attain the same Good: as *Distrust* or Diffidence is *Doubt* that maketh him endeavour to provide himself by other means." "Human Nature," in *The Moral and Political Works of Thomas Hobbes of Malmesbury* (London, 1750), quoted in John Dunn, "Trust and Political Agency," in *Trust: Making and Breaking Cooperative Relations*, ed. Diego Gambetta (Oxford: Basil Blackwell, 1988), p. 74.

8. At around the same time that the women's rights movement was launched by the Seneca Falls convention, free Blacks in the North began holding their own conventions for the purpose of formulating and articulating their claims for civil and political equality against both state and federal governments. Shortly after emancipation, a similar movement emerged among southern Blacks. The latter provided a proving ground for both the leaders and the ideas active in the constitutional conventions in the South after the war. Philip S. Foner and George E. Walker, eds., *Proceedings of the Black State*

Conventions, 1840–1865, vol. 1 (Philadelphia: Temple University Press, 1979), pp. xi–xviii.

9. In the words of one early fifth of July speaker, Peter Osborne, "I hope and trust that when the Declaration of Independence is fully executed, which declares that all men . . . were born free and equal, we may then have our Fourth of July on the fourth. . . . The Declaration of Independence has declared to man, without speaking of color, that all men are born free and equal. Has it not declared this freedom and equality to us too?" 5 July 1832; reprinted in P. Foner, *The Voice of Black America*, p. 48.

10. Peter Kolchin, *First Freedom: The Responses of Alabama's Blacks to Emancipation and Reconstruction* (Westport, CT: Greenwood, 1972), p. 153.

11. Quoted in E. Foner, *Reconstruction*, p. 114. The Declaration was also among the icons of republicanism placed on a table at meetings of the Union League, one of the organizations principally responsible for the political mobilization of Blacks during Reconstruction. Ibid., p. 283.

12. The statement is that of Richard H. Cain, a Black member of the U.S. House of Representatives. Speech before the U.S. House of Representatives, 10 January 1874, reprinted in Annjennette Sophie McFarlin, ed., *Black Congressional Reconstruction Orators and Their Orations, 1869–1879* (Metuchen, NJ: Scarecrow, 1976), p. 42.

13. Address to the People of Illinois, Illinois State Convention of Colored Men, October 1866, in Philip S. Foner and George E. Walker, eds., *Proceedings of the Black National and State Conventions, 1865–1900*, vol. 1 (Philadelphia: Temple University Press, 1986), p. 257.

14. Henry McNeal Turner, Speech before the Georgia Legislature, 3 September 1868, reprinted in P. Foner, *The Voice of Black America*, p. 360; see also, e.g., Turner's speech of 1 January 1866, reprinted in *The Colored American* (Augusta, Georgia), 13 January 1866 ("Was it then because we were not really human that we have not been recognized as a member of the nation's family? Are we not made as other men?"); *The Black Republican* (New Orleans, Louisiana), 13 May 1865, p. 2 (all men created free and equal by God).

15. *American Citizenship: The Quest for Inclusion* (Cambridge: Harvard University Press, 1991), pp. 16–17, 37.

16. Quoted in Roberta Sue Alexander, *North Carolina Faces the Freedmen: Race Relations During Presidential Reconstruction, 1865–67* (Durham, NC: Duke University Press, 1985), p. 19 (emphasis added).

17. Quoted in Alexander, *North Carolina Faces the Freedmen*, p. 18.

18. See Thomas Holt, *Black over White: Negro Political Leadership in South Carolina During Reconstruction* (Urbana: University of Illinois Press, 1977), p. 19. It is true, however, that property or no, the North Carolina legislature was soon to burden them with a tax on laborers. Alexander, *North Carolina Faces the Freedmen*, p. 51.

19. See, e.g., P. Foner and G. Walker, *Proceedings of the Black National and State Conventions, 1865–1900*, vol. 1, p. 194 (Arkansas, 1865); p. 202 (New England, 1865); p. 214 (Frederick Douglass to Andrew Johnson, 1866); p. 312 (Kentucky, 1867); p. 332 (Iowa, 1868); p. 369 (national convention, 1869); *The Black Republican* (New Orleans, Louisiana), 29 April 1865, p. 2.

20. See Shklar, *American Citizenship*, pp. 31, 51–53, for a discussion of the centrality of the idea of the "citizen soldier" in American political thought and of the use of this theme as a ground for the equal citizenship of Blacks.

21. Leon F. Litwack, *Been in the Storm So Long: The Aftermath of Slavery* (New York: Knopf, 1979), pp. 97, 98.

22. P. Foner and G. Walker, *Proceedings of the Black National and State Conventions, 1865–1900*, vol. 1, pp. 289–90.

23. Speech before the U.S. House of Representatives, 10 January 1874, in McFarlin, *Black Congressional Reconstruction Orators*, p. 44.

24. Quoted in Howard Brotz, ed., *Negro Social and Political Thought, 1850–1920: Representative Texts* (New York: Basic Books, 1966), p. 342.

25. The statement was that of U.S. Senator Richard Yates, quoted in E. Foner, *Reconstruction*, p. 278.

26. Address from the Colored Citizens of Norfolk, Virginia, to the People of the United States, 5 June 1865, reprinted in P. Foner and G. Walker, *Proceedings of the Black National and State Conventions, 1865–1900*, vol. 1, p. 85. See also Litwack, *Been in the Storm So Long*, p. 531, quoting the statement of another Virginia freedmen's meeting, in August 1865: "The only salvation for us besides the power of the Government . . . is in the *possession of the ballot.* Give us this, and we will protect ourselves" (emphasis in original).

27. For an interesting discussion of the connection in the American tradition between earning and full citizenship, see Shklar, *American Citizenship*.

28. See, e.g., *The Black Republican* (New Orleans), 15 April 1865, p. 2.

29. See, e.g., E. Foner, *Reconstruction*, pp. 70–71; Litwack, *Been in the Storm So Long*, pp. 399–404.

30. Quoted in Litwack, *Been in the Storm So Long*, p. 401.

31. Quoted in Brotz, *Negro Social and Political Thought*, pp. 211–12. As this suggests, Douglass thought the clearest route to Black economic independence was through learning artisans' crafts. His respect for artisans was shared by freedmen, as reflected by the prominence of artisans among Black leadership during Reconstruction. But his hope for their economic success was not borne out; Black artisans in the South were kept on the margins, and they shrank in numbers as the years went by. E. Foner, *Reconstruction*, pp. 287, 396–97.

32. *The Colored Citizen* (Cincinnati), 19 May 1866, p. 2.

33. "[W]ithout their own independent actions to secure their emancipation, elevation, and equality, black identity, equality, and self-confidence would be no more than an artificial product of white . . . tutelage." Leonard I. Sweet, *Black Images of America, 1784–1870* (New York: W. W. Norton, 1976), p. 5. However, some Black leaders rejected the formation of separate Black institutions as a violation of the principle of color blindness. They argued that Blacks should themselves practice what they asked of Whites. "It is as repugnant to the great principle of the brotherhood of man, to organize a church on the basis of a dark, as white skin, and just as anti-republican to encourage political organizations . . . for the *black* as the *white* man." Editorial in the Charleston *Advocate*, 11 May 1867, reprinted in Martin E. Dann, *The Black Press, 1827–1890: The Quest for National Identity* (New York: Putnam's, 1971), p. 150 (emphasis in original).

34. *Alabama State Sentinel*, 21 May 1867, quoted in E. Foner, *Reconstruction*, p. 288.

35. State Convention of the Colored People of Georgia, Jan. 10, 1866, reprinted in P. Foner and G. Walker, *Proceedings of the Black National and State Conventions, 1865–1900*, vol. 1, p. 232.

36. Benjamin Randolph at the South Carolina constitutional convention, quoted in Dorothy Sterling, ed., *The Trouble They Seen: Black People Tell the Story of Reconstruction* (Garden City, NY: Doubleday, 1976), p. 27; see also, e.g., "Freedmen's Convention," *The Colored American* (Augusta, Georgia), 6 January 1866, p. 3.

37. Quoted in E. Foner, *Reconstruction*, p. 288.

38. Quoted in P. Foner, *The Voice of Black America*, p. 355.

39. Frequently all these claims were strung together in a single demand for equality. See, e.g., R. I. Cromwell, "An Address to the Colored People of Louisiana," quoted in Sterling, *The Trouble They Seen*, p. 103: "We want every man to vote, hold office, sit on juries, travel on steamboats, eat in any restaurant, drink in any saloon, dine at any hotel, or educate our children at any school we choose." But true to the principle of equal political rights, most Blacks rejected Republican proposals to disenfranchise southern Whites who played active roles in the Confederacy. As one Black delegate to the Alabama constitutional convention put it, "I have no desire to take away the rights of the white man . . . All I want is equal rights in the court house and equal rights when I go to vote." Quoted in E. Foner, *Reconstruction*, p. 324.

40. See, e.g., Litwack, *Been in the Storm So Long*, chapter 6, for a description of the freed slaves' exuberant exercise of their freedom of mobility immediately after emancipation.

41. This ambivalence is reflected in a letter written by fifteen-year-old W.E.B. DuBois to the New York *Globe*, albeit after Reconstruction was over: "A political office should not be the goal of one's ambition, but still if anyone wishes an office and is worthy of it, it should not be denied him on account of his color." Reprinted in Dann, *The Black Press, 1827–1890*, pp. 166–67.

42. *New Orleans Tribune*, 13 April 1867, quoted in Sterling, *The Trouble They Seen*, pp. 107–8.

43. See also, e.g., Calvin Chase, editorial in *The Bee*, 15 January 1887 ("The race does not ask for special privileges and favors, and only insists upon a free and fair chance in the race of life offered to other people in this country."), quoted in Dann, *The Black Press, 1827–1890*, pp. 174–75; T. Thomas Fortune, editorial in the New York *Globe*, 17 February 1883 ("[N]o race, class or party has the right to claim to be the 'governing class.'"), quoted in Dann, *The Black Press, 1827–1890*, p. 163; *The Colored American* (Augusta, Georgia), 6 January 1866, p. 3 ("Make no class laws, or you sap the very foundation of the superstructure of republicanism").

44. Quoted in Brotz, *Negro Social and Political Thought*, p. 283.

45. Quoted in McFarlin, *Black Congressional Reconstruction Orators*, p. 55. See also, e.g., Address to the People of the United States, National Convention of Colored People, 18 October 1871: "We affirm that the colored people of the States represented by us have no desire to strike out a line of policy for their action involving interests not common to the whole people." Quoted in ibid., p. 237.

46. As noted in chapter 3, many woman suffrage activists reached the same conclusion from the premise of individual equality.

47. Quoted in P. Foner and G. Walker, *Black National and State Conventions*, vol. 1, p. 303.

48. *Reminiscences of an Active Life: The Autobiography of John Roy Lynch* (Chicago: University of Chicago Press, 1970), p. 507.

49. William Still, "A Defense of Independent Voting," March 1874, reprinted in P. Foner, *The Voice of Black America*, pp. 399–400.

50. "Office Holders," *The National Era* (Washington, D.C.), 13 January 1870.

51. Most notably, Frederick Douglass dissented sharply with Martin Delany's claim that Blacks should hold political offices in proportion to their population. Pointing out that Blacks comprised one-eighth of the population, he suggested that Delany's logic meant that "[t]hey should constitute one-eighth of the poets, scholars, authors, and philosophers of the country. . . . The Negro in black should mark every octave on the National piano." "Letter to Major Delany," *New National Era*, 31 August 1874, reprinted in P. Foner, *The Voice of Black America*, pp. 280–81. In fact, Douglass's rejection of this early proposal of quotas did rest on his view that slavery had left Blacks in an ignorant and degraded state. He was optimistic about their potential to raise themselves out of this condition, but he believed that the day when they would be equipped to share equally in political positions lay in the future.

52. Reprinted in McFarlin, *Black Congressional Reconstruction Orators*, p. 88.

53. *Black and White: Land, and Labor and Politics in the South* (1884), excerpted in Brotz, *Negro Social and Political Thought*, p. 338.

54. It is not anachronistic to suggest female representatives, as many Blacks during Reconstruction were avid supporters of equal political rights for women.

55. Speech of Joseph H. Rainey, U.S. Representative from South Carolina, 3 February 1875, reprinted in McFarlin, *Black Congressional Reconstruction Orators*, p. 227.

56. Quoted in ibid., p. 238.

57. Quoted in P. Foner and G. Walker, *Black National and State Conventions*, vol. 1, pp. 191–92.

58. Litwack, *Been in the Storm So Long*, p. 534.

59. From *The Loyal Georgian*, 10 April 1867, reprinted in Sterling, *The Trouble They Seen*, p. 100. As this illustrates, not only were freedmen determined to exercise the vote wisely, but they were positively excited about trying out their new political capacities. There was a flourishing of Black political organization during Reconstruction, some centering around Black churches and schools, and some generated by the Union League, a northern-sponsored political organization. Such efforts bore their first fruit in the southern state constitutional conventions of 1867–1869, most of which included significant numbers of Black delegates. At the Virginia convention, as ex-slave George Teamoh described it, "[I]n spite of their disqualifications, my people seems to have been possessed of a natural itching to meet, in open debate, every question which came up for discussion. Under all the circumstances, the colored members bore themselves very well." Quoted in ibid., pp. 119–20.

60. See Shklar, *American Citizenship*, pp. 57–58, for a discussion of this "darker side" to the quest for inclusion.

61. "The Present and Future of the Colored Race in America," June 1863, reprinted in Brotz, *Negro Social and Political Thought*, p. 273. Others, like John R. Lynch, a Black U.S. Representative from Mississippi, expressed this sentiment in the form of indignation at being classed with other marginal groups. Lynch chose to criticize comparisons between the "colored race" and the "Mongolian race." See McFarlin, *Black Congressional Reconstruction Orators*, p. 161.

62. 2 January 1873, quoted in Sterling, *The Trouble They Seen*, p. 176–77. Needless to say, a consciousness of their roles as symbolic representatives of the Black race put a great deal of psychic pressure on those who did hold public office. Robert Elliott remembered his first speech in Congress as burdened by White expectations of failure and fervent Black hopes for his success. See ibid., p. 178.

63. E. Foner, *Reconstruction*, p. 449.

64. The Enforcement Acts of 1870 and 1871 effectively eliminated the Klan, but violence directed against Black voters intensified again between 1874 and 1876. E. Foner, *Reconstruction*, pp. 458–59, 548–53.

65. Ibid., p. 556.

66. Address to the 1876 Republican National Convention, quoted in Harold M. Hyman, ed., *The Radical Republicans and Reconstruction, 1861–1870* (Indianapolis: Bobbs-Merrill, 1967), p. 522.

67. "From Ohio," *New National Era* (Washington, D.C.), 16 July 1874 (emphasis added).

68. *New National Era* (Washington, D.C.), 2 July 1874 (emphasis added); see also, in the same newspaper, "What Next Is to Be Done" and "Who Killed the Civil Rights Bill?" 9 July 1874.

69. Merline Pitre, *Through Many Dangers, Toils, and Snares: The Black Leadership of Texas, 1868–1900* (Austin, TX: Eakin, 1985), p. 162.

70. "The Civil-Rights Bill," *New National Era* 30 July 1874.

71. Although it was beyond the scope of this study to undertake a detailed statistical analysis of the trends of Black political arguments during Reconstruction, I did perform an analysis of the trends within a particularly important newspaper, Frederick Douglass's *New National Era*. That analysis supports the claim that, between 1870 and 1874, rhetoric shifted from the individualistic arguments toward the more group-oriented ones within the theme of betrayal. I examined all the paper's articles and editorials for arguments about Black political equality and political and civil rights for four months (January, February, June, and July) of each of these years, which came to a total of seventy-eight articles. I classified articles emphasizing color-blind equality, equal opportunity, and natural rights among the "individualist" arguments, whereas those stressing the Republican betrayal of Black citizens, the need for Black solidarity or political independence in the face of that betrayal, and the need for Black self-representation were classified among the "group-oriented" arguments. The number of individualist articles as a percentage of group-oriented articles in each year was as follows: 2.30 (1870); 1.25 (1871); 3.00 (1872); 0.38 (1873); 0.41 (1874).

72. "On the Nomination of Negroes," *New National Era*, 26 October 1871, reprinted in Philip Foner, ed., *The Life and Writings of Frederick Douglass*, vol. 4 (New York: International, 1955), p. 285.

73. "Colored Voters of the South Take Heed," *New National Era*, 1 February 1872, reprinted in ibid., p. 288.

74. T. Thomas Fortune, editorial in New York *Globe*, 2 June 1883, reprinted in Dann, *The Black Press, 1827–1890*, p. 164.

75. Litwack, *Been in the Storm So Long*, p. 512.

76. Ibid., pp. 512, 513. Douglass makes this point in defense of women's political rights, drawing a parallel between women and Blacks. "The man struck is the man to cry out. Woman knows and feels her wrongs as man cannot know and feel them, and she also knows as well as he can know, what measures are needed to redress them." "The Woman's Suffrage Movement," April 1888, reprinted in P. Foner, *Life and Writings of Frederick Douglass*, vol. 4, p. 449.

77. State Convention of the Colored Men of Alabama, 4 May 1867, quoted in P. Foner and G. Walker, eds., *Black National and State Conventions*, vol. 1, p. 304.

78. At pp. 166–68.

79. *New National Era and Citizen* (Washington, D.C.), 3 July 1873.

80. "A New Party," *The Echo* (St. Martinsville, LA), 15 March 1873.

81. Reprinted in *The Echo* (St. Martinsville, LA), 15 March 1873.

82. "The United States Senatorship," *New National Era* (Washington, D.C.), 12 January 1871, p. 3.

83. E. Foner, *Reconstruction*, p. 539.

84. For a discussion of the economy of trust, and the important role of *distrust* in sustaining legitimate government, see Dunn, "Trust and Political Agency," pp. 85–86; Judith N. Shklar, *Ordinary Vices* (Cambridge: Harvard University Press, 1984), p. 190.

85. *The Federalist Papers*, Number 10, ed. Clinton Rossiter (New York: Mentor, 1961), p. 80.

86. *Federalist 53*, p. 332.

87. *Federalist 52*, p. 330.

88. *Federalist 57*, p. 351; note that Madison explicitly employs the language of trust.

89. Ibid., p. 352.

90. Ibid. (emphasis added).

91. Ibid. Cf. Locke, *Second Treatise*, sec. 143, p. 364: "[T]he *Legislative* Power is put into the hands of divers Persons who duly Assembled, have . . . a Power to make Laws, which when they have done, being separated again, they are themselves subject to the Laws, they have made; which is a new and near tie upon them, to take care, that they make them for the publick good."

92. *Federalist 57*, p. 353.

93. Of course Madison would not have argued that the American spirit of liberty could ever sustain a social bond between freed Blacks and Whites. For this reason, although he did not attribute any natural inferiority to Blacks that would justify their enslavement, he opposed all schemes of emancipation in which freed slaves lived among White citizens:

> If the blacks, strongly marked as they are by physical and lasting peculiarities, be retained amid the whites, under the degrading privation of equal rights, political or social, they must be always dissatisfied with their condition, as a change only from one to another species of oppression; always secretly confederated against the ruling and privileged class. . . . Nor is it fair, in estimating the danger of collisions with the whites, to charge it wholly on the side of the Blacks. There would be reciprocal antipathies doubling the danger.

Letter from Madison to Robert J. Evans, 15 June 1819, quoted in Drew R. McCoy, *The Last of the Fathers: James Madison and the Republican Legacy* (Cambridge: Cambridge University Press, 1989), p. 279. Consequently Madison favored the emancipation of slaves followed by their colonization in the western territories of the United States. McCoy, pp. 280–85.

94. Clearly this is a presumption shared by both Madison and pluralist theorists like Dahl and Truman, although they construe the relationship between particular interests and the public interest differently.

95. Richard Fenno's study of federal representatives' behavior in their constituencies confirms that the reelection motive is a powerful one in contemporary politics. Even representatives from "safe" districts believe they have to work hard to preserve their

reputation for advancing constituent interests in order to keep their districts "safe." *Home Style: House Members in Their Districts* (Boston: Little, Brown, 1978), p. 233–34.

96. A recent study of Black political attitudes shows that this pattern continues to characterize Black party support: a large majority of Blacks now favor the Democratic to the Republican Party, but it seems to reflect a choice between the "lesser of two evils" rather than a sense that the Democratic Party represents Black interests. Blacks give the Democratic Party a thermometer rating of 75 as compared to 35.1 for the Republicans. Yet whereas 37 percent of the Black electorate believes that the Republican Party "does *not* work hard at all on issues black people care about," only 28 percent believe that the Democratic party *does* work "*very hard*" on issues black people care about." Patricia Gurin, Shirley Hatchett, and James S. Jackson, *Hope and Independence: Blacks' Response to Electoral and Party Politics* (New York: Russell Sage Foundation, 1989), pp. 55, 130–31.

97. Charles Backus, Sermon Preached at Long Meadow (1788), quoted in Gordon S. Wood, *The Creation of the American Republic, 1776–1787* (New York: W. W. Norton, 1969), p. 601.

98. Robert Putnam's important study provides the empirical evidence for the importance of civil society as the primary source of political trust. *Making Democracy Work: Civic Traditions in Modern Italy* (Princeton, NJ: Princeton University Press, 1993).

99. *Dred Scott v. Sandford* 60 U.S. (19 How.) 393 (1857).

100. *The Lincoln-Douglas Debates of 1858*, ed. Robert W. Johannsen (New York: Oxford University Press, 1965), p. 45.

101. Thomas Holt, *Black over White: Negro Political Leadership in South Carolina During Reconstruction* (Urbana: University of Illinois Press, 1977), chapter 6.

102. For journalistic accounts of the solidarity of the Congressional Black Caucus in attempting to protect African American interests, see "The Black Caucus," *Christian Science Monitor*, 16 July 1993, p. 18; "Clinton and the Caucus," *Christian Science Monitor*, 2 August 1993, p. 18; Kenneth J. Cooper and Ann Devroy, "Black Caucus's Coolness Delays Civil Rights Nomination of Payton," *Washington Post*, 5 November 1993, p. A10; Linda Feldmann, "Black Caucus Uses Its Clout Effectively but Also Carefully," *Christian Science Monitor*, 19 July 1994, p. 3.

103. Carol M. Swain, *Black Faces, Black Interests: The Representation of African Americans in Congress* (Cambridge: Harvard University Press, 1993). Compare Table 3.3, p. 57, to Table 7.2, p. 159. The one exception among White representatives was Peter Rodino (D - N.J.), who ranked as high on these indexes as any African American representative.

104. Fredrick C. Harris and James H. Lewis, *Who Supports Minority and Poor Interests? A Roll Call Voting Analysis of the Chicago City Council, 1988–1990* (Chicago: Chicago Urban League, 1991), p. 10. This finding is all the more striking because there are no partisan differences on the council. In the Illinois state legislature Harris found that partisan identification was the most important determinant of roll call voting behavior among legislators. Frederick C. Harris, *Who Supports Minority and Poor Interests? A Roll Call Voting Analysis of the 1989 Illinois General Assembly* (Chicago: Chicago Urban League, 1990).

105. For an analysis that measures the relative importance of race and party for legislative support for Black interests, see Charles Cameron, David Epstein, and Sharyn O'Halloran, "Do Majority-Minority Districts Maximize Substantive Black Representa-

tion in Congress?" *American Political Science Review* 90 (4) (1996), pp. 794–812, especially Table 4. It is important to note that the one published study of the descriptive representation of Latinos finds no statistically significant difference between Latino and Anglo representatives' voting in the 100th Congress. Rodney E. Hero and Caroline J. Tolbert, "Latinos and Substantive Representation in the U.S. House of Representatives: Direct, Indirect, or Nonexistent?" *American Journal of Political Science* 39 (3): 640–52 (1995). This finding, however, may well reflect the greater demographic diversity contained within the category "Latino."

106. Sue Thomas, *How Women Legislate* (New York: Oxford University Press, 1994), p. 69.

107. Ibid., pp. 70–72.

108. Ibid., pp. 72–77. See also Center for the American Woman and Politics, *The Impact of Women in Public Office: Findings at a Glance* (New Brunswick, NJ: Eagleton Institute of Politics, Rutgers, the State University of New Jersey, 1991).

109. See, e.g., Susan Gluck Mezey, "Increasing the Number of Women in Office: Does It Matter?" in *The Year of the Woman: Myths and Realities*, ed. Elizabeth Adell Cook, Sue Thomas, and Clyde Wilcox (Boulder, CO: Westview, 1994).

110. Thomas, *How Women Legislate*, chapter 4. Some evidence suggests that once women reach a threshold of about 25 percent of the legislative body, there is some decline in their investment of energy in women-focused policy areas. This may be because at that point women have had sufficient influence over their male colleagues that they can rely on the latter to advocate for women's issues, freeing them to focus their attention elsewhere. See ibid., p. 154, and sources cited.

111. Laurel Weldon makes this argument in "The Political Representation of Women: The Impact of a Critical Mass," paper presented at the annual meeting of the American Political Science Association, San Francisco, 29 August–1 September 1996.

112. Iris Young, "Difference as a Resource for Democratic Communication," in *Deliberation and Democracy*, ed. James Bohman and William Rehg (Cambridge: MIT Press, forthcoming).

113. Mary E. Bendyna and Celinda C. Lake, "Gender and Voting in the 1992 Presidential Election," in Cook, Thomas, and Wilcox, *The Year of the Woman*, pp. 252–53.

114. Mansbridge, "In Defense of 'Descriptive' Representation," p. 13.

115. Ibid., p. 14.

116. See the discussion in chapter 3, pp. 217–18; see also, e.g., Charles Beitz, *Political Equality* (Princeton, NJ: Princeton University Press, 1989), p. 157.

117. For further discussion see chapter 4, section VI, and chapter 7, section II.

118. Michael Ignatieff, *The Needs of Strangers* (London: Chatto and Windus, 1984), pp. 13–14. One might also state the need negatively, as a need to be emancipated from *misrecognition*. As Charles Taylor notes, "Nonrecognition or misrecognition can inflict harm, can be a form of oppression, imprisoning someone in a false, distorted, and reduced mode of being." Taylor, "The Politics of Recognition," in *Multiculturalism: Examining the Politics of Recognition*, ed. Amy Gutmann (Princeton, NJ: Princeton University Press, 1994), p. 25. I pursue the relationship between misrecognition and group identity in the next chapter.

119. As Anne Phillips has argued. See, e.g., *The Politics of Presence* (Oxford: Oxford University Press, 1995), pp. 42–43. For an argument along similar lines—that a history of marginalization gives rise to an especially strong need for symbolic recognition—see

Alan Cairns, "Constitutional Stigmatization: The Manufacture of 'Otherness,'" in *Identity, Rights and Constitutional Transformation*, ed. Patrick J. Hanafin and Melissa S. Williams (Hampshire, England: Dartmouth, forthcoming).

120. Cf. Putnam, *Making Democracy Work*, chapter 6.

121. See Gurin et al., *Hope and Independence*, introduction and chapter 1, for an overview of the way this pattern has been repeated in the history of African Americans.

Chapter 6
Memory: The Claims of History in Group Recognition

1. In addition, the theory of groups may serve the purpose of offering a brief for the political recognition of a particular group or set of groups. To do so effectively, however, it must relate the group's interest in recognition to political commitments or interests shared by the society as a whole.

2. The spirit of my argument in this chapter is similar to that of Jeremy Waldron's argument in his thought-provoking essay, "Historic Injustice: Its Remembrance and Supersession," in *Justice, Ethics, and New Zealand Society*, ed. Graham Oddie and Roy W. Perrett (Auckland: Oxford University Press, 1992), summarized on p. 167: "Often and understandably, claims based on rectification and claims based on forward-looking principles will coincide; for past injustice is not without its present effects. . . . All the same, it is worth stressing that it is the impulse to justice now that should lead the way in this process, not the reparation of something of which the wrongness is understood primarily in relation to conditions that no longer obtain."

3. Cf. John Rawls, *A Theory of Justice* (Cambridge: Harvard University Press, 1971), p. 86.

4. Abigail M. Thernstrom, *Whose Votes Count? Affirmative Action and Minority Voting Rights* (Cambridge: Harvard University Press, 1987), p. 124.

5. See, for example, the remarks of Chief Justice Burger and Justice Brennan in *United Jewish Organizations of Williamsburgh v. Carey*, quoted above in chapter 2, pp. 80–81 and 260 n. 96.

6. Rawls, *A Theory of Justice*, p. 74.

7. Shelby Steele, *The Content of Our Character: A New Vision of Race in America* (New York: Harper Perennial, 1991), passim, but see especially pp. 173–74.

8. See, e.g., Nathan Glazer, *Affirmative Discrimination: Ethnic Inequality and Public Policy* (New York: Basic Books, 1975), pp. 198–99.

9. See, e.g., Justice Powell's plurality opinion in *University of California Regents v. Bakke*, 438 U.S. 265, 298 (1978) ("[T]here is a measure of inequity in forcing innocent persons in respondent's position to bear the burdens of redressing grievances not of their making").

10. Against a policy of "affirmative gerrymandering," for example, Abigail Thernstrom writes, "Group membership counts as a qualification for office only where blacks and other minority citizens can prove themselves distinctly excluded from the electoral process." *Whose Votes Count?*, p. 240.

11. For other discussions of "balkanization," see the introduction, section I; section IV, below; and chapter 7, section I.

12. "The United States," in *Protection of Ethnic Minorities: Comparative Perspectives*, ed. Robert G. Wirsing (New York: Pergamon, 1981), p. 22.

13. 488 U.S. 469, 505 (1989). See also, e.g., Glazer, *Affirmative Discrimination*, pp. 30–31.

14. See the discussion in Larry May, *The Morality of Groups: Collective Responsibility, Group-Based Harm, and Corporate Rights* (Notre Dame: University of Notre Dame Press, 1987), pp. 135–38.

15. Christopher Nolan, *Under the Eye of the Clock: The Life Story of Christopher Nolan* (London: Weidenfeld and Nicolson, 1987), p. 3. Nolan developed the capacity to communicate verbally at the age of eleven, when a new drug loosened his muscles to the extent that he could strike the keys of a typewriter with a stick attached to his head, his "unicorn."

16. Ibid., p. 26.

17. T. S. Eliot explains the idea of the "objective correlative" as "a set of objects, a situation, a chain of events which shall be the formula of a *particular* emotion; such that when the external facts, which must terminate in sensory experience, are given, the emotion is immediately evoked." "Hamlet," in *Selected Essays* (London: Faber and Faber, 1951), p. 145.

18. Steele retells Black comedian Richard Pryor's account of his terror when, during a holiday in Hawaii in a remote cabin, such a cry resounded through the night-shrouded woods. To Pryor—though not to the frolickers—that shout could only conjure up the image of a lynching party. *The Content of Our Character*, p. 153.

19. Ibid., pp. 153, 151. Steele argues that this powerful memory functions as an enemy to Black progress, as it heightens Blacks' sensitivity to White actions that are not discriminatory in intent, and diverts energy and resources away from efforts materially to improve Blacks' social position.

20. Bill Hendrick and Robert Anthony Watts, "Crushing Blow in a Losing Battle," *The Globe and Mail* (Toronto) 6 May 1992, p. A8. The same article quotes Adrian Tibbs, a graduating senior at Clark Atlanta University, stating that the King verdict "threw me back into the lynching time period. It made me say, 'Right here and now, minorities on this Earth are not safe.' It seemed the white sheets and hoods were around."

21. Isabel Wilkerson, "Acquittal in Beating Raises Fears over Race Relations," *New York Times*, 1 May 1992, p. A13. Note the similarity here to Burke's use of the term *description*, discussed in chapter 1 at pp. 34–37.

22. Bruce Weber, "Students Talk about Race, Violence, and Rodney King," *New York Times*, 4 May 1992, p. A13.

23. W.E.B. DuBois, *Darkwater: Voices from within the Veil* (New York: Schocken, 1969), p. 44.

24. Iris Young, *Justice and the Politics of Difference* (Princeton, NJ: Princeton University Press, 1990), p. 129.

25. For further discussion, see Charles Lawrence, "The Id, the Ego, and Equal Protection: Reckoning with Unconscious Racism," *Stanford Law Review* 39 (2) (1987), p. 330: "Racism in America is much more complex than either the conscious conspiracy of a power elite or the simple delusion of a few ignorant bigots. It is a part of our common historical experience and, therefore, a part of our culture. It arises from the assumptions we have learned to make about the world, ourselves, and others as well as from the patterns of our fundamental social activities."

26. 347 U.S. 483, 494 (1954). The Court stated that this finding was "amply supported by modern authority." Ibid. (citing Kenneth B. Clark, *Effect of Prejudice and*

Discrimination on Personality Development [Washington, D.C.: Midcentury White House Conference on Children and Youth, 1950]).

27. Steele, *The Content of Our Character*, p. 25.

28. Research suggests that the phenomenon of learned helplessness is more common among women than men. See, e.g., Ivan W. Miller III and William H. Norman, "Learned Helplessness in Humans: A Review and Attribution Theory Model," *Psychological Bulletin* 86 (1) (1979), pp. 93–118.

29. See, e.g., Justice Bradley's separate opinion in *Bradwell v. Illinois*, 83 U.S. (16 Wall.) 130, 141 (1873) (upholding a decision to exclude women from the practice of law): "Man is, or should be, woman's protector and defender. The natural and proper timidity and delicacy which belongs to the female sex evidently unfits it for many of the occupations of civil life. The constitution of the family organization, which is founded in the divine ordinance, as well as in the nature of things, indicates the domestic sphere as that which properly belongs to the domain and functions of womanhood."

30. See, e.g., Young's lucid discussion in *Justice and the Politics of Difference*, pp. 148–51.

31. Quoted in Young, *Justice and the Politics of Difference*, p. 39. See also, e.g., John Hart Ely, *Democracy and Distrust* (Cambridge: Harvard University Press, 1980), pp. 158–59.

32. "[I]n certain moral circumstances, the relevant description of the self may embrace more than a single, individual human being, as when we attribute responsibility or affirm an obligation to a family or community or class or nation rather than to some particular human being." Michael Sandel, *Liberalism and the Limits of Justice* (Cambridge: Cambridge University Press, 1982), pp. 63–64.

33. Will Kymlicka, *Liberalism, Community, and Culture* (Oxford: Clarendon, 1991), p. 175.

34. Sandel, *Liberalism and the Limits of Justice*, pp. 152–53.

35. Patricia Williams, *The Alchemy of Race and Rights* (Cambridge: Harvard University Press, 1991), p. 10. This point is made in more theoretical terms by Henri Tajfel: for some groups, "it is impossible, or at least difficult, for a member of the minority to move out *individually* from the group and become a member of the 'majority' indistinguishable from others. In other words, it is the belief that individual social mobility . . . will not affect, in many important social situations, the identification of the individual by others as a member of the minority." "The Social Psychology of Minorities," in *Human Groups and Social Categories: Studies in Social Psychology* (Cambridge: Cambridge University Press, 1981), p. 314.

36. Cf. Elizabeth Spelman, *Inessential Woman: Problems of Exclusion in Feminist Thought* (Boston: Beacon, 1988), pp. 124–25, and sources cited.

37. Kymlicka, *Liberalism, Community, and Culture*, p. 166.

38. Yael Tamir, *Liberal Nationalism* (Princeton, NJ: Princeton University Press, 1993), p. 35.

39. Rawls, *A Theory of Justice*, p. 440.

40. Hannah Arendt, *Men in Dark Times* (San Diego: Harcourt Brace Jovanovich, 1983 [1955]), p. 18.

41. Stephen Cornell, *The Return of the Native: American Indian Political Resurgence* (New York: Oxford University Press, 1988), p. 217.

42. Recall Anne Martin's statement that the day would come when "we [shall] have,

not a man-made or a woman-made world, but a *human* world," when "sex is put out of politics, and the world made human." "Woman's Inferiority Complex," *The New Republic* 27 (29 July 1921), p. 210.

43. "How do you protest a socially imposed categorization, except by organizing around the category? Just as blacks cannot fight the arbitrariness of racial classification without organizing *as blacks,* so gays could not advocate the overthrow of the sexual order without making their gayness the very basis of their claims." Stephen Epstein, "Gay Politics, Ethnic Identity: The Limits of Social Constructionism," *Socialist Review* 17 (May–August 1987), p. 19.

44. See, e.g., Sam Stanley, ed., *American Indian Economic Development* (The Hague: Mouton, 1978), p. 6: "Indians have a perspective toward modern life which involves their own past deeply. The treaties, which most non-Indians regard trivially, are a sacred part of their life. . . . They had their roots here thousands of years before Europeans arrived. They are acutely aware of the specific ways in which they lost possession of over 98 percent of the land to non-Indians. All of this involves history, and it is living history to Indians—handed down orally in every tribe, a part of their collective bitter experience."

45. Sara Evans, *Personal Politics: The Roots of Women's Liberation in the Civil Rights Movement and the New Left* (New York: Vintage, 1980), p. 219.

46. *Plessy v. Ferguson,* 163 U.S. 537, 551 (1896).

47. See, e.g., Judith Shklar, *The Faces of Injustice* (New Haven: Yale University Press, 1990), pp. 3–4: "To take the victims' view seriously does not . . . mean that they are always right when they perceive injustice. We often blame ourselves and each other for no good reason."

48. See especially Steele, *The Content of Our Character,* chapter 1.

49. Mill accomplished this by delegating legislative powers to a "Commission for Legislation" rather than to the Parliament, and left the expression of suffering or discontent to the latter as a deliberative but not legislating body. Burke's notion of virtual representation ensured (he thought) that all the important social "descriptions" would have at least one advocate in Parliament, who would be familiar with any deep grievances developing among the people. However, the power of judging whether the grievances were well founded would lie first with the representative and then with the Parliament as a whole, not left to the judgment of the aggrieved parties.

50. 488 U.S., at 506.

51. United States Bureau of the Census, *Statistical Abstract of the United States: 1996* (Washington, D.C.: Government Printing Office, 1996), Table 728, p. 471. This ratio has been fairly constant since 1920. Mary Ann Mason, *The Equality Trap* (New York: Simon and Schuster, 1988), p. 124.

52. United States Bureau of the Census, *Statistical Abstract of the United States: 1996,* Table 664, p. 413.

53. Ibid., Table 52, p. 50; Table 49, p. 48.

54. Ibid., Table 442, p. 279.

55. Sara E. Rix, ed., *American Woman, 1990–91: A Status Report* (New York: W. W. Norton, 1990), appendix, Table 22.

56. United States Bureau of the Census, *Statistical Abstract of the United States: 1996,* Table 450, p. 283.

57. Ibid., Table 442, p. 279.

58. William Julius Wilson, *The Declining Significance of Race: Blacks and Changing American Institutions* (Chicago: University of Chicago Press, 1978).

59. *The Truly Disadvantaged: The Inner City, the Underclass, and Public Policy* (Chicago: University of Chicago Press, 1987), p. 10.

60. For other arguments that link the history of Black oppression to contemporary social, economic, and political equality, see Christopher Jencks, *Rethinking Social Policy: Race, Poverty and the Underclass* (Cambridge: Harvard University Press, 1992), p. 34; Andrew Hacker, *Two Nations: Black and White, Separate, Hostile, Unequal* (New York: Charles Scribner's, 1992), pp. 12, 17–20. With regard to women, Barbara Ehrenreich and Deirdre English have written an influential history of women in medicine that offers good reasons for believing that women's current unequal status in the medical profession is a product of a history of discrimination against them. *For Her Own Good: 150 Years of the Experts' Advice to Women* (Garden City, NY: Anchor, 1978), chapters 2 and 3. Other accounts of the enduring effects of women's explicit exclusion from well-paying positions include, among many others, Miriam Slater and Penina Migdal Glazer, "Prescriptions for Professional Survival," *Daedalus* 116 (1987), p. 126, and Nancy Gabin, "Women Workers and the UAW in the Post-World War II Period: 1945–1954," in *Our American Sisters: Women in American Life and Thought*, ed. Jean E. Friedman, William G. Shade, and Mary Jane Capozzoli (Lexington, MA: D. C. Heath, 1987), pp. 469–92.

61. Mary R. Jackman and Michael J. Muha, "Education and Intergroup Attitudes: Moral Enlightenment, Superficial Democratic Commitment, or Ideological Refinement?" *American Sociological Review* 49 (6) (1984), p. 760.

62. Robert B. Hill, "Structural Discrimination: The Unintended Consequences of Institutional Processes," in *Surveying Social Life: Papers in Honor of Herbert H. Hyman*, ed. Hubert J. O'Gorman (Middletown, CT: Wesleyan University Press, 1988), p. 366.

63. Ibid., p. 367; see also Susan Okin's discussion of the reproduction of gender inequality from the domestic sphere in both civil society and political life. *Justice, Gender, and the Family* (New York: Basic Books, 1989), chapter 6.

64. Hill, "Structural Discrimintation," pp. 367–68.

65. See the discussion in Tajfel, "The Social Psychology of Minorities," p. 318.

66. 395 U.S. 285 (1969).

67. Shklar, *Faces of Injustice*, p. 81 (emphasis added).

68. Lee Sigelman and Susan Welch. *Black Americans' Views of Racial Inequality: The Dream Deferred* (Cambridge: Cambridge University Press, 1991), p. 65.

69. Although the existence of distinct social groups does not in itself create a legitimate claim for their representation, it is a prerequisite of such a claim. Current Supreme Court doctrine implicitly acknowledges as much in its emphasis on the definition of discrete voting blocs along group lines in racial (and now partisan) gerrymandering cases.

70. Thomas Scanlon, "Contractualism and Utilitarianism," in *Utilitarianism and Beyond*, ed. Amartya Sen and Bernard Williams (Cambridge: Cambridge University Press, 1982).

71. Williams, *The Alchemy of Race and Rights*, p. 121.

72. For this reason, even the "representation-reinforcing" approach to constitutional interpretation that John Hart Ely advocates in *Democracy and Distrust* would be inadequate to a group-based view of fair representation.

73. See, e.g., the discussion in Kymlicka, *Liberalism, Community, and Culture*, pp. 76–77.

74. Native American communities might come closest, but even they are clearly not homogeneous, as evidenced by native women's groups' concerns that native self-government will further entrench women's subordinate position in some communities. See the discussion in Will Kymlicka, *Multicultural Citizenship: A Liberal Theory of Minority Rights* (Oxford: Clarendon, 1995), p. 39.

75. Young, *Justice and the Politics of Difference*, pp. 102–7.

76. See the discussion in chapter 4, section V.

77. I am indebted to Rainer Bauböck for this way of expressing the point.

78. To be fair, Young does offer criteria for group recognition in her important discussion of the "five faces of oppression." *Justice and the Politics of Difference*, chapter 2. Illuminating as that chapter is in helping us to understand the multifacetedness of inequality, however, it is not a great deal of help in deciding how to allocate scarce resources. As Will Kymlicka has noted, perhaps a little tendentiously, Young's "list of 'oppressed groups' in the United States would seem to include 80 per cent of the population, . . . [i]n short, everyone but relatively well-off, relatively young, able-bodied, heterosexual white males." *Multicultural Citizenship*, p. 145. Although Young explicitly eschews the distributive model of justice (see *Justice and the Politics of Difference*, chapter 1), there are some problems of distribution that are inescapable, and among them is the distribution of legislative seats.

79. I am thus in strong sympathy with Anne Phillips's claim that arguments for a group's legislative presence must be grounded in a "historically specific analysis of existing structures of exclusion and existing arrangements for representation." *The Politics of Presence*, p. 31; see also p. 46.

80. Marginalized groups, like all social groups, are characterized by internal diversity. A group's claim to recognition does not depend on its members' unanimous agreement that its identity is politically salient.

81. Kymlicka, *Multicultural Citizenship*, p. 143.

82. I am grateful to Will Kymlicka for his challenges on these points, which persuaded me that any claims I might make for the self-representation of Native Americans in legislative bodies would be premature without further study.

83. Peter Feaver is the source of this suggestion.

84. Cf. the introduction, section III, where I explain that it is the mutual reinforcement of cultural and material injustice that is the particular focus of my concern in this book.

85. For a discussion on this topic, see Samuel Bowles and Herbert Gintis, *Democracy and Capitalism: Property, Community, and the Contradictions of Modern Social Thought* (New York: Basic Books, 1986), especially chapter 2.

86. See especially Wilson, *The Declining Significance of Race*.

Chapter 7
The Institutions of Fair Representation

1. An exception to this tendency is Pamela S. Karlan, "Maps and Misreadings: The Role of Geographic Compactness in Racial Vote Dilution Litigation," *Harvard Civil Rights–Civil Liberties Law Review* 24 (1) (1989), pp. 173–248.

2. See, e.g., Anne Phillips, *Engendering Democracy* (University Park, PA: Pennsylvania State University Press, 1991), pp. 90–91, 153; *Democracy and Difference* (University Park, PA: Pennsylvania State University Press, 1993), pp. 99, 150–56. In her most recent treatment of the subject, *The Politics of Presence* (Oxford: Clarendon, 1995), she does a great deal to overcome this tendency by attempting to trace the relationship between the representation of groups' substantive concerns and interests (what she calls the "politics of ideas") with their legislative presence.

3. Abigail Thernstrom, *Whose Votes Count? Affirmative Action and Minority Voting Rights* (Cambridge: Harvard University Press, 1987); Carol M. Swain, *Black Faces, Black Interests: The Representation of African Americans in Congress* (Cambridge: Harvard University Press, 1993).

4. This is not to suggest that the normative critique, by itself, is not worthwhile. Indeed, the profoundest works of political theory—Plato's *Republic*, Rousseau's *Social Contract*—have been critiques of existing practice, not guides to reform.

5. The empirical evidence shows, however, that the concentration of minority voters required to elect a minority candidate is higher for Latinos than for African Americans. For Blacks, a plurality of Black voters plus a combined minority population of 50 percent usually suffices to elect the Black community's candidate of choice, and a 65 percent majority Black population virtually guarantees Black electoral success. For a Latino community's candidate to win, there must be a Latino plurality plus a combined minority population of 55 percent. A safe Latino district requires a 60 percent Latino majority and a combined minority population of 70 percent. Bernard Grofman and Lisa Handley, "Preconditions for Black and Hispanic Congressional Success," in *United States Electoral Systems: Their Impact on Women and Minorities*, ed. Wilma Rule and Joseph F. Zimmerman (New York: Greenwood, 1992), pp. 31–39.

6. Frank R. Parker, "*Shaw v. Reno*: A Constitutional Setback for Minority Representation," in *PS: Political Science and Politics* 28 (1) (1995), p. 47. See also Steven A. Holmes, "Voting Rights Experts Say Challenges to Political Maps Could Cause Turmoil." *New York Times*, 30 June 1995, p. A23.

7. Ibid. See also Bernard Grofman, "*Shaw v. Reno* and the Future of Voting Rights," in *PS: Political Science and Politics* 28 (1) (1995), pp. 27–36.

8. 115 S. Ct. 2475, at 2486 (1995) (quoting *Shaw v. Reno*, 509 U.S. 630, at 647 (1993).

9. I have discussed this point in some detail in chapter 3, section III, and the appendix.

10. Swain, *Black Faces, Black Interests*, p. 72.

11. Lani Guinier, "Groups, Representation, and Race Conscious Districting: A Case of the Emperor's Clothes," in *Tyranny of the Majority: Fundamental Fairness in Representative Democracy* (New York: Free Press, 1994), p. 121; see also the discussion at pp. 134–35. The argument that single-member district systems are antidemocratic because they waste votes is, however, by no means a new argument in democratic theory. Recall from the discussion in chapter 1 that it was among Mill's reasons for advocating a switch to the single transferable vote.

12. See, e.g., Douglas Amy, *Real Choices/New Voices: The Case for Proportional Representation in the United States* (New York: Columbia University Press), pp. 24–26.

13. See, e.g., Kenneth J. Cooper, "Black Caucus Tries to Cushion the Fall from Its Height of Influence." *Washington Post*, 16 December 1994, p. A21.

14. See, e.g., discussion in Bernard Grofman, Lisa Handley, and Richard G. Niemi, *Minority Representation and the Quest for Voting Equality* (New York: Cambridge University Press, 1992), pp. 105–6.

15. Enid Lakeman, "The Case for Proportional Representation," in *Choosing an Electoral System: Issues and Alternatives*, ed. Arend Lijphart and Bernard Grofman (New York: Praeger, 1984), p. 50; Enid Lakeman, *Power to Elect: The Case for Proportional Representation* (London: Heinemann, 1982), p. 136. Welch and Herrick contest this finding, claiming that women do only marginally better in at-large systems than in single-member district systems. Susan Welch and Rebekah Herrick, "The Impact of At-Large Elections on the Representation of Minority Women," in Rule and Zimmerman, *United States Electoral Systems*, p. 161.

16. Wilma Rule and Pippa Norris, "Anglo and Minority Women's Underrepresentation in Congress: Is the Electoral System the Culprit?" in Rule and Zimmerman, *United States Electoral Systems*, pp. 49–50.

17. Peggy Lamson, *Few Are Chosen: American Women in Political Life Today* (Boston: Houghton Mifflin, 1968), p. xxiii.

18. See, e.g., Wilma Rule, "Women's Underrepresentation and Electoral Systems," in *PS: Political Science and Politics* 27 (4) (1994), p. 690 ("With PR, political parties have an *incentive* to place women on their respective lists to broaden their appeal. But in single-member districts where only one person is elected, political elites have a *disincentive* to risk backing a woman candidate"); M. Margaret Conway, "Creative Multimember Redistricting and Representation of Women and Minorities in the Maryland Legislature," in Rule and Zimmerman, *United States Electoral Systems,* p. 105; Phillips, *Engendering Democracy,* p. 80. Enid Lakeman argues that this logic applies as well to racial minorities. "The Case for Proportional Representation," p. 50. However, in the American case, minority men achieve greater electoral success within single-member district systems than in plurality multimember district systems. Victor DeSantis and Tari Renner, "Minority and Gender Representation in American Country Legislatures: The Effect of Election Systems," in Rule and Zimmerman, *United States Electoral Systems*, pp. 143–52; Albert Karnig and Susan Welch, "Electoral Structure and Black Representation on City Councils," in *Social Science Quarterly* 63 (1) (1982), pp. 99–114; Amy, *Real Choices/New Voices*, p. 119.

19. For a history of Maori representation in New Zealand, see Augie Fleras, "From Social Control towards Political Self-Determination? Maori Seats and the Politics of Separate Maori Representation in New Zealand," in *Canadian Journal of Political Science* 18 (3) (1985), pp. 551–76.

20. Joan Rydon, "Representation of Women and Ethnic Minorities in the Parliaments of Australia and New Zealand," in Rule and Zimmerman, *Electoral Systems in Comparative Perspective*, pp. 230.

21. Fleras, "From Social Control towards Political Self-Determination," pp. 563–64.

22. Ibid., p. 566.

23. Raj Vasil, *What Do the Maori Want? New Maori Political Perspectives* (Auckland, New Zealand: Random Century, 1990), p. 129.

24. Fleras, "From Social Control towards Political Self-Determination," p. 568.

25. "Your Guide to MMP: The Basic Facts," and "More About MMP," New Zealand Electoral Commission, Wellington, January 1996.

26. Royal Commission on Electoral Reform, *Reforming Electoral Democracy*, vol. 1 (Ottawa: Minister of Supply and Services Canada, 1991), p. 173.

27. The term *Aboriginal*, in the Canadian context, encompasses so-called status Indians in southern Canada and Inuit in the north, as well as Métis (those who have mixed French and Indian ancestry). The term *First Nations* is also common in Canadian parlance.

28. It is important to note here that the Canadian Supreme Court has allowed much greater deviations from average district size than has the U.S. Supreme Court: districts may diverge by as much as 25 percent from that figure. The Royal Commission on Electoral Reform, however, recommends that deviations be limited to 15 percent. *Reforming Electoral Democracy*, pp. 154–55. Under the Commission's proposals, then, Aboriginal communities could be as small as 85 percent of a province's electoral quotient (number of voters/seats) and still receive parliamentary representation. Ibid., p. 189.

29. *Reforming Electoral Democracy*, pp. 169–93.

30. Bih-Er Chou and Janet Clark, "Electoral Systems and Women's Representation in Taiwan: The Impact of the Reserved-Seat System," in Rule and Zimmerman, *Electoral Systems in Comparative Perspective*, pp. 161–70.

31. Ibid., p. 161.

32. For a related discussion of Aboriginal women's concerns about the protection of their rights within schemes of Aboriginal self-government, see Will Kymlicka, *Multicultural Citizenship: A Liberal Theory of Minority Rights* (Oxford: Clarendon, 1995), p. 39, and sources cited.

33. The counterthesis is that ethnic conflict in the former Yugoslavia would not have been so pervasive or destructive if the Yugoslav regime had treated all ethnic groups even-handedly.

34. The issues of stability and "balkanization" are discussed at greater length in chapter 6, sections I and V.

35. See Philips, *Engendering Democracy*, chapter 3, and *Politics of Presence*, chapter 3.

36. This limitation could be overcome by the direct legal requirement that parties run a certain percentage of women candidates. Argentina adopted a law requiring parties to compose candidate lists in which at least 30 percent of candidates are women. In 1993 Italy adopted a women's quota for the 25 percent of its seats that are elected from party lists. Mark P. Jones, "Gender Quotas and PR in Argentina," in *Voting and Democracy Report* (Washington, D.C.: Center for Voting and Democracy, 1995), p. 176.

37. I am indebted to Dominique Leydet for encouraging me to reflect on this issue.

38. For further discussion of Calhoun's concept of concurrent majorities, see chapter 1, section VI.

39. Arend Lijphart, *Democracy in Plural Societies: A Comparative Exploration* (New Haven: Yale University Press, 1977), p. 25.

40. Phillips, *Engendering Democracy*, p. 153. It is because consociational arrangements secure a balanced legislative presence for subnational blocs that I include it here, under the category of constituency definition, rather than in the next section, on the dynamics of legislative decision making; that is, although consociational systems are compatible with a variety of electoral schemes, they share the feature that constituencies are defined *within* subnational-groupings based on ethno-linguistic identity, not across them, and that this foundation of constituency definition has constitutional status.

While consociationalism, like the group-based theory of fair representation that I defend, aims at a deliberative mode of governmental decision making across the lines of group difference, it does so by entrenching group identity at the electoral stage and by giving priority to ethno-linguistic forms of identity over other forms. As I note in the text below, consociationalism thus shares both the strengths and weaknesses of Calhoun's theory of concurrent majorities.

41. See, e.g., Pierre du Toit, "Consociational Democracy and Bargaining Power," in *Comparative Politics* 19 (July 1987), pp. 422–23.

42. The same is true of representation in the United States Senate, in which citizens of more populous states are underrepresented in comparison with citizens from sparsely populated states. The American solution to the problem was to layer this institution of state representation on top of an institution of representation by population, which recognizes the principle of individual equality. Many consociational systems lack this feature, and so provide no place within institutions of representation for the principle of equal citizenship.

43. Recent defenses of proportional and semiproportional representation include Amy, *Real Choices/New Voices*; and Guinier, "Groups, Representation, and Race Conscious Districting," in *Tyranny of the Majority*, and "Good Government? Fairness? Or Vice Versa. Or Both," *Economist*, 1 May 1993, pp. 19–21.

44. Michael Gallagher, "Comparing Proportional Representation Electoral Systems: Quotas, Thresholds, Paradoxes and Majorities," *British Journal of Political Science* 22 (4) (1992), p. 476.

45. Douglas Amy offers a helpful technical overview of alternative systems of proportional and semi-proportional representation in the appendix to *Real Choices/New Voices*. For a briefer but useful discussion, see also Joseph F. Zimmerman, "Alternative Voting Systems for Representative Democracy," in *PS: Political Science and Politics* 27 (4) (1994), pp. 674–77; and "A Wide Choice of Ways to Choose," *Economist*, 1 May 1993, p. 20.

46. For a more detailed discussion, see Amy, *Real Choices/New Voices*, pp. 227–28.

47. This section presents a simplified explanation of STV systems. For a more technical and precise account, see Douglas W. Rae, *The Political Consequences of Electoral Laws* (New Haven: Yale University Press, 1971), pp. 36–38; or Amy, *Real Choices/New Voices*, pp. 230–32.

48. This method of voting has been in place in Cambridge, Massachusetts, since 1941. The city now has a site on the worldwide web that describes the history and operation of the system (which it calls "proportional voting"), complete with an interactive demonstration of STV in the form of a simulated election. For those interested in the mechanics of the system, this site is worth a visit. It is located at: ⟨http://www.ai.mit.edu/projects/iiip/Cambridge/prop-voting/prop-voting.html⟩

49. For further discussion of cumulative voting and limited voting, see Edward Still, "Cumulative Voting and Limited Voting in Alabama," in Rule and Zimmerman, *United States Electoral Systems*, pp. 183–96.

50. Joseph F. Zimmerman, "Equity in Representation for Women and Minorities," in Rule and Zimmerman, *Electoral Systems in Comparative Perspective*, pp. 3–13.

51. Arend Lijphart argues that the German system is not, properly speaking, a mixed system but is better characterized as a party-list PR system. Arend Lijphart, "Trying to Have the Best of Both Worlds: Semi-Proportional and Mixed Systems," in

Lijphart and Grofman, *Choosing an Electoral System*, pp. 207–13. Insofar as the final balance of the parties in the Bundestag is determined by the PR half of the ballot, this is correct, but the system does preserve some of the advantages of single-member district systems which PR systems otherwise fail to secure, such as a direct relationship between constituents and legislators whom they can clearly identify as "their representative." To the extent that constituency service constitutes an important element of political representation, this seems a significant difference between the German and other party-list systems.

52. See, e.g., Lisa Young, *Electoral Systems and Representative Legislatures: Consideration of Alternative Electoral Systems*, Canadian Advisory Council on the Status of Women, Pub. No. 94-L-206 (Ottawa, 1994).

53. On the general effectiveness of the single transferable vote, limited voting, and cumulative voting for minority representation, see Bernard Grofman, "Criteria for Redistricting: a Social Science Perspective," *UCLA Law Review* 33 (1) (1985), pp. 167–70.

54. Rule, "Women's Underrepresentation and Electoral Systems," pp. 689–90.

55. Amy, *Real Choices/New Voices*, p. 107.

56. Rule, "Women's Underrepresentation and Electoral Systems," pp. 690–91.

57. Pippa Norris, "Women's Legislative Participation in Western Europe," in *Women and Politics in Western Europe*, ed. Sylvia Bashevkin (London: Frank Cass, 1985), pp. 71–89.

58. Amy, *Real Choices/New Voices*, p. 127.

59. For an overview of this history, see Amy, *Real Choices/New Voices*, pp. 133–38. See also, e.g., Leon Weaver and Judith Baum, "Proportional Representation on New York City Community School Boards," in Rule and Zimmerman, *United States Electoral Systems*, pp. 197–205; Joseph F. Zimmerman, "Enhancing Representational Equity in Cities," in ibid., p. 214; George S. Blair, *Cumulative Voting: An Effective Electoral Device in Illinois Politics* (Urbana: University of Illinois Press, 1960).

60. Richard L. Engstrom, "The Voting Rights Act: Disfranchisement, Dilution, and Alternative Election Systems," *PS: Political Science and Politics* 27 (4) (1994), p. 687; see also Dave Kaplan, "Controversial Way to Vote Ordered." *Congressional Quarterly Weekly Report*, 9 April 1994, p. 857.

61. Richard L. Engstrom and Charles J. Barilleaux, "Native Americans and Cumulative Voting: The Sisseton-Wahpeton Sioux," *Social Science Quarterly* 72 (2) (1991), p. 388; see also Dave Kaplan, "Alternative Election Methods: A Fix for a Besieged System?" *Congressional Quarterly Weekly Report*, 2 April 1994, pp. 812–13.

62. See Richard L. Engstrom, Delbert A. Taebel, and Richard L. Cole, "Cumulative Voting as a Remedy for Minority Vote Dilution: The Case of Alagmogordo, New Mexico," *Journal of Law and Politics* 5(3) (1989), pp. 469–97; Richard L. Cole, Delbert A. Taebel, and Richard L. Engstrom, "Cumulative Voting in a Municipal Election: A Note on Voter Reaction and Electoral Consequences," *Western Political Quarterly* 43 (1) (1990), pp. 191–99; and Richard L. Engstrom and Charles J. Barilleaux, "Native Americans and Cumulative Voting," *Social Science Quarterly* 72 (2) (1991), pp. 388–93.

63. Rein Taagepera, "The Effect of District Magnitude and Properties of Two-Seat Districts," in Lijphart and Grofman, *Choosing an Electoral System*, p. 92.

64. Rule and Norris, "Anglo and Minority Women's Underrepresentation in Congress," pp. 44–45.

65. I use the terms *equality* and *equity* here in the same sense as in chapter 2, where they designate the different normative standards of the two strands of liberal representation.

66. Lani Guinier, "No Two Seats: The Elusive Quest for Political Equality," in *Tyranny of the Majority*, pp. 96–97, 251, n. 75.

67. Beitz argues against the notion that equality requires PR in *Political Equality: An Essay in Democratic Theory* (Princeton, NJ: Princeton University Press, 1989), p. 140. More recently he has articulated the view that the historical exclusion of some groups from full political equality requires remedial action, whether in the form of race-conscious districting or reforms that institute some elements of PR.

68. Amy, *Real Choices/New Voices*, pp. 140–52.

69. Ibid., pp. 21–26.

70. See ibid., p. 159, and sources cited.

71. Michel Duverger, "Which Is the Best Electoral System?," in Lijphart and Grofman, *Choosing an Electoral System*, pp. 31–39.

72. Phillips, *Engendering Democracy*, pp. 83–89.

73. In his essay, "The Metamorphoses of Representative Government," *Economy and Society* 23(2) (1994), pp. 133–71, Bernard Manin distinguishes "parliamentarianism" from "party democracy" and "tribunal of the public" as ideal types of representative government. In particular, his distinction between parliamentarianism (by which he means parliamentary government before the emergence of mass-based parties) and party democracy is instructive and brings out some of the themes I have in mind here in the distinction between candidate-focused and party-focused electoral systems.

74. I have discussed the importance of a spirit of impartiality in democratic deliberation in "Justice Toward Groups: Political Not Juridical," *Political Theory* 23 (1) (1995), pp. 85–87.

75. Phillips, *The Politics of Presence*, p. 146. See also, e.g., Jack Knight and James Johnson, "Aggregation and Deliberation: On the Possibility of Democratic Legitimacy," *Political Theory* 22 (2) (1994), p. 288.

76. The norm of reciprocity is among the most important. In relationships that extend across time and involve multiple points of decision, as do relationships between legislators, an actor must either support others' interests sometimes or reliably and persuasively ground one's decision in a common interest; otherwise others will simply ignore his or her priorities.

77. "The Rise and Fall of Self-Interest in the Explanation of Political Life," in *Beyond Self-Interest*, ed. Jane J. Mansbridge (Chicago: University of Chicago Press, 1990), especially pp. 13–14.

78. See Knight and Johnson, "Aggregation and Deliberation," p. 282.

79. I also discussed this point in chapter 4, section VI.

80. In chapter 4, section VI.

81. This strategy for enhancing their strength within Congress is clearly in the minds of minority legislators. See, e.g., Kenneth J. Cooper, "Congress's Hispanic Membership Likely to Grow 50% for Next Term," *Washington Post*, 3 October 1992, p. A11, quoting Nydia Velazquez, then a Democratic candidate for a House of Representatives seat from New York: "'I intend to fill the breach between the African-American and Latino community, and the breach between the African-American and Latino leadership in this

country . . . If we can work together, I think we can have more political leverage." See also Juan Williams, "From Caucus to Coalition: Can the Black Freshman Class in Congress Shape the Clinton Program?" *Washington Post*, 10 January 1993, p. C2.

82. For journalistic accounts of the policy influence of the Congressional Black Caucus, see, e.g., Susan B. Garland and Richard S. Dunham, "The Black Caucus Has Clinton Running Scared," *Business Week*, 8 August 1994, p. 33; Linda Feldmann, "Black Caucus Uses Its Clout Effectively but Also Carefully," *Christian Science Monitor*, 19 July 1994, p. 3; "As the Black Caucus Grows, So Does Its Pull with Clinton," *New York Times*, 13 February 1993, p. A9; Steven A. Holmes, "With Persuasion and Muscle, Black Caucus Reshapes Haiti Policy," *New York Times*, 14 July 1994, p. A10; "Women Remain on Periphery Despite Electoral Gains," *Congressional Quarterly Weekly Report*, 9 October 1993, p. 2712.

83. See John E. Yang, "Black Caucus Adjusts to New Political Scene," *Washington Post*, 23 September 1995, p. A15.

84. John C. Calhoun, *A Disquisition on Government*, reprinted in *Union and Liberty: The Political Philosophy of John C. Calhoun*, ed. Ross M. Lence (Indianapolis: Liberty Fund, 1992), p. 50.

85. See, e.g., Mark Rush, "In Search of a Coherent Theory of Voting Rights: Challenges to the Supreme Court's Vision of Fair and Effective Representation," *Review of Politics* 56 (3) (1994), pp. 504–5, 514–18 (criticizing Lani Guinier).

86. Iris Marion Young, *Justice and the Politics of Difference* (Princeton, NJ: Princeton University Press, 1990), p. 184.

87. Ibid.

88. See discussion in section I, above.

89. Lani Guinier, "No Two Seats," in *Tyranny of the Majority*, pp. 107–8.

90. See, e.g., Guinier, *The Tyranny of the Majority*, pp. 17, 116, 260 n. 119.

91. Young, *Justice and the Politics of Difference*, pp. 187–88.

92. Kymlicka, *Multicultural Citizenship*, p. 147.

93. I am grateful to Joe Carens for prodding me on this point.

94. Lani Guinier, "No Two Seats," in *Tyranny of the Majority*, pp. 92–93.

95. See, e.g., Swain, *Black Faces, Black Interests*; Phillips, *The Politics of Presence*; Lani Guinier, "The Triumph of Tokenism," in *Tyranny of the Majority*, pp. 41–70.

96. See, e.g., Melancton Smith's speech of 25 June 1788 to the New York ratification convention: "[T]he nearer the representative is to his constituent, the more attached and dependent he will be—In the states, the elections are frequent, and the representatives numerous." In Herbert J. Storing, ed., *The Anti-Federalist* (Chicago: University of Chicago Press, 1985), p. 351.

97. Phillips, *The Politics of Presence*, p. 80.

98. Ibid., p. 78.

99. Ibid., p. 80.

100. Ibid., p. 83.

101. We need not assume, however, that political constituencies cannot be formed along the lines of marginalized group identities, despite the fact that contemporary electoral systems do not organize constituencies in this way. As I discuss below in section IV, the attraction of some forms of semi-proportional representation is precisely that they open up the possibility that marginalized groups may mobilize around candi-

dates who share their experience and who they believe will effectively represent their interests.

102. Phillips, *The Politics of Presence*, p. 160.

103. See, e.g., Phillips's discussion in ibid., pp. 43, 77, and 156.

104. Hanna Pitkin, *The Concept of Representation* (Berkeley: University of California Press, 1967), p. 209.

105. See the discussion at p. 206, above, of Carol Swain's critique of "safe" majority-minority districts.

106. See, e.g., David Weaver, "Media Agenda Setting and Elections: Voter Involvement or Alienation?" in *Political Communication* 11 (4) (1994), pp. 347–56.

107. For a detailed discussion of citizen consultations in the last round of Canadian constitutional discussions, see Wendy F. Porteous, *Citizens' Forum on Canada's Future: Report on the Consultative Process* (Ottawa: Canadian Centre for Management Development, March 1992).

108. Both governments and private organizations have recently conducted consultations with citizens that could serve as a model for representatives' interactions with constituents. On the Canadian government's consultations with citizens concerning the federal budget, see Evert A. Lindquist, "Citizens, Experts and Budgets: Evaluating Ottawa's Emerging Budget Process," in *How Ottawa Spends: 1994–95*, ed. Susan D. Phillips (Ottawa: Carleton University Press, 1994), pp. 91–128. During the 1992 U.S. presidential campaign, the Jefferson Center for Democratic Values sponsored deliberative panels of citizens to discuss key policy questions, particularly that of the federal budget. For journalistic reports, see Robert L. Jackson, "Unofficial 'Juries' Program Renders Verdicts on Politics," *Los Angeles Times*, 6 January 1993, Washington ed., p. A7; "Making the Voices of Ordinary Citizens Count," *USA Today*, 7 January 1993, p. 15A; William Raspberry, "'Citizens' Juries,'" *Washington Post*, 23 January 1993 (op-ed). Finally, James Fishkin's proposals for "deliberative opinion polls" could be used within legislative constituencies to inform representatives' choices, as well as on the state and national levels of politics. For a general description and discussion of his approach, see James S. Fishkin, *Democracy and Deliberation: New Directions for Democratic Reform* (New Haven: Yale University Press, 1991).

109. Benjamin Barber, *Strong Democracy: Participatory Politics for a New Age* (Berkeley: University of California Press, 1984), chapter 10.

110. See Beitz, *Political Equality*, p. 99.

111. See also the related discussion in the introduction, section IV.

112. Constitution of Hawaii, Section 6(8), reproduced in Ann Feder Lee, *The Hawaii State Constitution: A Reference Guide* (Westport, CT: Greenwood, 1993), p. 102.

113. Leroy Hardy, Alan Heslop, and Stuart Anderson, eds., *Reapportionment Politics: The History of Redistricting in the 50 States* (Beverly Hills, CA: Sage, 1981).

114. Currently only Colorado, Hawaii, and Montana have districting or reapportionment commissions whose decisions are binding without final legislative approval. Six states (Arkansas, Connecticut, Illinois, Iowa, Michigan, and New Jersey) have commissions that are partially independent of the legislature. In the remaining forty-one states, districting decisions are indistinct from any other legislative enactment, and so are subject to manipulation in the interests of incumbents and partisan majorities. Information compiled from ibid.

115. See section II, above.

116. Current law requires single-member districts, but multimember districts have been used in the past. There is no constitutional bar to the use of multimember districts in congressional elections.

117. Amy, *Real Choices/New Voices*, p. 113.

Conclusion
Descriptive Representation with a Difference

1. *Making All the Difference: Inclusion, Exclusion, and American Law* (Ithaca: Cornell University Press, 1990).

2. "What is Equality? Part 2: Equality of Resources," *Philosophy and Public Affairs* 10 (4) (1981), p. 311; see also the discussion in Will Kymlicka, *Contemporary Political Philosophy: An Introduction* (Oxford: Clarendon, 1990), pp. 75–85.

3. Michael J. Sandel, *Liberalism and the Limits of Justice* (Cambridge: Cambridge University Press, 1982).

4. For a discussion of the neglect of histories of marginalization in jurisprudence, see Aviam Soifer, "Involuntary Groups and the Role of History in American Law," in *Law and the Company We Keep* (Cambridge: Harvard University Press, 1995).

5. Rawls, *A Theory of Justice* (Cambridge: Harvard University Press, 1971), p. 440.

6. Rawls, "Justice as Fairness: Political not Metaphysical," *Philosophy and Public Affairs* 14 (1985), p. 242.

7. Mill second-guesses the shared agency of representer and represented by allocating the ultimate power of decision to the committee of legislation. To this extent he shares the other theorists' suspicion that the experiential basis of political judgment is radically distinct from the skill of designing sound legislation, and that these two virtues are not likely to be contained within the same person. The theory I offer here supposes that representatives are likely to possess both competences to the requisite degree.

8. I particularly have in mind the work of Will Kymlicka and Yael Tamir.

9. Stuart Hampshire, *Innocence and Experience* (Cambridge: Harvard University Press, 1989), p. 68.

10. For the most succinct presentation of a negative view of liberalism, see Judith Shklar, "The Liberalism of Fear," in *Liberalism and the Moral Life*, ed. Nancy L. Rosenblum (Cambridge: Harvard University Press, 1989), pp. 21–38.

11. In this I join company with Judith Shklar, who argues, in *Faces of Injustice* (New Haven: Yale University Press, 1990), that we have more to learn from the nature of injustice than from positive ideals of justice, and with Ian Shapiro's view of democracy as "opposition to unjust social arrangements." *Democracy's Place* (Ithaca: Cornell University Press, 1996), p. 6.

12. Shklar, *The Faces of Injustice*, p. 118.

13. Two Letters to Gentlemen in Bristol (1778), in *The Works of the Right Hon. Edmund Burke*, 4th ed., vol. 2 (Boston: Little, Brown, 1871; 12 vols.), p. 251.

Bibliography

Cases

Abate v. Mundt, 403 U.S. 182 (1971).
Abrams v. Johnson, 117 S. Ct. 1925 (1997).
Adarand Constructors, Inc., v. Pena, 115 S. Ct. 2097 (1995).
Allen v. State Board of Elections, 393 U.S. 544 (1969).
Baker v. Carr, 369 U.S. 186 (1962).
Bradwell v. Illinois, 83 U.S. (16 Wall.) 130 (1873).
Brown v. Board of Education, 347 U.S. 483 (1954).
Bush v. Vera, 116 S. Ct. 1941 (1996).
City of Cleburne v. Cleburne Living Center, Inc., 473 U.S. 432 (1985).
City of Mobile v. Bolden, 446 U.S. 55 (1980).
City of Richmond v. J. A. Croson Co., 488 U.S. 469 (1989).
Davis v. Bandemer, 478 U.S. 109 (1986).
Dred Scott v. Sandford, 60 U.S. (19 How.) 393 (1857).
Fortson v. Dorsey, 379 U.S. 433 (1965).
Gaston County v. United States, 395 U.S. 285 (1969).
Gomillion v. Lightfoot, 364 U.S. 399 (1960).
Gray v. Sanders, 372 U.S. 368 (1963).
Holder v. Hall, 114 S. Ct. 2581 (1994).
Johnson v. De Grandy, 114 S. Ct. 2647 (1994).
Karcher v. Daggett, 462 U.S. 725 (1983).
Kirkpatrick v. Preisler, 394 U.S. 526 (1969).
Mahan v. Howell, 410 U.S. 315 (1973).
Miller v. Johnson, 115 S. Ct. 2475 (1995).
Plessy v. Ferguson, 163 U.S. 537 (1896).
Reno v. Bossier Parish School Board, 117 S. Ct. 1491 (1997).
Reynolds v. Sims, 377 U.S. 533 (1964).
Rogers v. Lodge, 458 U.S. 613 (1982).
Shaw v. Reno (Shaw I), 509 U.S. 630 (1993).
Shaw v. Hunt (Shaw II), 116 S. Ct. 1894 (1996).
Thornburg v. Gingles, 478 U.S. 30 (1986).
United Jewish Organizations of Williamsburgh v. Carey, 430 U.S. 144 (1977).
United States v. Carolene Products Co., 304 U.S. 144 (1938).
University of California Regents v. Bakke, 438 U.S. 265 (1978).
Wesberry v. Sanders, 376 U.S. 1 (1964).
Whitcomb v. Chavis, 403 U.S. 124 (1971).
White v. Regester, 412 U.S. 755 (1973).
Wygant v. Jackson Board of Education, 476 U.S. 267 (1986).
Zimmer v. McKeithen, 485 F. 2d 1297 (5th Cir. 1973).

Newspapers and Weeklies

The Black Republican
Business Week
The Christian Science Monitor
The Colored American
The Colored Citizen
Congressional Quarterly Weekly Report
The Economist
The Globe and Mail
The Los Angeles Times
The National Era
The New National Era
The New York Times
The Washington Post

Books and Articles

Adams, John. 1856. *Works*. Boston: Little. 10 vols.

Addams, Jane. 1914. "The Larger Aspects of the Women's Movement." *Annals of the American Academy of Political and Social Science* 56 (November): 1–8.

Alexander, Roberta Sue. 1985. *North Carolina Faces the Freedmen: Race Relations During Presidential Reconstruction, 1865–67*. Durham, NC: Duke University Press.

Amy, Douglas J. 1993. *Real Choices/New Voices: The Case for Proportional Representation Elections in the United States*. New York: Columbia University Press.

Anderson, Kathryn. 1988. "Anne Martin and the Dream of Political Equality for Women." *Journal of the West* 27 (2): 28–34.

Arendt, Hannah. 1983. *Men in Dark Times*. San Diego: Harcourt Brace Jovanovich.

Baker, Gordon E. 1966. *The Reapportionment Revolution: Representation, Political Power, and the Supreme Court*. New York: Random House.

Barber, Benjamin R. 1984. *Strong Democracy: Participatory Politics for a New Age*. Berkeley: University of California Press.

Barry, Brian. 1988. "Equal Opportunity and Moral Arbitrariness." In *Equal Opportunity*. Edited by Norman E. Bowie. Boulder, CO: Westview Press.

Beard, Mary R. 1914. "The Legislative Influence of Unenfranchised Women." *Annals of the American Academy of Political and Social Science* 56 (November): 54–61.

Beer, Samuel H. 1957. "The Representation of Interests in British Government: Historical Background." *American Political Science Review* 51 (3): 613–50.

Beitz, Charles R. 1989. *Political Equality: An Essay in Democratic Theory*. Princeton, NJ: Princeton University Press.

Bell, Derrick. 1987. *And We Are Not Saved: The Elusive Quest for Racial Justice*. New York: Basic Books.

Bendyna, Mary E., and Celinda C. Lake. 1994. "Gender Voting in the 1992 Presidential Election." In *The Year of the Woman: Myths and Realities*. Edited by Elizabeth Adell Cook, Sue Thomas, and Clyde Wilcox. Boulder, CO: Westview Press.

Benhabib, Seyla. 1987. "The Generalized and the Concrete Other: The Kohlberg-Gilligan Controversy in Feminist Theory." In *Feminism as Critique: On the Politics of*

Gender. Edited by Seyla Benhabib and Drucilla Cornell. Minneapolis: University of Minnesota Press.

Bentley, Arthur F. [1908] 1967. *The Process of Government.* Cambridge: Harvard University Press.

Birch, A. H. 1971. *Representation.* New York: Praeger.

Black, Max. 1975. "The Elusiveness of Sets." In *Caveats and Critiques: Philosophical Essays in Language, Logic, and Art.* Edited by Max Black. Ithaca: Cornell University Press.

Blackwell, Alice Stone. 1893. "Twelve Reasons Why Women Want to Vote." *The Woman's Journal,* May 6.

Blair, George S. 1960. *Cumulative Voting: An Effective Electoral Device in Illinois Politics.* Urbana: University of Illinois Press.

Boies, Fannie Catherine. 1917. "Democracy and Woman Suffrage." *The New Republic,* October 27.

Bowles, Samuel, and Herbert Gintis. 1986. *Democracy and Capitalism: Property, Community, and the Contradictions of Modern Social Thought.* New York: Basic Books.

Briffault, Richard. 1995. "Race and Representation after *Miller v. Johnson.*" *University of Chicago Legal Forum* 1995: 23–82.

Brotz, Howard, ed. 1966. *Negro Social and Political Thought, 1850–1920: Representative Texts.* New York: Basic Books.

Browning, Rufus P., Dale Rogers Marshall, and David H. Tabb. 1984. *Protest Is Not Enough: The Struggle of Blacks and Hispanics for Equality in Urban Politics.* Berkeley: University of California Press.

Burke, Edmund. 1871. *The Works of the Right Honorable Edmund Burke,* 4th edition. Boston: Little, Brown. 12 vols.

———. [1790] 1955. *Reflections on the Revolution in France.* Edited by Thomas H. D. Mahoney. Indianapolis, IN: Bobbs-Merrill.

Bybee, Keith. 1998. *Mistaken Identity: The Supreme Court and the Politics of Minority Representation.* Princeton, NJ: Princeton University Press.

Cain, Bruce, John Ferejohn, and Morris Fiorina. 1987. *The Personal Vote: Constituency Service and Electoral Independence.* Cambridge: Harvard University Press.

Cairns, Alan. Forthcoming. "Constitutional Stigmatization: The Manufacture of 'Otherness.'" In *Identity, Rights and Constitutional Transformation.* Edited by Patrick J. Hanafin and Melissa S. Williams. Hampshire, England: Dartmouth Publishing Co.

Calhoun, John C. [1850] 1953. *A Disquisition on Government, and Selections from the Discourse.* New York: Liberal Arts Press.

———. [1837] 1992. Speech on the Reception of Abolition Petitions. In *Union and Liberty: The Political Philosophy of John C. Calhoun.* Edited by Ross M. Lence. Indianapolis: Liberty Fund.

Cameron, Charles, David Epstein, and Sharyn O'Halloran. 1996. "Do Majority-Minority Districts Maximize Substantive Black Representation in Congress?" *American Political Science Review* 90 (4): 794–812.

Campbell, Karlyn Kohrs. 1989. *Man Cannot Speak for Her: A Critical Study of Early Feminist Rhetoric.* Vol. 1. New York: Greenwood Press.

Canada. Royal Commission on Electoral Reform and Party Financing. 1991. *Reforming Electoral Democracy: Final Report.* Ottawa: Minister of Supply and Services Canada.

Carens, Joseph H. 1990. "Difference and Domination: Reflections on the Relation Between Equality and Pluralism." In *NOMOS 32: Majorities and Minorities.* Edited by John W. Chapman and Alan Wertheimer. New York: New York University Press.

Carens, Joseph H., and Melissa S. Williams. 1996. "Muslim Minorities in Liberal Democracies: The Politics of Misrecognition." In *The Challenge of Diversity: Integration and Pluralism in Societies of Immigration.* Edited by Rainer Bauböck, Agnes Heller, and Aristide R. Zolberg. Aldershot: Avebury Press.

Catt, Carrie Chapman. 1918. *Address to the Congress of the United States.* New York: National Woman Suffrage Publishing Co.

Center for the American Woman and Politics. 1991. *The Impact of Women in Public Office: Findings at a Glance.* New Brunswick, NJ: Eagleton Institute of Politics, Rutgers, the State University of New Jersey.

Chou, Bih-Er, and Janet Clark. 1994. "Electoral Systems and Women's Representation in Taiwan: The Impact of the Reserved-Seat System." In *Electoral Systems in Comparative Perspective: Their Impact on Women and Minorities.* Edited by Wilma Rule and Joseph F. Zimmerman. Westport, CT: Greenwood Press.

Clancy, Sandra J. 1997. "Imagining Affirmative Action and Equal Opportunity: American Failures, Canadian Challenges." Ph.D. diss., University of Toronto.

Cohen, Joshua. 1989. "Deliberation and Democratic Legitimacy." In *The Good Polity: Normative Analysis of the State.* Edited by Alan Hamlin and Philip Pettit. Oxford: Basil Blackwell.

Cole, Richard L., Delbert A. Taebel, and Richard L. Engstrom. 1990. "Cumulative Voting in a Municipal Election: A Note on Voter Reaction and Electoral Consequences." *Western Political Quarterly* 43 (1): 191–99.

Commons, John R. 1950. *The Economics of Collective Action.* New York: Macmillan.

Conway, M. Margaret. 1992. "Creative Multimember Redistricting and Representation of Women and Minorities in the Maryland Legislature." In *United States Electoral Systems: Their Impact on Women and Minorities.* Edited by Wilma Rule and Joseph F. Zimmerman. New York: Greenwood Press.

Cornell, Stephen. 1988. *The Return of the Native: American Indian Political Resurgence.* New York: Oxford University Press.

Cott, Nancy F. 1987. *The Grounding of Modern Feminism.* New Haven: Yale University Press.

———. 1987. "Women and the Ballot." *Reviews in American History* 15 (2): 290–96.

Crawson, Alan. 1986. *Corporatism and Political Theory.* Oxford: Basil Blackwell.

Crenshaw, Kimberlé W. 1988. "Race, Reform, and Retrenchment: Transformation and Legitimation in Antidiscrimination Law." *Harvard Law Review* 101 (7): 1331–87.

Dahl, Robert A., and Charles E. Lindblom. 1953. *Politics, Economics, and Welfare: Planning and Politico-Economic Systems Resolved into Basic Social Processes.* New York: Harper Torchbooks.

Dahl, Robert A. 1956. *A Preface to Democratic Theory.* Chicago: University of Chicago Press.

———. 1970. *After the Revolution? Authority in a Good Society.* New Haven: Yale University Press.

———. 1982. *Dilemmas of Pluralist Democracy: Autonomy vs. Control.* New Haven: Yale University Press.

———. 1984. "Polyarchy, Pluralism, and Scale." *Scandinavian Political Studies* 7 (4): 225–40.

———. 1989. *Democracy and Its Critics*. New Haven: Yale University Press.

Dann, Martin E. 1971. *The Black Press, 1827–1890: The Quest for National Identity*. New York: G. P. Putnam's Sons.

Davidson, Chandler. 1992. "The Voting Rights Act: A Brief History." In *Controversies in Minority Voting: The Voting Rights Act in Perspective*. Edited by Bernard Grofman and Chandler Davidson. Washington, D.C.: Brookings Institution.

Davidson, Chandler, and Bernard Grofman, eds. 1994. *Quiet Revolution in the South: The Impact of the Voting Rights Act, 1965–1990*. Princeton, NJ: Princeton University Press.

Deardorff, Neva R. 1914. "Women in Municipal Activities." *Annals of the American Academy of Political and Social Science* 56 (November): 71–77.

De Grazia, Alfred. 1951. *Public and Republic: Political Representation in America*. New York: Alfred A. Knopf.

DeSantis, Victor, and Tari Renner. 1992. "Minority and Gender Representation in American County Legislatures: The Effect of Election Systems." In *United States Electoral Systems: Their Impact on Women and Minorities*. Edited by Wilma Rule and Joseph F. Zimmerman. New York: Greenwood Press.

Dixon, Robert G. 1968. *Democratic Representation: Reapportionment in Law and Politics*. New York: Oxford University Press.

Dodson, Debra L., and Susan J. Carroll. 1991. *Reshaping the Agenda: Women in State Legislatures*. New Brunswick, NJ: Center for the American Woman and Politics.

Dorris, Michael. 1989. *The Broken Cord*. New York: Harper and Row.

du Toit, Pierre. 1987. "Consociational Democracy and Bargaining Power." *Comparative Politics* 19 (July): 419–30.

DuBois, Ellen Carol. 1987. "Outgrowing the Compact of the Fathers: Equal Rights, Woman Suffrage, and the United States Constitution, 1820–1878." *Journal of American History* 74 (3): 836–62.

DuBois, W.E.B. 1969. *Darkwater: Voices from within the Veil*. New York: Schocken Books.

Dunn, John. 1988. "Trust and Political Agency." In *Trust: Making and Breaking Cooperative Relations*. Edited by Diego Gambetta. Oxford: Basil Blackwell.

Duverger, Maurice. 1954. *Political Parties*. Translated by Barbara North and Robert North. London: Methuen.

———. 1984. "Which Is the Best Electoral System?" In *Choosing an Electoral System: Issues and Alternatives*. Edited by Arend Lijphart and Bernard Grofman. New York: Praeger.

———. 1986. "Duverger's Law: Forty Years Later." In *Electoral Laws and Their Political Consequences*. Edited by Bernard Grofman and Arend Lijphart. New York: Agathon Press.

Dworkin, Ronald. 1978. *Taking Rights Seriously*. Cambridge: Harvard University Press.

———. 1981. "What is Equality? Part 2: Equality of Resources." *Philosophy and Public Affairs* 10 (4): 283–345.

Ehrenreich, Barbara, and Deirdre English. 1978. *For Her Own Good: 150 Years of the Experts' Advice to Women*. Garden City, NY: Anchor Press.

Eisenstein, Zillah R. 1986. *The Radical Future of Liberal Feminism*. Boston: Northeastern University Press.

Eliot, T. S. 1951. "Hamlet." In *Selected Essays*, 3rd edition. London: Faber and Faber.

Elster, Jon. 1995. "Strategic Uses of Argument." In *Barriers to Conflict Resolution*. Edited by Kenneth J. Arrow. New York: W. W. Norton.

Ely, John Hart. 1980. *Democracy and Distrust: A Theory of Judicial Review.* Cambridge: Harvard University Press.

Engstrom, Richard L. 1980. "Racial Discrimination in the Electoral Process: The Voting Rights Act and the Vote Dilution Issue." In *Party Politics in the South.* Edited by Robert P. Steed, Lawrence W. Moreland, and Tod A. Baker. New York: Praeger.

———. 1994. "The Voting Rights Act: Disfranchisement, Dilution, and Alternative Election Systems." *PS: Political Science and Politics* 27 (4): 685–88.

Engstrom, Richard L., Delbert A. Taebel, and Richard L. Cole. 1989. "Cumulative Voting as a Remedy for Minority Vote Dilution: The Case of Alagmogordo, New Mexico." *Journal of Law and Politics* 5 (3): 469–97.

Engstrom, Richard L., and Charles J. Barrilleaux. 1991. "Native Americans and Cumulative Voting: The Sisseton-Wahpeton Sioux." *Social Science Quarterly* 72 (2): 388–93.

Epstein, Stephen. 1987. "Gay Politics, Ethnic Identity: The Limits of Social Constructionism." *Socialist Review* 17 (May–August): 9–54.

Estlund, David M. 1993. "Who's Afraid of Deliberative Democracy? On the Strategic/ Deliberative Dichotomy in Recent Constitutional Jurisprudence." *Texas Law Review* 71 (7): 1437–77.

Eulau, Heinz. 1978. "Changing Views of Representation." In *The Politics of Representation: Continuities of Theory and Research.* Edited by Heinz Eulau and John C. Wahlke. Beverly Hills: Sage Publications.

Eulau, Heinz, and Paul D. Karps. 1978. "The Puzzle of Representation: Specifying the Components of Responsiveness." In *The Politics of Representation: Continuities in Theory and Research.* Edited by Heinz Eulau and John C. Wahlke. Beverly Hills: Sage Publications.

Evans, Sara. 1980. *Personal Politics: The Roots of Women's Liberation in the Civil Rights Movement and the New Left.* New York: Vintage Books.

Fenno, Richard F. 1978. *Home Style: House Members in Their Districts.* Boston: Little, Brown.

Fishkin, James S. 1991. *Democracy and Deliberation: New Directions for Democratic Reform.* New Haven: Yale University Press.

Fleras, Augie. 1985. "From Social Control towards Political Self-Determination? Maori Seats and the Politics of Separate Maori Representation in New Zealand." *Canadian Journal of Political Science* 18 (3): 551–76.

Flexner, Eleanor. 1975. *Century of Struggle: The Women's Rights Movement in the United States.* Cambridge, MA: Belknap Press.

Foner, Eric. 1988. *Reconstruction: America's Unfinished Revolution, 1863–1877.* New York: Harper and Row.

Foner, Philip S., ed. 1955. *The Life and Writings of Frederick Douglass.* New York: International Publishers. 4 vols.

———, ed. 1972. *The Voice of Black America: Major Speeches by Negroes in the United States, 1797–1971.* New York: Simon and Schuster.

Foner, Philip S., and George E. Walker, eds. 1979. *Proceedings of the Black State Conventions, 1840–1865.* Vol. 2. Philadelphia: Temple University Press.

———, eds. 1986. *Proceedings of the Black National and State Conventions, 1865–1900.* Vol. 1. Philadelphia: Temple University Press.

Fraser, Nancy. 1997. *Justice Interruptus: Critical Reflections on the "Postsocialist" Condition.* New York: Routledge.

Gabin, Nancy. 1987. "Women Workers and the UAW in the Post-World War II Period: 1945–1954." In *Our American Sisters: Women in American Life and Thought*, 4th edition. Edited by Jean E. Friedman, William G. Shade, and Mary Jane Capozzoli. Lexington, MA: D. C. Heath.

Gallagher, Michael. 1992. "Comparing Proportional Representation Systems: Quotas, Thresholds, Paradoxes and Majorities." *British Journal of Political Science* 22 (4): 469–96.

George, W. L. 1919. "Woman in Politics." *Harper's Magazine*, June.

Gilligan, Carol. 1982. *In a Different Voice: Psychological Theory and Women's Development*. Cambridge: Harvard University Press.

Glazer, Nathan. 1975. *Affirmative Discrimination: Ethnic Inequality and Public Policy*. New York: Basic Books.

———. 1981. "The United States." In *Protection of Ethnic Minorities: Comparative Perspectives*. Edited by Robert G. Wirsing. New York: Pergamon Press.

Gordon, Felice D. 1986. *After Winning: The Legacy of the New Jersey Suffragists, 1920–1947*. New Brunswick, NJ: Rutgers University Press.

Gregor, James A. 1968. "Political Science and the Uses of Functional Analysis." *American Political Science Review* 62 (2): 425–39.

Grofman, Bernard. 1985. "Criteria for Redistricting: A Social Science Perspective." *UCLA Law Review* 33 (1): 77–184.

———. 1995. "*Shaw v. Reno* and the Future of Voting Rights." *PS: Political Science and Politics* 28 (1): 27–36.

Grofman, Bernard, and Lisa Handley. 1992. "Preconditions for Black and Hispanic Congressional Success." In *United States Electoral Systems: Their Impact on Women and Minorities*. Edited by Wilma Rule and Joseph F. Zimmerman. New York: Greenwood Press.

Grofman, Bernard, Lisa Handley, and Richard G. Niemi. 1992. *Minority Representation and the Quest for Voting Equality*. New York: Cambridge University Press.

Guinier, Lani. 1994. *The Tyranny of the Majority: Fundamental Fairness in Representative Democracy*. New York: Free Press.

Gurin, Patricia, Shirley Hatchett, and James S. Jackson. 1989. *Hope and Independence: Blacks' Response to Electoral and Party Politics*. New York: Russell Sage Foundation.

Gutmann, Amy. 1980. *Liberal Equality*. Cambridge: Cambridge University Press.

Gutmann, Amy, and Dennis Thompson. 1990. "Moral Conflict and Political Consensus." *Ethics* 101 (1): 64–88.

———. 1996. *Democracy and Disagreement*. Cambridge: Harvard University Press.

Hacker, Andrew. 1992. *Two Nations: Black and White, Separate, Hostile, Unequal*. New York: Charles Scribner's Sons.

Hall, Richard L., and Frank W. Wayman. 1990. "Buying Time: Moneyed Interests and the Mobilization of Bias in Congressional Committees." *American Political Science Review* 84 (3): 797–820.

Hampshire, Stuart. 1989. *Innocence and Experience*. Cambridge: Harvard University Press.

Hardy, Leroy, Alan Heslop, and Stuart Anderson, eds. 1981. *Reapportionment Politics: The History of Redistricting in the 50 States*. Beverly Hills: Sage Publications.

Harris, Frederick C. 1990. *Who Supports Minority and Poor Interests? A Roll Call Voting Analysis of the 1989 Illinois General Assembly*. Chicago: Chicago Urban League.

Harris, Frederick C., and James H. Lewis. 1991. *Who Supports Minority and Poor Interests? A Roll Call Voting Analysis of the Chicago City Council, 1988–1990*. Chicago: Chicago Urban League.

Hero, Rodney E., and Caroline J. Tolbert. 1995. "Latinos and Substantive Representation in the U.S. House of Representatives: Direct, Indirect, or Nonexistent?" *American Journal of Political Science* 39 (3): 640–52.

Hill, Robert B. 1988. "Structural Discrimination: The Unintended Consequences of Institutional Processes." In *Surveying Social Life: Papers in Honor of Herbert H. Hyman*. Edited by Hubert J. O'Gorman. Middletown, CT: Wesleyan University Press.

Hoffman, Ross J. S., and Paul Levack, eds. 1959. *Burke's Politics: Selected Writings and Speeches on Reform, Revolution and War*. New York: Alfred A. Knopf.

Hofstadter, Richard. 1948. "John C. Calhoun: The Marx of the Master Class." In *The American Political Tradition*. New York: Vintage Books.

Holt, Thomas. 1977. *Black over White: Negro Political Leadership in South Carolina During Reconstruction*. Urbana: University of Illinois Press.

Hyman, Harold M. 1967. *The Radical Republicans and Reconstruction, 1861–1870*. Indianapolis: Bobbs-Merrill.

Ignatieff, Michael. 1984. *The Needs of Strangers*. London: Chatto and Windus.

Issacharoff, Samuel. 1992. "Polarized Voting and the Political Process: The Transformation of Voting Rights Jurisprudence." *Michigan Law Review* 90 (7): 1833–91.

———. 1993. "Judging Politics: The Elusive Quest for Judicial Review of Political Fairness." *Texas Law Review* 71 (7): 1643–1703.

Jackman, Mary, and Michael J. Muha. 1984. "Education and Intergroup Attitudes: Moral Enlightenment, Superficial Democratic Commitment, or Ideological Refinement?" *American Sociological Review* 49 (6): 751–69.

Jacobi, Mary Putnam. 1902. "The Status and Future of the Woman Suffrage Movement." Mary Putnam Jacobi Papers. Schlesinger Library, Radcliffe College, Cambridge, MA.

Jagger, Allison. 1990. "Sexual Difference and Sexual Equality." In *Theoretical Perspectives on Sexual Difference*. Edited by Deborah L. Rhode. New Haven: Yale University Press.

Jencks, Christopher. 1992. *Rethinking Social Policy: Race, Poverty, and the Underclass*. Cambridge: Harvard University Press.

Johannsen, Robert W., ed. 1965. *The Lincoln-Douglas Debates of 1858*. New York: Oxford University Press.

Johnson, Alvin S. 1915. "The Effect on Labor." *The New Republic*, October 9.

Johnson, James. 1995. "Arguing for Deliberation: Some Skeptical Considerations." Department of Political Science, University of Rochester. Photocopy.

Jones, Mark P. 1995. "Gender Quotas and PR in Argentina." In *Voting and Democracy Report: 1995*. Washington, D.C.: Center for Voting and Democracy.

Karlan, Pamela S. 1989. "Maps and Misreadings: The Role of Geographic Compactness in Racial Vote Dilution Litigation." *Harvard Civil Rights–Civil Liberties Law Review* 24 (1): 173–248.

———. 1993. "The Rights to Vote: Some Pessimism about Formalism." *Texas Law Review* 71 (7): 1705–40.

———. 1995. "Our Separatism? Voting Rights as an American Nationalities Policy." *University of Chicago Legal Forum* 1995: 83–109.

Karlan, Pamela, and Daryl Levinson. 1996. "Why Voting Is Different." *California Law Review* 84 (4): 1201–32.

Karnig, Albert, and Susan Welch. 1982. "Electoral Structure and Black Representation on City Councils." *Social Science Quarterly* 63 (1): 99–114.

King, Gary, John Bruce, and Andrew Gelman. 1995. "Racial Fairness in Legislative Redistricting." In *Classifying by Race*. Edited by Paul E. Peterson. Princeton, NJ: Princeton University Press.

Knight, Jack, and James Johnson. 1994. "Aggregation and Deliberation: On the Possibility of Democratic Legitimacy." *Political Theory* 22 (2): 277–96.

Kolchin, Peter. 1972. *First Freedom: The Responses of Alabama's Blacks to Emancipation and Reconstruction*. Westport, CT: Greenwood Press.

Kraditor, Aileen S. 1981. *The Ideas of the Woman Suffrage Movement, 1890–1920*. New York: W. W. Norton.

Kuhn, Thomas S. 1970. *The Structure of Scientific Revolutions*. Chicago: University of Chicago Press.

Kymlicka, Will. 1990. *Contemporary Political Philosophy: An Introduction*. Oxford: Clarendon Press.

———. 1991. *Liberalism, Community, and Culture*. Oxford: Clarendon Press.

———. 1995. *Multicultural Citizenship: A Liberal Theory of Minority Rights*. Oxford: Oxford University Press.

Lakeman, Enid. 1982. *Power to Elect: The Case for Proportional Representation*. London: Heinemann.

———. 1984. "The Case for Proportional Representation." In *Choosing an Electoral System: Issues and Alternatives*. Edited by Arend Lijphart and Bernard Grofman. New York: Praeger.

Lamson, Peggy. 1968. *Few Are Chosen: American Women in Political Life Today*. Boston: Houghton Mifflin.

Larmore, Charles E. 1987. *Patterns of Moral Complexity*. Cambridge: Cambridge University Press.

Lawrence, Charles. 1987. "The Id, the Ego, and Equal Protection: Reckoning with Unconscious Racism." *Stanford Law Review* 39 (2): 317–88.

Lee, Ann Feder. 1993. *The Hawaii State Constitution: A Reference Guide*. Westport, CT: Greenwood Press.

Lijphart, Arend. 1977. *Democracy in Plural Societies: A Comparative Exploration*. New Haven: Yale University Press.

———. 1984. *Democracies: Patterns of Majoritarian and Consensus Government in Twenty-One Countries*. New Haven: Yale University Press.

———. 1984. "Trying to Have the Best of Both Worlds: Semi-Proportional and Mixed Systems." In *Choosing an Electoral System: Issues and Alternatives*. Edited by Arend Lijphart and Bernard Grofman. New York: Praeger.

Lindquist, Evert A. 1994. "Citizens, Experts and Budgets: Evaluating Ottawa's Emerging Budget Process." In *How Ottawa Spends: 1994–95*. Edited by Susan D. Phillips. Ottawa: Carleton University Press.

Lippmann, Walter. 1915. "The Vote as a Symbol." *The New Republic*, October 9.

Litwack, Leon F. 1979. *Been in the Storm So Long: The Aftermath of Slavery*. New York: Alfred A. Knopf.

Locke, John. [1679?] 1988. *Two Treatises of Government*. Edited by Peter Laslett. Cambridge: Cambridge University Press.

Lynch, John Roy. 1970. *Reminiscences of an Active Life: The Autobiography of John Roy Lynch*. Chicago: University of Chicago Press.

MacKinnon, Catharine A. 1990. "Legal Perspectives on Sexual Difference." In *Theoretical Perspectives on Sexual Difference*. Edited by Deborah L. Rhode. New Haven: Yale University Press.

Manin, Bernard. 1987. "On Legitimacy and Political Deliberation." *Political Theory* 15 (3): 338–68.

———. 1994. "The Metamorphoses of Representative Government." *Economy and Society* 23 (2): 133–71.

Mansbridge, Jane J. 1980. *Beyond Adversary Democracy*. New York: Basic Books.

———. 1981. "Living with Conflict: Representation in the Theory of Adversary Democracy." *Ethics* 91 (3): 466–76.

———. 1990. "The Rise and Fall of Self-Interest in the Explanation of Political Life." In *Beyond Self-Interest*. Edited by Jane J. Mansbridge. Chicago: University of Chicago Press.

———. 1992. "A Deliberative Theory of Interest Representation." In *The Politics of Interests: Interest Groups Transformed*. Edited by Mark P. Petracca. Boulder, CO: Westview Press.

———. 1996. "In Defense of 'Descriptive' Representation." Paper read at American Political Science Association, San Francisco, August 29–September 1.

March, James G., and Johan P. Olsen. 1989. *Rediscovering Institutions: The Organizational Basis of Politics*. New York: Free Press.

Marshall, Gordon, ed. 1994. *The Concise Oxford Dictionary of Sociology*. New York: Oxford University Press.

Martin, Anne. 1921. "Woman's Inferiority Complex." *The New Republic*, July 20.

———. 1924. "Political Methods of American and British Feminists." *Current History* 20 (3): 396–401.

Mason, Mary Ann. 1988. *The Equality Trap*. New York: Simon and Schuster.

May, Larry. 1987. *The Morality of Groups: Collective Responsibility, Group-Based Harm, and Corporate Rights*. Notre Dame: University of Notre Dame Press.

Mayhew, David R. 1974. *Congress: The Electoral Connection*. New Haven: Yale University Press.

McCoy, Drew R. 1989. *The Last of the Fathers: James Madison and the Republican Legacy*. Cambridge: Cambridge University Press.

McDonald, Laughlin. 1992. "The 1982 Amendments of Section 2 and Minority Representation." In *Controversies in Minority Voting: The Voting Rights Act in Perspective*. Edited by Bernard Grofman and Chandler Davidson. Washington, D.C.: Brookings Institution.

McFarlin, Annjennette Sophie, ed. 1976. *Black Congressional Reconstruction Orators and Their Orations, 1869–1879*. Metuchen, NJ: Scarecrow Press.

Mezey, Susan Gluck. 1994. "Increasing the Number of Women in Office: Does It Matter?" In *The Year of the Woman: Myths and Realities*. Edited by Elizabeth A. Cook, Sue Thomas, and Clyde Wilcox. Boulder, CO: Westview Press.

Mill, John Stuart. [1861] 1958. *Considerations on Representative Government*. Edited by Currin V. Shields. Indianapolis: Bobbs-Merrill.

————. [1859] 1973. "Recent Writers on Reform." In *Essays on Politics and Culture*. Edited by Gertrude Himmelfarb. Gloucester, MA: Peter Smith.

Miller, Ivan W. III, and William H. Norman. 1979. "Learned Helplessness in Humans: A Review and Attribution Theory Model." *Psychological Bulletin* 86 (1): 93–118.

Minow, Martha. 1990. *Making All the Difference: Inclusion, Exclusion, and American Law*. Ithaca: Cornell University Press.

Nedelsky, Jennifer. 1990. *Private Property and the Limits of American Constitutionalism: The Madisonian Framework and Its Legacy*. Chicago: University of Chicago Press.

New Zealand Electoral Commission. 1996. *Your Guide to MMP: The Basic Facts*.

————. 1996. *More About MMP.*

Nolan, Christopher. 1987. *Under the Eye of the Clock: The Life Story of Christopher Nolan*. London: Weidenfeld and Nicolson.

Norris, Pippa. 1985. "Women's Legislative Participation in Western Europe." In *Women and Politics in Western Europe*. Edited by Sylvia Bashevkin. London: Frank Cass.

O'Rourke, Timothy G. 1992. "The 1982 Amendments and the Voting Rights Paradox." In *Controversies in Minority Voting: The Voting Rights Act in Perspective*. Edited by Bernard Grofman and Chandler Davidson. Washington, D.C.: Brookings Institution.

Offen, Karen. 1989. "Reply to DuBois." *Signs: Journal of Women in Culture and Society* 15 (1): 198–202.

Okin, Susan M. 1989. *Justice, Gender, and the Family*. New York: Basic Books.

Olson, Mancur. 1971. *The Logic of Collective Action: Public Goods and the Theory of Groups*. Cambridge: Harvard University Press.

Parker, Frank R. 1995. "*Shaw v. Reno*: A Constitutional Setback for Minority Representation." *PS: Political Science and Politics* 28 (1): 47–50.

Phillips, Anne. 1991. *Engendering Democracy*. University Park, PA: Pennsylvania State University Press.

————. 1993. *Democracy and Difference*. University Park, PA: Pennsylvania State University Press.

————. 1995. *The Politics of Presence*. Oxford: Clarendon Press.

Pildes, Richard H., and Richard G. Niemi. 1993. "Expressive Harms, 'Bizarre Districts,' and Voting Rights: Evaluating Election-District Appearances after *Shaw v. Reno*." *Michigan Law Review* 92 (3): 483–587.

Pitkin, Hanna F. 1967. *The Concept of Representation*. Berkeley: University of California Press.

Pitre, Merline. 1985. *Through Many Dangers, Toils, and Snares: The Black Leadership of Texas, 1868–1900*. Austin, TX: Eakin Press.

Pole, J. R. 1966. *Political Representation in England and the Origins of the American Republic*. New York: St. Martin's Press.

————. 1978. *The Pursuit of Equality in American History*. Berkeley: University of California Press.

Porteous, Wendy F. 1992. *Citizens' Forum on Canada's Future: Report on the Consultative Process*. Ottawa: Canadian Centre for Management Development.

Putnam, Robert D. 1993. *Making Democracy Work: Civic Traditions in Modern Italy*. Princeton, NJ: Princeton University Press.

Rae, Douglas W. 1971. *The Political Consequences of Electoral Laws*. New Haven: Yale University Press.

Rae, Douglas W., et al. 1981. *Equalities*. Cambridge: Harvard University Press.

Rawls, John. 1971. *A Theory of Justice*. Cambridge: Harvard University Press.

———. 1985. "Justice as Fairness: Political Not Metaphysical." *Philosophy and Public Affairs* 14 (3): 223–51.

———. 1993. *Political Liberalism*. New York: Columbia University Press.

Rhode, Deborah L. 1990. "Definitions of Difference." In *Theoretical Perspectives on Sexual Difference*. Edited by Deborah L. Rhode. New Haven: Yale University Press.

Rix, Sara E., ed. 1990. *The American Woman, 1990–91: A Status Report*. New York: W. W. Norton.

Rogowski, Ronald. 1981. "Representation in Political Theory and in Law." *Ethics* 91 (3): 395–430.

Rossiter, Clinton, ed. 1961. *The Federalist Papers*. New York: New American Library.

Rule, Wilma, and Pippa Norris. 1992. "Anglo and Minority Women's Underrepresentation in Congress: Is the Electoral System the Culprit?" In *United States Electoral Systems: Their Impact on Women and Minorities*. Edited by Wilma Rule and Joseph F. Zimmerman. New York: Greenwood Press.

Rule, Wilma. 1994. "Women's Underrepresentation and Electoral Systems." *PS: Political Science and Politics* 27 (4): 689–92.

Rush, Mark E. 1990. "The Supreme Court's Approach to Gerrymandering and Representation." *Journal of Law and Politics* 6 (4): 683–722.

———. 1993. *Does Redistricting Make a Difference? Partisan Representation and Electoral Behavior*. Baltimore, MD: The Johns Hopkins University Press.

———. 1994. "In Search of a Coherent Theory of Voting Rights: Challenges to the Supreme Court's Vision of Fair and Effective Representation." *Review of Politics* 56 (3): 503–23.

———. 1994. "Gerrymandering: Out of the Political Thicket and into the Quagmire." *PS: Political Science and Politics* 27 (4): 682–85.

Rydon, Joan. 1994. "Representation of Women and Ethnic Minorities in the Parliaments of Australia and New Zealand." In *Electoral Systems in Comparative Perspective: Their Impact on Women and Minorities*. Edited by Wilma Rule and Joseph F. Zimmerman. Westport, CT: Greenwood Press.

Sandel, Michael J. 1982. *Liberalism and the Limits of Justice*. Cambridge: Cambridge University Press.

Scanlon, Thomas M. 1982. "Contractualism and Utilitarianism." In *Utilitarianism and Beyond*. Edited by Amartya Sen and Bernard Williams. Cambridge: Cambridge University Press.

Schattschneider, E. E. 1975. *The Semisovereign People: A Realist's View of Democracy in America*. Hinsdale, IL: Dryden Press.

Schwartz, Nancy L. 1988. *The Blue Guitar: Political Representation and Community*. Chicago: University of Chicago Press.

Shapiro, Ian. 1996. *Democracy's Place*. Ithaca: Cornell University Press.

Shaw, Anna Howard. 1914. "Equal Suffrage—A Problem of Political Justice." *Annals of the American Academy of Political and Social Science* 56 (November): 93–98.

Shklar, Judith N. 1984. *Ordinary Vices*. Cambridge: Harvard University Press.

———. 1989. "The Liberalism of Fear." In *Liberalism and the Moral Life*. Edited by Nancy L. Rosenblum. Cambridge: Harvard University Press.

———. 1990. *The Faces of Injustice*. New Haven: Yale University Press.

————. 1991. *American Citizenship: The Quest for Inclusion*. Cambridge: Harvard University Press.

Sigelman, Lee, and Susan Welch. 1991. *Black Americans' Views of Racial Inequality: The Dream Deferred*. Cambridge: Cambridge University Press.

Silver, Allan. 1985. "'Trust' in Social and Political Theory." In *The Challenge of Social Control: Citizenship and Institution Building in Modern Society*. Edited by Gerald D. Suttles and Mayer N. Zald. Norwood, NJ: Ablex Publishing Corporation.

Sitkoff, Harvard. 1989. Review of *Whose Votes Count? Affirmative Action and Minority Voting Rights*. *American Historical Review* 94 (1): 242.

Slater, Miriam, and Penina Migdal Glazer. 1987. "Prescriptions for Professional Survival." *Daedalus* 116 (4): 119–35.

Soifer, Aviam. 1995. *Law and the Company We Keep*. Cambridge: Harvard University Press.

Spelman, Elizabeth V. 1988. *Inessential Woman: Problems of Exclusion in Feminist Thought*. Boston: Beacon Press.

Stanley, Sam, ed. 1978. *American Indian Economic Development*. The Hague: Mouton.

Stanton, Elizabeth Cady. [1892] 1981. "The Solitude of Self." In *Elizabeth Cady Stanton/ Susan B. Anthony: Correspondence, Writings, Speeches*. Edited by Ellen Carol Dubois. New York: Schocken Books.

Stanton, Elizabeth Cady, Susan B. Anthony, and Matilda Joslyn Gage. 1985. *History of Woman Suffrage*. Salem, NH: Ayer. 5 vols.

Steele, Shelby. 1991. *The Content of Our Character: A New Vision of Race in America*. New York: Harper Perennial.

Sterling, Dorothy, ed. 1976. *The Trouble They Seen: Black People Tell the Story of Reconstruction*. Garden City, NY: Doubleday.

Stewart, Ella Seass. 1914. "Woman Suffrage and the Liquor Traffic." *Annals of the American Academy of Political and Social Science* 56 (November): 143–52.

Still, Edward. 1992. "Cumulative Voting and Limited Voting in Alabama." In *United States Electoral Systems: Their Impact on Women and Minorities*. Edited by Wilma Rule and Joseph F. Zimmerman. New York: Greenwood Press.

Stills, Jonathan. 1981. "Political Equality and Election Systems." *Ethics* 91 (3): 375–94.

Storing, Herbert J., ed. 1985. *The Anti-Federalist: An Abridgment, By Murray Dry, of the Complete Anti-Federalist*. Chicago: University of Chicago Press.

Sunstein, Cass. 1988. "Beyond the Republican Revival." *Yale Law Journal* 97 (8): 1539–90.

Swain, Carol M. 1992. "Some Consequences of the Voting Rights Act." In *Controversies in Minority Voting: The Voting Rights Act in Perspective*. Edited by Bernard Grofman and Chandler Davidson. Washington, D.C.: Brookings Institution.

————. 1993. *Black Faces, Black Interests: The Representation of African Americans in Congress*. Cambridge: Harvard University Press.

Sweet, Leonard I. 1976. *Black Images of America, 1784–1870*. New York: W. W. Norton.

Taagepera, Rein. 1984. "The Effect of District Magnitude and Properties of Two-Seat Districts." In *Choosing an Electoral System: Issues and Alternatives*. Edited by Arend Lijphart and Bernard Grofman. New York: Praeger.

Tajfel, Henri. 1981. "The Social Psychology of Minorities." In *Human Groups and Social Categories: Studies in Social Psychology*. Cambridge: Cambridge University Press.

Tamir, Yael. 1993. *Liberal Nationalism*. Princeton, NJ: Princeton University Press.

Tate, Katherine. 1993. *From Protest to Politics: The New Black Voters in American Elections*. Cambridge: Harvard University Press.

Taylor, John. [1814] 1950. *An Inquiry into the Principles and Policy of the Government of the United States*. London: Routledge and Kegan Paul.

Taylor, Charles. 1994. "The Politics of Recognition." In *Multiculturalism: Examining the Politics of Recognition*. Edited by Amy Gutmann. Princeton, NJ: Princeton University Press.

Theodorson, George A., and Achilles G. Theodorson, eds. 1969. *A Modern Dictionary of Sociology*. New York: Thomas Y. Crowell.

Thernstrom, Abigail M. 1987. *Whose Votes Count? Affirmative Action and Minority Voting Rights*. Cambridge: Harvard University Press.

Thomas, Sue. 1994. *How Women Legislate*. New York: Oxford University Press.

Thompson, Dennis F. 1976. *John Stuart Mill and Representative Government*. Princeton, NJ: Princeton University Press.

Truman, David B. 1953. *The Governmental Process: Political Interests and Public Opinion*. New York: Alfred A. Knopf.

United States Bureau of the Census. 1995. *Statistical Abstract of the United States: 1995*. Washington, D.C.: Government Printing Office.

United States Senate Judiciary Committee. 1982. *Voting Rights Act Amendments of 1982*, 97th Cong., 2d sess. S. Rept. 97–417. Reprinted in *United States Code Congressional and Administrative News 1982*. Vol. 2. St. Paul, MN: West Publishing Co., 1982. Pp. 177–410.

Vasil, Raj. 1990. *What Do the Maori Want? New Maori Political Perspectives*. Auckland, New Zealand: Random Century.

Waldron, Jeremy. 1992. "Historic Injustice: Its Remembrance and Supersession." In *Justice, Ethics, and New Zealand Society*. Edited by Graham Oddie and Roy W. Perrett. Auckland: Oxford University Press.

Weale, Albert P. 1981. "Representation, Individualism, and Collectivism." *Ethics* 91 (3): 457–65.

Weaver, Leon, and Judith Baum. 1992. "Proportional Representation on New York City Community School Boards." In *United States Electoral Systems: Their Impact on Women and Minorities*. Edited by Wilma Rule and Joseph F. Zimmerman. New York: Greenwood Press.

Weaver, David. 1994. "Media Agenda Setting and Elections: Voter Involvement or Alienation?" *Political Communication* 11 (4): 347–56.

Welch, Susan, and Rebekah Herrick. 1992. "The Impact of At-Large Elections on the Representation of Minority Women." In *United States Electoral Systems: Their Impact on Women and Minorities*. Edited by Wilma Rule and Joseph F. Zimmerman. New York: Greenwood Press.

Weldon, Laurel. 1996. "The Political Representation of Women: The Impact of a Critical Mass." Paper read at American Political Science Association, San Francisco, August 29–September 1.

Weyl, Walter E. 1915. "Working for the Inevitable." *The New Republic*, October 9.

Williams, Patricia J. 1991. *The Alchemy of Race and Rights*. Cambridge: Harvard University Press.

Williams, Melissa S. 1995. "Justice Toward Groups: Political Not Juridical." *Political Theory* 23 (1): 67–91.

———. 1996. "Burkean 'Descriptions' and Political Representation: A Reappraisal." *Canadian Journal of Political Science* 29 (1): 23–45.

Wilson, William Julius. 1978. *The Declining Significance of Race: Blacks and Changing American Institutions.* Chicago: University of Chicago Press.

———. 1987. *The Truly Disadvantaged: The Inner City, the Underclass, and Public Policy.* Chicago: University of Chicago Press.

Wood, Gordon S. 1969. *The Creation of the American Republic, 1776–1787.* New York: W. W. Norton.

Wright, John R. 1990. "Contributions, Lobbying, and Committee Voting in the U.S. House of Representatives." *American Political Science Review* 84 (2): 417–38.

Young, Iris Marion. 1990. *Justice and the Politics of Difference.* Princeton, NJ: Princeton University Press.

———. 1993. "Justice and Communicative Democracy." In *Radical Philosophy: Tradition, Counter-Tradition, Politics.* Edited by Roger S. Gottlieb. Philadelphia: Temple University Press.

———. 1997. "Deferring Group Representation." In *NOMOS 39: Ethnicity and Group Rights.* Edited by Will Kymlicka and Ian Shapiro. New York: New York University Press.

———. Forthcoming. "Difference as a Resource for Democratic Communication." In *Deliberation and Democracy.* Edited by James Bohman and William Rehg. Cambridge: MIT Press.

Young, Lisa. 1994. *Electoral Systems and Representative Legislatures: Consideration of Alternative Electoral Systems.* Ottawa: Canadian Advisory Council on the Status of Women.

Zimmerman, Joseph F. 1992. "Enhancing Representational Equity in Cities." In *United States Electoral Systems: Their Impact on Women and Minorities.* Edited by Wilma Rule and Joseph F. Zimmerman. New York: Greenwood Press.

———. 1994. "Alternative Voting Systems for Representative Democracy." *PS: Political Science and Politics* 27 (4): 674–77.

———. 1994. "Equity in Representation for Women and Minorities." In *Electoral Systems in Comparative Perspective: Their Impact on Women and Minorities.* Edited by Wilma Rule and Joseph F. Zimmerman. Westport, CT: Greenwood Press.

Index